BOULDER RUNNING JOURNAL
2016

BoulderRunning.com
@2016 Boulder Running & Bäuu Publishers

CONTENTS

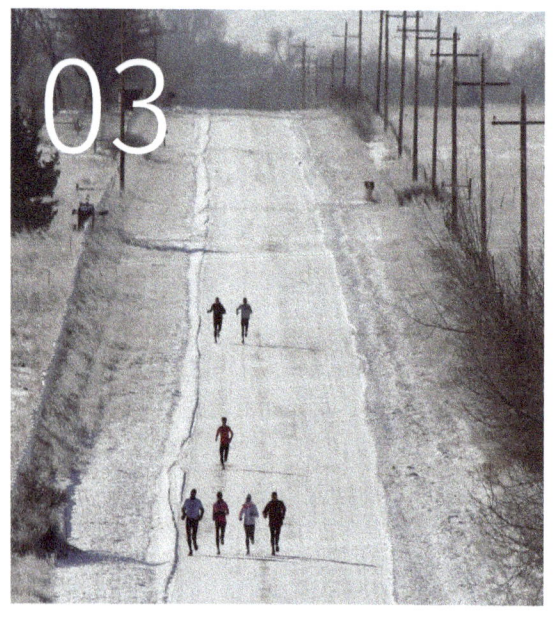

03

WINTER

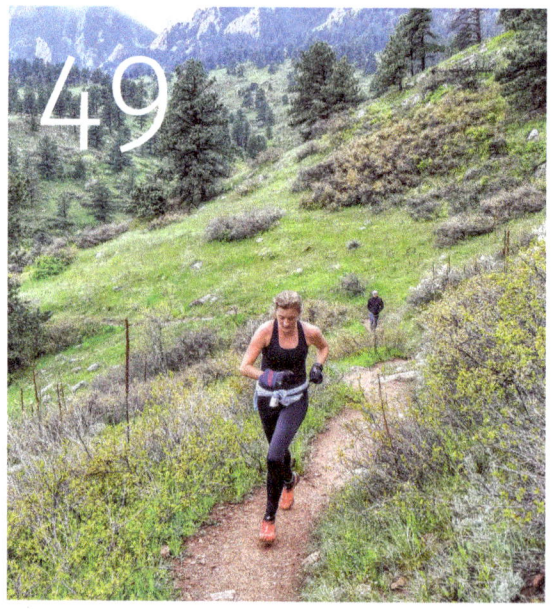

49

SPRING

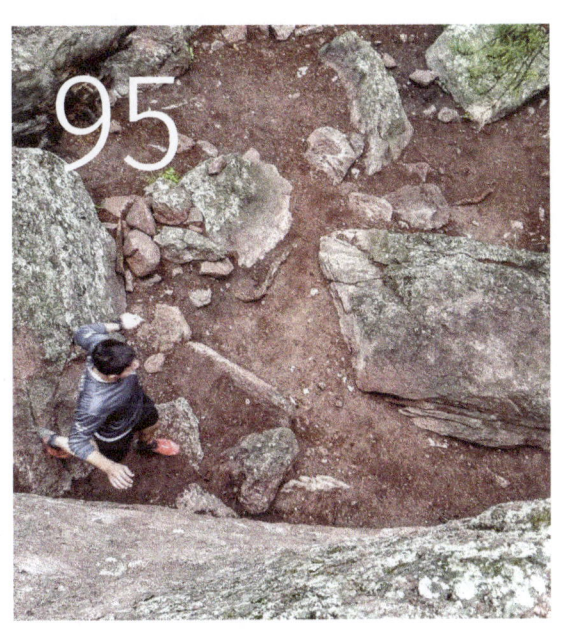

95

SUMMER

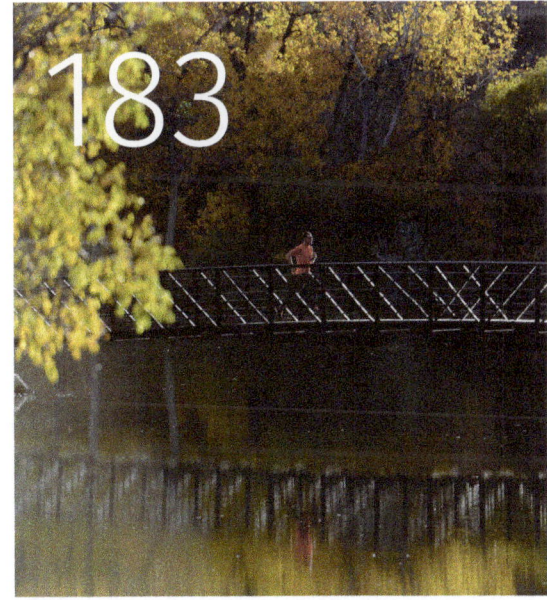

183

FALL

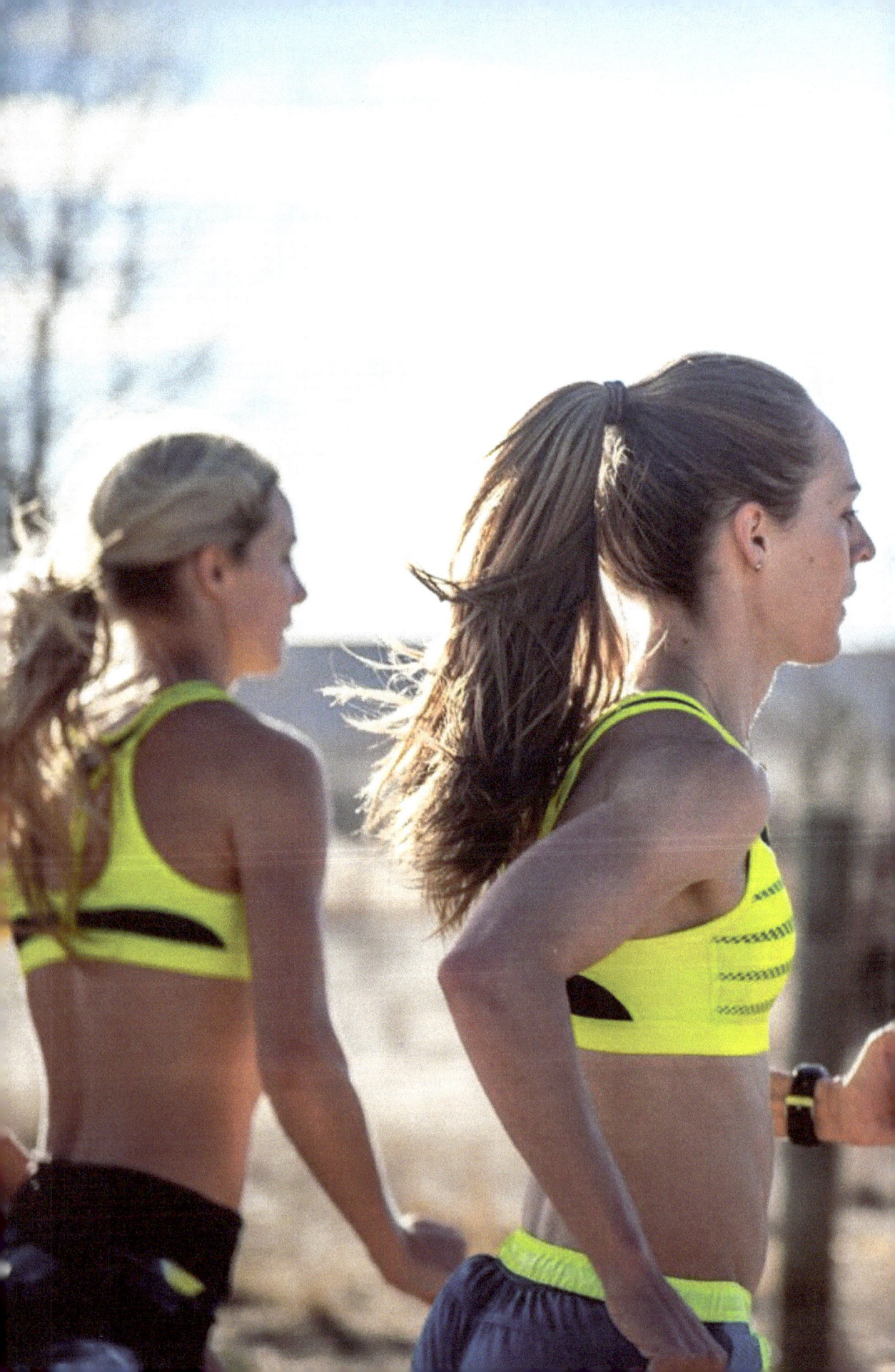

PURSUIT OF
EXCELLENCE

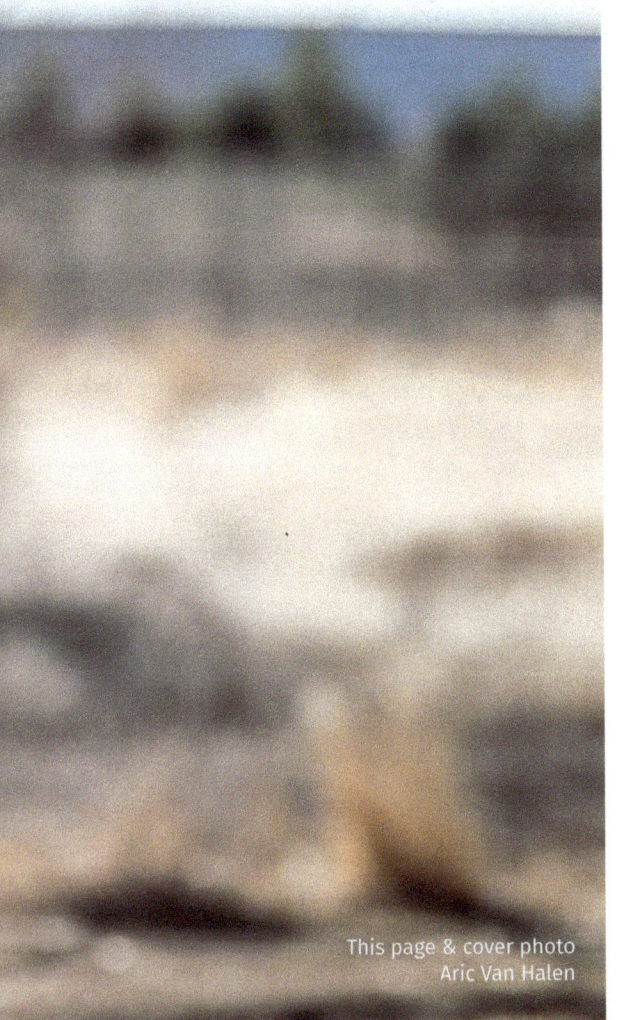

There is so much to be said about the friendship and goals shared by these two, striving towards excellence each day.

Keep your eye on the prize. Get what you can out of each quality of effort. In each of their races they ran as fast as they could, and ran within themselves. Valuable lessons we can bring into our own running or racing.

In many ways, it's fitting that they both were able to become bronze medalists, the first Americans to do so in the 1500 meters and the steeplechase. Then to bring home those medals and, instead of putting them into a display case, to share them with our community so we too can celebrate their success.

We are what we repeatedly do. Excellence, then, is not an act, but a habit. - Aristotle

Go forth and dream big.
- The editors

This page & cover photo
Aric Van Halen

WINTER

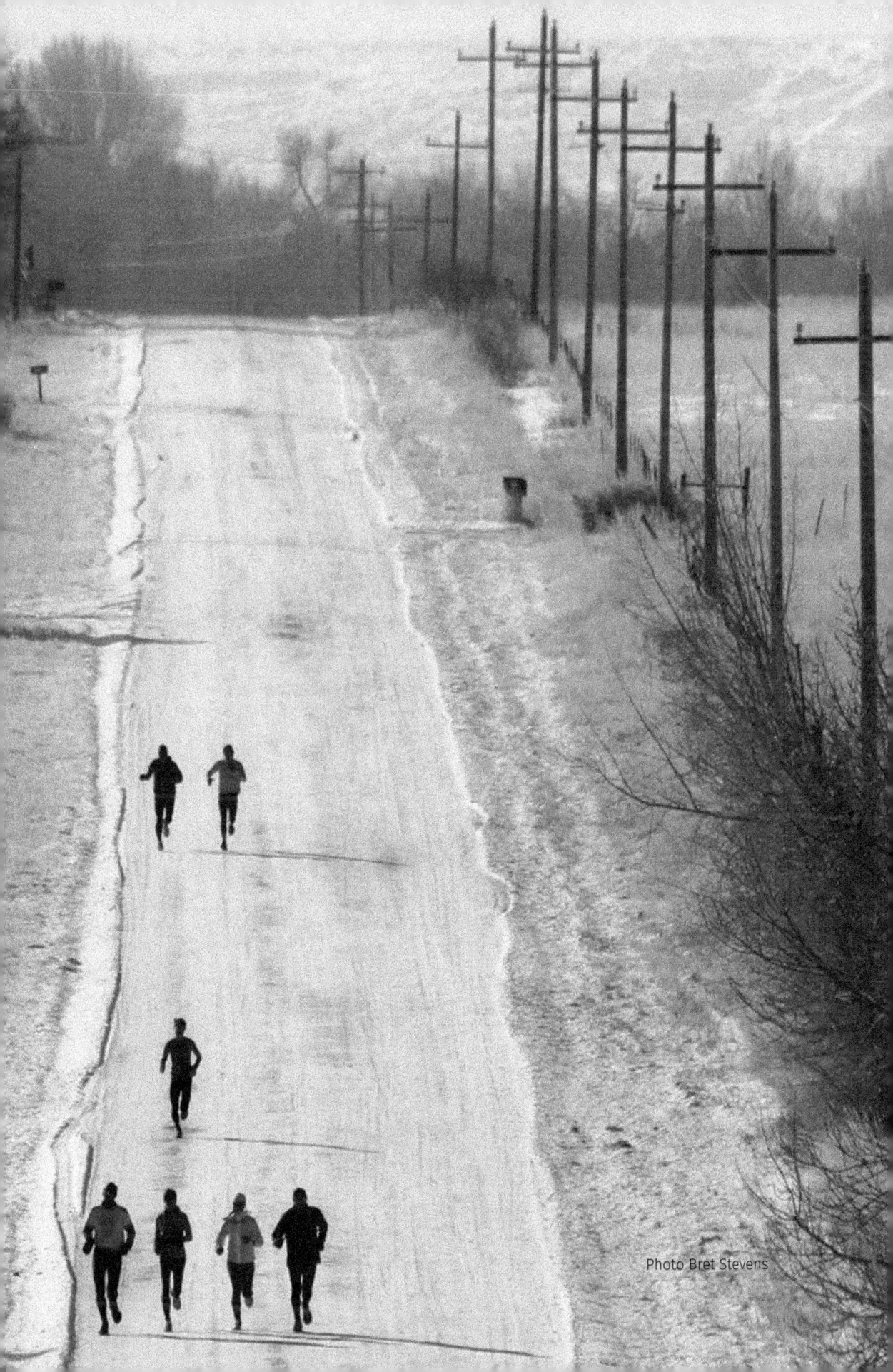
Photo Bret Stevens

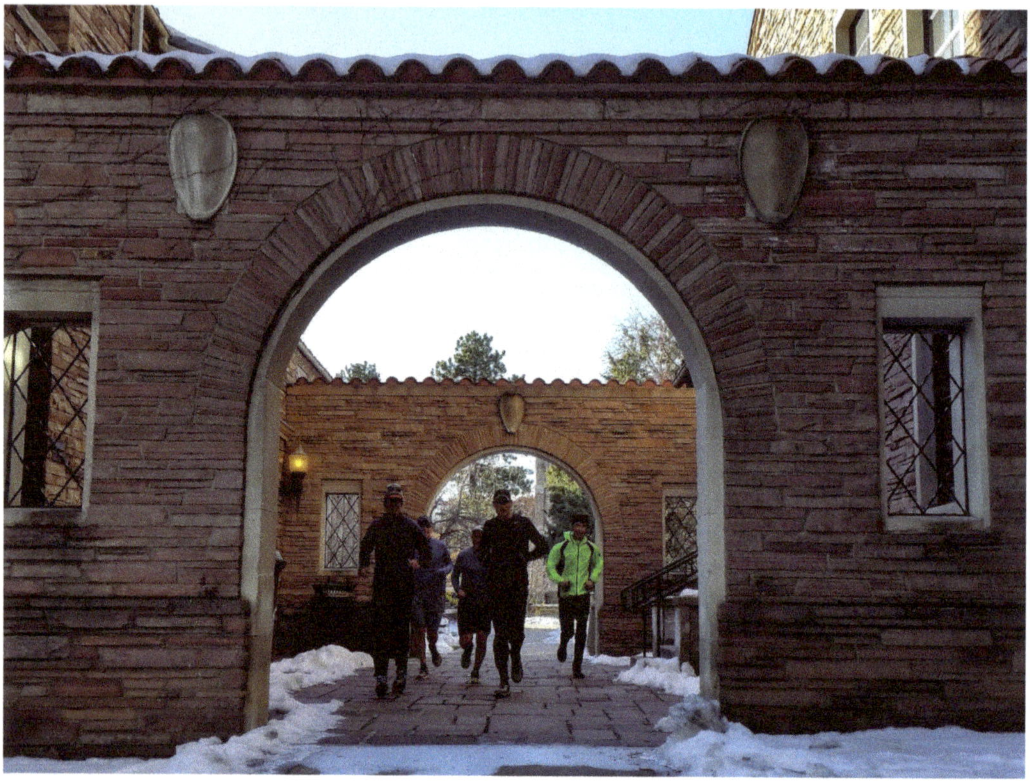

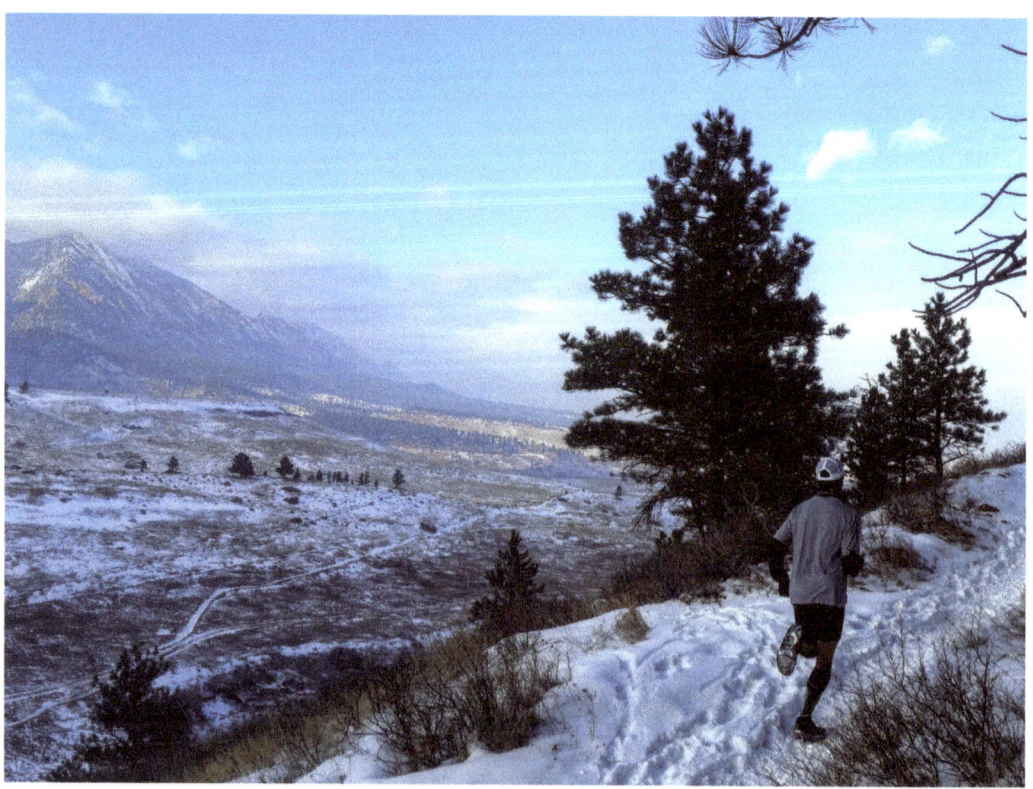

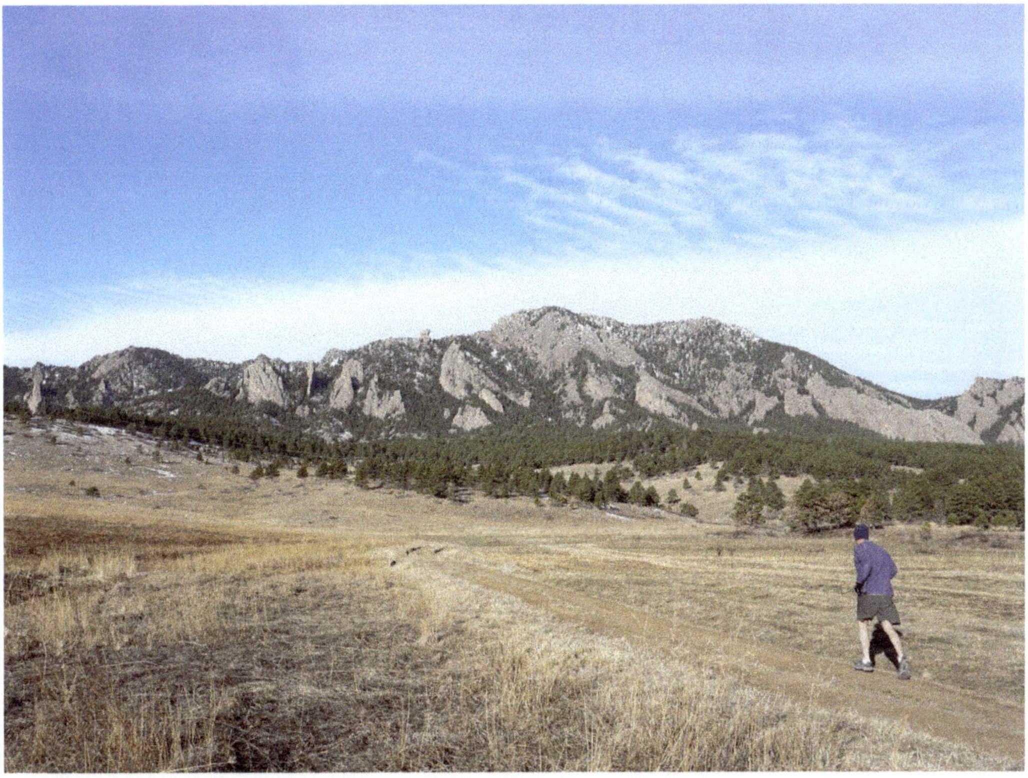

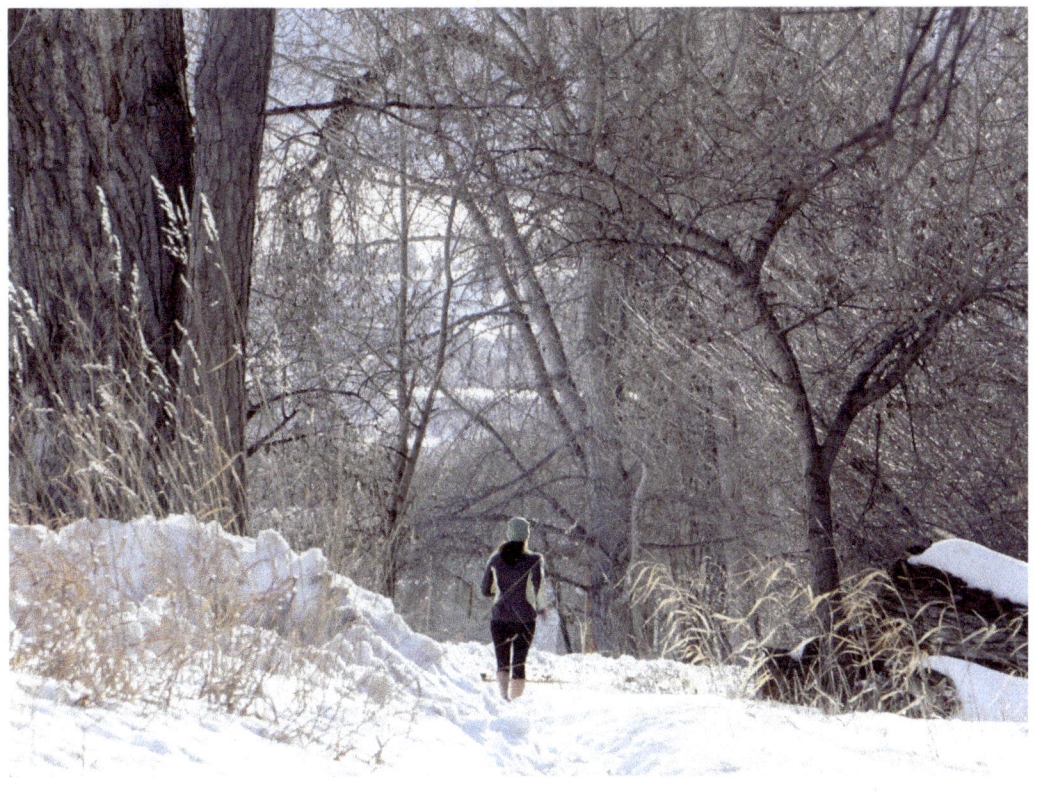

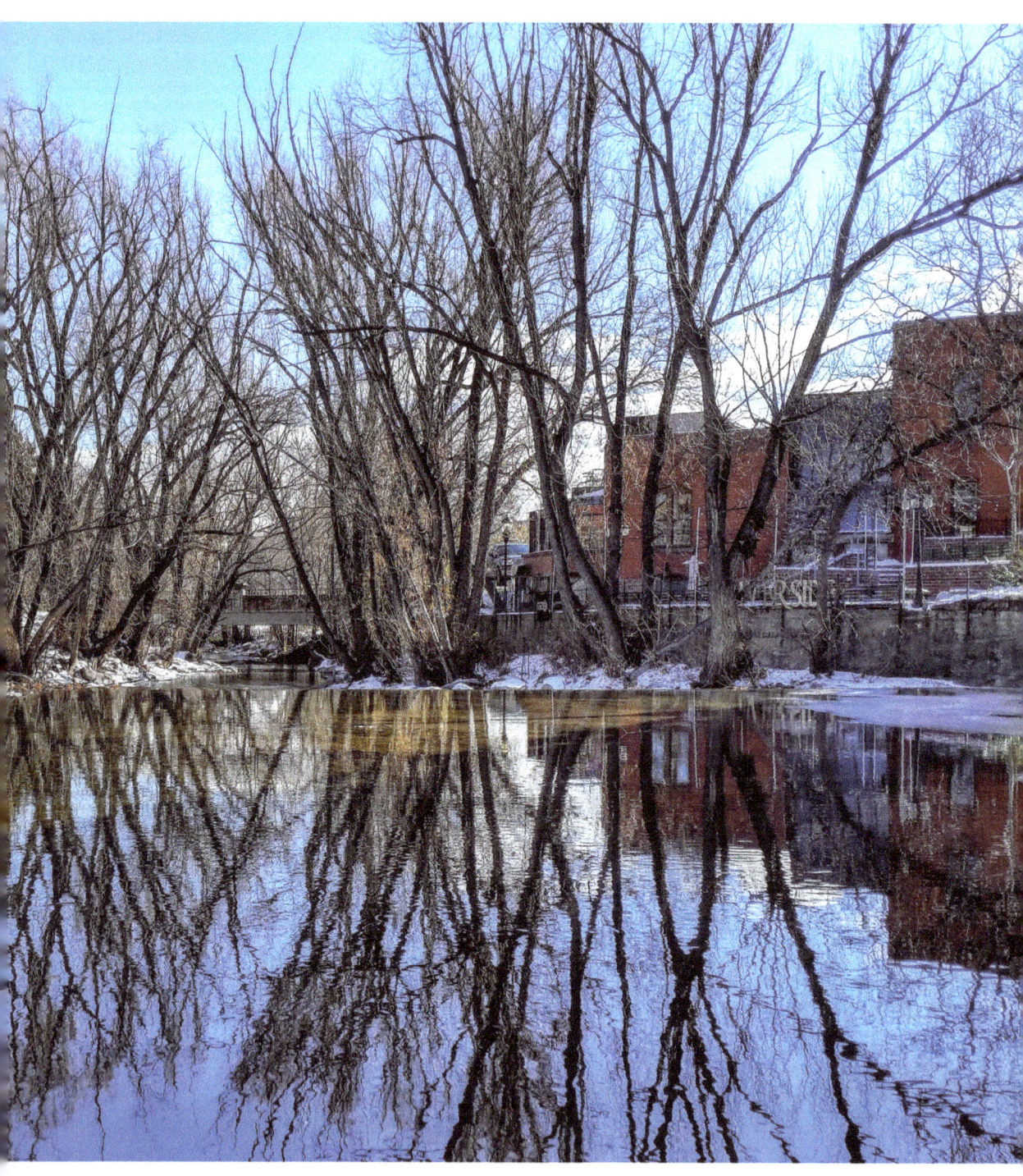

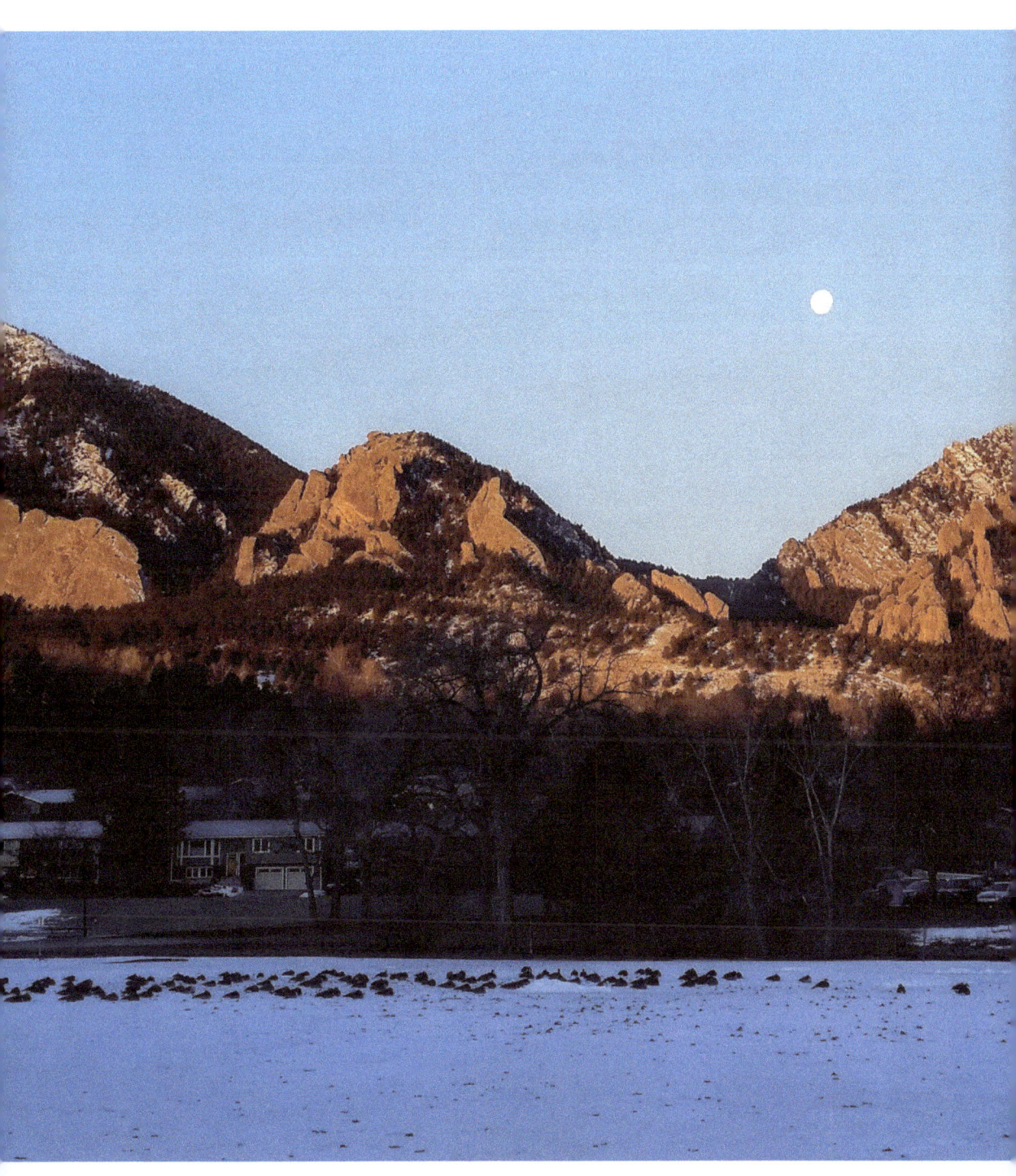

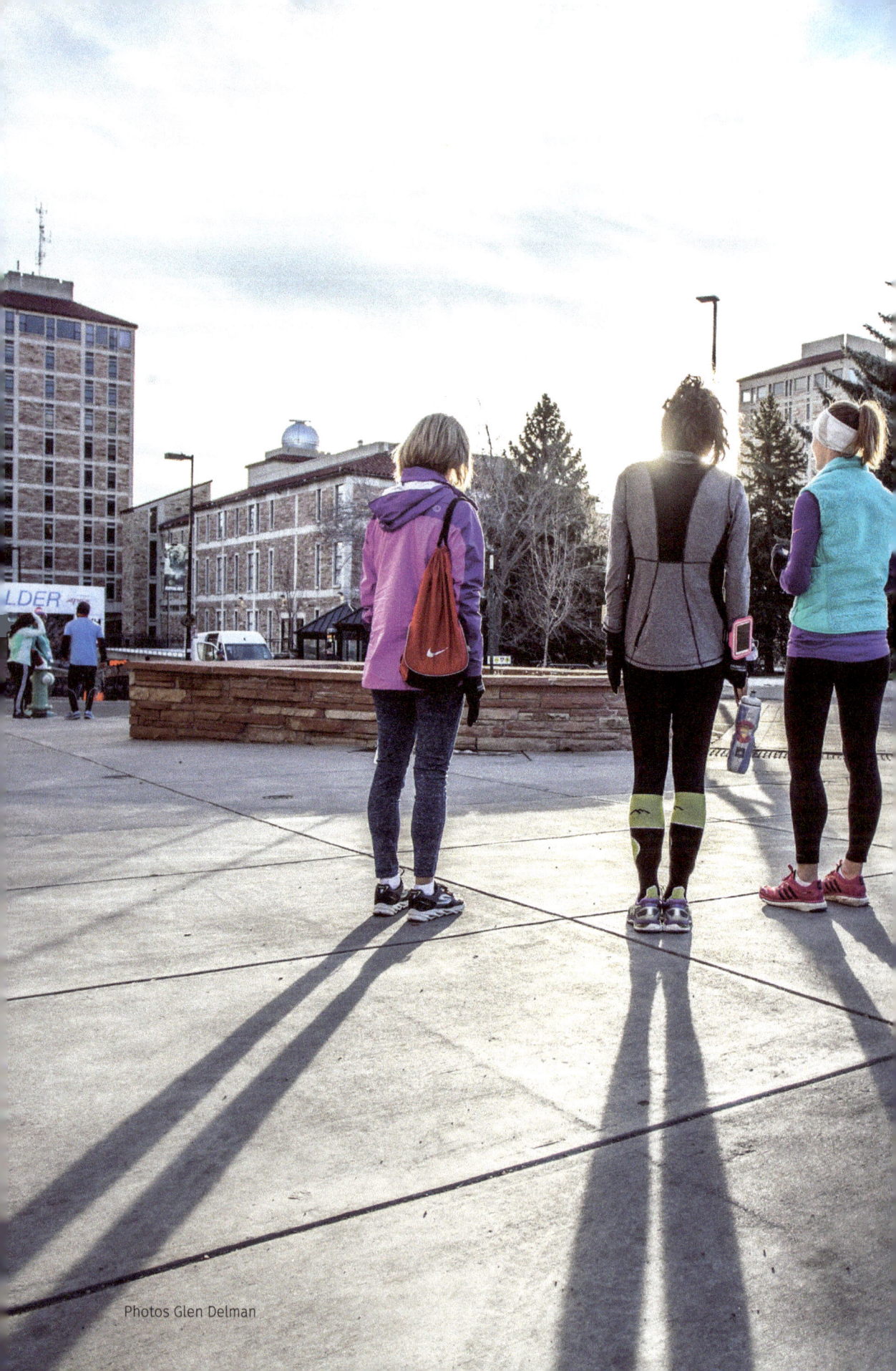
Photos Glen Delman

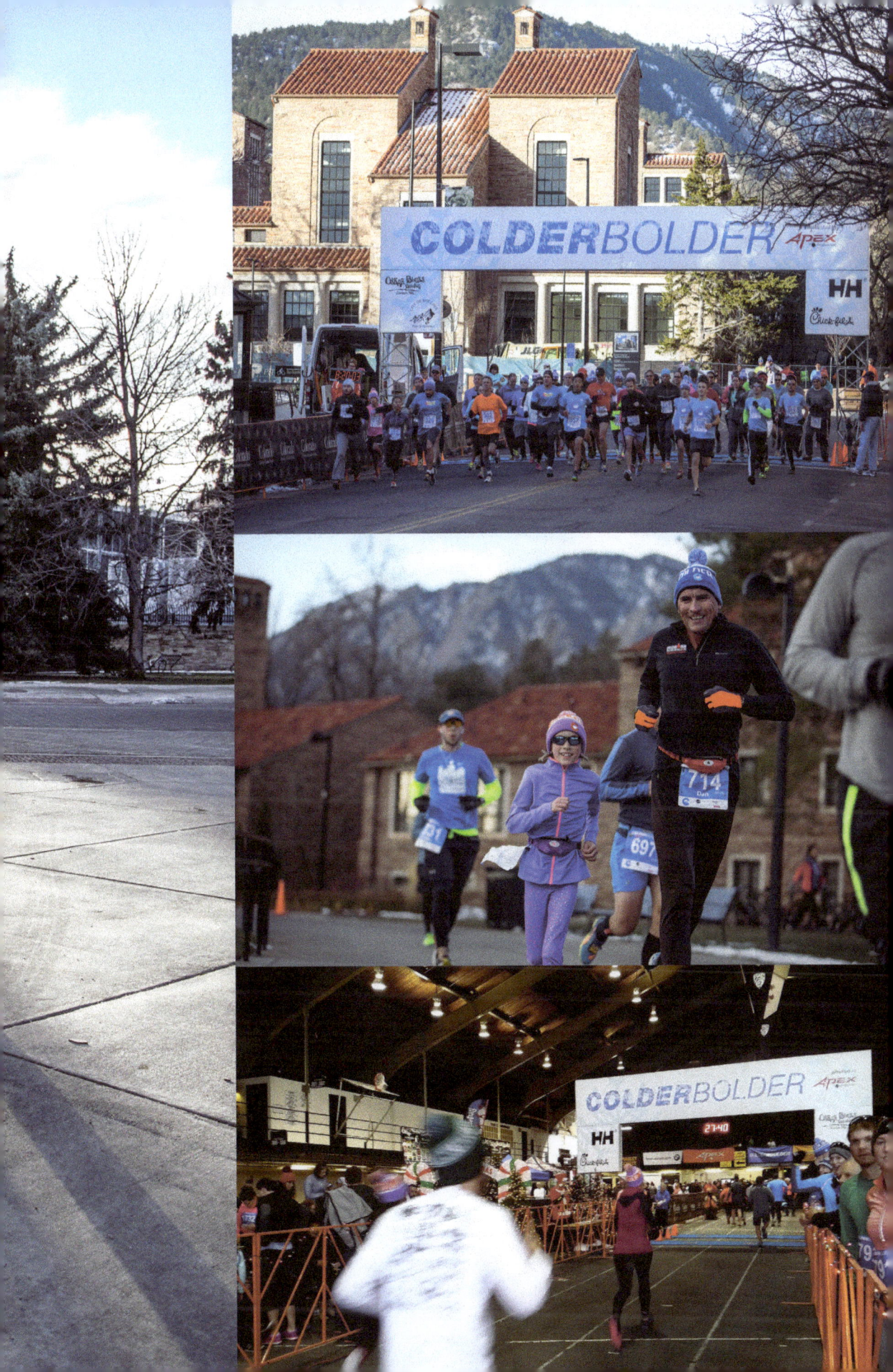

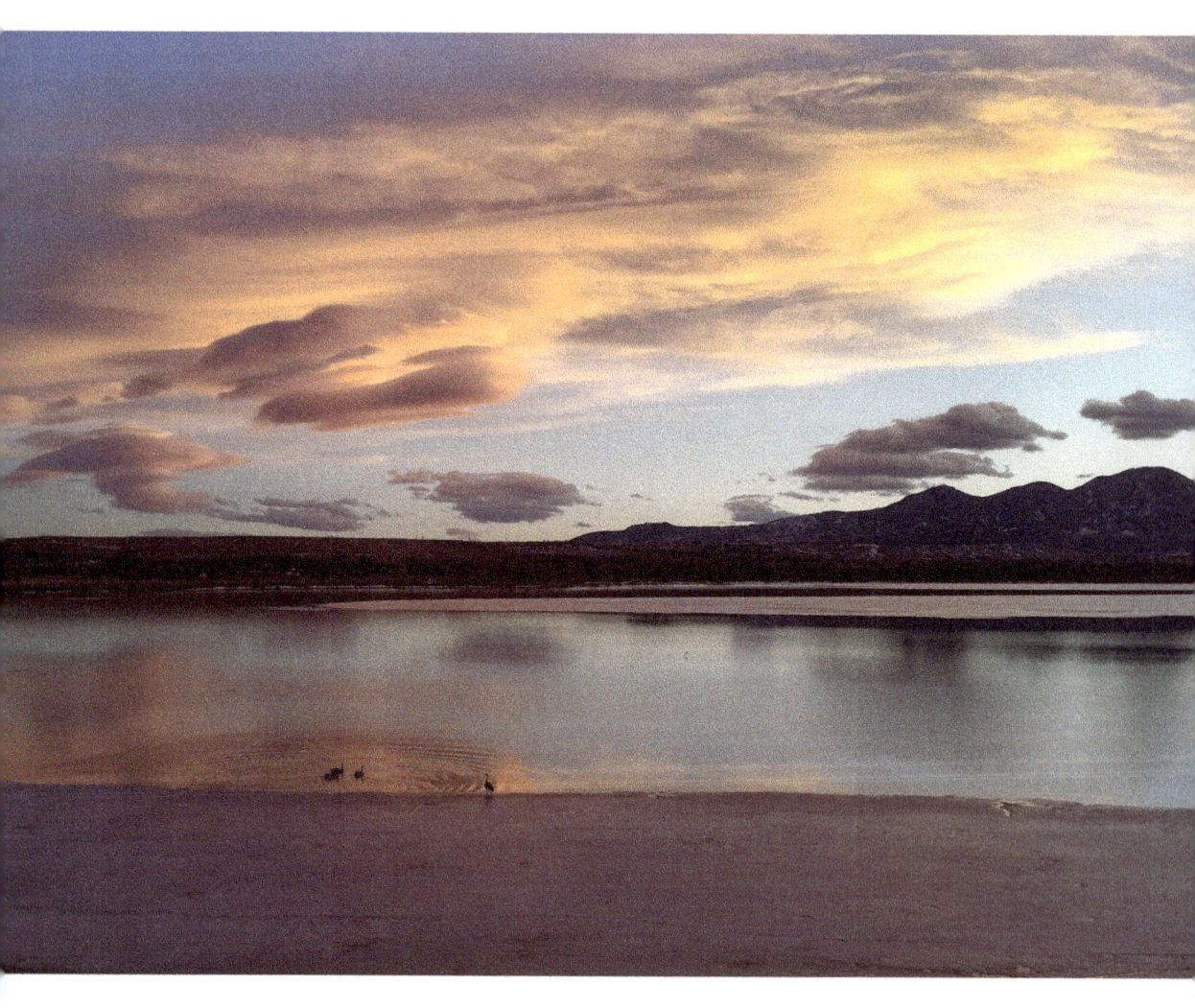

January 1

There are many paths to greatness and you, you will have your own path. #HappyNewYear

Jenny Simpson @TrackJenny

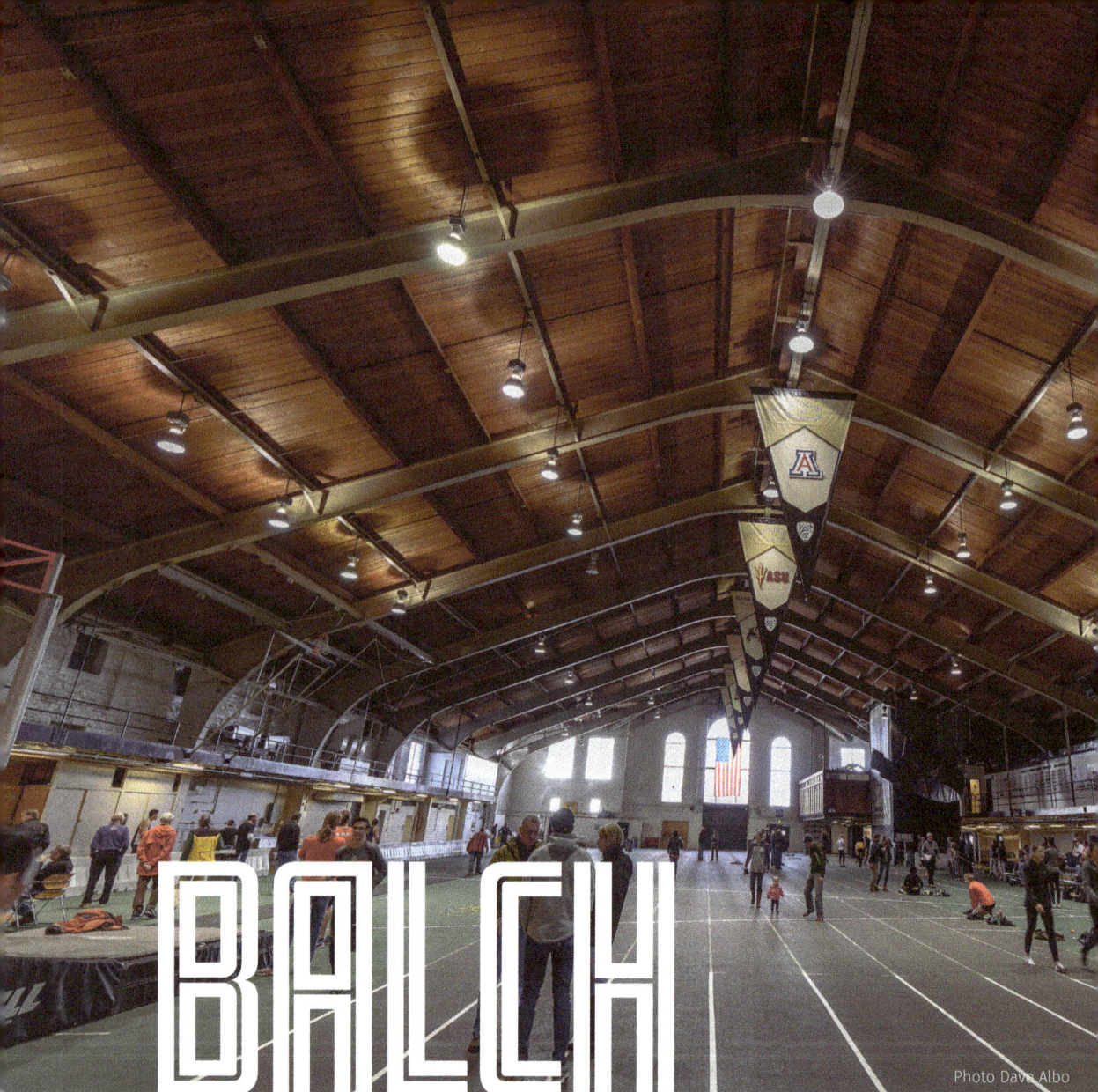

BALCH

Photo Dave Albo

The overhead lights in the fieldhouse are off during the winter break. Only dim light slips through it's cathedral windows, providing just enough illumination for a few athletes to work on their form with throws coach Casey Malone. It may be easier to reflect on its glory days in the quiet and darkness.

The southern upper bleachers are pulling away from the wall and have been deemed unsafe but the hallowed names of NCAA All Americans and Olympians remain looking down on the field below. It's three flat, narrow lanes, measuring a tight 200 meters per lap, have served many a runner over the years since it was built in 1936 but are now tired and worn.

Frank Shorter chose Boulder specifically, not only because of its altitude, but because CU's Fieldhouse was the only indoor track in the region. He spent many a winter training here, rolling out hard workouts like 200m repeats preparing for the 1976 Olympics. The fieldhouse was open to the public back then. Amateur and elite athetes alike flocked to the warmth of the gym on cold winter days.

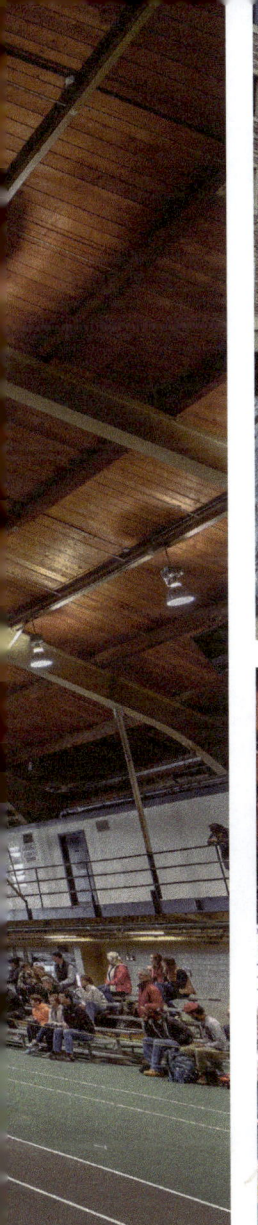
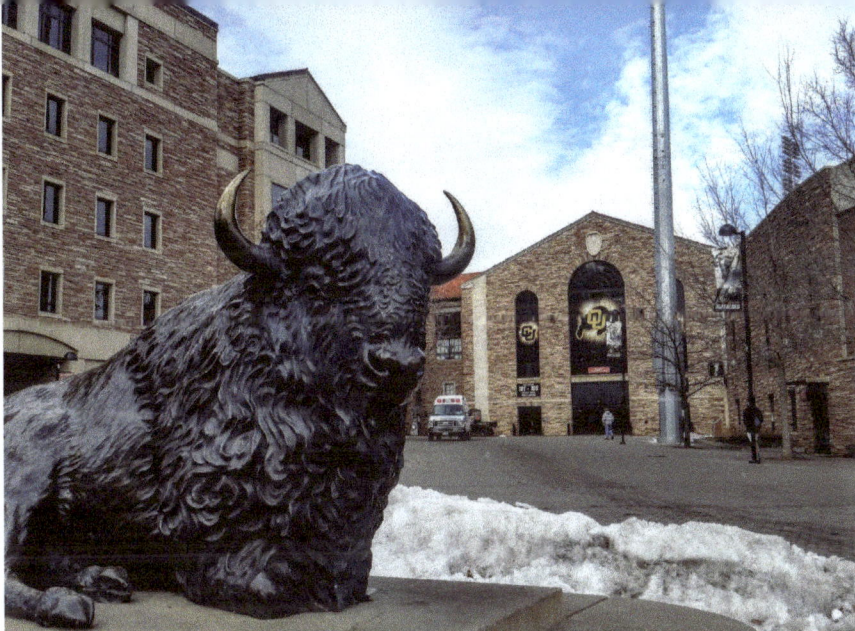
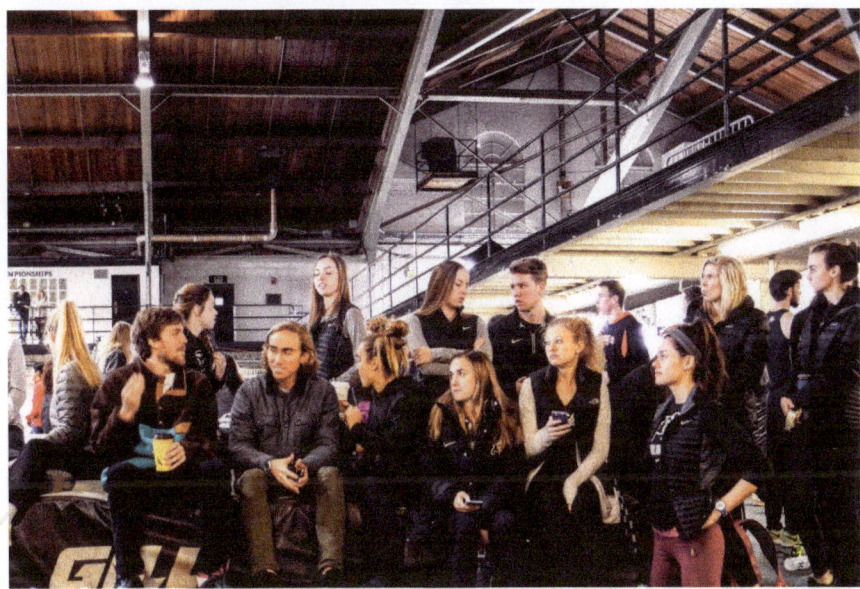
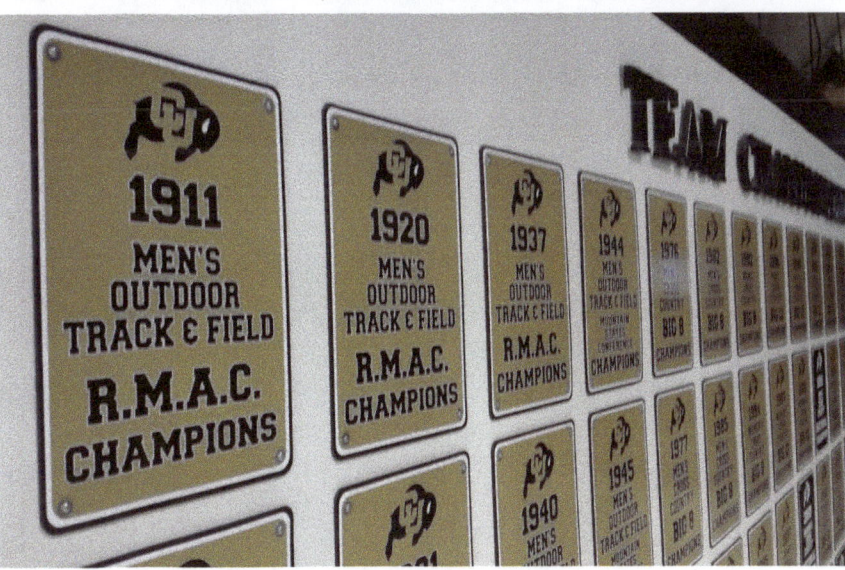

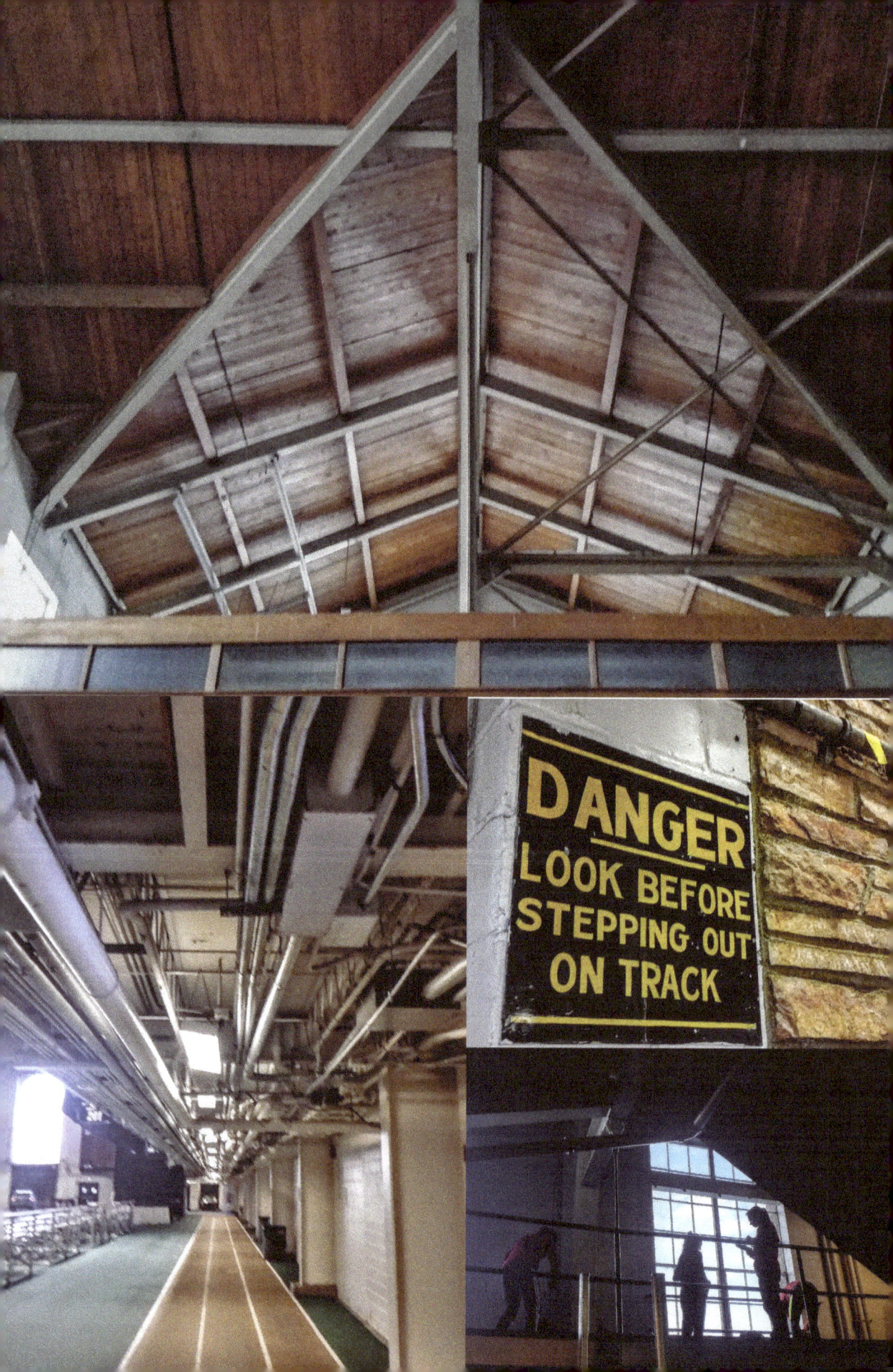

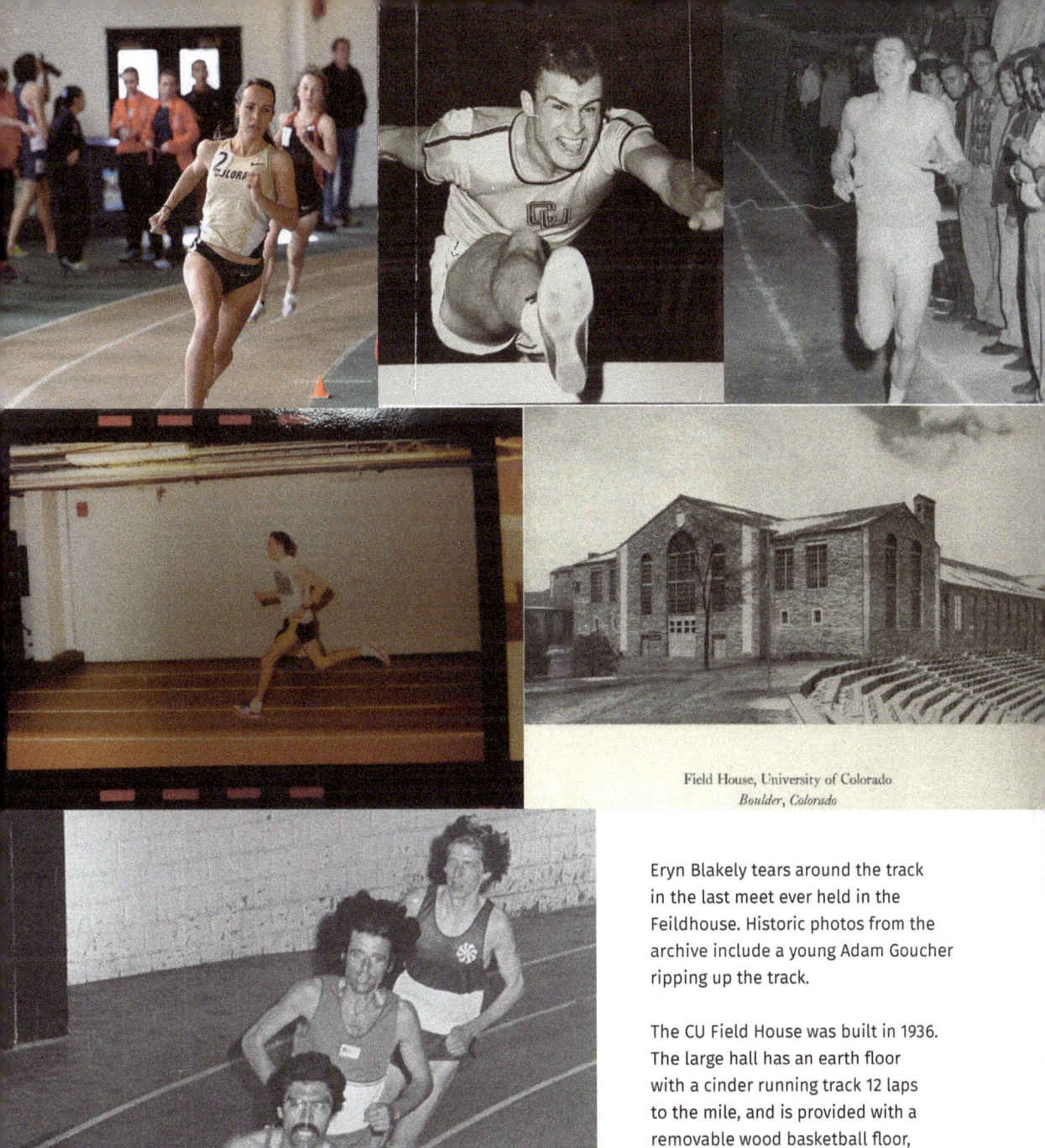

Eryn Blakely tears around the track in the last meet ever held in the Feildhouse. Historic photos from the archive include a young Adam Goucher ripping up the track.

The CU Field House was built in 1936. The large hall has an earth floor with a cinder running track 12 laps to the mile, and is provided with a removable wood basketball floor, 60 by 90 feet. Permanent bleachers seat approximately 2,000, and removable bleachers on both sides of the basketball court can seat approximately 1,900.

Photos courtesy of University of Colorado Archives.

Ric Rojas leads Frank Shorter and Stan Mavis in the Potts Invitational 2 mile circa 1980.
Photo courtesy of Ric Rojas

VOLUNTEERS
RUNNING'S OTHER HALF

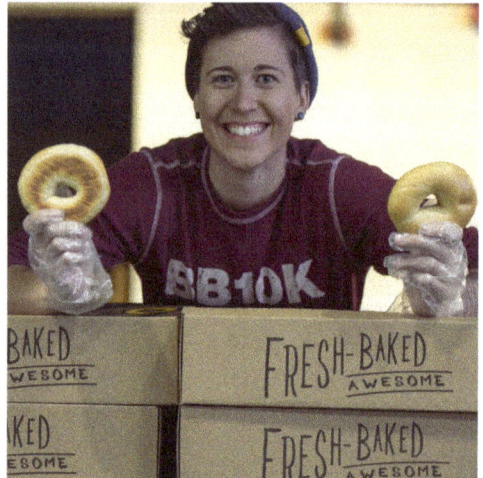
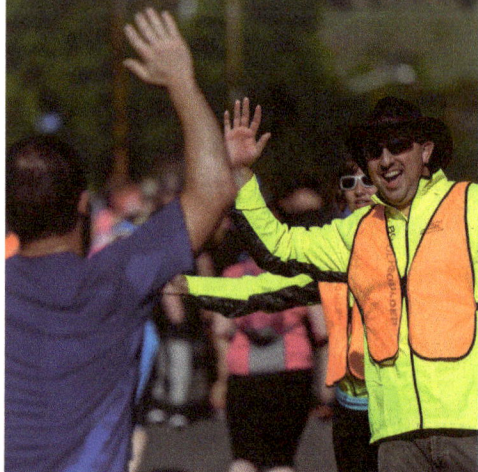
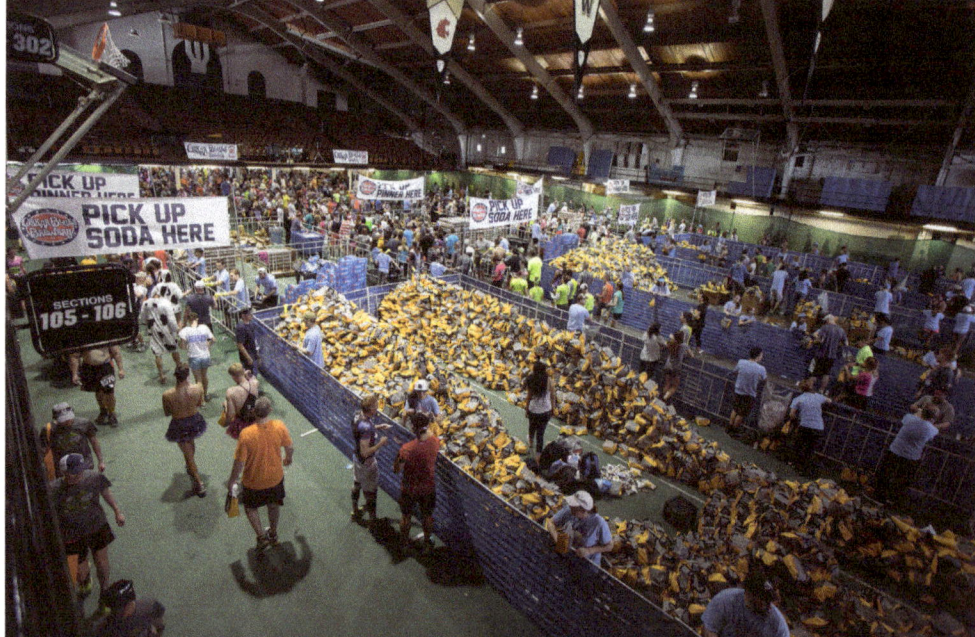

Volunteers are a vital part and essential backbone of the running community. Whether it's helping make races go smoothly, keeping you hydrated and fed during a race, or working behind the scenes, volunteers are key to a strong community. They help deliver shoes, build trails, time races, and more. Without volunteers, we would not be the community we are today.

We wanted to take a moment to thank the thousands of volunteers in our amazing running community.

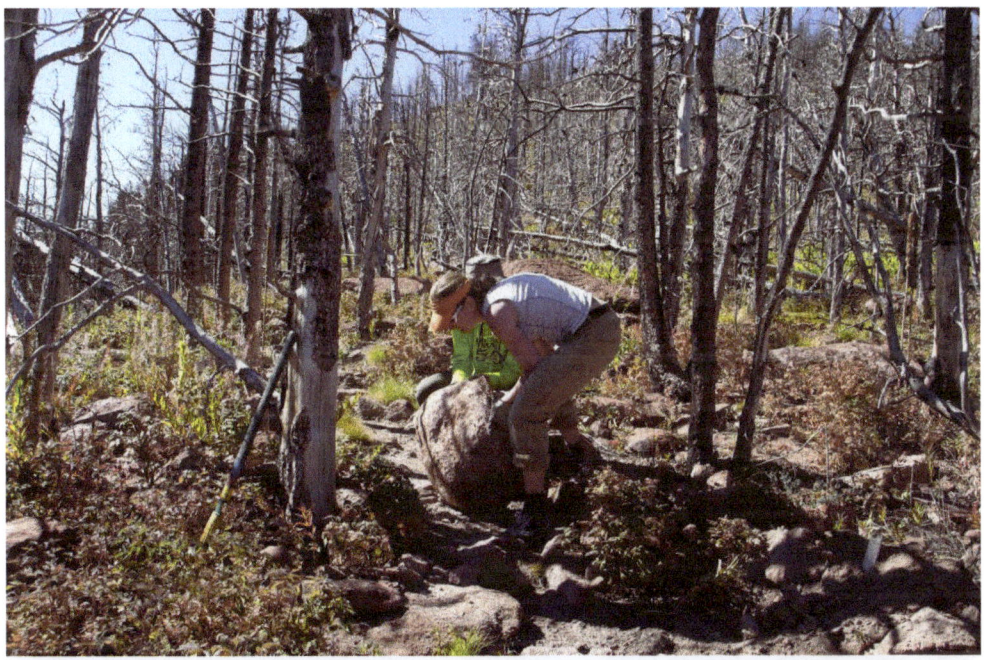

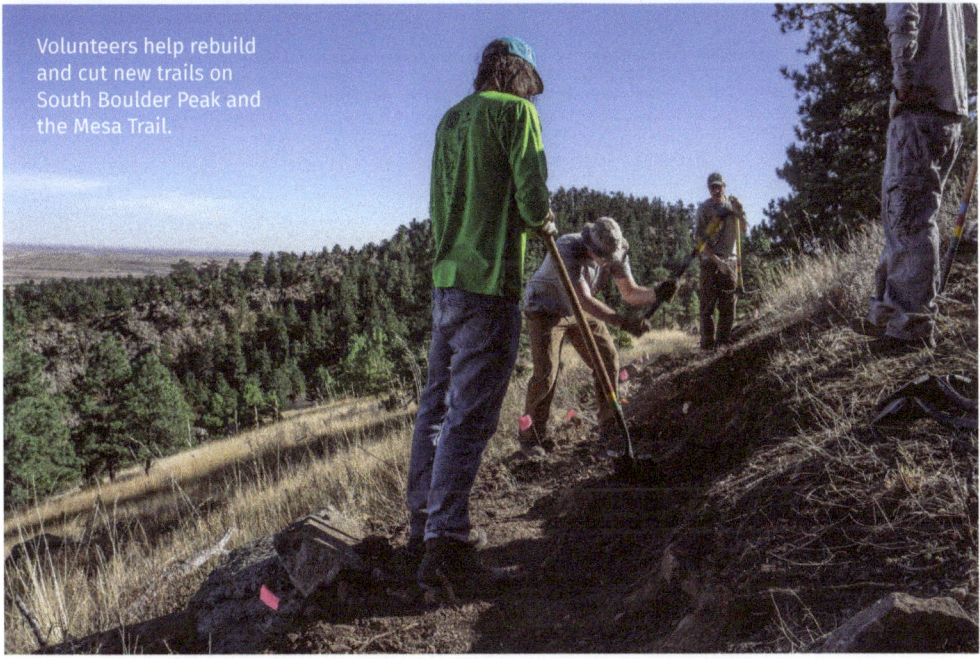

Volunteers help rebuild and cut new trails on South Boulder Peak and the Mesa Trail.

Photos - Opposite page: Glen Delman and Dave Albo. This page courtesy of OSMP and Todd Straka

COLBY HARMON

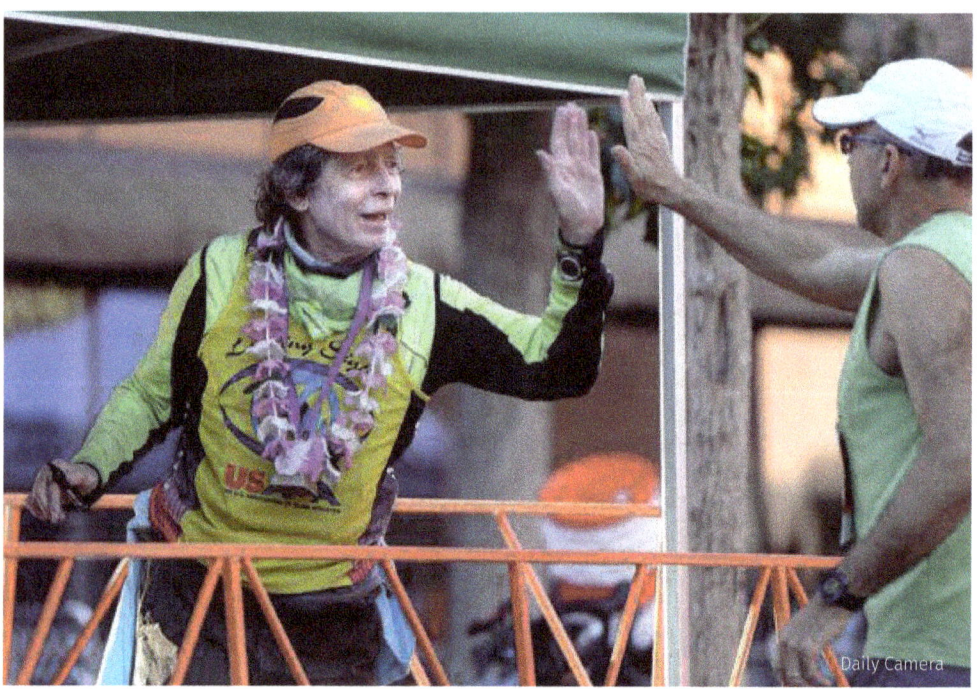

Colby (Charles) Harmon passed away Tuesday March 22, 2016 just over a week after celebrating his 75th birthday. He was a member of the Boulder Road Runners, Fast Forward and Revolution Running for several years. Deb Conley met Colby on a Boulder Road Runner Sunday run when he first came to Boulder and remembered him in these ways:

He lived an amazing life that many were not aware of. He spoke Thai fluently. He talked about his favorite memories as a young adult serving in the Peace Corps for two years in Thailand. He was among the first classes of the Peace Corps and was personally thanked by John F. Kennedy for his service. He applied six times before being accepted. Those years and experiences shaped his beliefs in living simply and in having peace, and his enthusiasm for animal and human instincts. He was a dedicated father, raising his son as a single parent and working three jobs. Colby retired from Cal Poly after some 30 years of work.

BOULDER ROAD RUNNERS

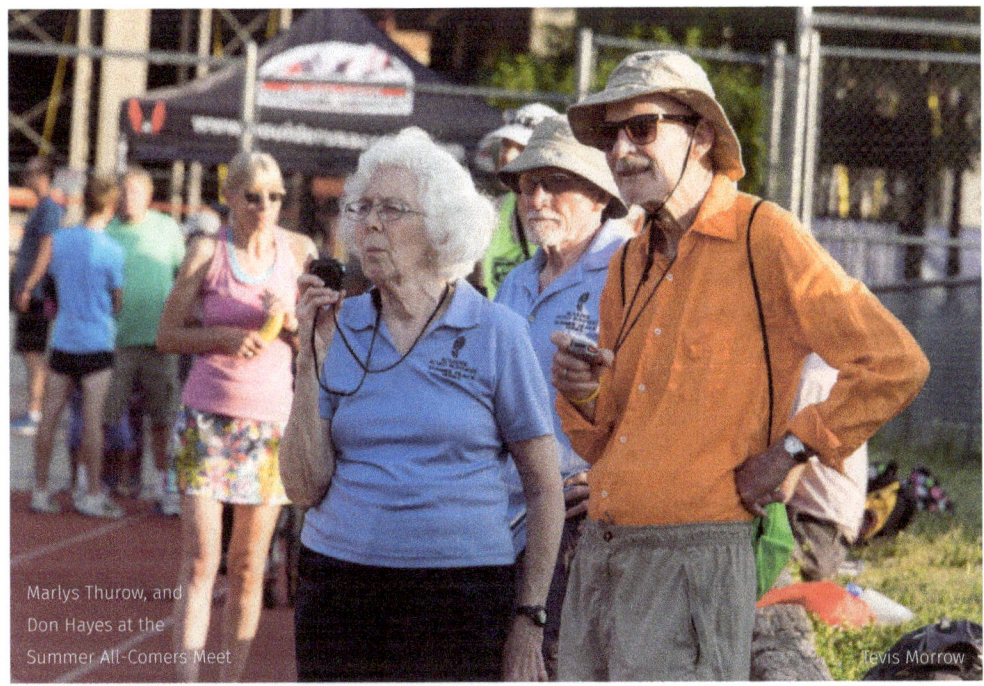

Marlys Thurow, and Don Hayes at the Summer All-Comers Meet — Tevis Morrow

Super Volunteers

Bill Buffum
Tom LeMire
Chuck Lowrie
Don Janicki
Joyce LeMire
John Bridges
Terry Femmer
Terry Haran
Ellen Moeller
Tom O'Banion
Mary Poole
Frank Shafer
Ken Thurow
Marlys Thurow

Stacy Apple
DeeDee Beard
Steve Carlson
Sue Carlson
Deb Conley
Sandy Edmundson
Bill Faulkner
Karen Fuchs
Lorraine Green
Don Hayes
Vinny Juliano
Lynne Kidder
Karen Lechman
Nancy Peter
Dan Pierce
Lyle Rosbotham
Gavin Slater
Judy Smythe
Pat Toleson
JoAnn Wolbier

Steve Ackman, David Apple, Anne Bartuszerge, Mo Baselli, Quin Baselli, Steve Baselli, Angela Bryan, Laird Cagan, John Caldwell, Vern Carlson, Johnny Chapin, Austin Connolly, Sharon Connolly, Devin Croft, Jeff Dumas, Andy Edmundson, Lance Evans, David Femmer, Patty Femmer, Mike Fenerty, Brent Friesth, Bob Fuchs, Eugene Gaub, Ryan Hale, Anne Hammond, Harry Hammond, Sara Handing, David Hardwick, Chris Hayes, Scott Hooten, Gail Hunter, Kirsten Kindt, Bruce Kirschner, Duane Klenk, Jeanette Kornreich, Scott Kornreich, Tom Kunstman, Jody Manning, Kristin McLauren, Carl Mohr, Sally Mohr, Lisa Munsch, Rick Nastico, Tarrance, O'Connor, Bob Parizek, Jean Pierce, Alec Pott, Don Price, Peter Richards, Pat Robak, Neesha Schnepf, Nick Schnepf, Pam Slater, Rod Smythe, Edie Stevenson, Michelle Van Pelt, Cindy Van SchouWen, Jennifer Vincent, Katie Walkden, John Zamora

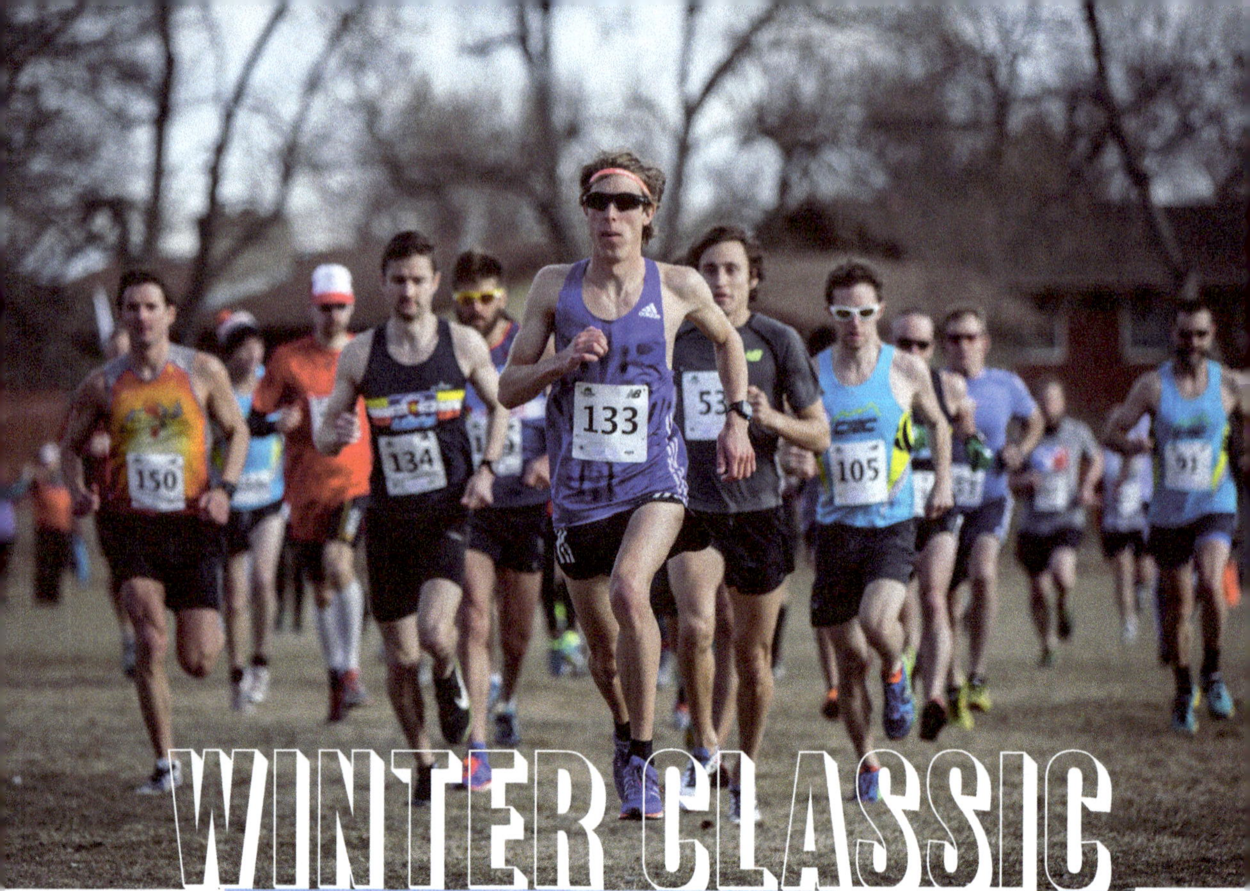

WINTER CLASSIC

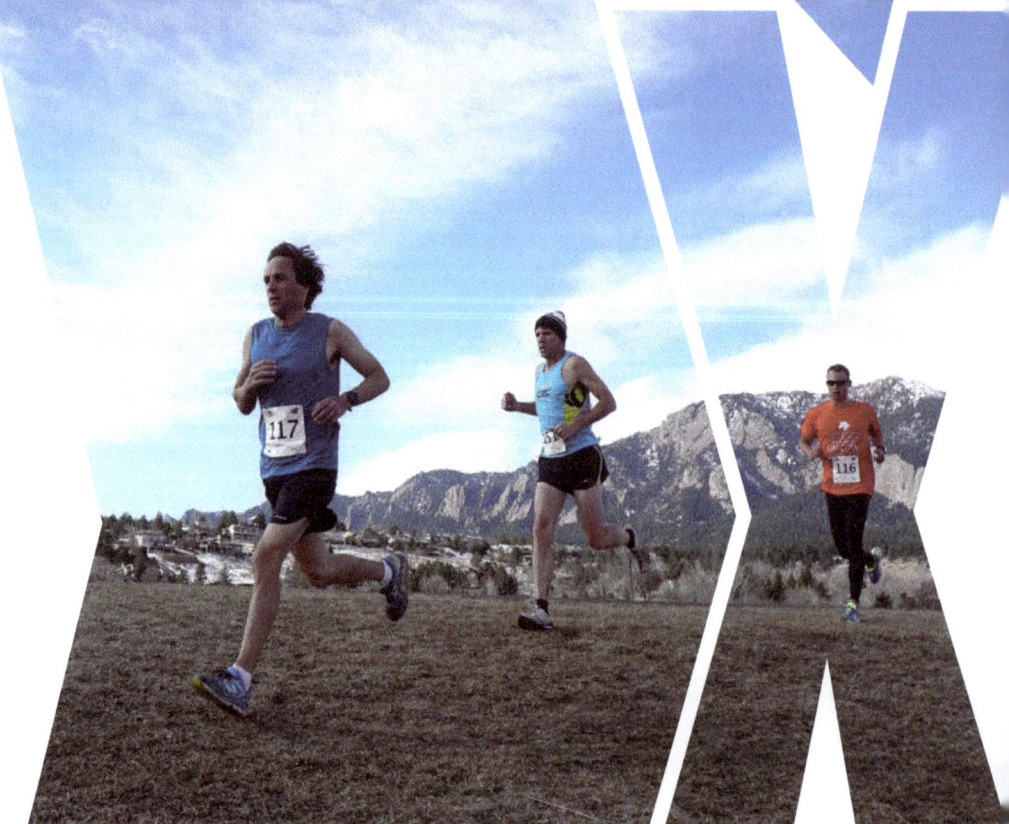

Photos Glen Delman and Todd Straka

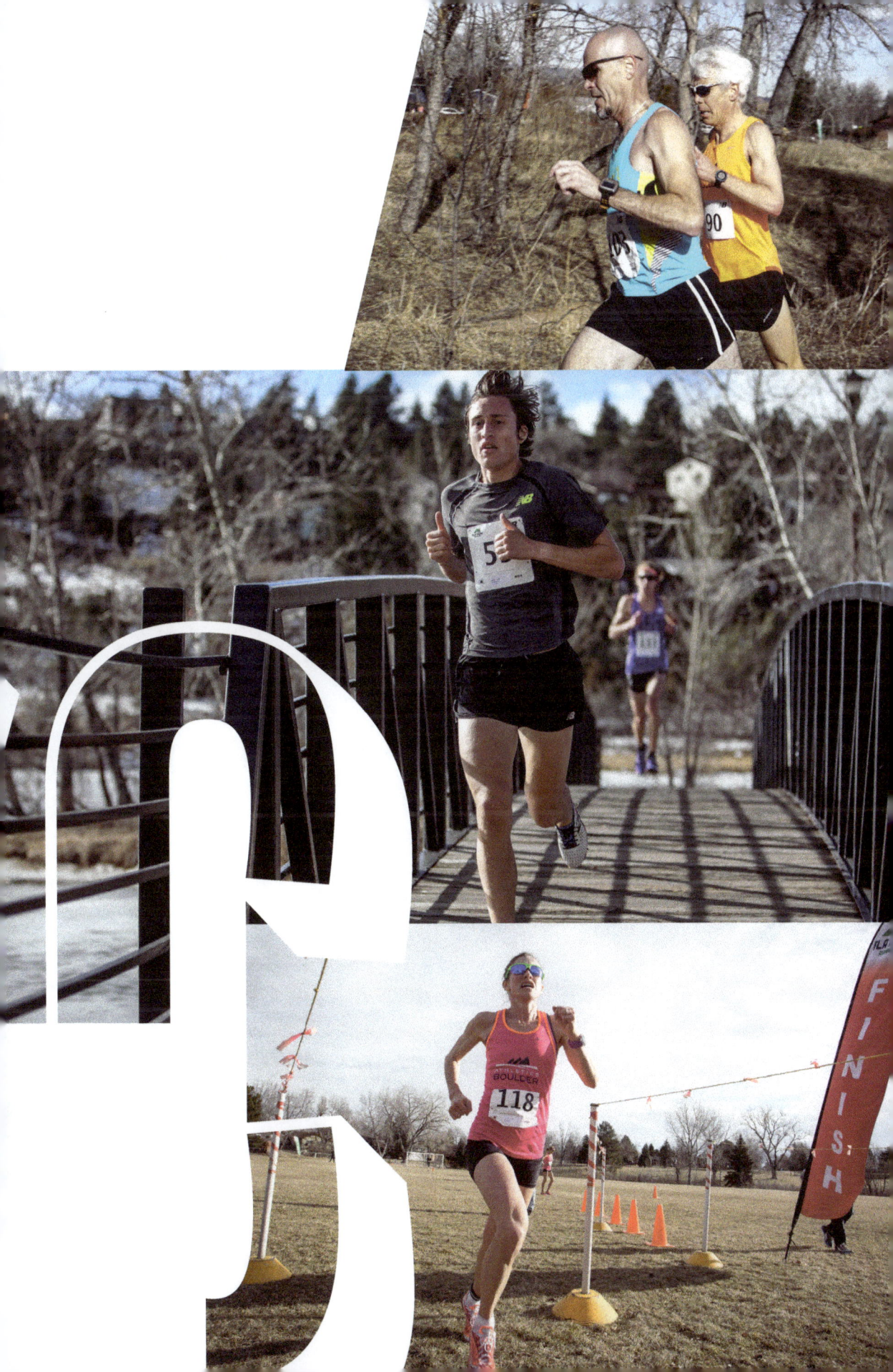

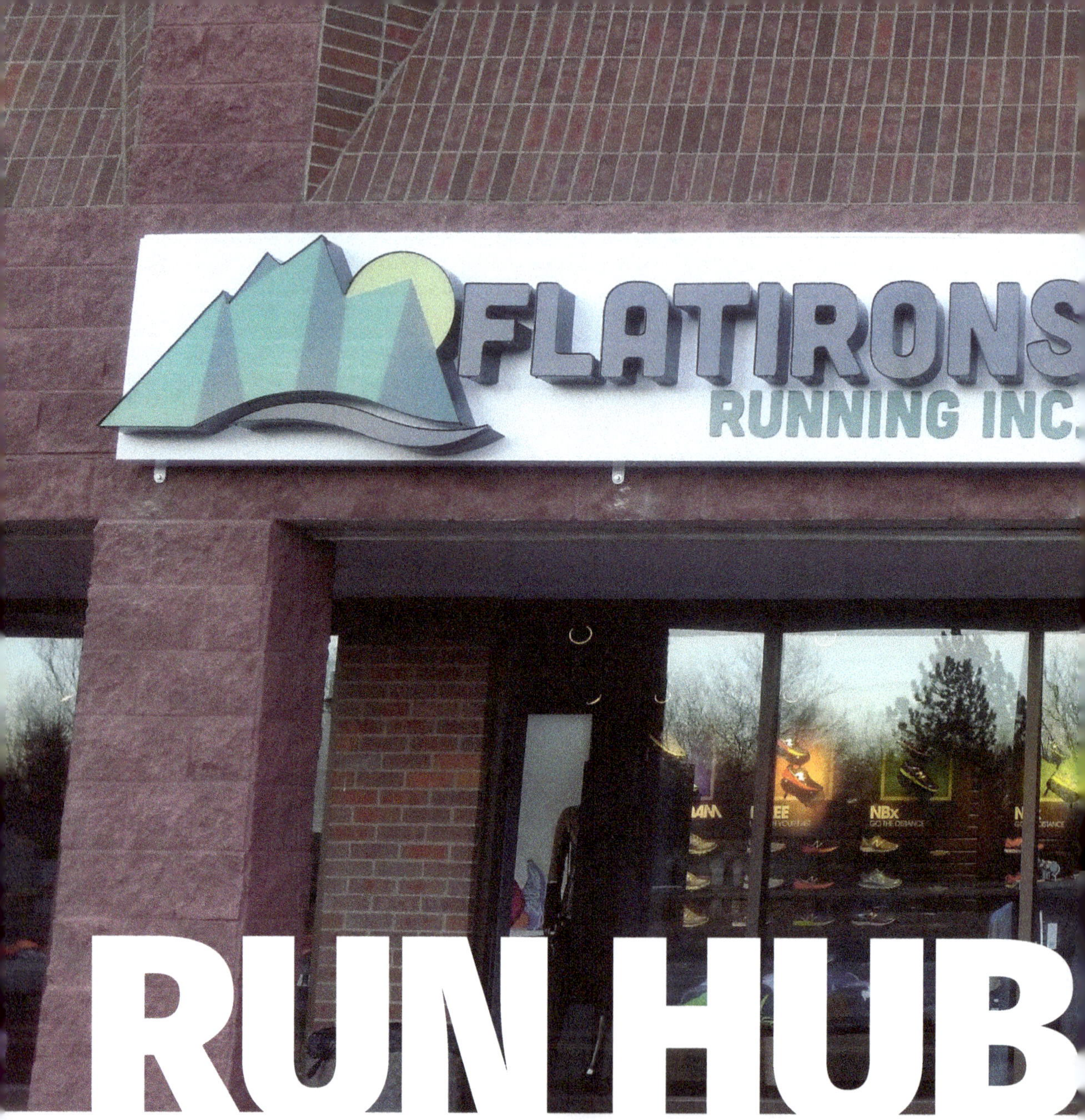

RUN HUB

Flatirons Running partners with New Balance to create a unique gathering place for runners.

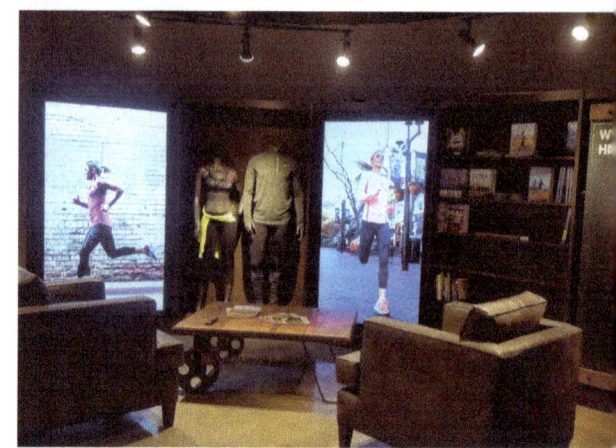

23

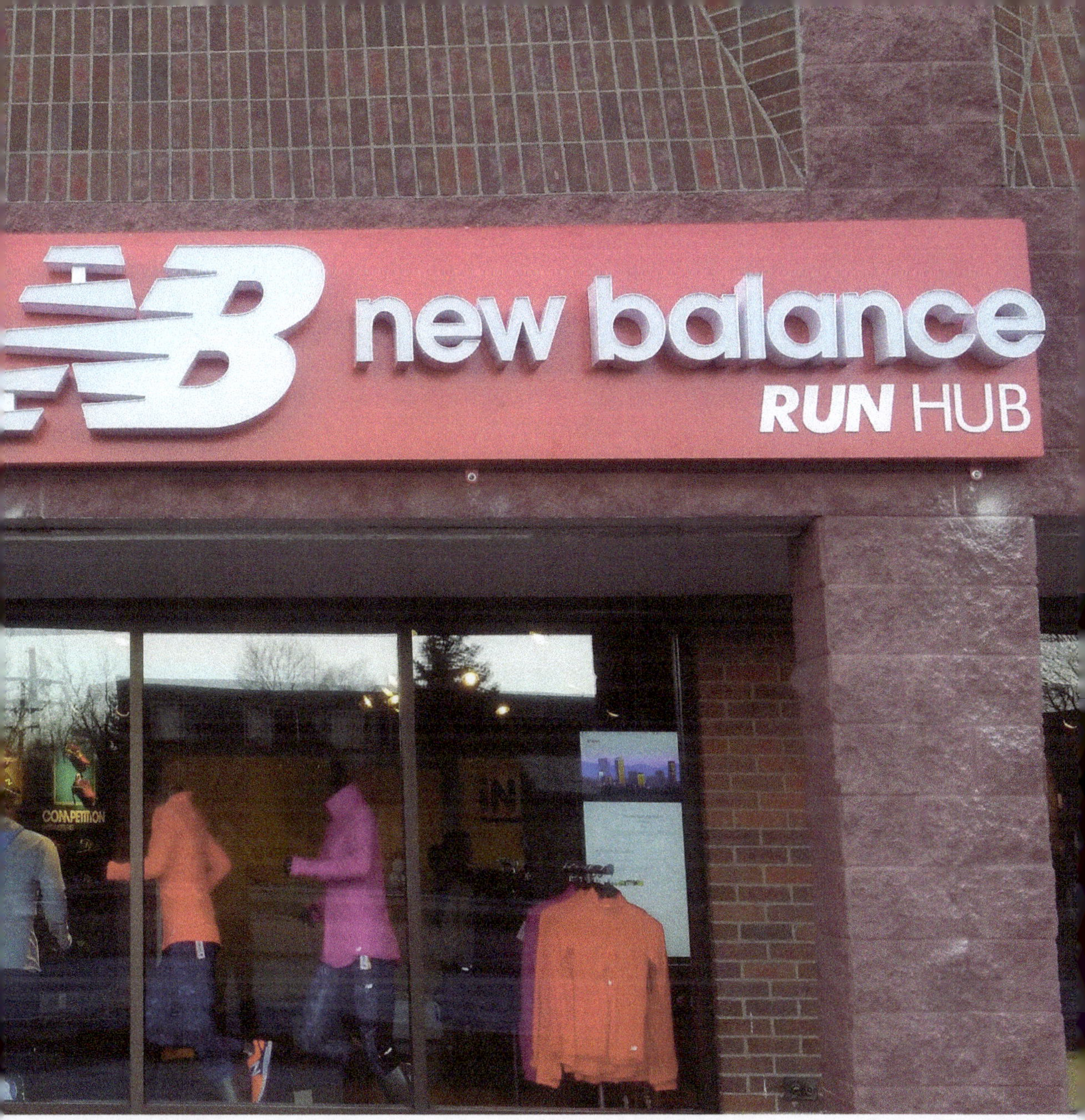

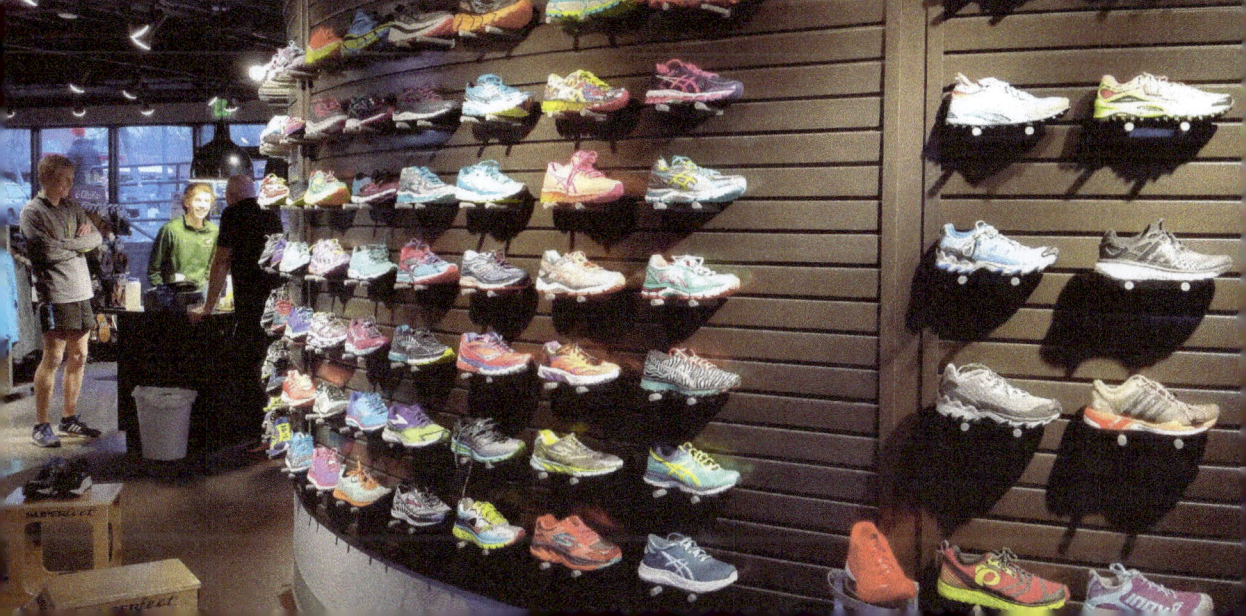

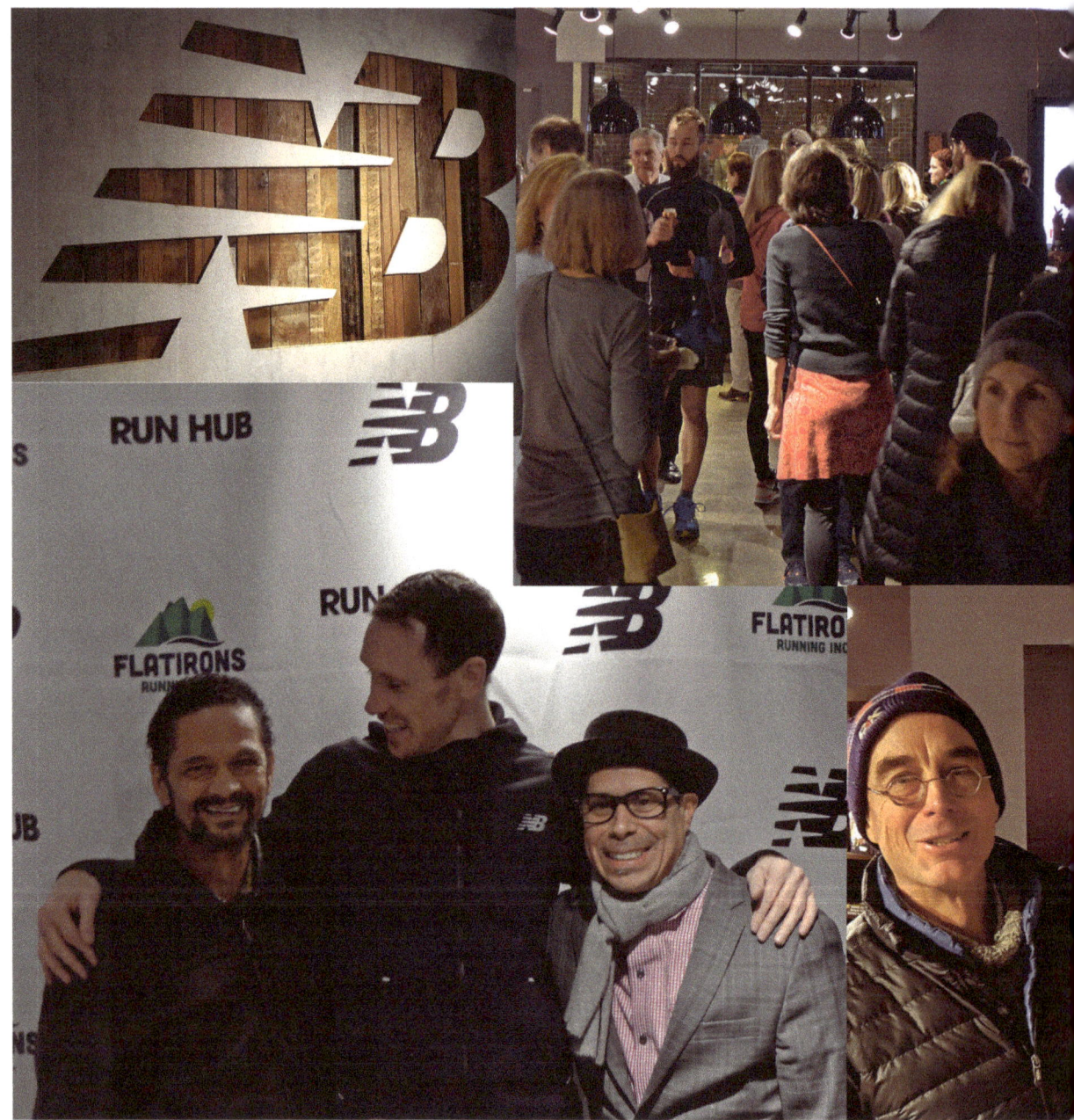

Grand Opening Gala

In January, the final touches on the freshly expanded and redesigned space were complete and it was time to celebrate.

Photos Peter Jones, Glen Delman, and Todd Straka

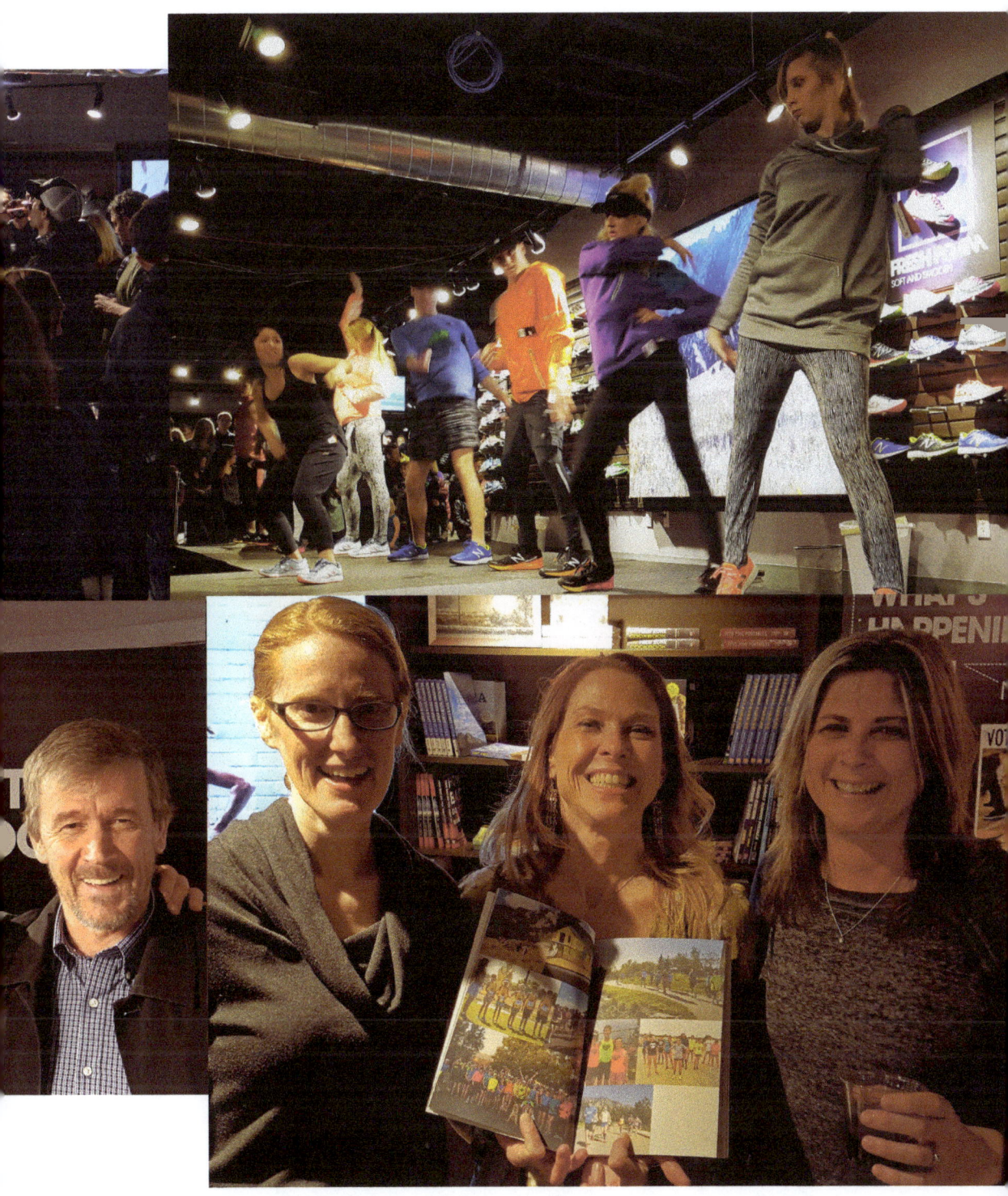

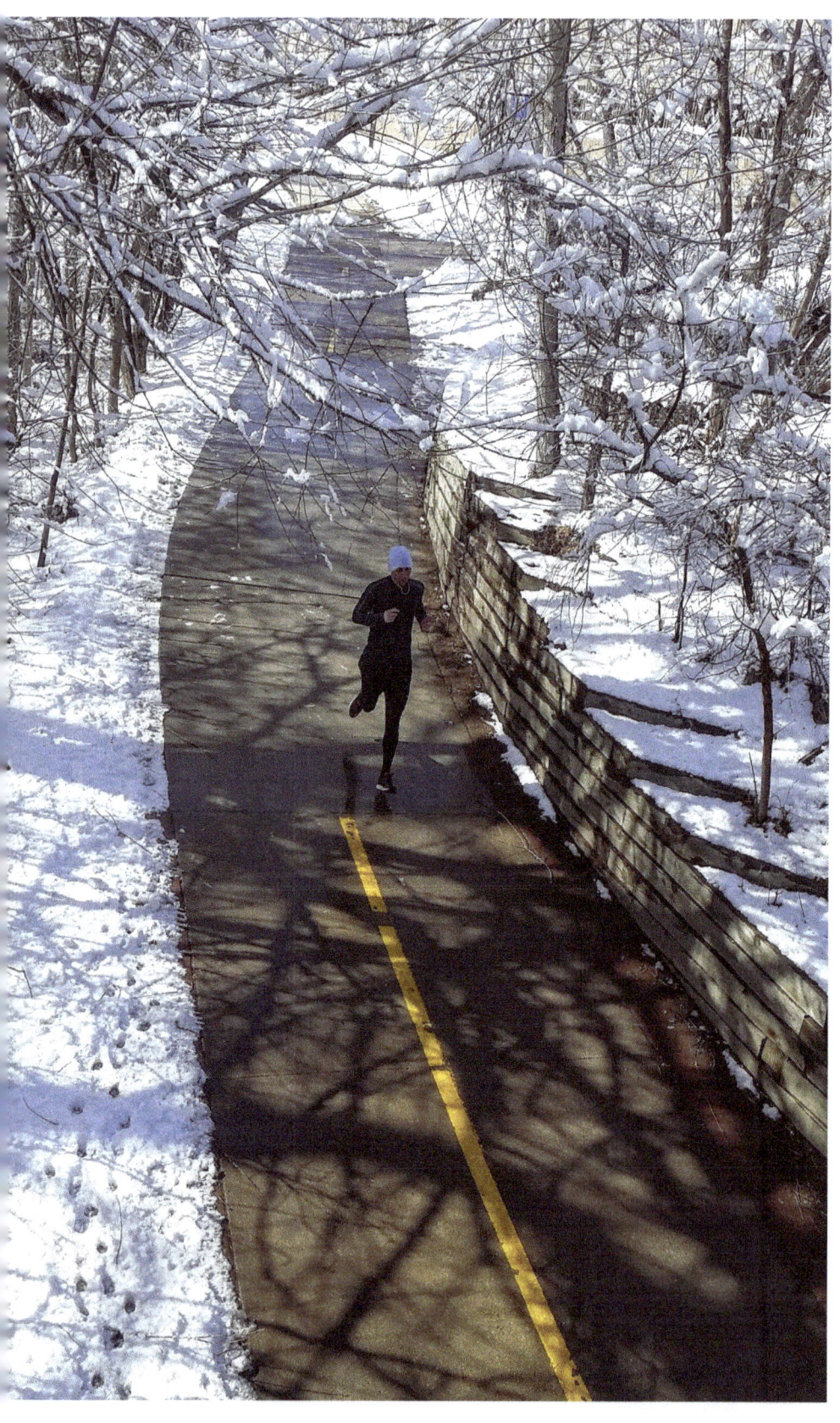

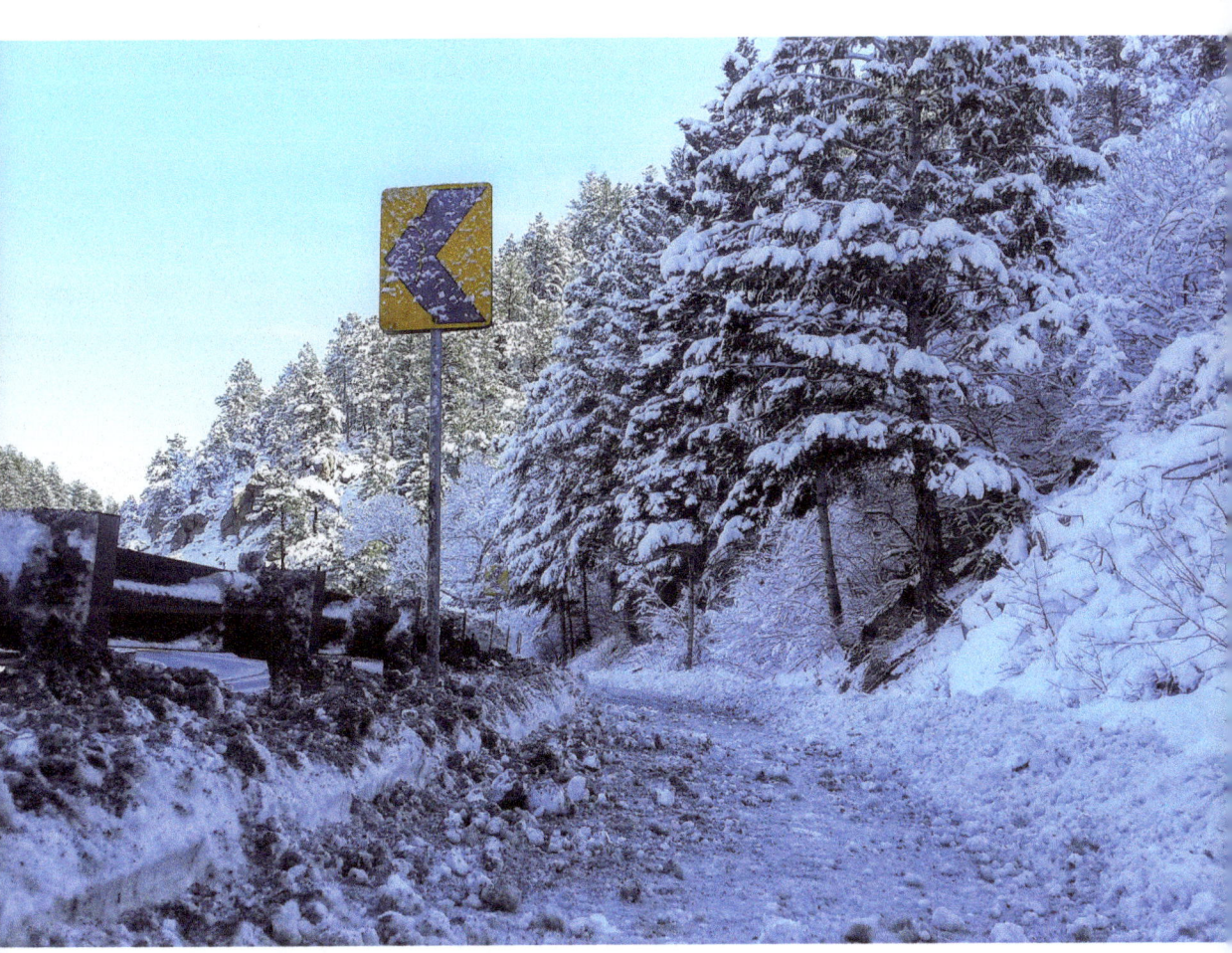

Words by John O'Dea
CLOSE CALL

It happens all too often on the roads around Boulder: a close encounter between a runner or cyclist and a car that (at best) leaves us feeling helpless as we shout at a rapidly departing vehicle and marvel at the indifference to our lives.

Close Call

For me, that moment came in February 2016 as I was training for my first full marathon. My race was a month out and while I much prefer to run trails, I had a number of long runs that could only be accomplished on the road.

The fateful Thursday found me running north on 63rd street past the Boulder Reservoir and towards Niwot. I was in reflective gear, which was still more than adequate in the late afternoon light. As I was running, I suddenly heard the roar of tires behind me and I lurched to the left. As I did, I was immediately struck by the windblast of a vehicle that was overtaking a long line of cars. At first blush, I thought that it had hit my right arm.

My head spun around in time to see a lifted 4x4 with aftermarket bumpers, lifted suspension and oversized mud tires fly past just inches away. I watched as the truck continued past the remaining cars. After screaming a few choice expletives, I stopped on the side of the road and shook, knowing how close I had just come to being killed. I estimated that the truck had been travelling at 70 plus miles per hour as it was overtaking the string of afternoon commuters.

For the rest of my run that day, I looked for that truck in every driveway along the route. When I arrived home for dinner, I recounted the story for my family, but there was no way to adequately express how close I had come to being another two-paragraph story in the Daily Camera without jeopardizing my ability to do the remaining long runs I needed for my race.

As I thought about it that night, it occurred to me that given the time of day, the person driving was likely heading home from school or work. I further surmised that Gunbarrel would be a likely place for that person to be coming from. The next morning, immediately after dropping my (not freshly fatherless) kids off at school, I drove out to 63rd Street and set up in a place where I could see the in-bound traffic. I watched traffic for an hour without result and logged the time in my journal.

That afternoon, I had another window between 3:00 and 4:00. My years as a private investigator taught me that if I simply covered the available slots, at some point over a period of days or weeks, my suspect vehicle would drive by. Alas, on this Friday it was not to be.

Saturday morning found me at the kitchen table with my laptop. The truck was pretty distinctive. As an off road enthusiast myself, I knew exactly was I was looking for. The truck had an uncommon aftermarket rear bumper with swing away rear tire carrier and a Hi-Lift jack mounted at an odd angle. After a few hours trolling through offroad forums, I found the truck (or so I thought). Same color, same lift, same rear bumper. Working backwards from the screen name and town, I was able to attach a name and address to the truck.

The owner and his wife were well-established business people. The driving style I'd witnessed was incongruous with someone who owned a business and who had two small children. Nevertheless, I kept digging until I found another picture of that truck. It had oversized tires, but all terrain tread, not the mud tires that were still roaring in my head. Still, I continued reading the forum posts by that person until I saw this exchange:

Screen Name 1: "I saw you driving on Arapaho Avenue yesterday. I flashed my lights, but you didn't wave.

Screen Name 2: "It wasn't me. You must have seen [Screenname X], he has the identical truck. People confuse us all the time."

Sure enough, [Screenname X] did have the identical truck. Working backwards from his screen name, I found a picture of his well-built truck, with the mud tires and distinctive rear bumper.

Over the course of the weekend, I was able to stitch together a pretty complete portrait of [Screenname X]s life. He had grown up in a rural state where he and his brother shared a passion for anything with wheels on it including bikes, motorcycles, cars and trucks. He had been an athlete in college, raced bikes and motorcycles while earning an engineering degree. From there, I was able to identify his employer... located right in the heart of Gunbarrel.

Monday morning, after dropping the kids off at school, I drove to the employer's facility and located the truck in the parking lot. What I hadn't seen the preceding Thursday was the home made front bumper made from a 10" piece of steel C channel. I shivered at the thought of getting whacked in the kidney by that bumper moving at 70 mph.

I walked inside the office and asked the receptionist if I could speak with "Paul". She took my name and asked if he was expecting me. "Oh yes," I replied. "He has been waiting for me since Thursday."

A few minutes later, Paul came around the corner. He was a typical late 20's engineer... right down to the safety glasses. He said "Do I know you?" I said "No, but I know you. I am here as a courtesy because we have some mutual friends in the bike world and in the off-road community. I am the person you almost killed last week."

"I don't know what you are talking about."

"Let me clarify. On Thursday, you cleared the parking lot here at 4:10 p.m. By 4:18, you were headed north on 63rd and overtook a string of cars. I am the runner you almost struck as you were passing". His face went ashen and he said, "I am so sorry, I am..." I put my hand up and stopped him. I told "Paul" that because of our mutual friends, I had chosen to come speak with him instead of swearing out a complaint at the sheriff's office... or worse.

I explained that I too was a motorhead with similar interests who identified with his life growing up in [his small town in his home state]. I also told him if he had struck me, as he had come so close to doing, that my wife and two children would be burying me that very day and that his life would have been forever changed as well.

He said "I feel so sorry" and I put my hand up again and stopped him.

I said "If we'd met another way, you and I would probably be friends. Now that we know each other, if we are ever in the same place again, your job, unlike the last time, is to see me first... and bring me a cold beer. He grinned, stuck out his hand and said "fair enough."

We never know which run will be our last. I often think about how close I came to getting scrubbed out that February day. Had I done so, my friends and family would have consoled themselves by saying that I died doing what I loved. All of us who pine for the trail, or the open road, would prefer to do what we love and live.

Let's make 2017 the year that we strive for more accountability from our fellow motorists and, as a community of runners, set an example of how we want to be interacted with on the road. This includes leading by example and waiting to text until we are out of the car. As for "Paul", I hope that the next time he is hot footing it down some 2-lane road, he is mindful of the new "friends" he could meet along the way.

The names have been changed and several key details have been omitted. The author can be found running the trails, and occasionally the roadways, of Boulder County.

OLYMPIC MARATHON TRIALS

LOS ANGELES

With over 50 qualifiers from Colorado attending, many from the Boulder area, there was much excitement around the Olympic Marathon Trials held in Los Angeles on February 13. While many Boulderites put in early bids in hot conditions for the coveted Team spots, there were three Top 10 performances from Boulder area runners, starting with Kara Goucher just missing the Team with a strong 4th place finish.

Sean Quigley of the Boulder Track Club was 9th in the men's field, while Alia Gray of Roots Running Project was 10th in the women's field and ran a PR of 2:35:47. Other notable top performances were Adriana Nelson, Co-Founder of Roll Recovery in 12th, Boulder Track Club's Wendy Thomas of Windsor who took 17th, Whitney Bevins of Roots Running Project in 31st, and BRC/adidas' Brianne Nelson who was 35th. For the men, Jeffrey Eggleston was 13th overall while Boulder Track Club's Jonathan Grey was 36th in his marathon debut which also happened to be his birthday.

Heat and injuries proved to be too much for many of the competitors, even on what may have been the biggest race of their life.

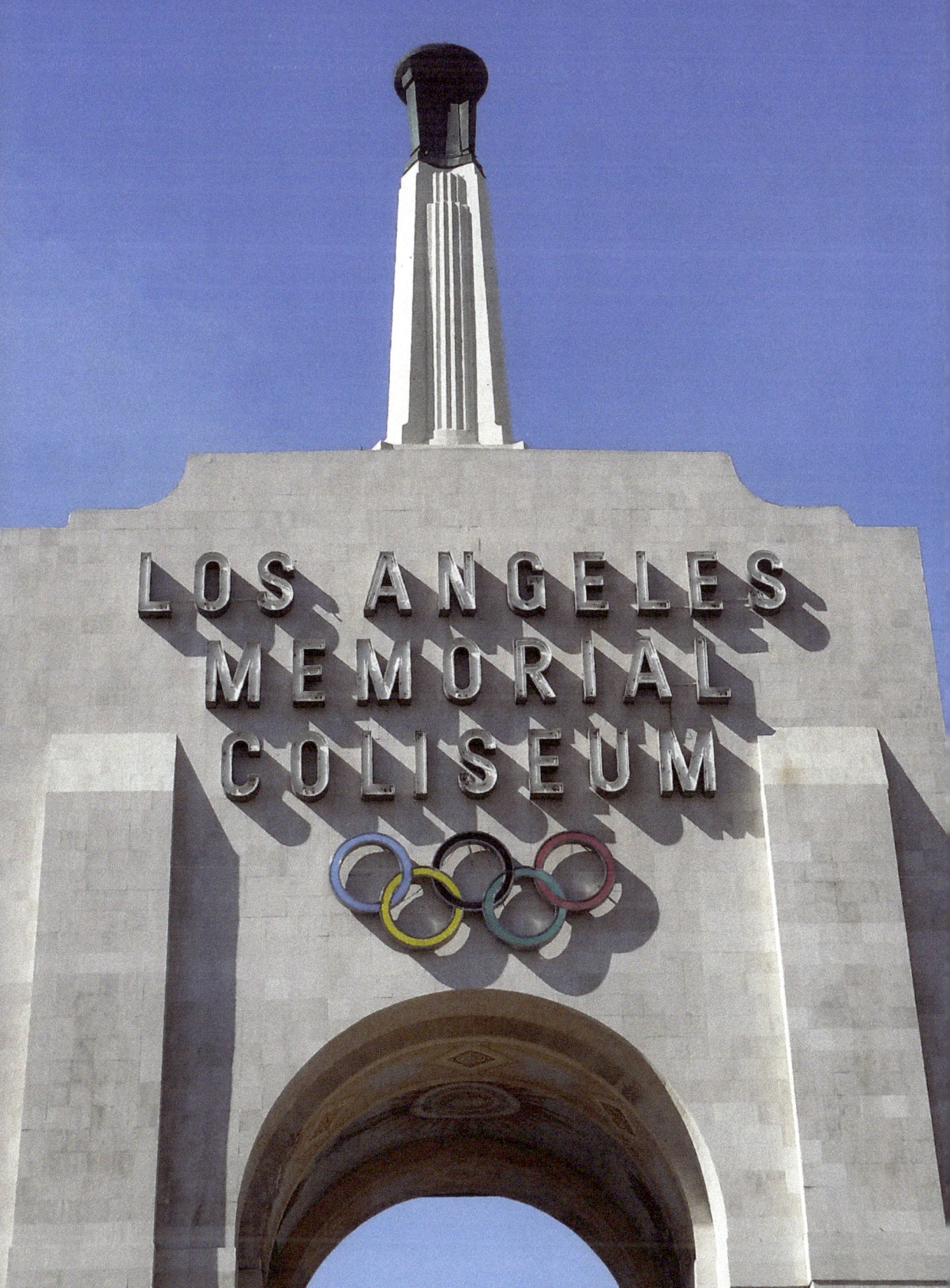

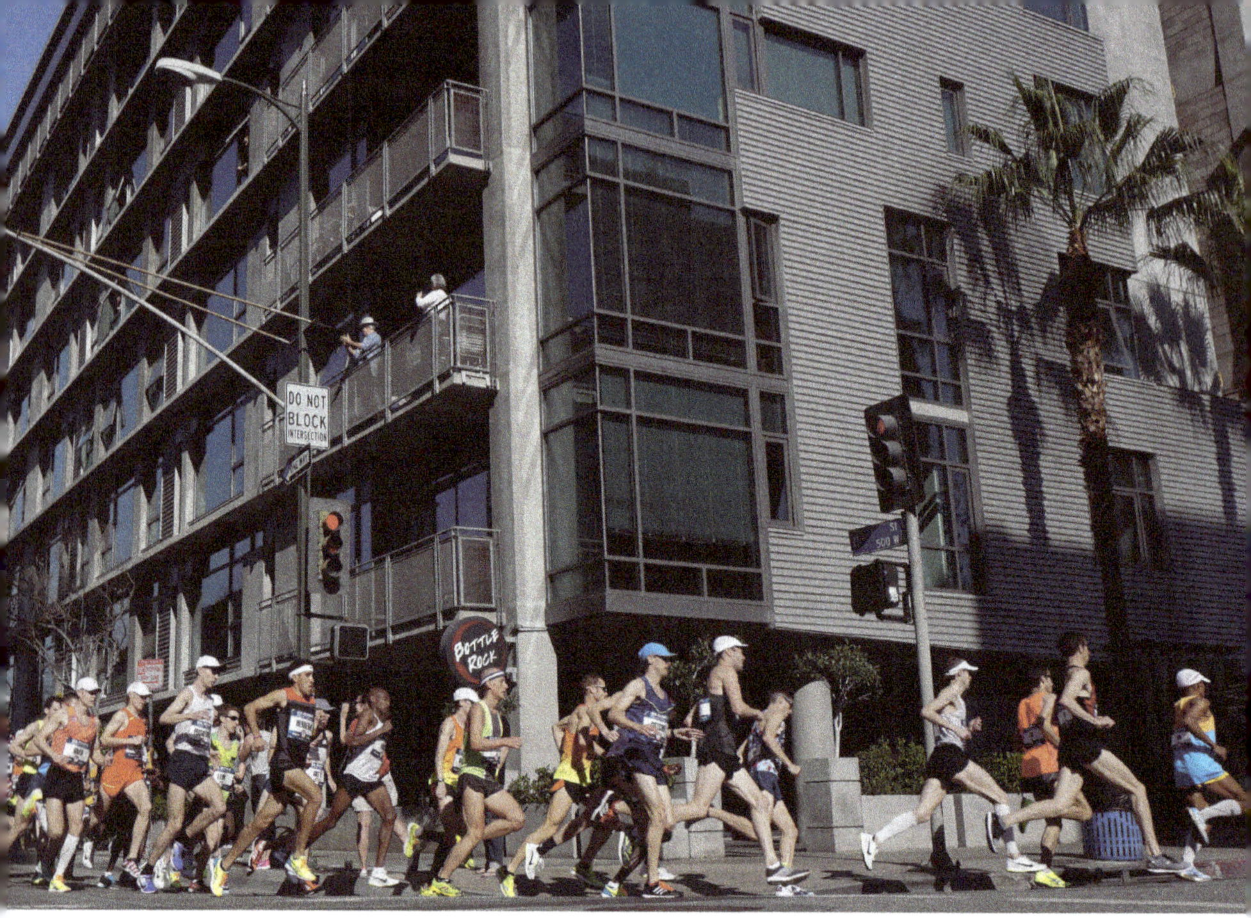

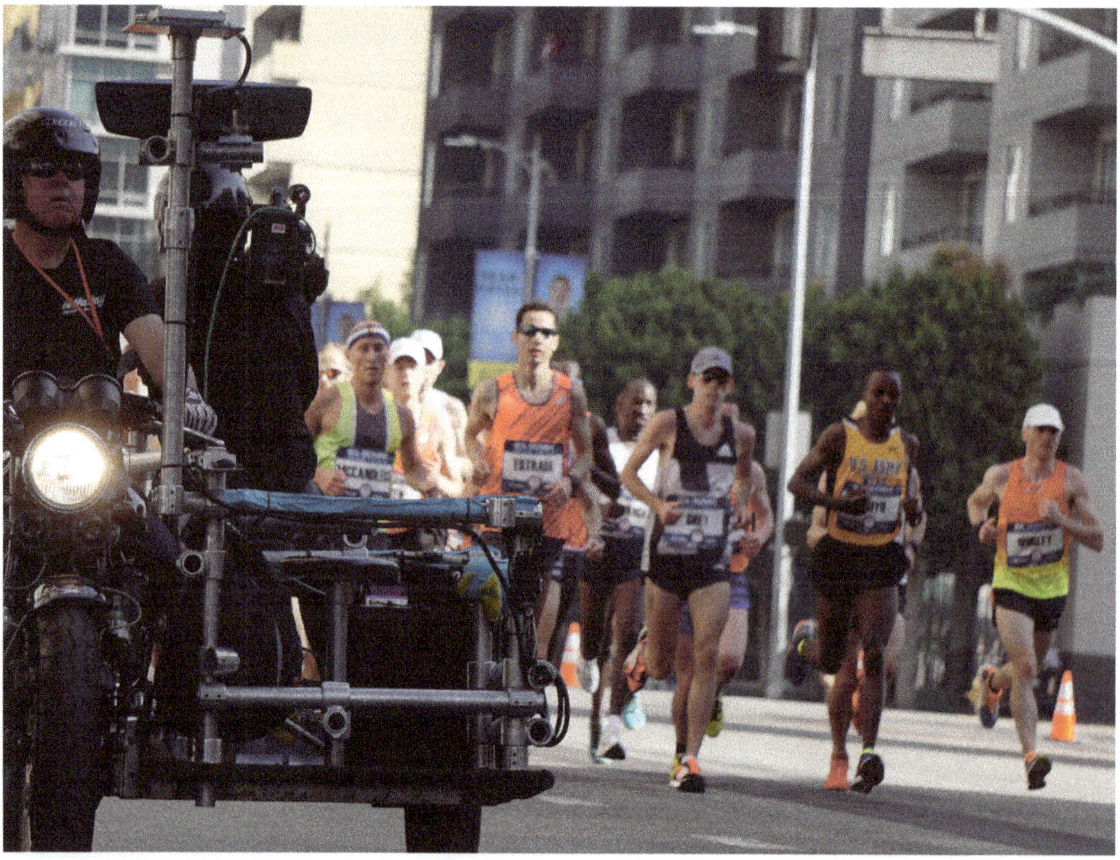

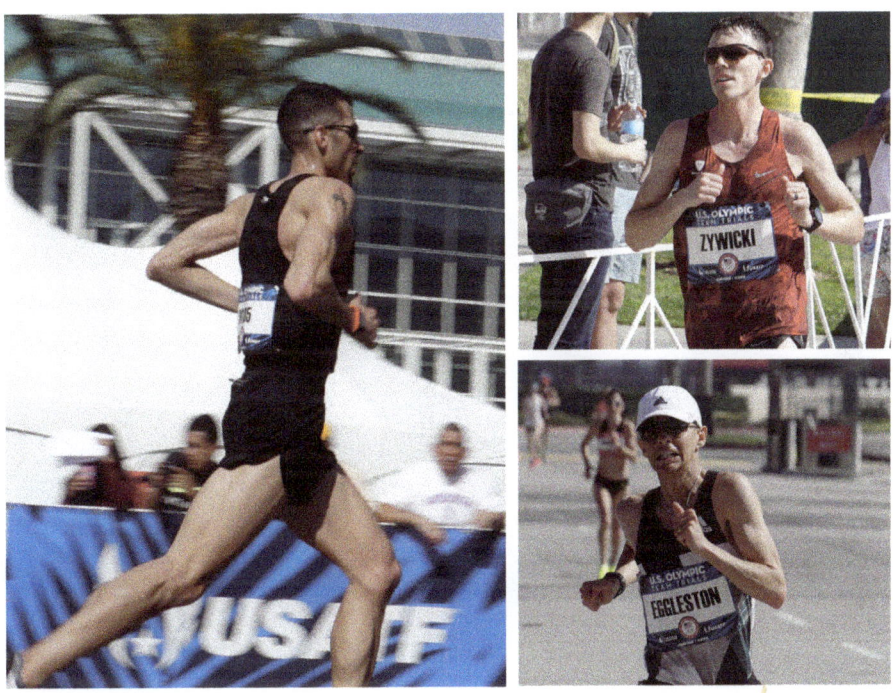

Stephen Pifer, Ben Zywicki, Jeff Eggleston.

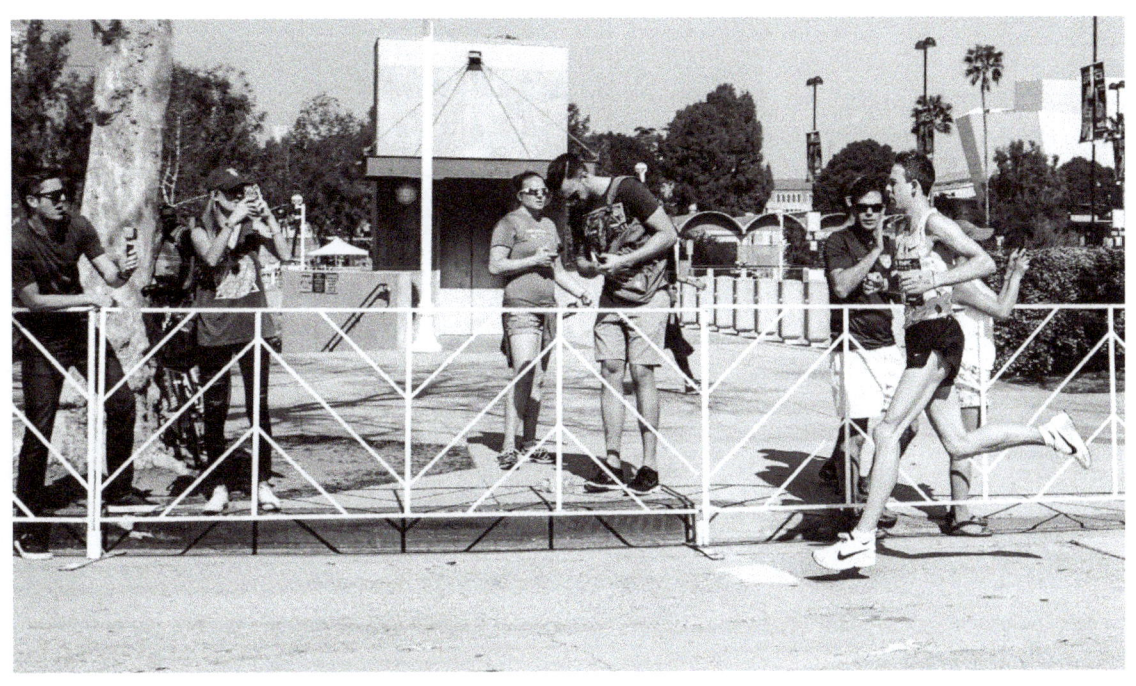

Galen Rupp takes the lead in stride.

PROFILE
JON GREY

Empty plastic water bottles pile over the edges of the host hotel room's trash cans and spill over onto available countertops and bedsides. Preparation for a warm morning of racing seem checked off. Now he dons headphones, listening to music while scanning the social feeds and reading texts of encouragement.

It is Jon's 30th birthday. The hair on his head is freshly cut short, lean and clean, his head covered only by his light grey adidas cap. While there is no "Flat Jon" race day kit, any marathoner would likely identify with his preparations. He is quietly confident. You have to have gumption to put yourself in a position to compete.

At the athlete breakfast that morning, the conversation around the table is lighthearted. With teammates and fellow competitors, Jon picks at his oatmeal and coffee, remaining calm on the outside. But his thoughts would return to the literal Trials ahead.

Down the escalator, on the way to the staging area, he exchanges high fives with a friend going the opposite way. Athletes take a moment to relax before being escorted in groups to the Athletes Village and starting line, a 1/2 mile walk to the Staples Center.

The stakes are high in the heat of the streets of L.A.

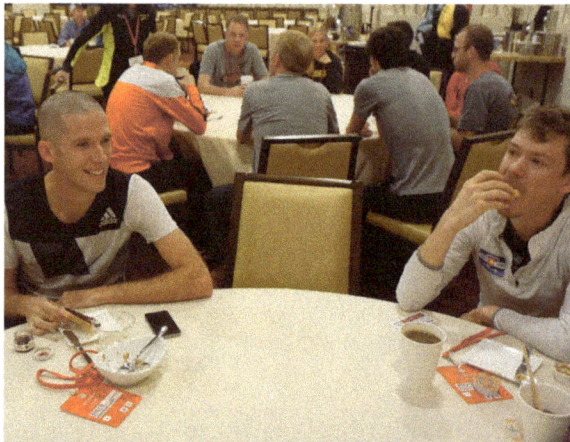

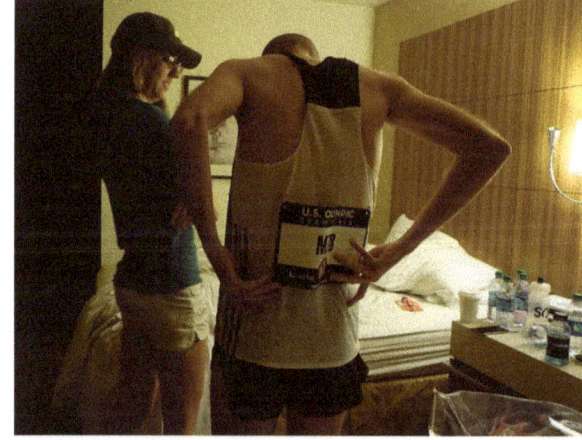

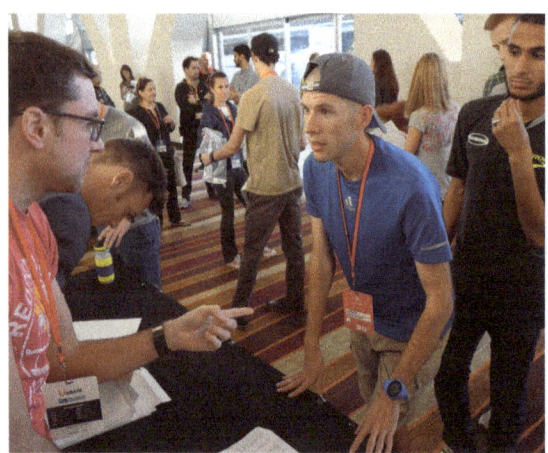

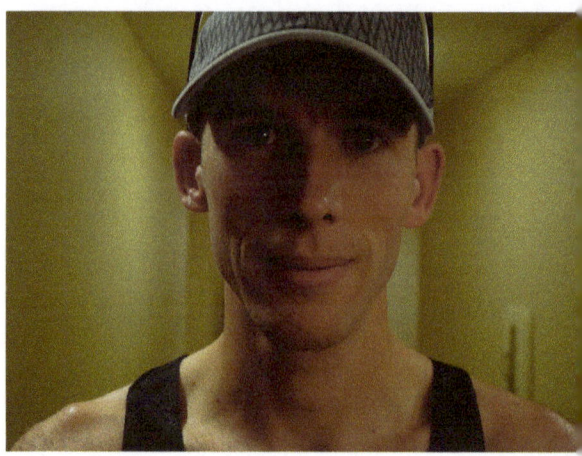

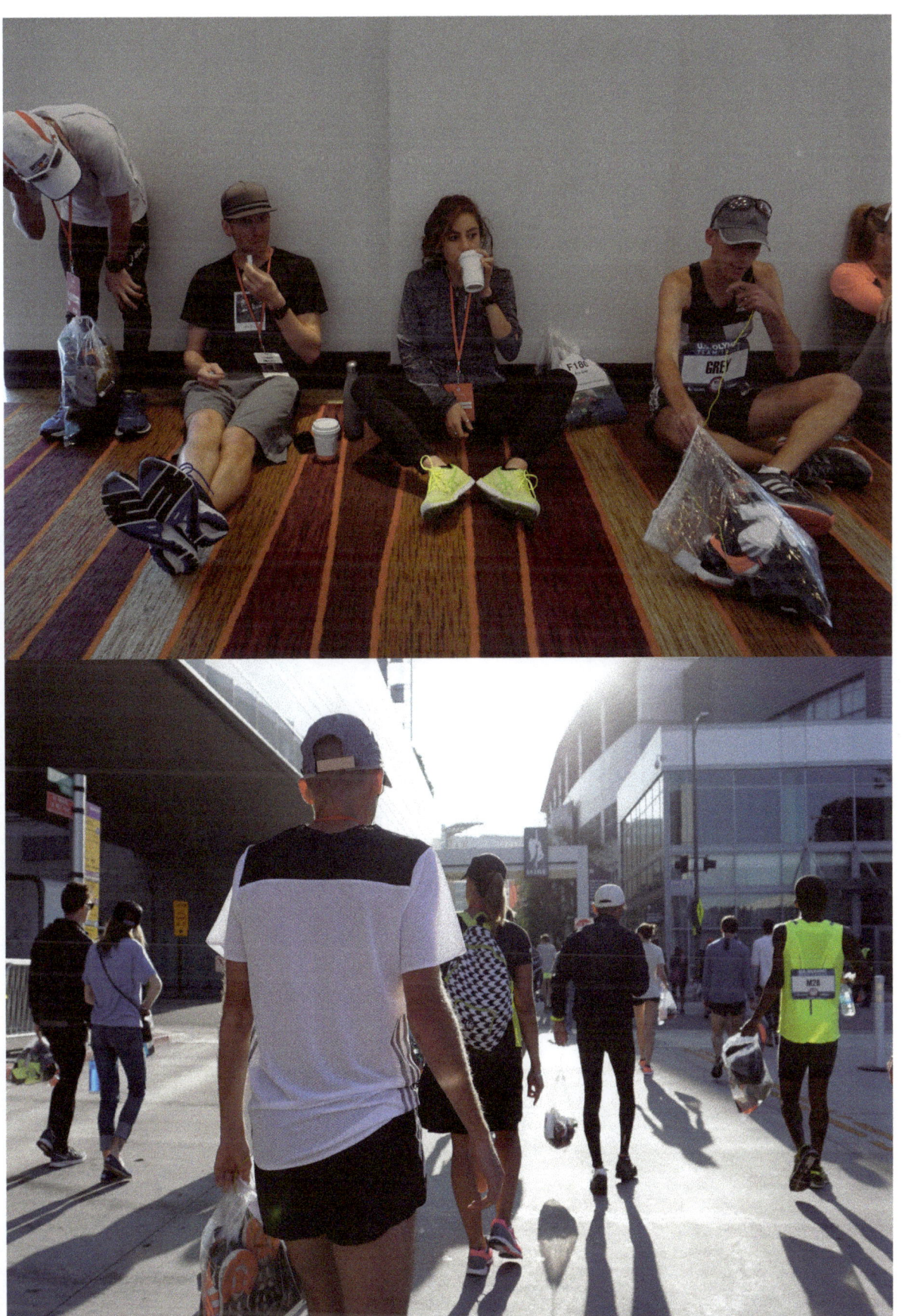

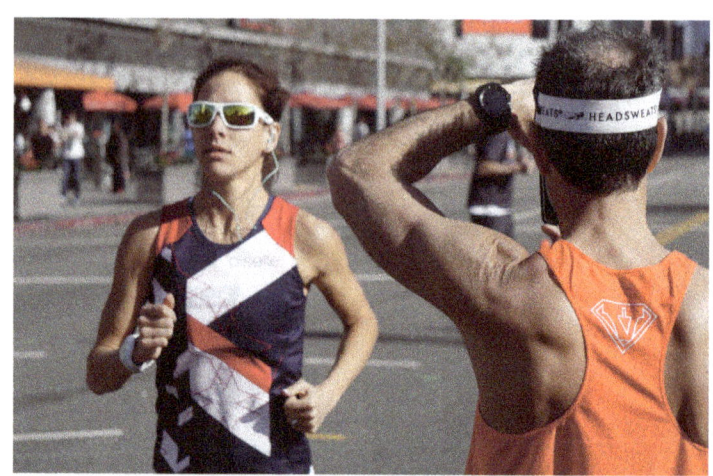

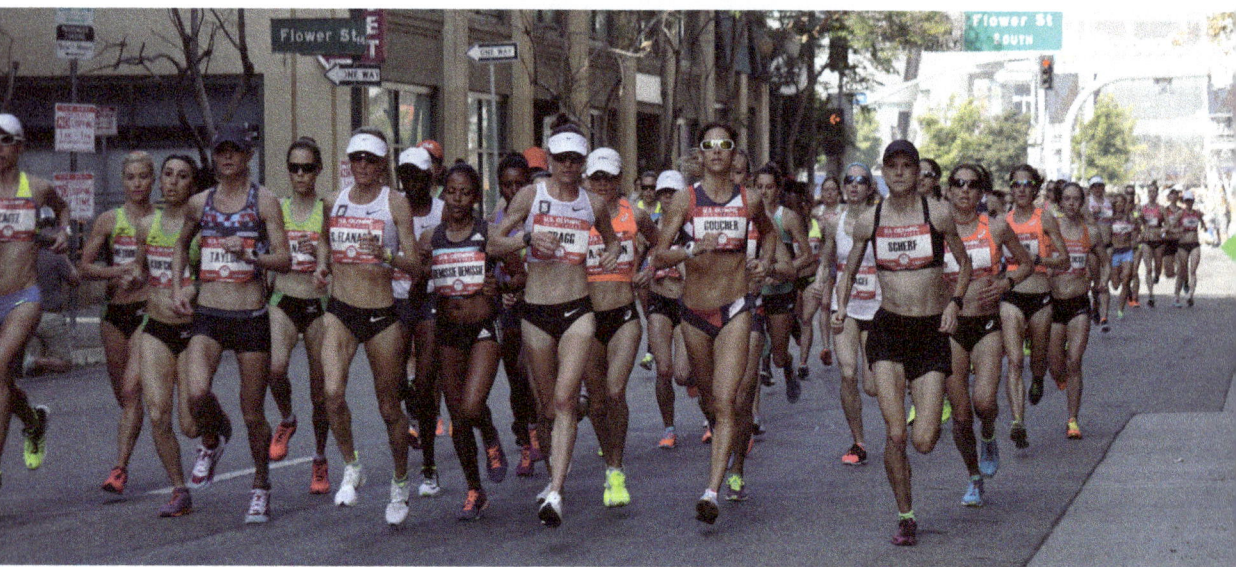

Jay Survil of Denver captures the moment as Kara Goucher warms up. The field at the start of the race. Alia Gray toughs out a personal best to finish 10th.

Opposite page: Shalane Flanagan and Amy Cragg stride for stride later in the race. Nicole Camp, Amanda Scott and Coach Lee Troop encouraging Lauren Fog down the long straight aways. Kara Goucher with 3 miles to go, with Desi Linden in her sights.

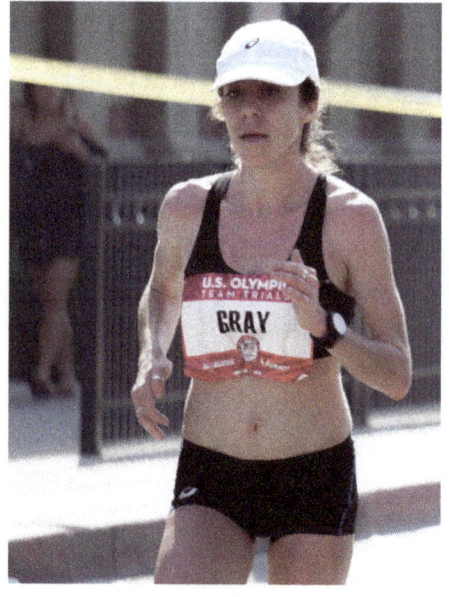

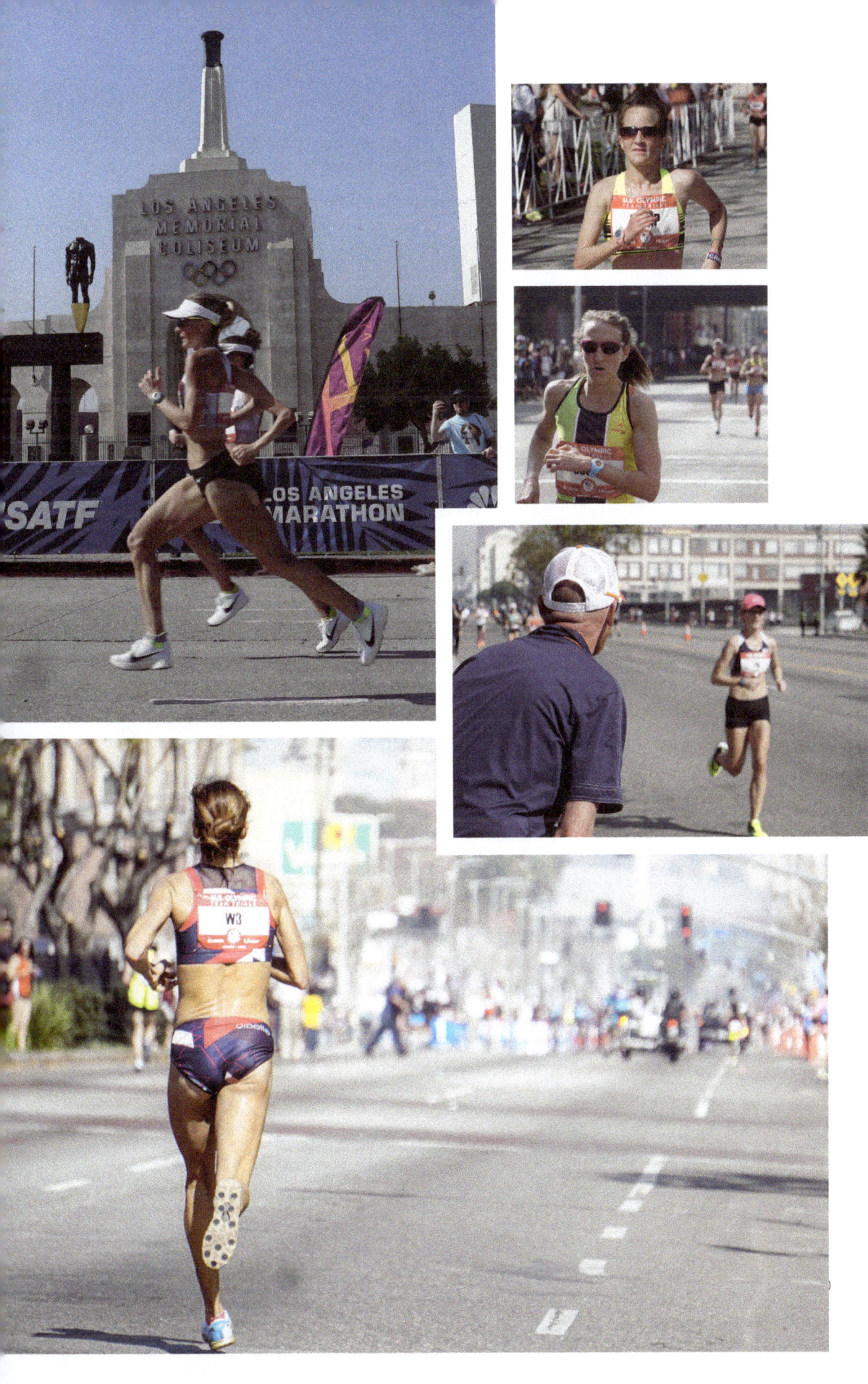

POWER TRIO
3 Women - 3 Decades - 12 Olympic Trials

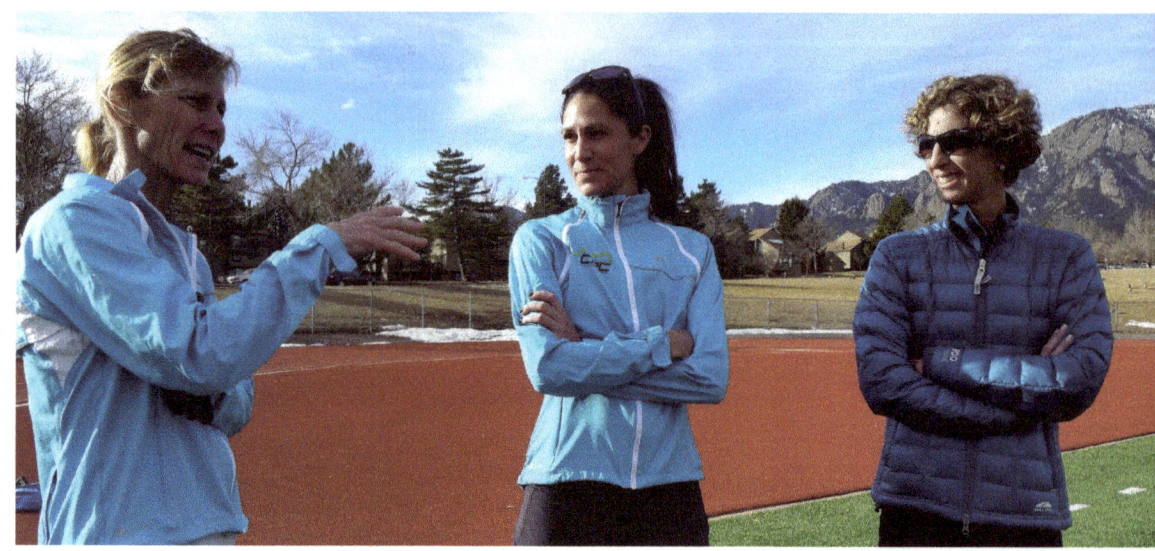

The Colorado Racing Club trio of Colleen De Reuck, Joanna Zeiger and Shawna Han all lined up at the Olympic Trials Marathon in Los Angeles in February. For De Reuck it was her 5th time on the Marathon start line, she won it in 2004 to make her 4th Olympic Team. Joanna, who started in Triathlon, has been to 7 Olympic Trials, first in swimming, then Triathlon, and now running as a master. This was Han's first Olympic Trials.

Joanna had the honor of making headlines as the last woman on the course as many others dropped out due to the heat and/or injuries. She also cheered on Amy Cragg as she passed the finish line at the same time.

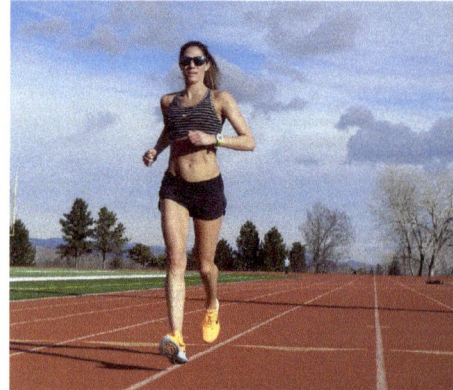

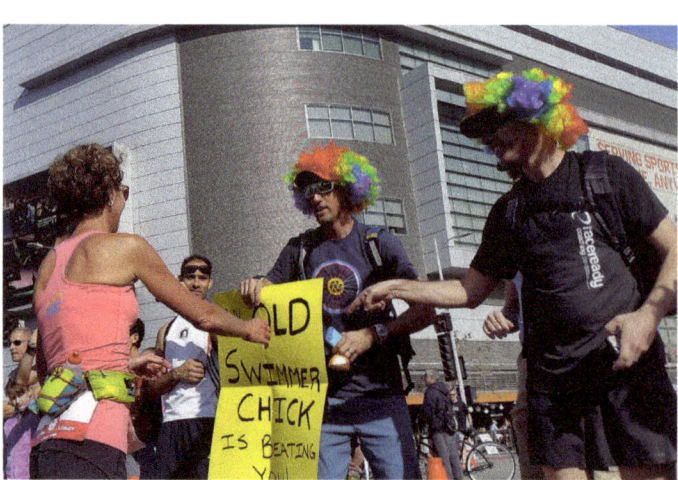

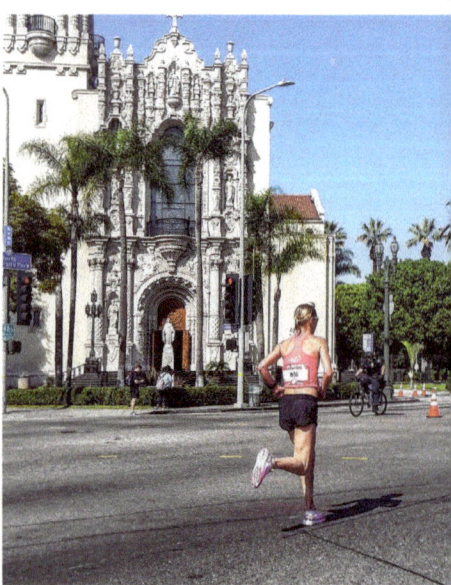

SUPPORTING ATHLETES

Supporting athletes pursuing their dreams is nothing new for Roll Recovery. In fact the company was pretty much founded on it. Founder Jeremy Nelson's wife, and Co-Founder Adriana Nelson, along with Jeremy's sister-in-law, Brianne Nelson, competed in the Olympic marathon trials while ROLL Recovery staffers Andy Wacker, Nuta Olaru, Carlos Trujillo and Justin Young all hit OT qualifying marks.

Not only do they employ top-level runners but they support runners locally and nationally. That support was extended out even further when they announced that Roll Recovery would reimburse the $30 entry fee that Olympic Marathon qualifiers pay to enter the Trials.

"Having family and staff competing in the Olympic Trials, it strikes me as odd they would have to pay for an event that will be televised nationally and is expected to draw significant revenue. Extending sponsorships, hosting premiere events in mass media markets and gaining broadcasting partners is great for the sport, but shouldn't some of that success be extended to the athletes competing? After all, isn't it them we're watching?"

- Jeremy Nelson, Co-Founder ROLL Recovery

Well done @ROLLRecovery. Great to see a Company standing behind the athletes in which they support. #Digdeeper

Laura Thweatt @Thweatt11

Love seeing companies getting behind athletes. An awesome show of support from @ROLLRecovery for OT qualifiers.

Mod Craft @modcraftstudio

42

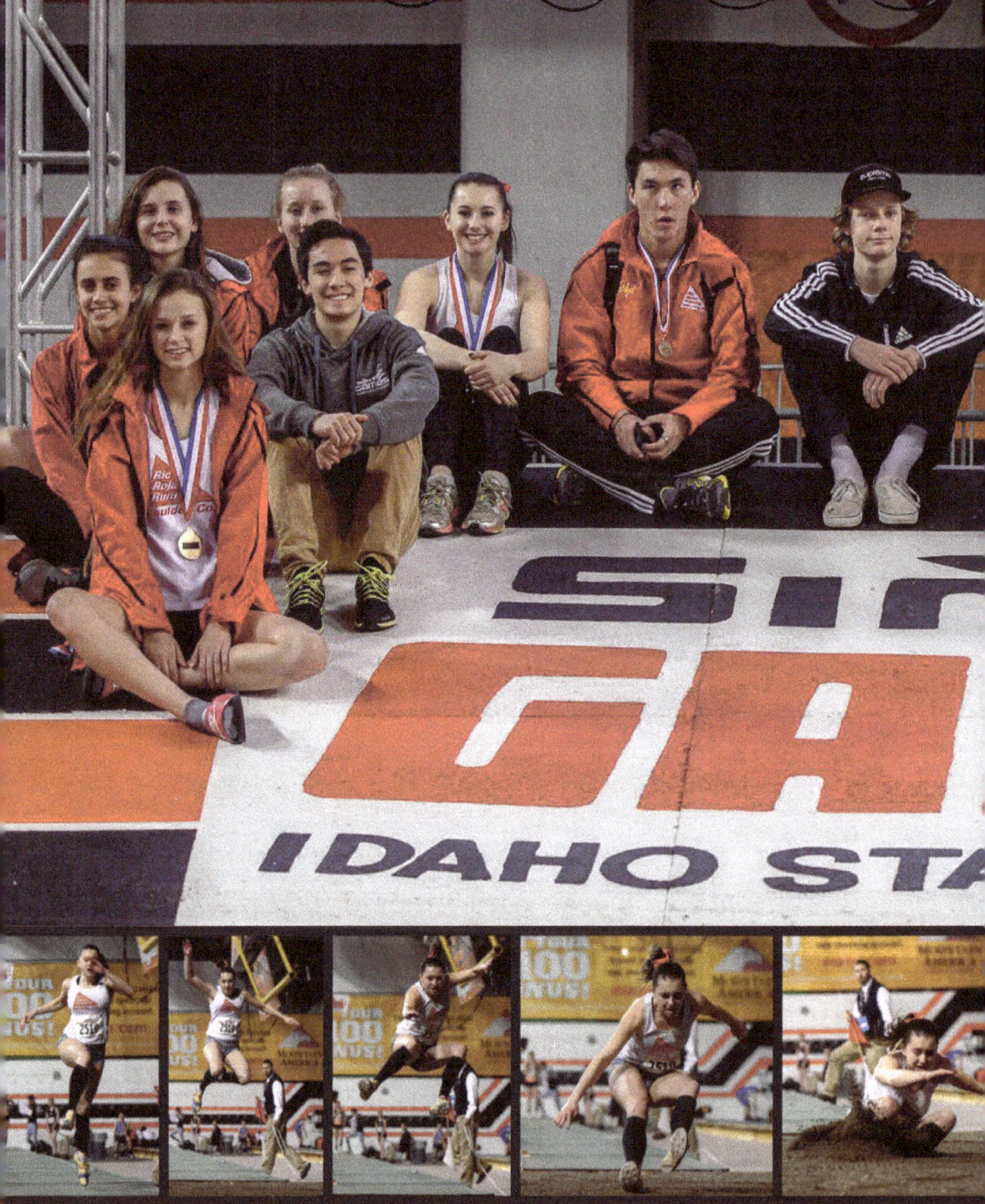

Photos by Dave Albo

Fourteen Boulder area High School preps training with the Ric Rojas Running group traveled to Pocatello, ID to compete at the prestigious Simplot Games held February 18-20, 2016 at Idaho State University's Holt Arena. This high school track meet attracts top nationwide talent and is considered to be the Olympics for High School track and field athletes. This is the 20th year that Rojas has taken his teams to the Games.

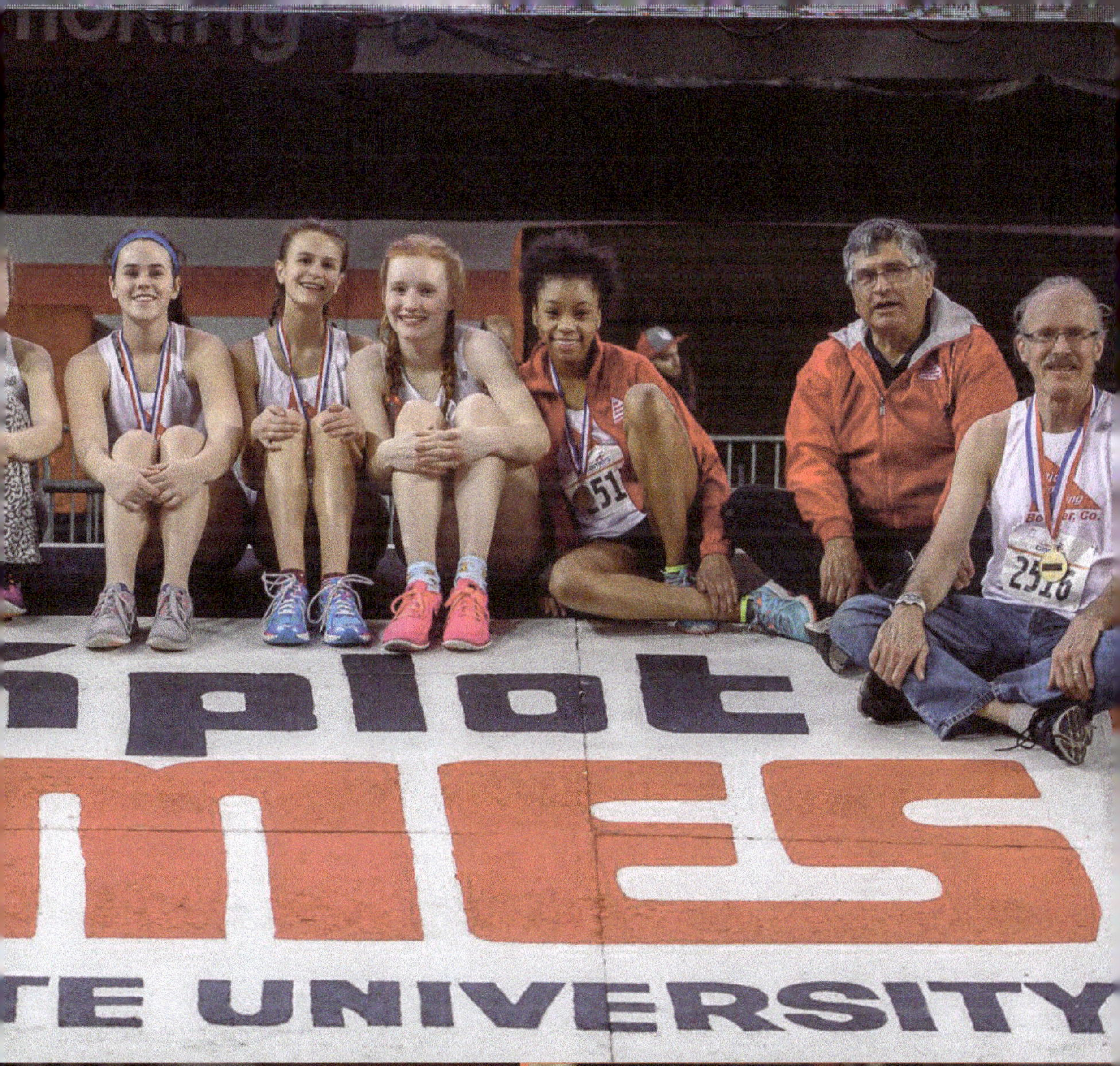

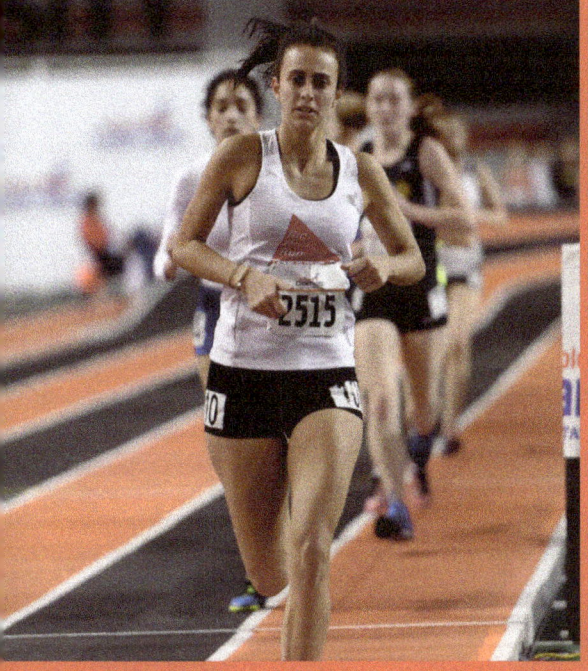
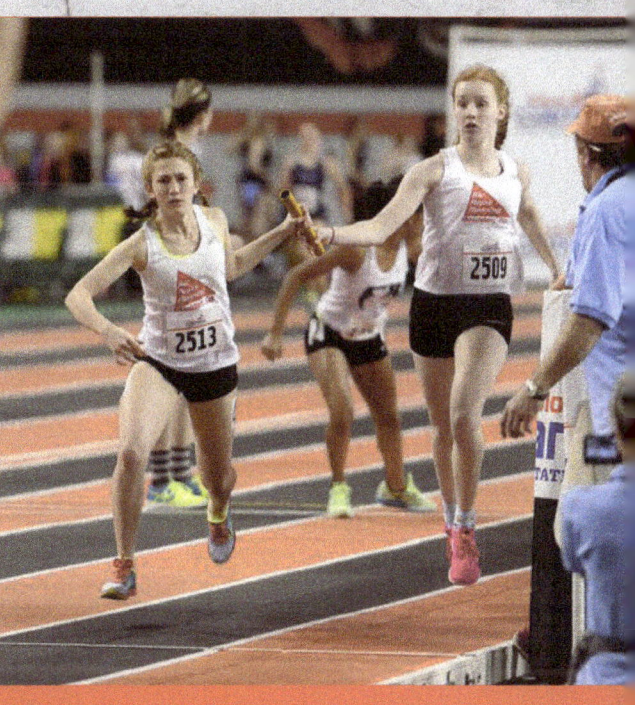

Top Results
January - March

On January 3rd, after six days of running, **Greg Salvesen** of Boulder threw in the hat at 402.08 miles at the Across the Years Footrace, held in Phoenix, Arizona. Starting on December 28th Greg ran, walked, and crawled his way to 7th place overall on a 1.0498 loop course consisting of dirt paths and asphalt/concrete.

At a much shorter race – the Jacksonville Bank Half Marathon – held on January 3rd in Florida, Boulder runners once again ran well. **Jon Grey** came away with the win and a new course record in a time of 62:47, while **Sean Quigley** ran in for 4th place with a time of 63:45. **Ashley Brasovan** of Golden ran a personal best in 1:14:30 for 9th place and **Brianne Nelson** of Golden came in close behind in a time of 1:14:34. **Wendy Thomas**, running for the Boulder Track Club but technically residing in Windsor, came in 14th with a time of 74:52. All five runners were well under the Olympic Trials Qualifying Standards.

On January 9th in Bandera, Texas, Boulder ultrarunner **Cassie Scallon** scorched up the trail at the Bandera 100K Endurance Run, blazing to a new course record in a time of 9:19:46.

Back home, in Lafayette, the Lafayette Quaker Oatmeal Festival and Quicker Quaker 5K Run was held on January 9th. **Brittni Hutton** out raced everyone in the field, including the men, winning in a time of 18:05.

Across the pond, Boulder's **Alex Monroe** ran in his first international race representing the United States at the Great Edinburgh Cross Country race, held at Holyrood Park in Edinburgh, Scotland on January 9th. In a highly competitive field, Alex held his own on the 8K course and finished in a time of 25:57 for 10th place overall.

In Phoenix, Arizona on January 17th at the Rock 'n' Roll Arizona Half Marathon, Boulder's **Noah Droddy** ran a personal best, finishing the 13.1 mile course in 1:04:17 for 7th place, and making the Olympic Qualifying Standard. **Maggie Callahan** and **Addie Bracy**, both of Longmont, also had excellent races, finishing in 1:16:57 and 1:17:14 respectively.

Also on January 17th at the Tri-City Medical Center Carlsbad Marathon, held in Carlsbad, California, **Mario Macias** of Boulder ran to a 4th place finish in a time of 2:26:16.

In Colorado Springs on January 23rd, at the Air Force Invitational, Boulder athletes made the trip down to run some fast laps around the track. In the 800 meters, **Nick Harris** had the fastest legs and came away with the win in a time of 1:51.63. Boulder's **Alex Monroe** was 4th in the 1 mile with a time of 4:18.22 and then came back for 2nd in the 3000 meters with a time of 8:47.18. **Lindsey Putman** of Boulder was 3rd in the 800 meters with a time of 2:14.73, while **Maor Tiyouri** was 2nd in the 3000 meters with a time of 10:18.68 and **Lucy Cheadle** was 3rd in a time of 10:23.19.

Out east, at the Frank Sevigne Husker Invitation held in Lincoln, Nebraska on February 5th and 6th Boulder's **Laura Thweatt** started the day out with a win in the mile running 4:41.5 off a very slow first 800m (2:22) and then running 2:18 in the second 800m. Just 50 minutes later she came back and won the 3K in 9:09.48 in racing flats. **Maor Tiyouri** bounced back to form and had a great 3K placing 4th in 9:40.3 while **Alex Monroe** ran a huge PR in the 3K placing 2nd in 8:04.66. **Lindsey Putman** ran a very aggressive first 400m in the 800m but tightened up finishing in 2:16.33 for 13th overall.

At the 2016 USATF Cross Country Championships, held in Bend, OR on February 6th two Boulder runners had solid races, placing 6th and 7th overall in the competitive men's field. **Joe Bosshard** ran to 6th place in a time of 32:26 on the 10K course, while **Andy Wacker** came in just one second behind for 7th place in 32:27.

Also on February 6th in sunny California, ultrarunner **Timmy Olson** put down a fast time in the 50K event at the Sean O'Brien races, running away with the win in a time of 4:39:10.

On Friday night, February 12th at the Husky Classic and Indoor Open held at the University of Washington, Boulder runners had strong showings. **Pierce Murphy** ran a time of 13:40.12 in the 5,000m for 2nd place, while **Morgan Pearson** ran 13:48.18 for 8th overall in the 5,000m. **Alex Monroe** ran a 13:51.07 for 10th place in the 5,000m while **Maor Tiyouri** ran 16:07.77 in the 5,000m for 13th place. Both times were personal records for each runner. CU athletes **Erin Clark** and **Kaitlyn Benner** ran fast times as well, finishing 9th and 11th overall in times of 15:54.01 and 16:01.53 respectively. The following day, **Jordan Jennings** ran a 1:54.69 in the 800m event.

Over in Utah on the same day, local ultrarunners tested out their legs in the early season classic Red Hot 55k and 33k. Held just outside of Moab on the famous slickrock of the area, several local runners had strong showings. In the 55K distance, **Dan Berteletti** of Golden ran a time of 4:22:07 for 5th place, while **Jeff Schuler** of Boulder ran to 5th place in the 33K distance in a time of 2:20:09. **Jeanne Cooper** of Lafayette was second for the women in the 33K distance with a time of 2:46:08.

The same day down in Mayer, AZ, Boulder's **Sage Canaday** had a spectacular race, winning and setting the course record in the Black Canyon 100K with a time of 7:52:26.

On February 14th at the New Balance Indoor Games, Boulder's **Laura Thweatt** ran a stellar race in the 3,000m, finishing 3rd in a time of 8:57.11.

On Sunday, February 28th at the Rock 'n' Roll New Orleans Half-Marathon, Boulder's **Neely Spence Gracey** came away with a solid win, running the course in 1:14:10. "I'm pleased with my effort," Gracey told race organizers. "It's exactly what I wanted to get out of it. I stayed controlled and pushed the last three miles, getting out of my comfort zone, something you can't simulate in training."

Down in Woodlands, Texas ultra runner **Cassie Scallon** tested out her speed at the Woodlands Marathon, held on Saturday, March 5th. Apparently running on trails prepared one well for the roads, as Cassie came in 2nd place with a time of 2:56:58.

The following day in Phoenix, Golden's **Monica Folts** ran a solid race at the SWSSFire Mountain to Fountain 15K, crossing the line in 57:36 for 5th place.

On March 12th at the highly competitive Gate River Run 15K in Jacksonville, Florida, which served as the US 15K Championships, Lyons' **Alex Monroe** raced to 7th place in a time of 45:12. **Andy Wacker** of Boulder was 13th with a time of 46:25. **Alisha Williams** of Golden came in 6th with a time of 52:32.

More locally, at the 28th Runnin' of the Green 7K in Denver, local runners dominated the race. Golden's **Jordan Jones** came in 2nd with a time of 22:21, while **Benjamin Zywicki** of Louisville was right behind for 3rd in a time of 23:04. For the women, Boulder's **Krystalanne Curwood** came away with the win in a time of 25:41.

In beautiful Monument Valley, Arizona on March 19th Golden's **Zach Hermsen** had a strong race at the Monument Valley 50K, running a time of 4:36:56 for 2nd place.

At the Towne Bank 8K held in Virginia Beach, VA, Longmont's **Kristen Arendt** ran to a third place finish with a time of 27:44 while Boulder's **Amanda Scott** came in just under a minute behind for 5th place in 28:41.

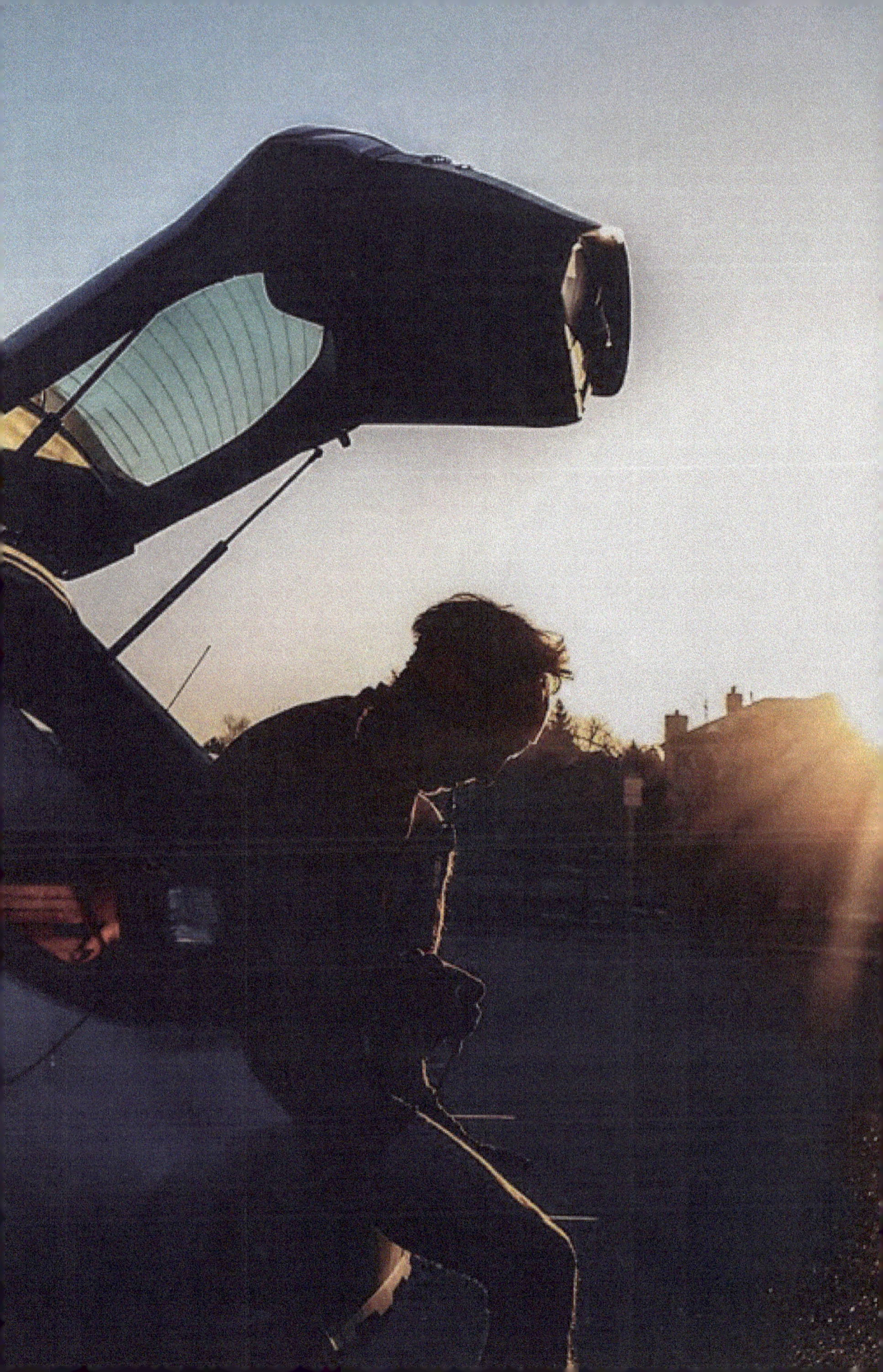

WRITING PROMPT
WINTER
What kept you motivated this season?

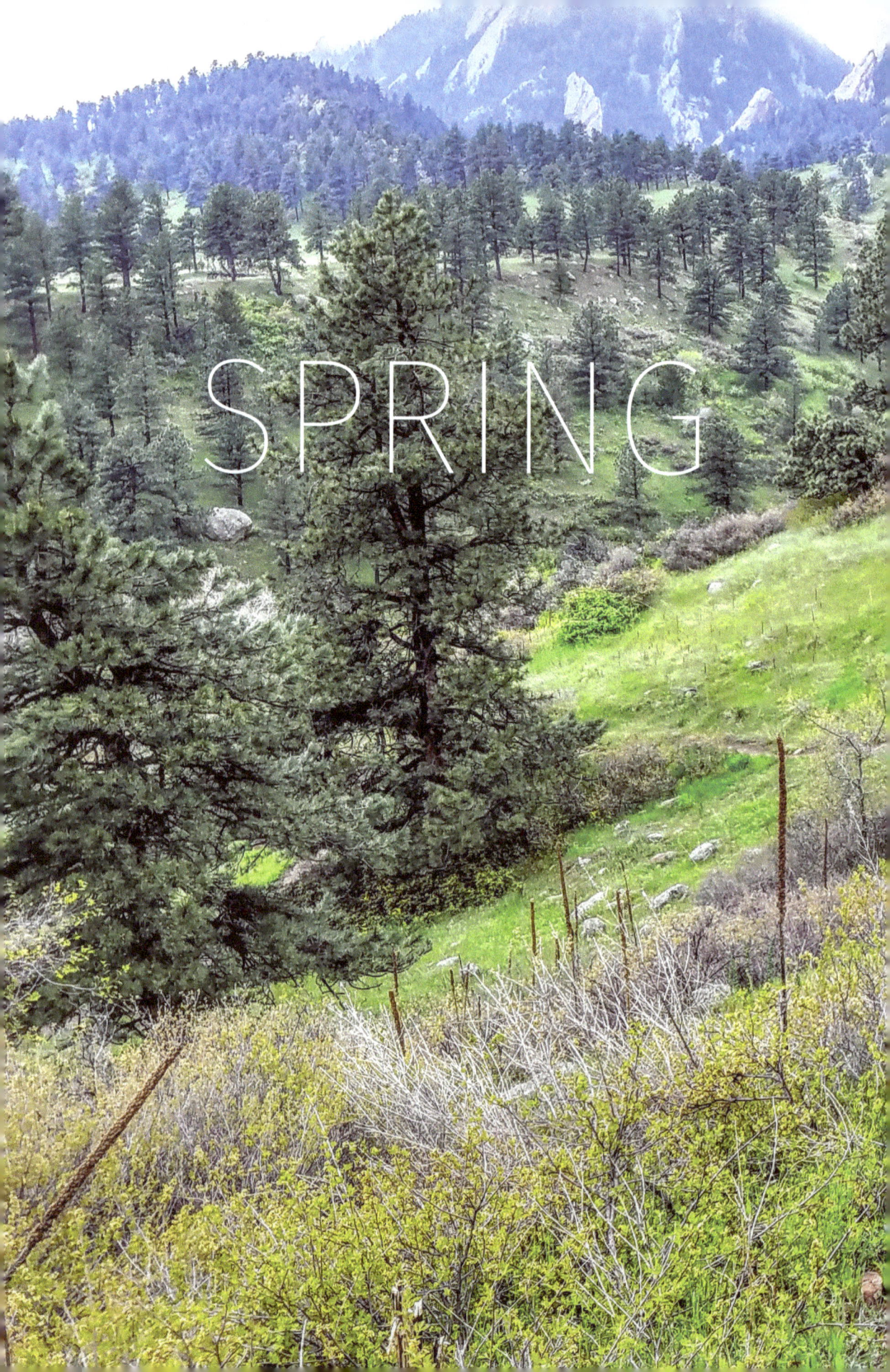

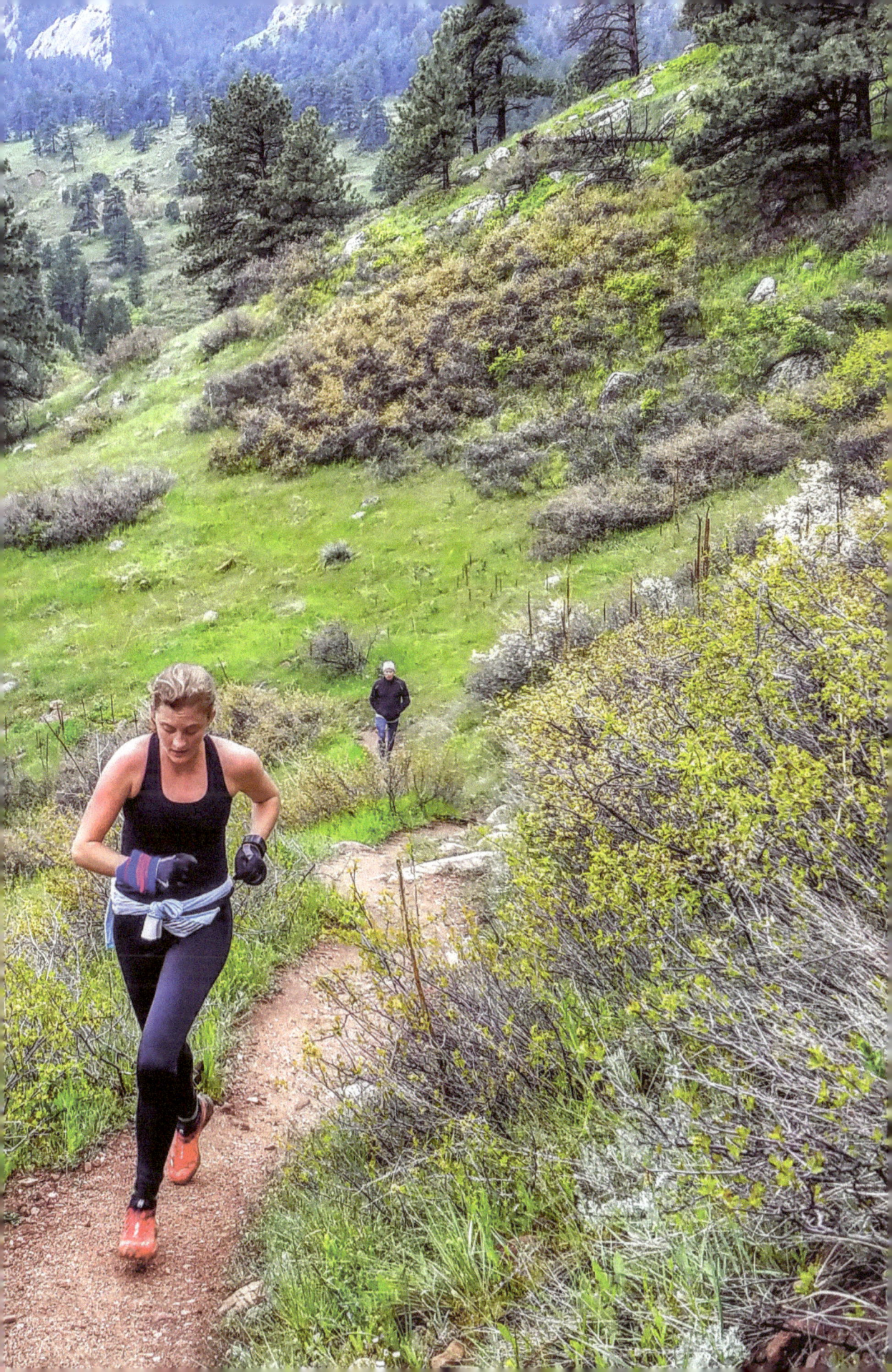

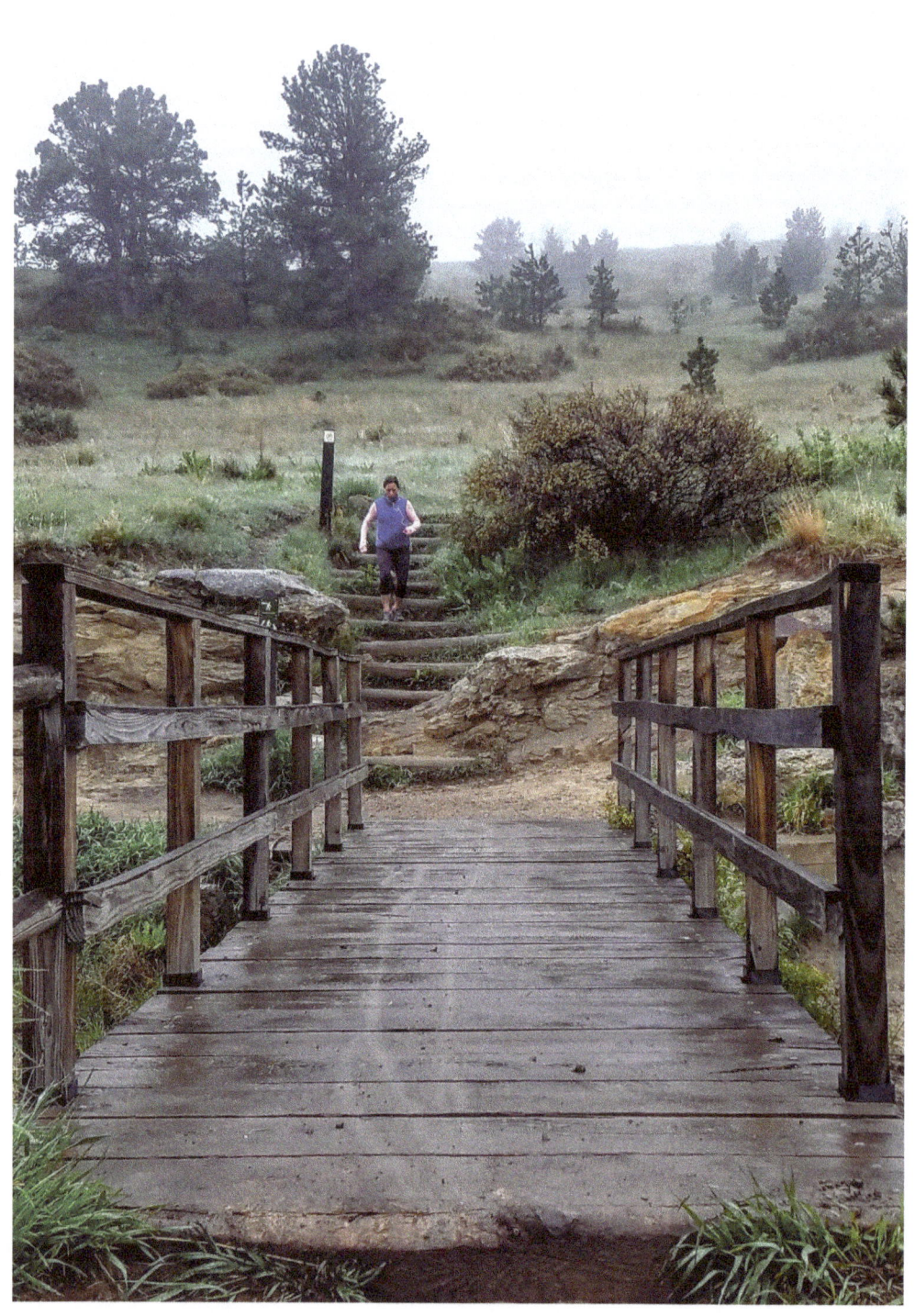

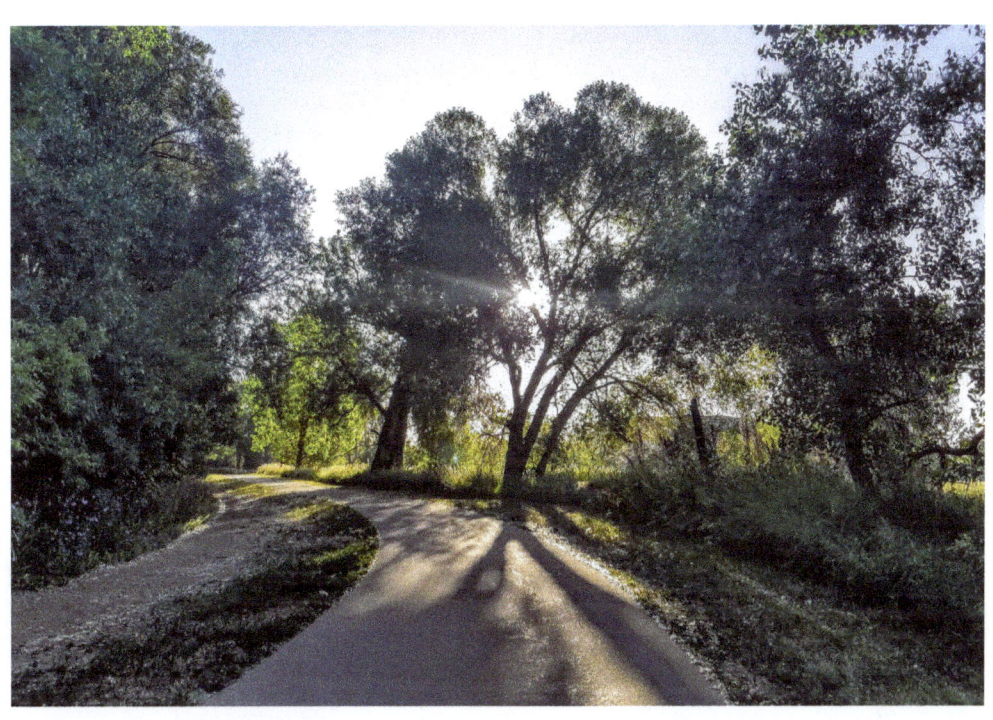

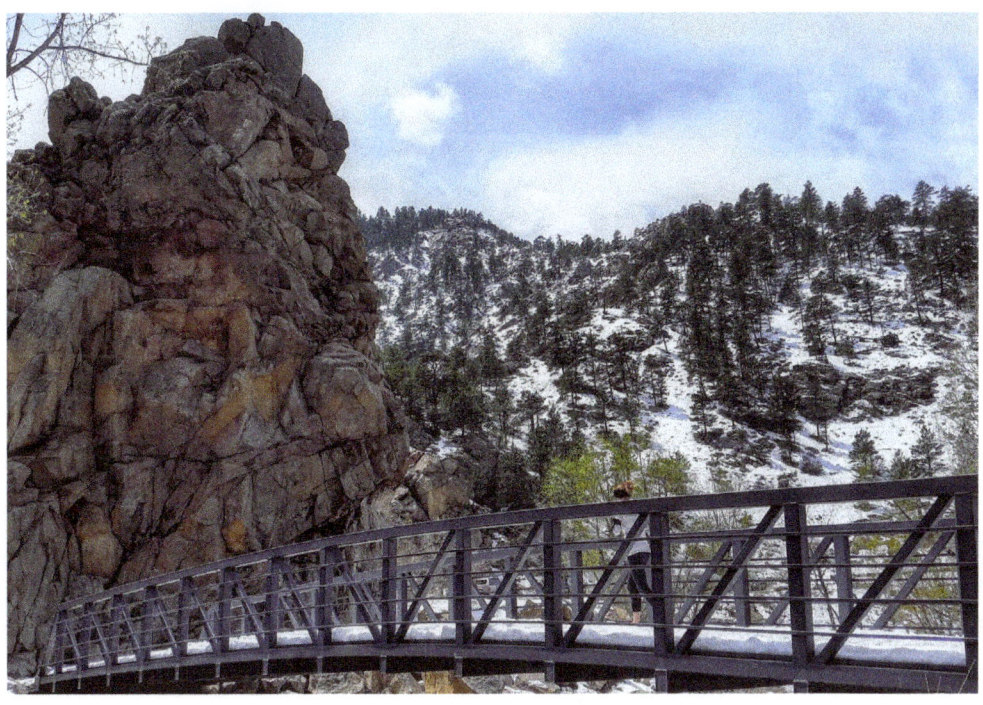

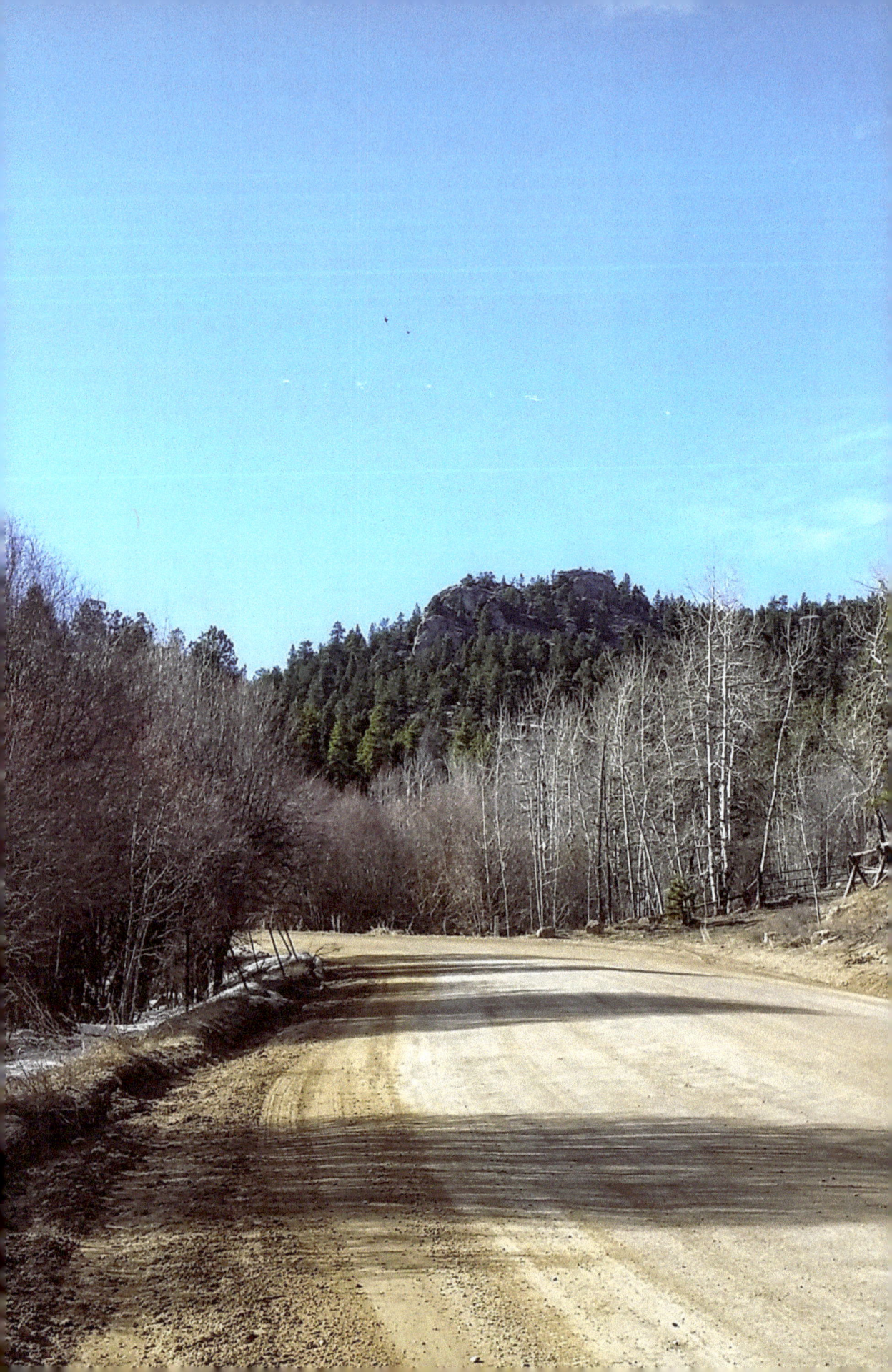

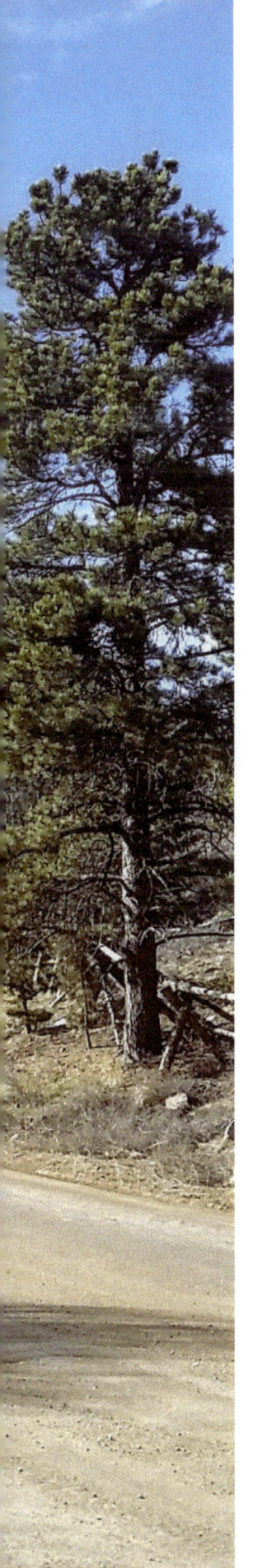

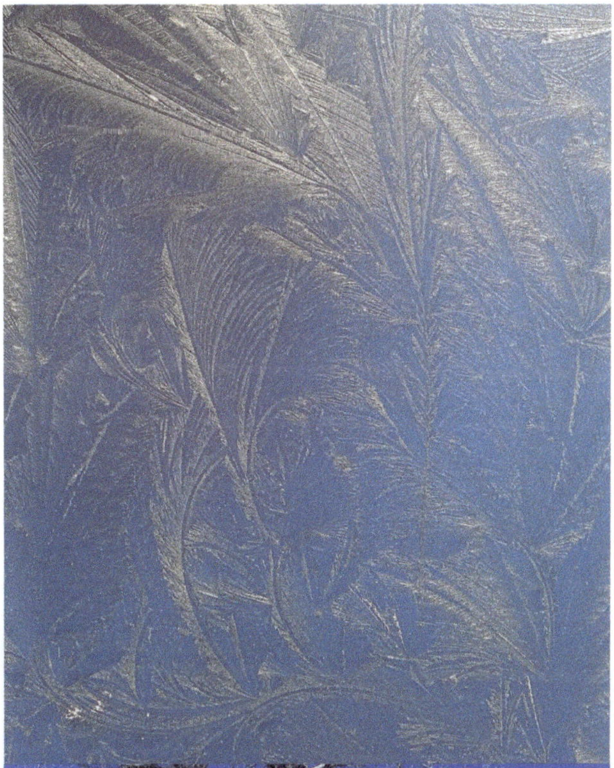

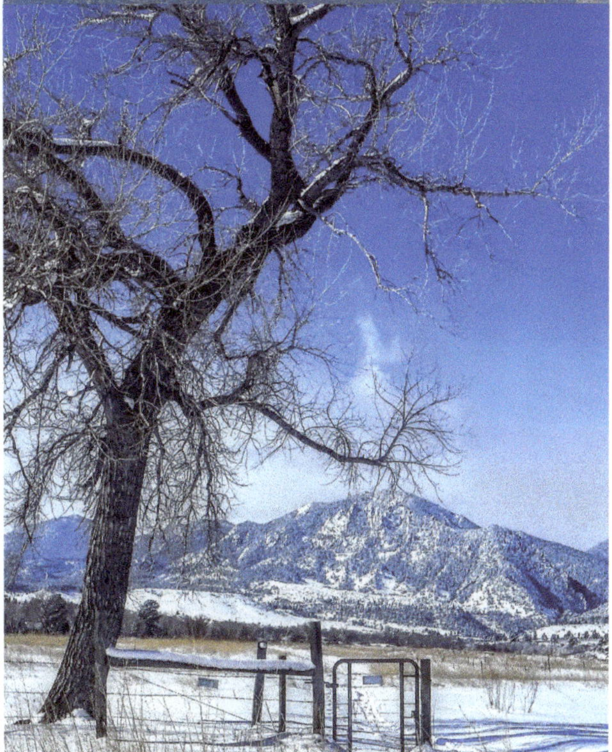

54

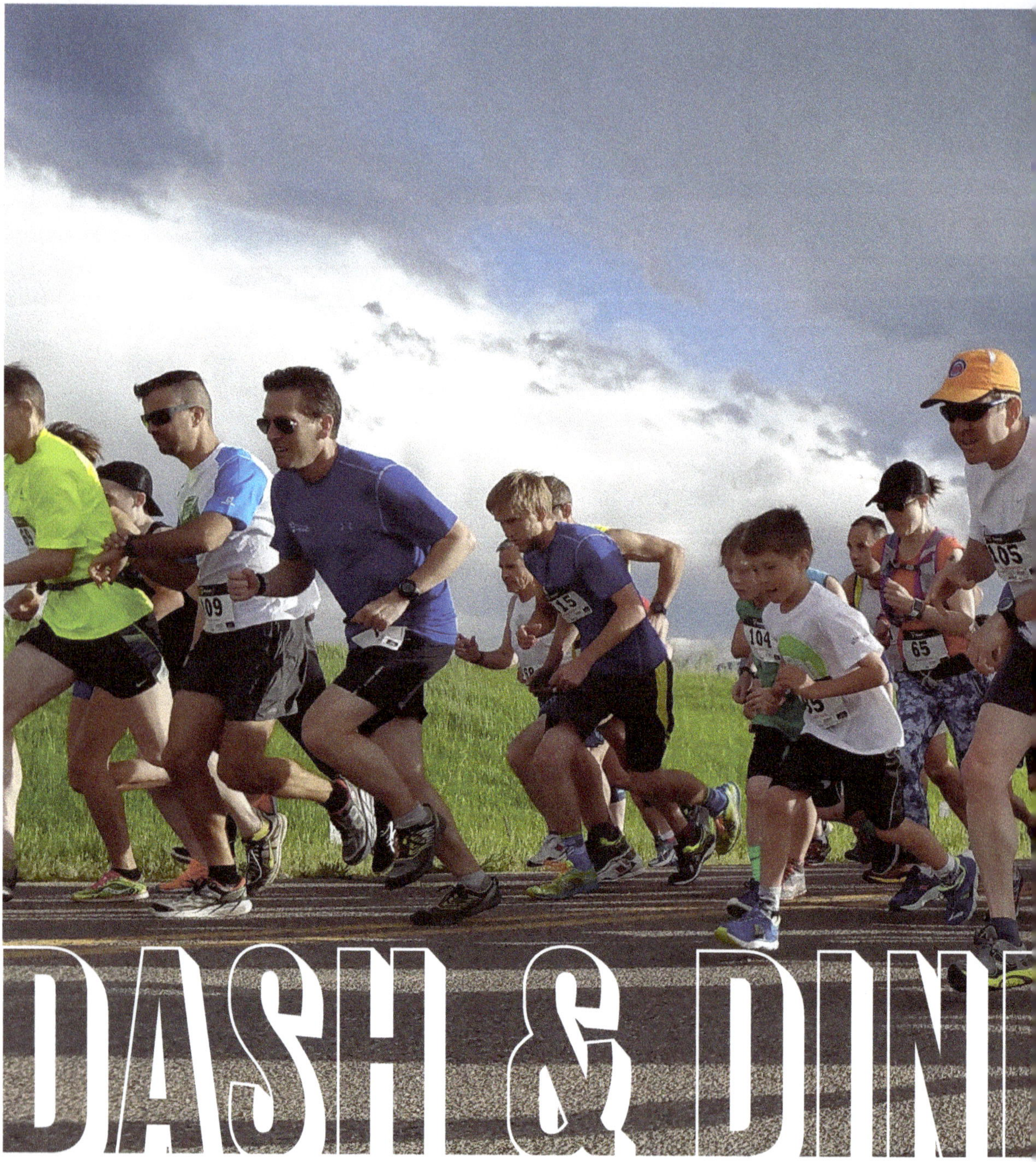

DASH & DINE

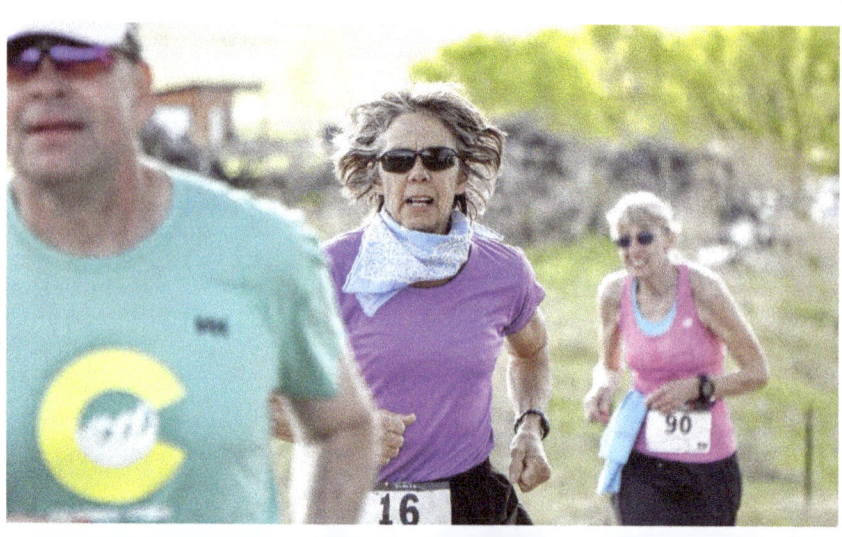
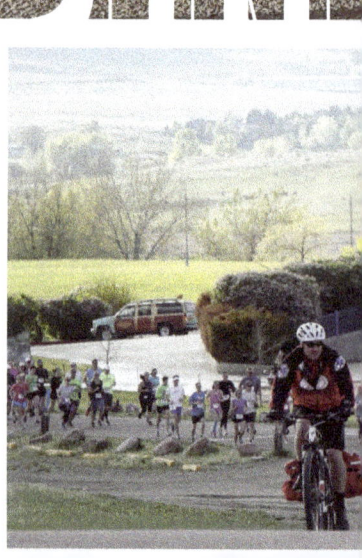

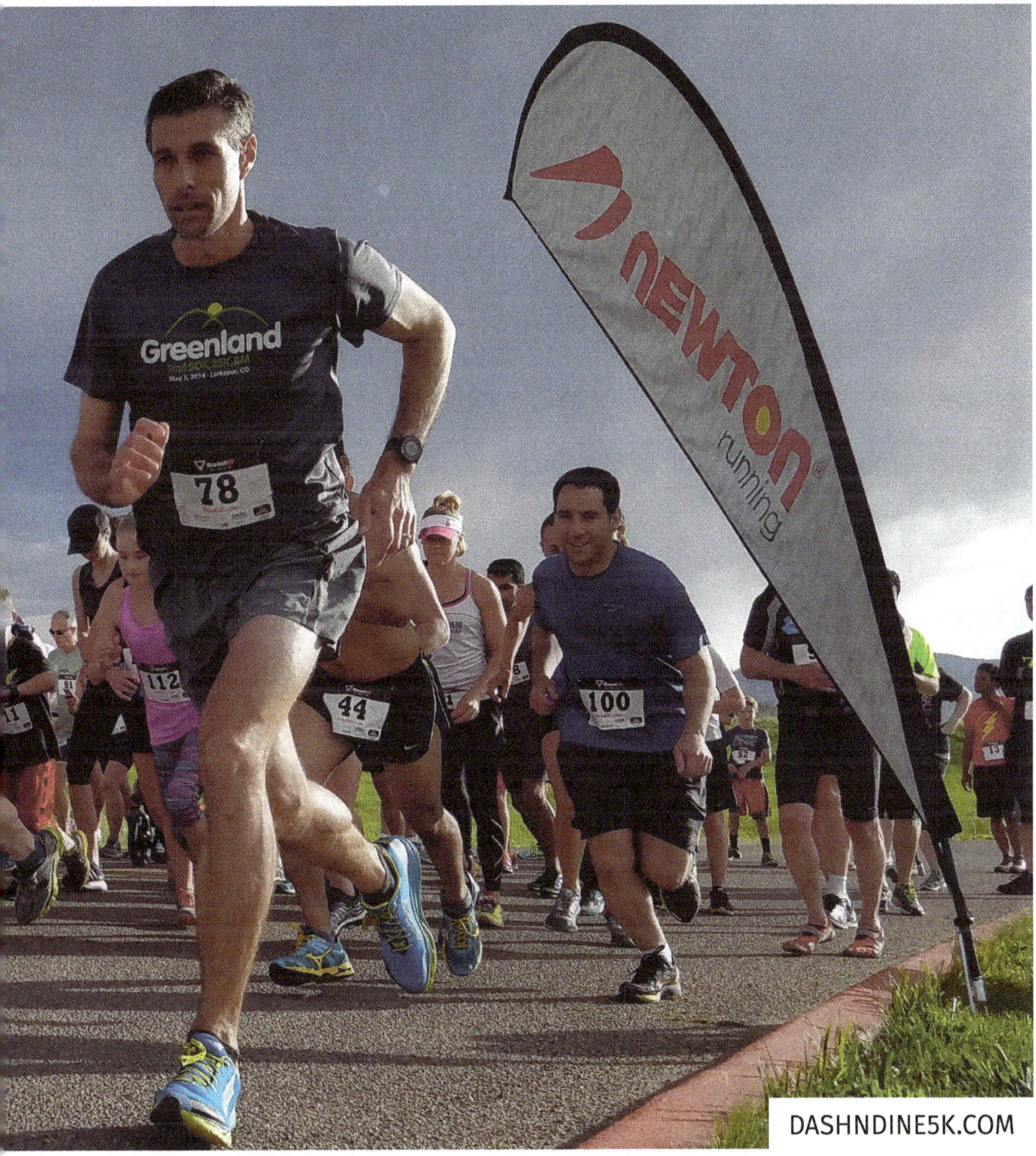

DASHNDINE5K.COM

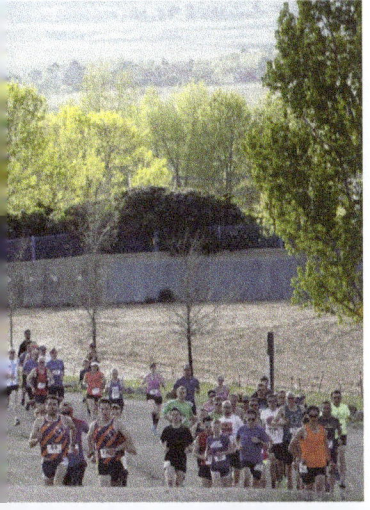
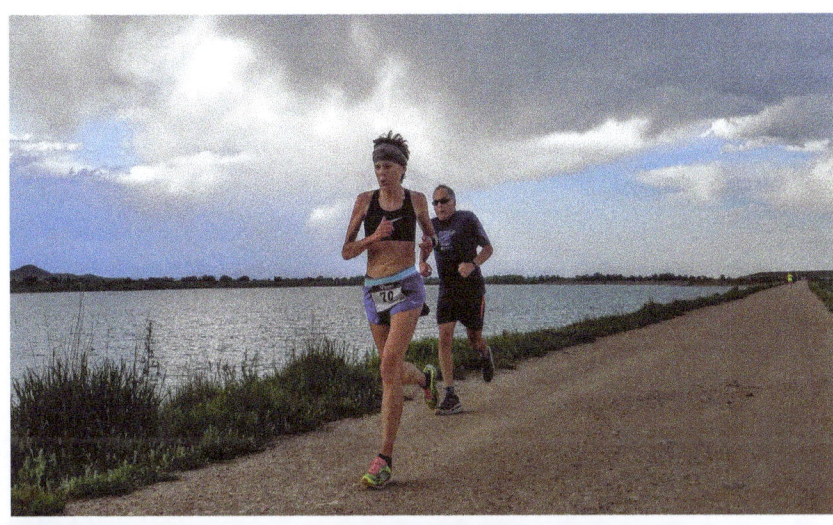

Neely Spence Gracey

For Neely Spence Gracey, destiny is tied up in the Boston Marathon. She was born on Patriot's Day as her father – 1991 World Champion Marathon Bronze medalist Steve Spence – was out running the event.

"Every year, I hear the story of the day I was born while my Dad was running the Boston Marathon in 1990. When I knew I couldn't run in the Olympic Trials this year, the next thing was Boston, and it just fell into place and seemed like a perfect fit."

Neely to Mike Sandrock in a Competitor.com article.

While Neely just moved to Boulder a year ago, she is no stranger to the area as she used to come to Colorado as a kid so her father could train at altitude.

"I grew up knowing that being a professional runner was an option. Until I was 7, we'd come out to Boulder for my Dad's training every summer. I did not know everyone didn't do that — that kids don't go to Colorado for their dad's altitude training."

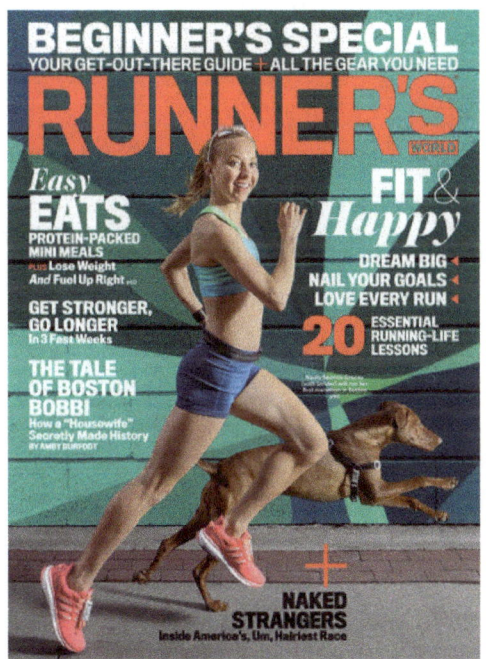 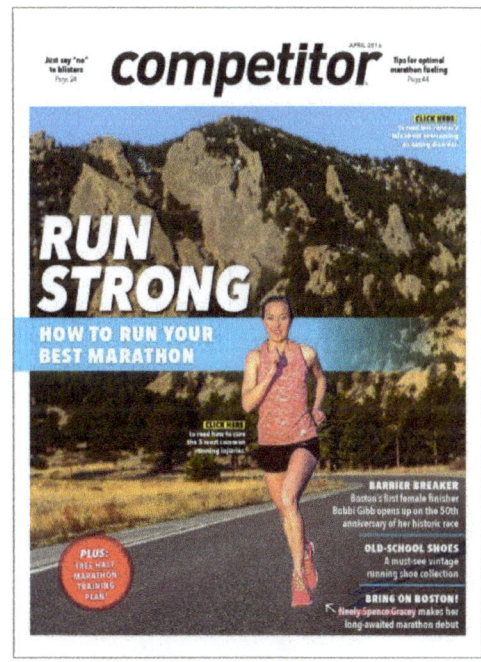

You can see her smiling face, along with her trusty training partner, Strider, on the May 2016 cover of Runner's World (shot by Denver photographer Matte Trappe) and Competitor Magazine (shot by Boulder's James Carney).

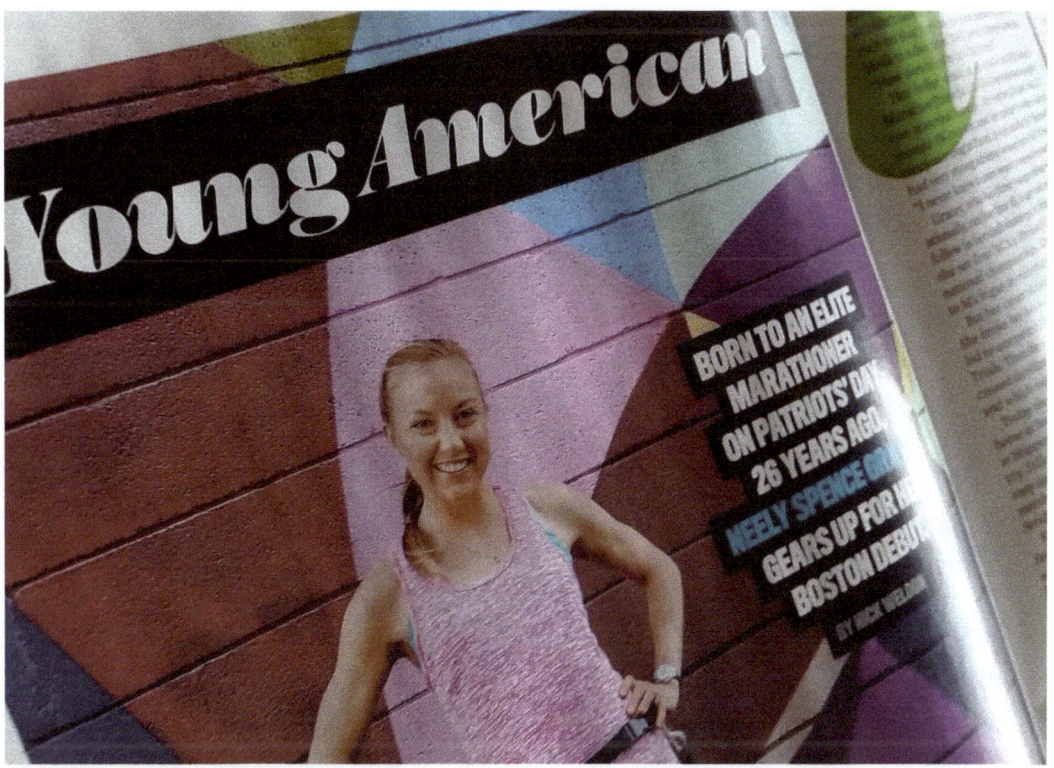

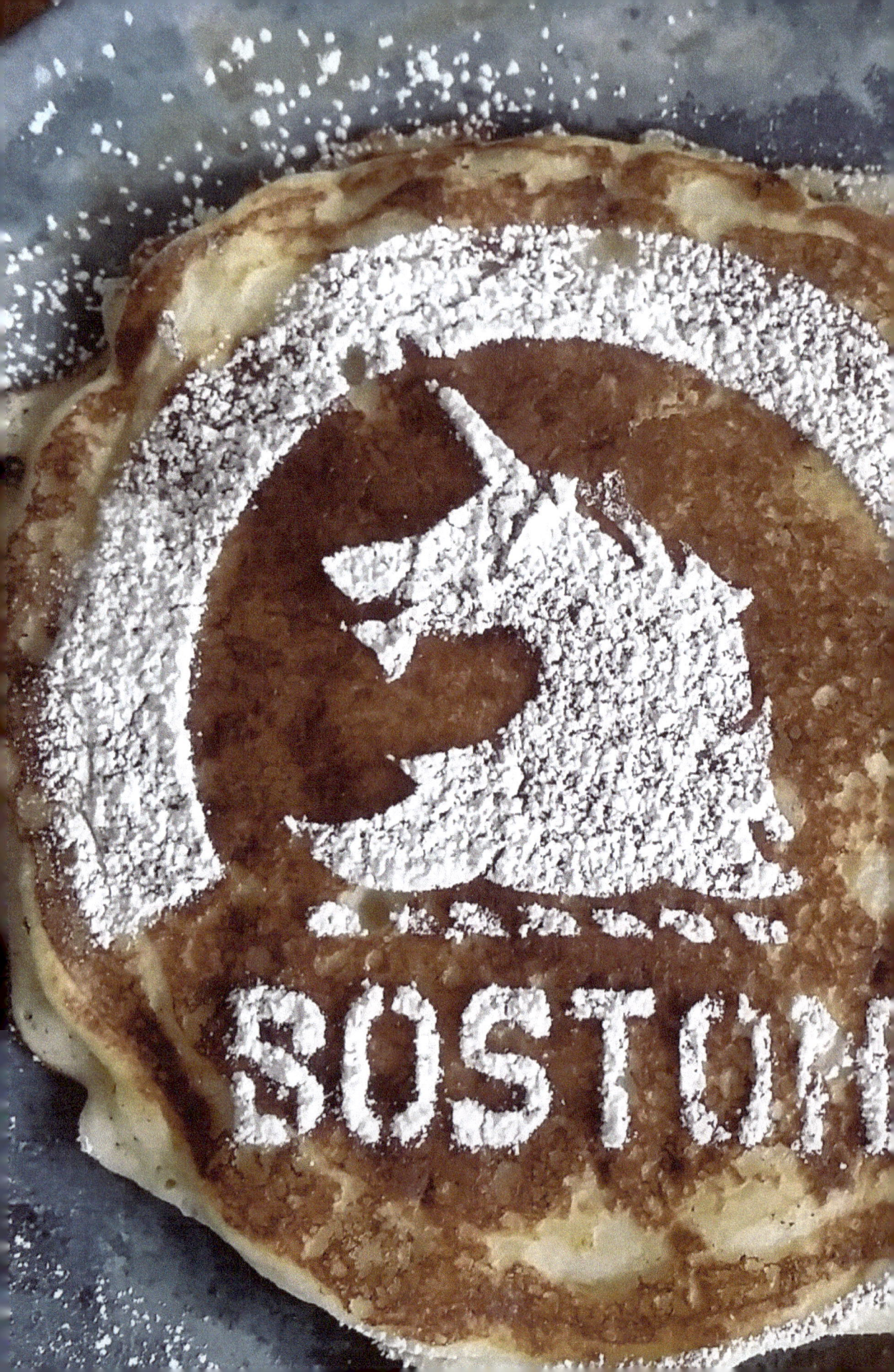

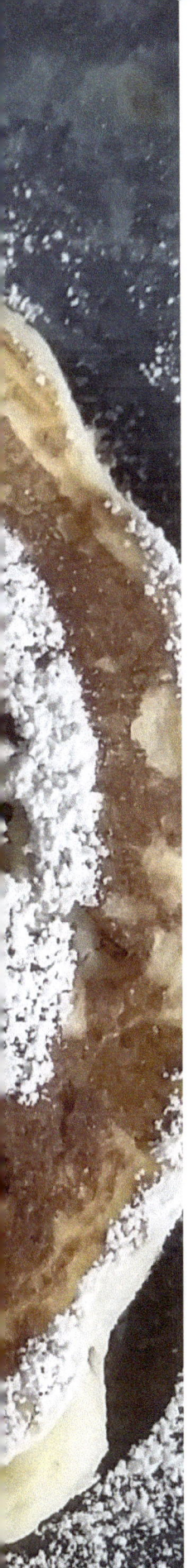
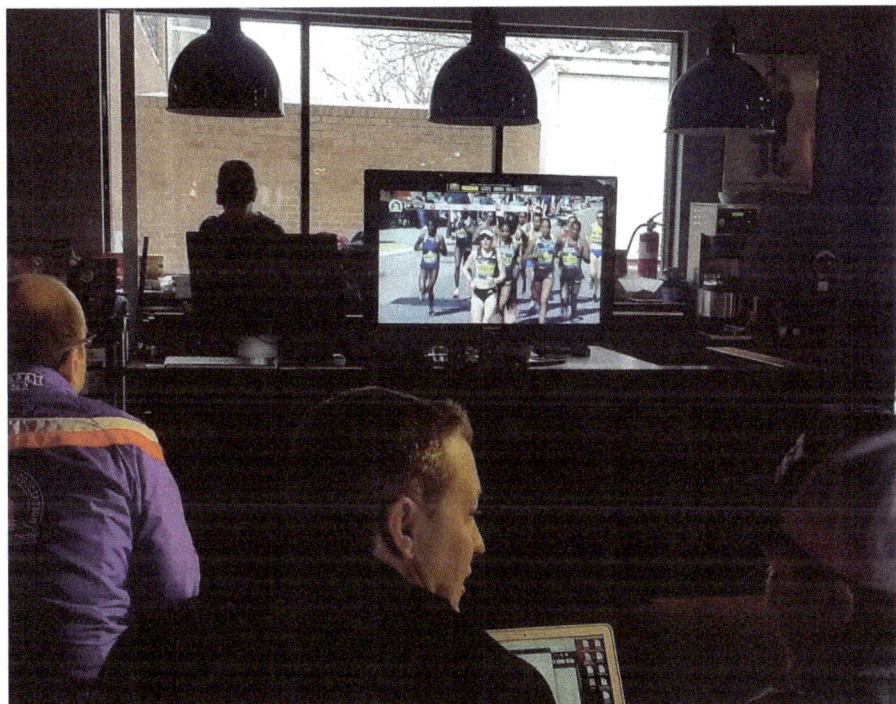
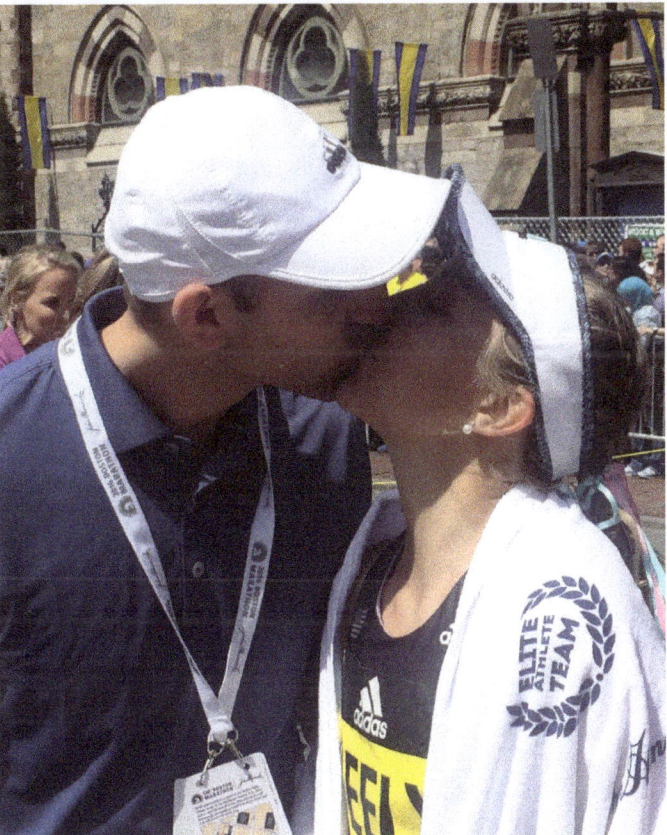

Running fans gathered at Flatirons Running on Marathon Monday to cheer on local athletes including Neely who finished as the first American and 9th overall in her Marathon debut. She kisses her husband post race. Bottom photo courtesy of Brian Metzler.

Boulder to Boston

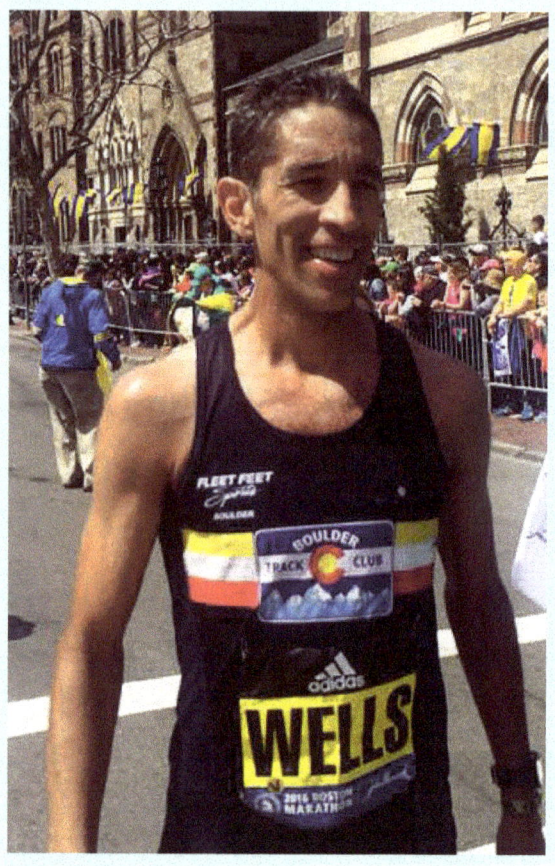

Photo by Brian Metzler

Clint Wells has returned to running after a successful post-collegiate stint with renewed vigor, getting after his training and it's paying off. Now a masters runner, Clint was the 3rd American overall at Boston and was the first Masters in the race.

"Turning the corner on Boylston Street and seeing the thousands of spectators and the finish line was the best part!!"

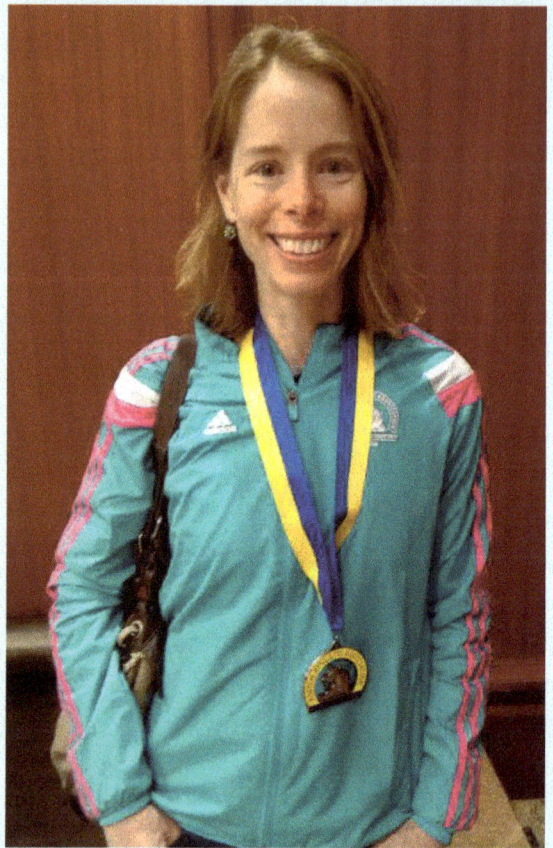

Photo courtesy Terzah Becker

Terzah Becker was looking to qualify for Boston by the time she reached 40. She managed to do just that, but was denied an entry as her age group filled with faster runners. So she qualified again with the new tighter standard. Again the demand for entries was so high that her new time still wasn't fast enough. Through the luck of a Facebook contest put on by Clif Bar, she won one of five spots granted back to runners who qualified but were not able to get in. Terzah finally got to run Boston and ran a PR to boot.

"For two years I had to tell my kids that I qualified and then explain to them later why I couldn't run it. It's a good feeling to be able to tell them that because I didn't quit and didn't give up I was able to fulfill my dream — it's nice to be able to show them even a nerdy girl can one day grow up to achieve all her athletic dreams."

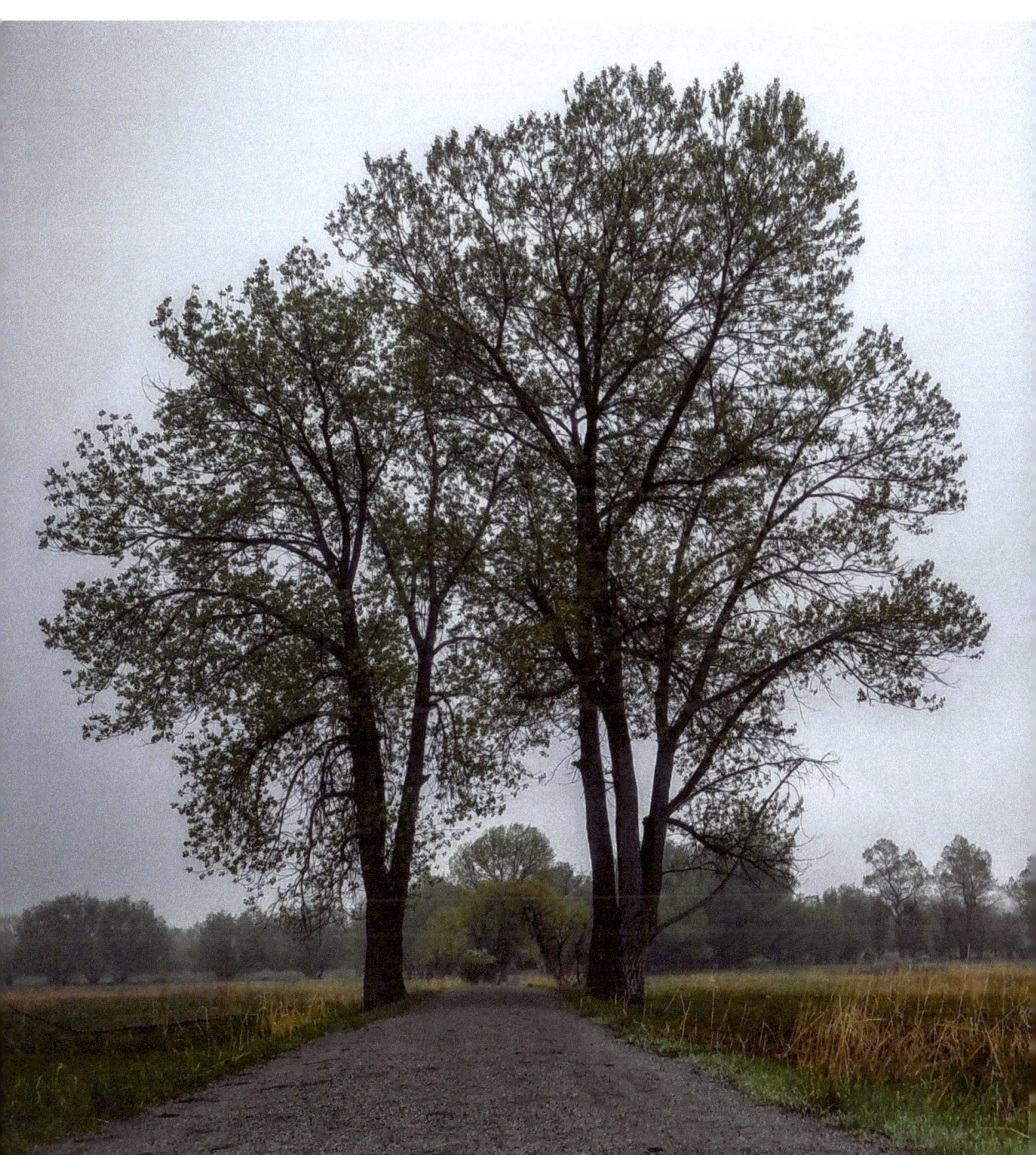

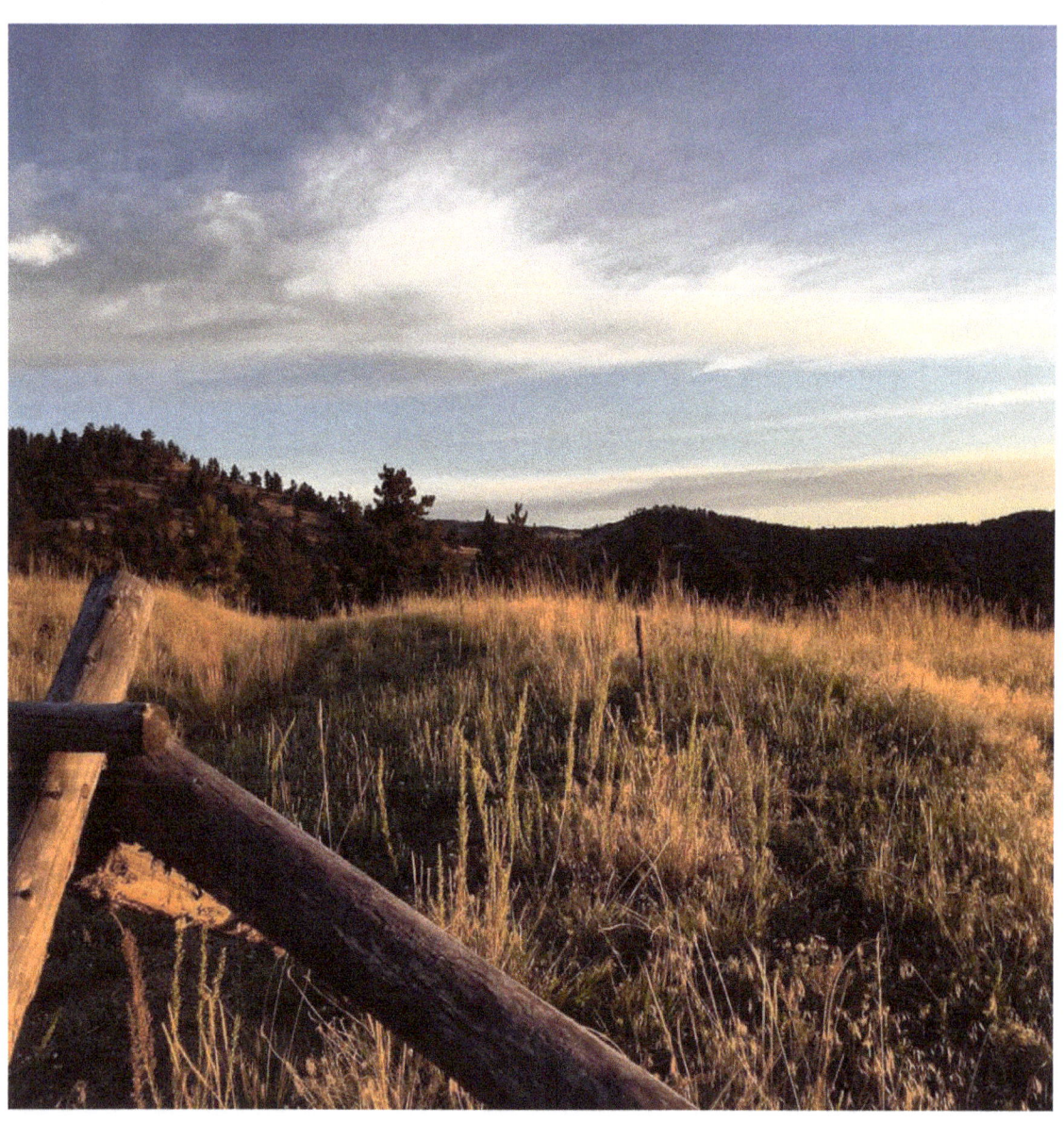

Scratching the Epic Itch

Words by Cheri Felix

When I was a little girl growing up in Oregon, it rained a lot. One of my favorite things to do was to go mud sliding at the park. It involved lots of standing water and lots of mud. I played baseball back then so I think it was my way of getting dirty and working on skills all at the same time. When I was 17, I moved to Southern California to live with my dad, who had left when I was six. Looking back, we barely knew each other. All I knew was that I could leave my makeup and blush behind because I'd be tan all the time. California dreamin'. Land of milk and honey and all those old notions. When I was 26, I sold everything I owned and bought a one-way ticket to Cairo, Egypt. I spent the next two years learning Arabic, drinking coffee, dancing, dating and watching the sun set on the Nile. I've been to Morocco and Tunisia, and although I love Italy and Spain and anywhere else the passport can take me, I really love North Africa. It's epic.

Now, at 48, happily married with three kids, my epic itch is still there. But my life is full. Not a lot of time for mud sliding because really, who has time for that kind of laundry? But it has to be something because I'm still fundamentally the same person I was at 12, 17, and 26. And so, it's running. It's become the scratch for my epic itch. It's not floating on the Nile or mud sliding or negotiating a taxi fare in Morocco. It's not figuring out how to tell a doctor in Arabic what's wrong with my belly or getting into an argument with a soldier and a gun about the proper way to insert my ticket into the subway machine. It's not a sunset or a sunrise over a city of 17 million people as the call to prayer elevates from the ground to the clouds. And it's okay. Because for the last few years I've had running. I added it to my other love, mountain biking. They have something in common; they both get me back into the trees and the dirt. Away from cars and streets and people. They both, if only for an hour or two, allow me to believe that I can do anything I want. No one is the boss of me and I really can carry all that I need on my back. For two hours, the world will continue to spin. The world will survive without me. The kids will be alright. And I believe once again that my epic itch can be scratched.

By running.

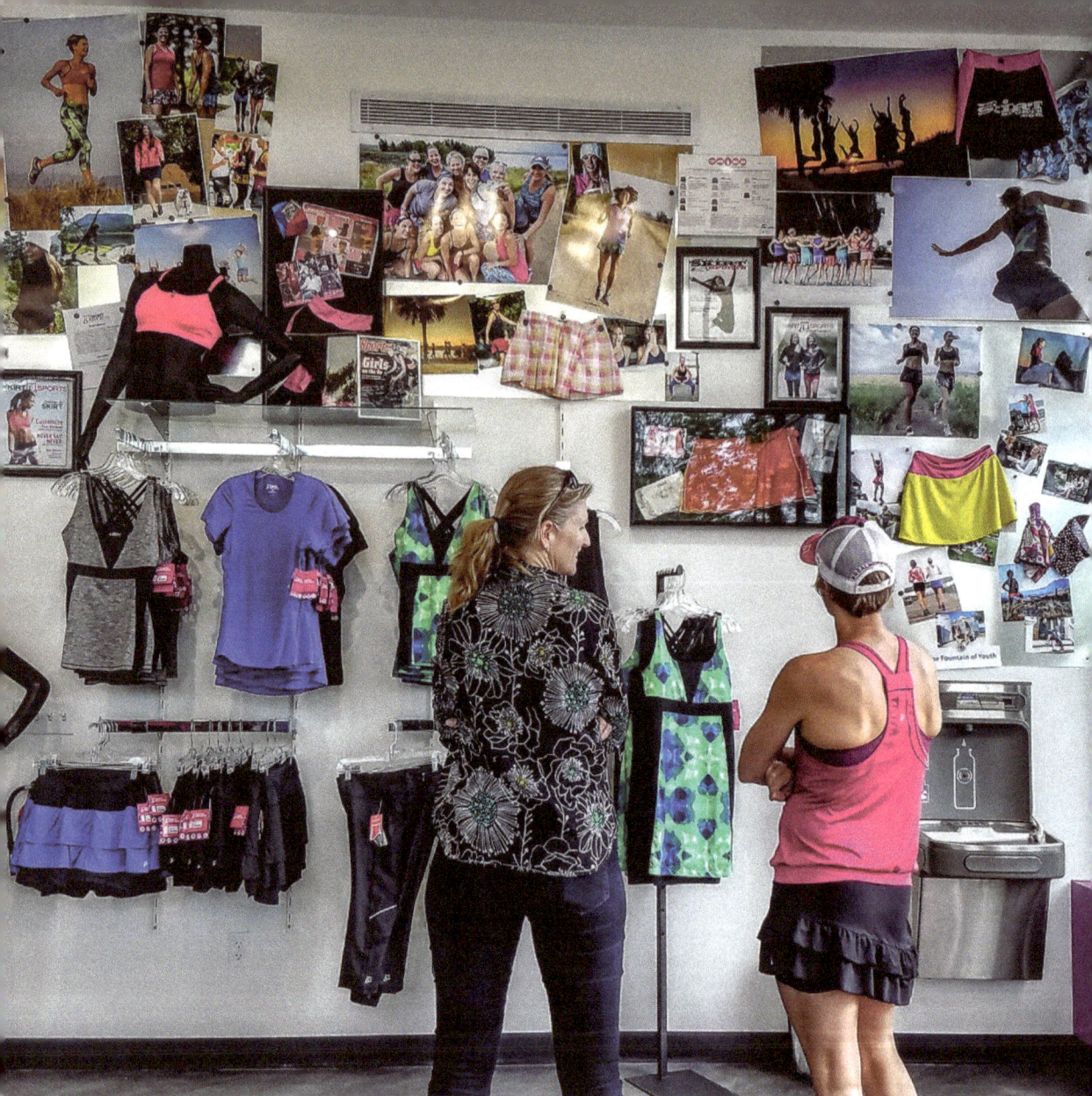

SKIRT SPORTS

"Our vision for the store is to create an environment of inspiration and acceptance. A woman's relationship with her body is very personal, so having the ability to try everything on in a welcoming environment is so important."

Founder Nicole DeBoom on the opening of their first retail location

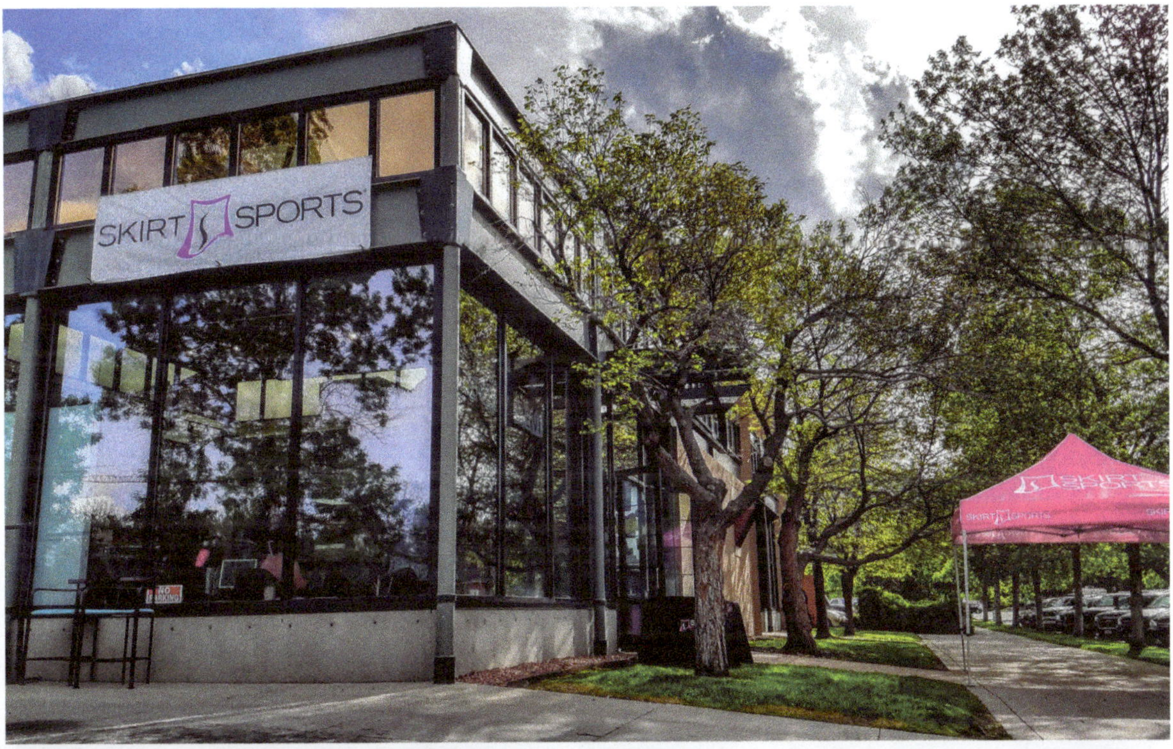

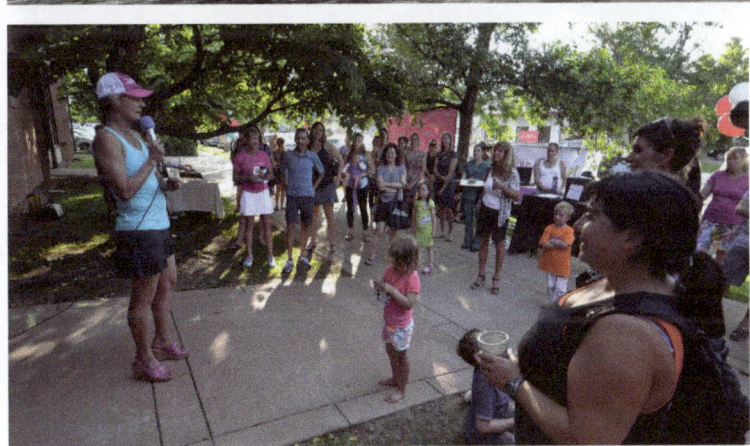
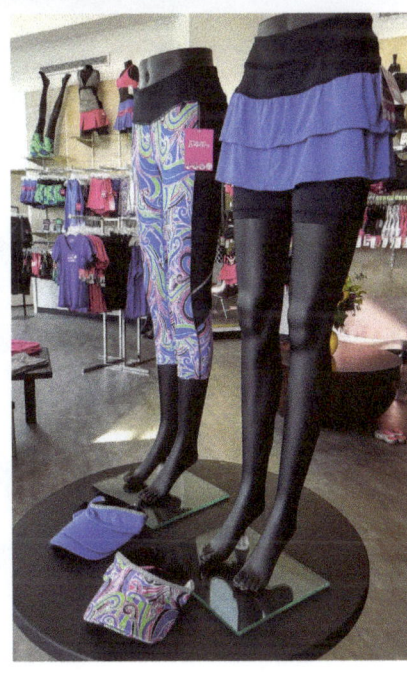
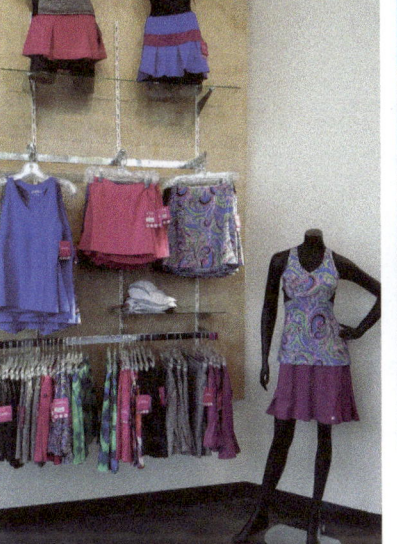
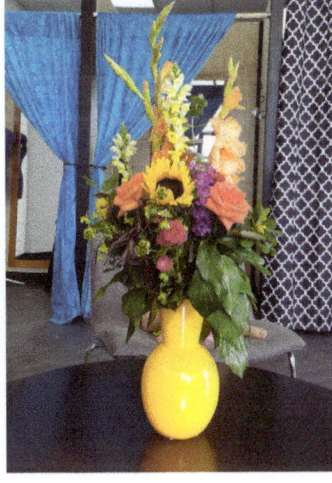

COLORADO RUNNING HALL OF FAME INDUCTS THREE OF BOULDER'S BEST

Three of Boulder's running elite were inducted into the Colorado Running Hall of Fame on April 20: Adam Chase, Don Janicki and Billy Nelson. They joined Susan Weeks and Jennifer Michel in the class of 2016 for their achievements and contributions to the sport of running.

Chase for his adventure and ultrarunning achievements and his long time contributions to running journalism. Janicki for his lifetime achievements in road racing and as the Elite Coordinator for the Bolder Boulder and Nelson for his achievements as runner and assistant coach at CU Boulder.

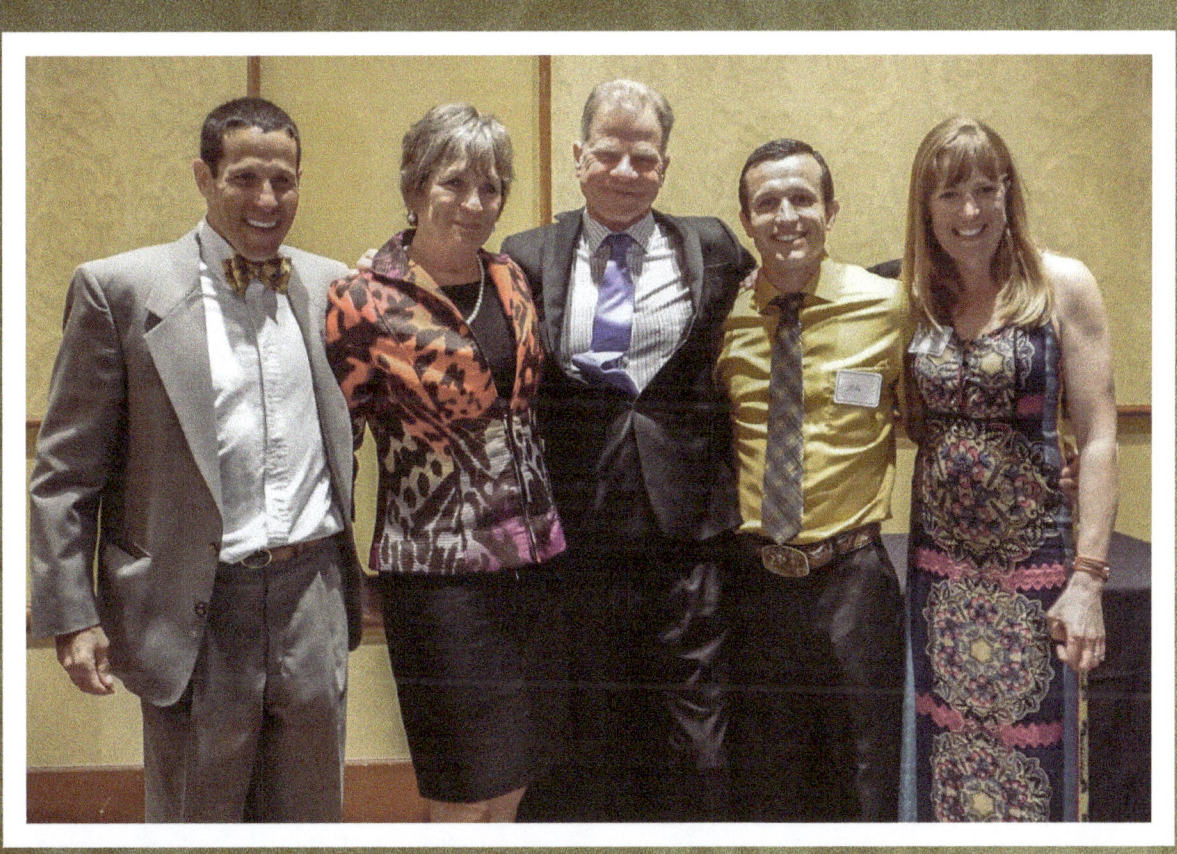

BOULDER

There has never been any question of Colleen De Reuck's ties to the Comrades Marathon. The South African native's dad, Frank Lindeque, ran it when she was young, and her entire family would drive along the course to provide him fluids ("water and Coke and maybe a brandy halfway," she recalls). Her younger brother, Henry, eventually joined him. The two each earned green numbers, with Henry running ten Comrades and Frank 15. Her speedy older brother, Colin, ran it four times, with a best finish of seventh place overall for a gold medal; her sister-in-law Kerry-Jane ran it too.

But De Reuck herself, despite being the family's four-time Olympian and international distance running star, had never run Comrades.

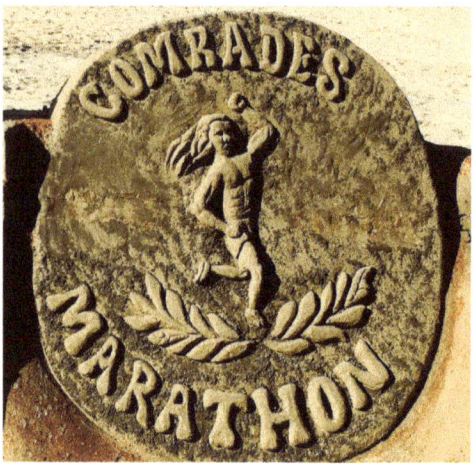

Until this year.

Now also a master's Ironman triathlon champion and U.S. citizen, De Reuck is always looking for new challenges, and, she says, "being a South African runner, you are drawn to this incredible race." Things fell into place when KPMG, the international accounting company, offered to sponsor her first Comrades.

That's how she found herself lined up in the pre-dawn darkness as the strains of "Shosholoza," an African folk song, poured over the waiting runners. "You feel the excitement and energy," she says. "It really is so powerful." A crowing rooster sent them off. At last, De Reuck was following in the footsteps of her father and brothers.

She wasn't sure what to expect from the race, though she had done a shorter ultra earlier in the spring and had worked hard back in Boulder, logging four-hour long runs and training on Mt. Sanitas.

"The most unexpected thing was that I experienced cramping with 14 miles to go. That was new to me, and I had to walk and run to the finish. The Comrades is the toughest event I have done so far; I found it harder than an Ironman."

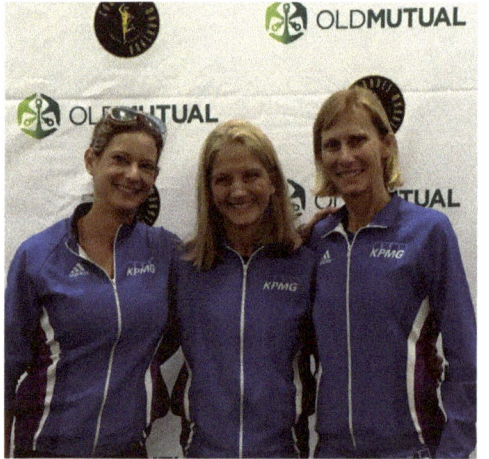

Courtesy photo - De Reuck with Caroline Wostmann (2nd) and Kerry-Ann Marshall (6th)

Despite that, the experience was hugely satisfying for De Reuck. She finished seventh, earning a gold medal, but more important to her, her whole family came out to watch her. "Even my brother, Colin, from Perth, [Australia], flew in, and I had many friends along the course that I hadn't seen in years," she says.

She plans to return next year, when the course reverses direction and heads "up." But she isn't worried about trying for more gold medals or a green number. "I feel I need to do both the up and down run to have the full Comrades Experience," she says. "And I will leave it at that."

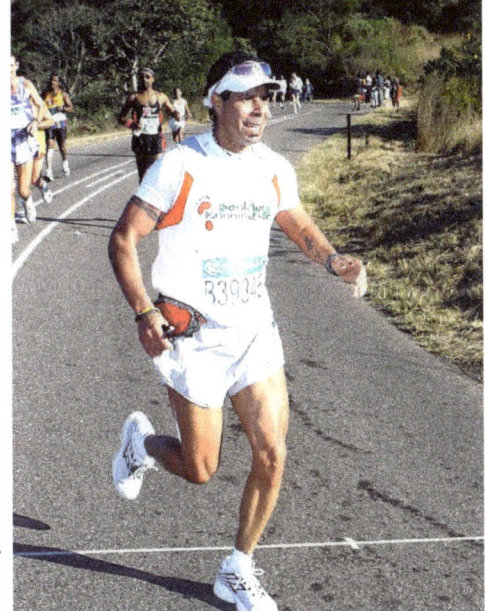

Words by Terzah Becker

When Henry Guzman boarded a plane to South Africa to run his first Comrades Marathon in 1999, he had no idea that he was about to start a relationship as much as a race. Nor did he have any idea what the notoriously tough 56-mile ultra had in store for him physically.

He was there because his colleague Mark Plaatjes, a South African native and marathon world champion, had talked him into it. The two had run the Tucson Marathon the prior December, Guzman in 2:43.

"I figured I was in good shape. I didn't understand the lore of Comrades at all."

That first go—a "downhill" year—left Guzman, now co-owner of Flatirons Running, unable to walk "for literally three days." But he went back. Again. And again. And despite nearly going into kidney failure after the 2001 race, DNFing in 2002, and skipping the race for a period before resuming in 2012, Guzman persevered, earning his 10th Comrades medal in May 2016.

The feat placed him on the Green Number Roll of Honour, an exclusive list of athletes who have earned their Comrades number in perpetuity (Guzman's number is 39346). To get a Green Number, runners must finish the race 10 times under 12 hours, win it outright three times or garner five gold medals (gold medalists finish in the top ten for their gender).

Comrades was founded in 1921 to honor South Africa's World War I veterans (the name derives from the League of Comrades of the Great War), and it boasts a history at least as rich as the Boston Marathon's. While early records are spotty, Guzman appears to be the first American to have earned a Green Number.

2016's was a finish he will not forget. Race spectators and volunteers knew he was gunning for his 10th due to a special stripe on his bib. At the end, he says, "I had 30 minutes to run 2K, so I said, 'Screw this. I'll walk.'" As he got closer to the finish in Kingsmead Cricket Stadium in Durban and realized the green number was a reality, emotion overcame him. Volunteers rushed him to a special tent after he crossed the line.

"It was something," he said, shaking his head at the understatement. "It was something."

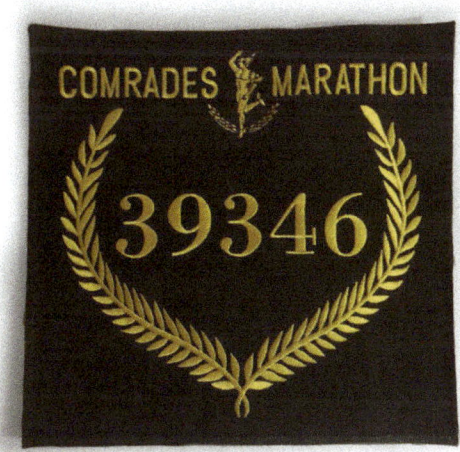

COMRADES

TRAIL SISTERS

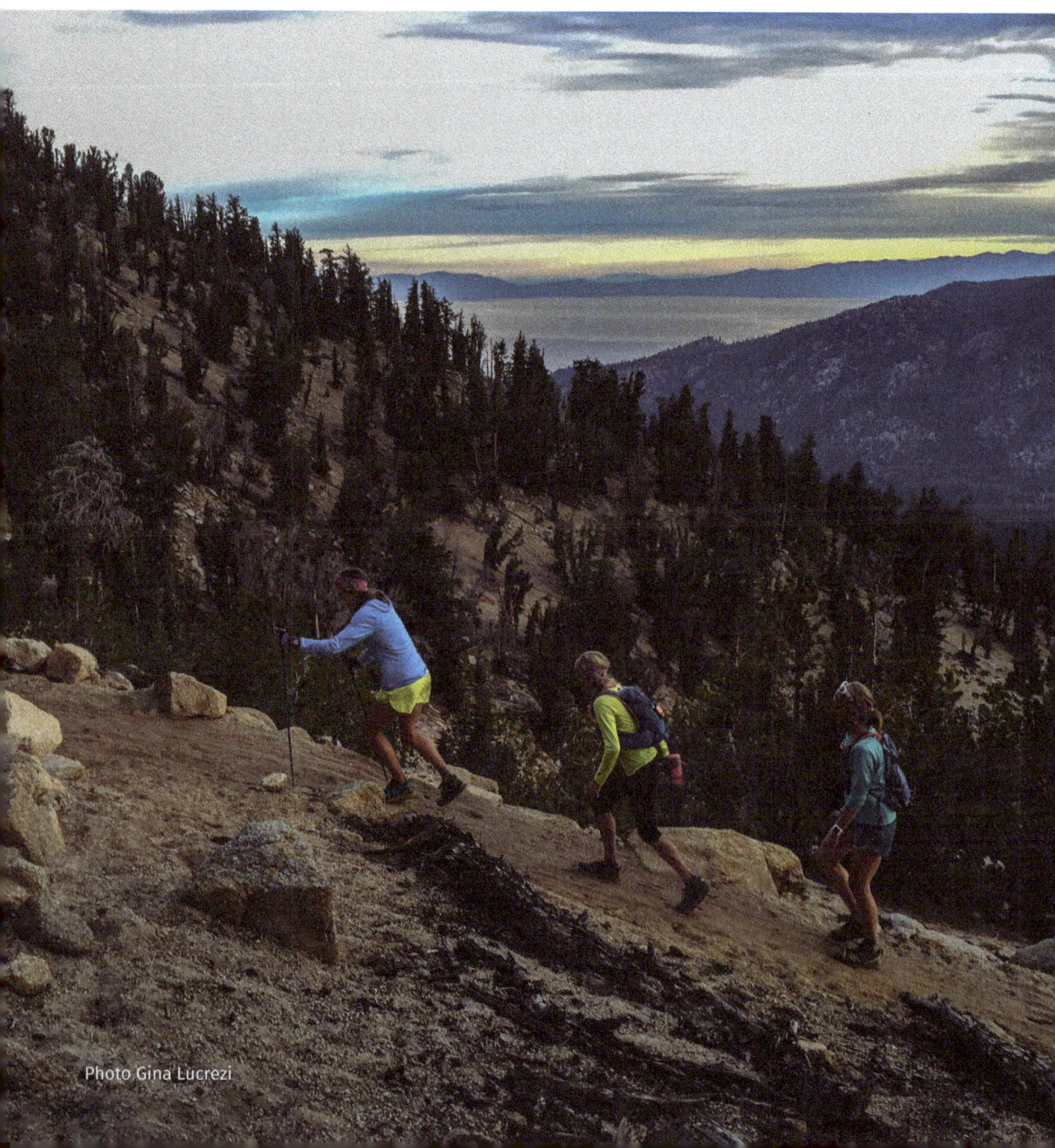

Photo Gina Lucrezi

Ultrarunner Gina Lucrezi has been in the outdoor industry for many years and couldn't help but notice the lack of female voices as compared to the amount of female participation in trail and ultra races. "It's certainly gotten better than it was 10 years ago," she notes, but there is still room for more. So she started **TrailSisters.net** with a collection of female trail badasses with the mission to support women and four pillars: community, health/well-being, outdoor sport, and conservational awareness.

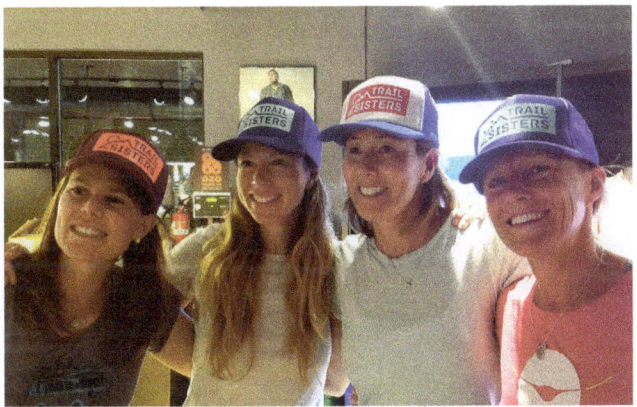

In May, Flatirons Running hosted a fun run and panel with Darcy Piceu, Lisa Jhung, and Elinor Fish, all experienced trail running veterans who shared their secrets and fielded questions from those looking to find out more about how to get into trail running or racing.

The TrailSisters website is full of content exploring topics ranging from preparing for races to divorce to mindfulness, adventure, and inspiration. All of these women are highly accomplished in the world of trail running but are humble and relatable.

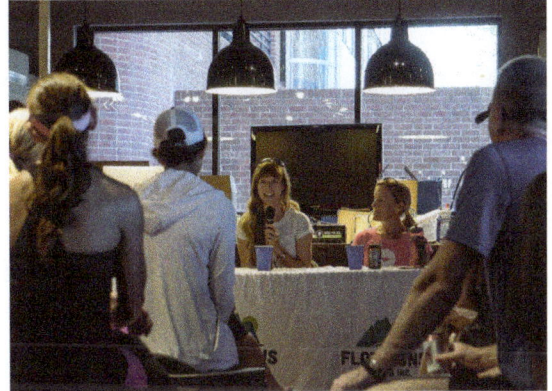

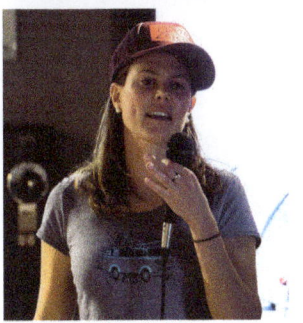

72

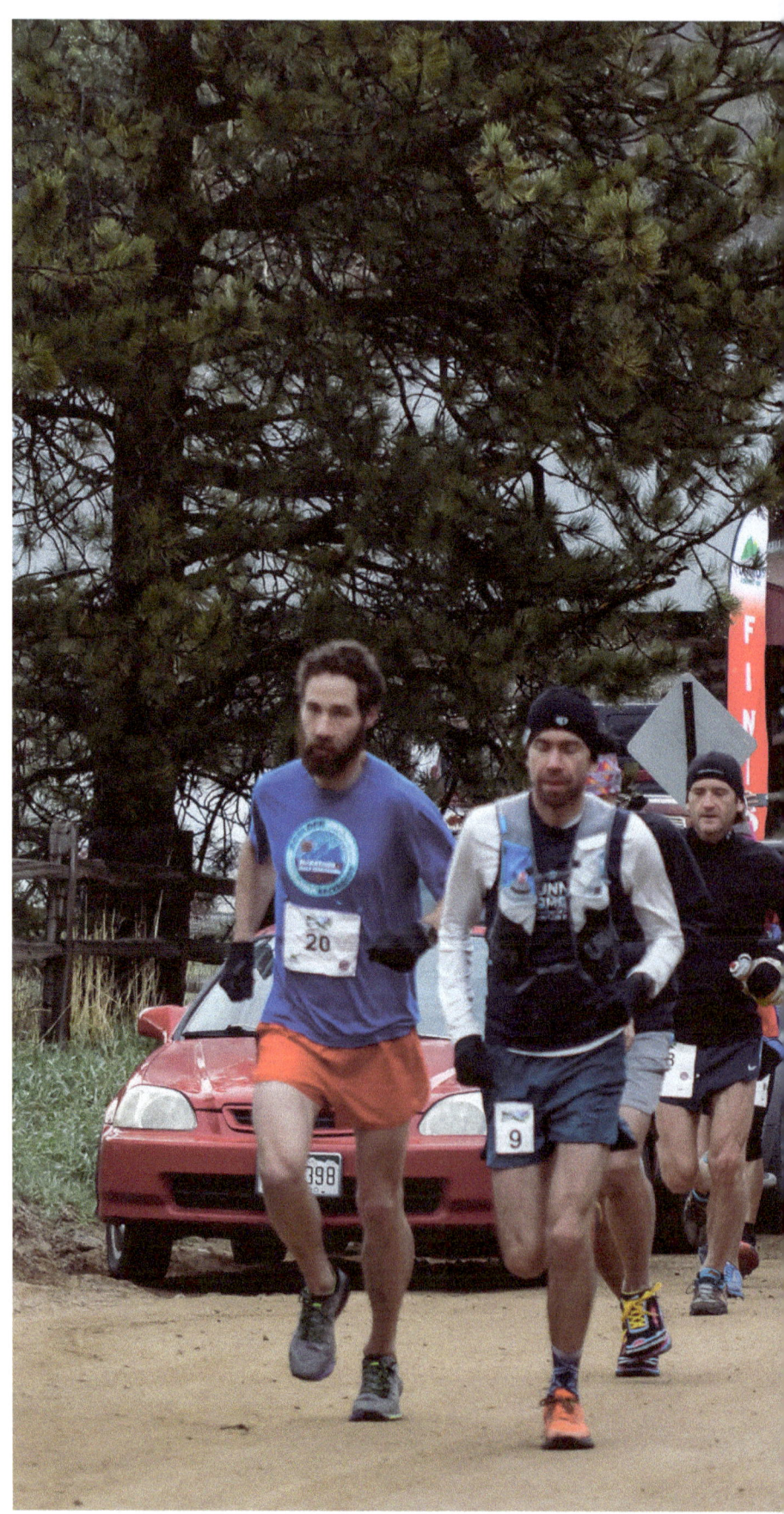

Boulder Mountain Marathon

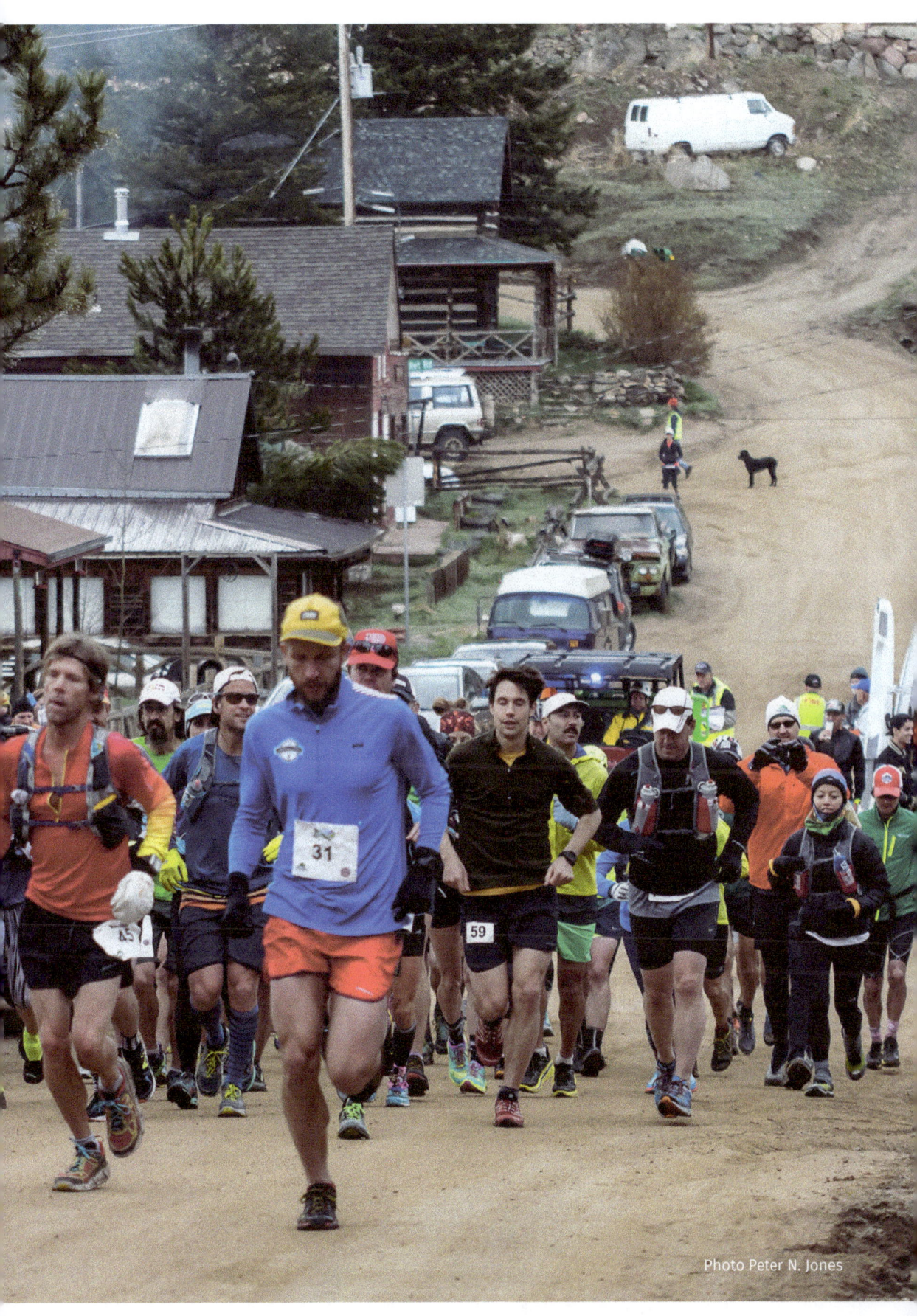
Photo Peter N. Jones

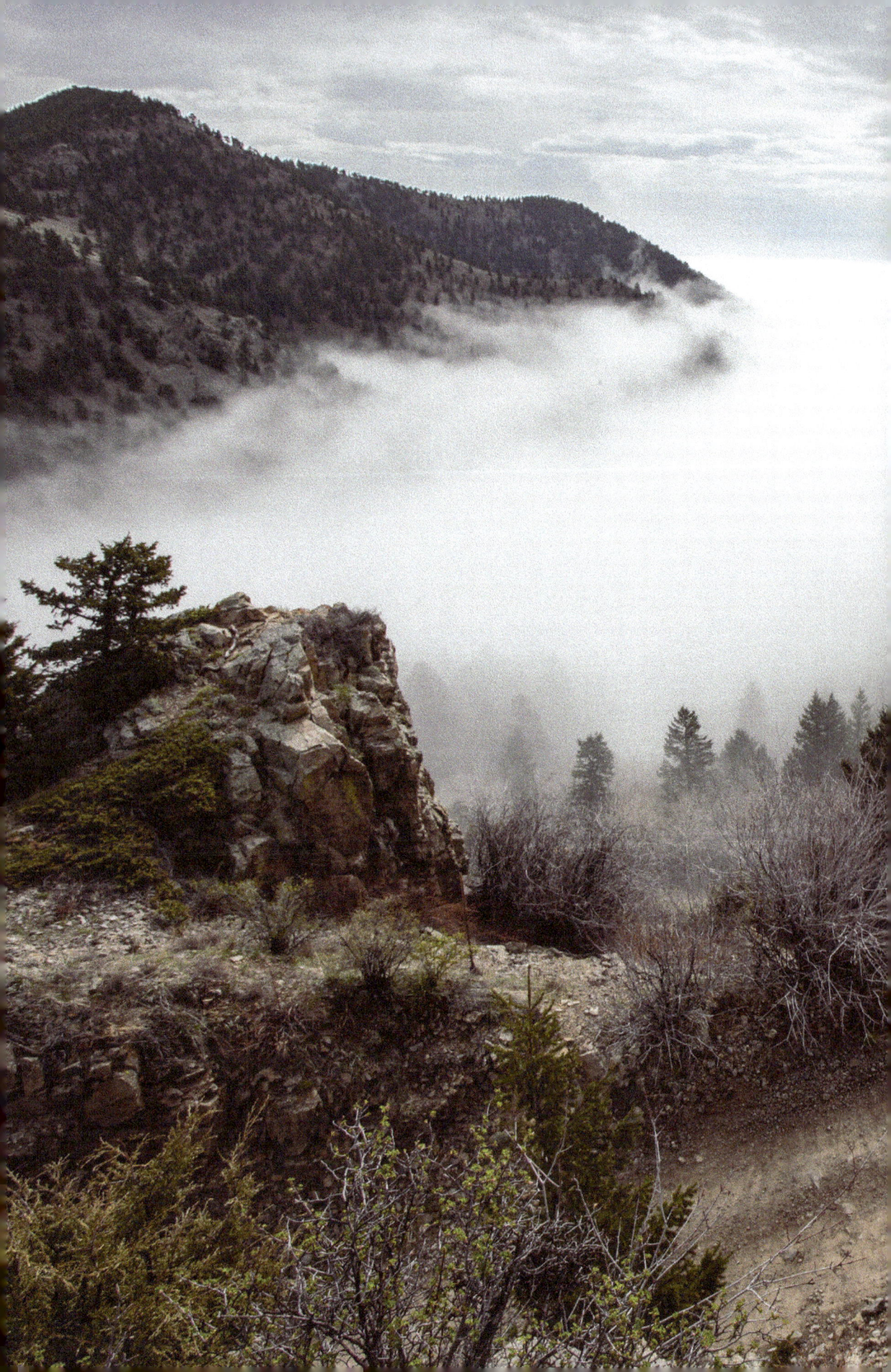

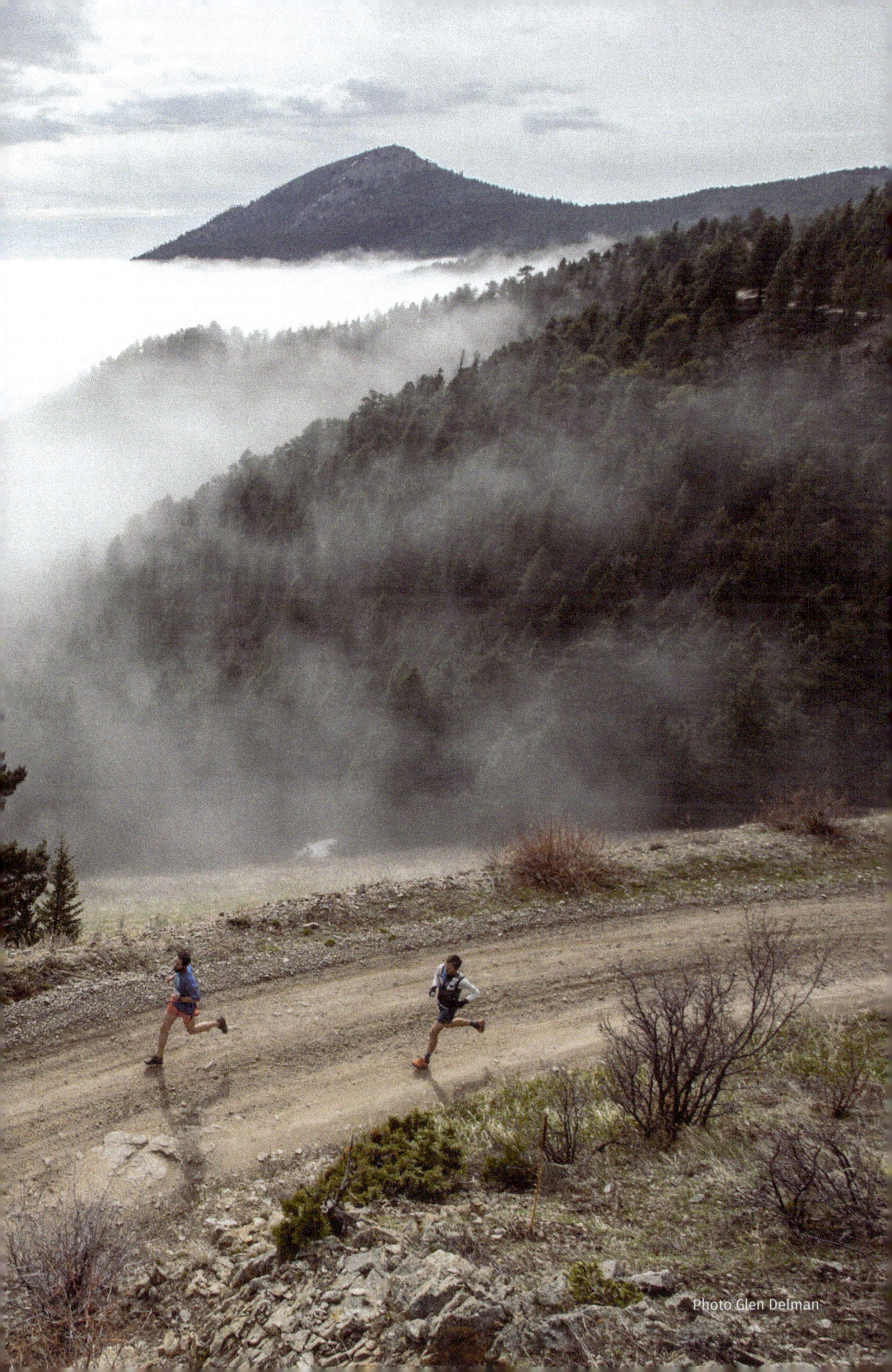
Photo Glen Delman

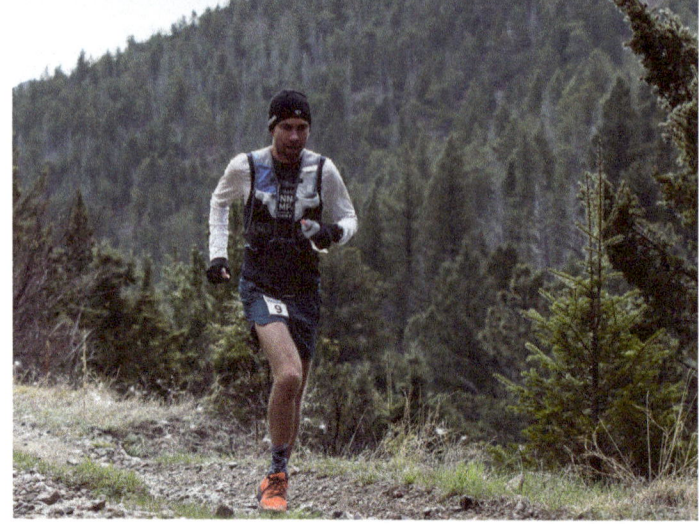
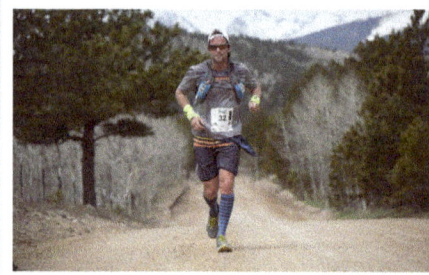
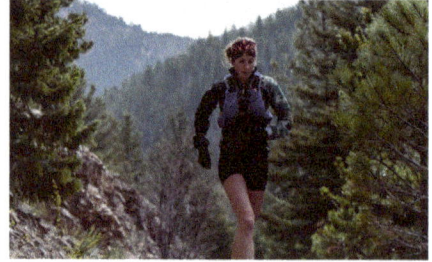
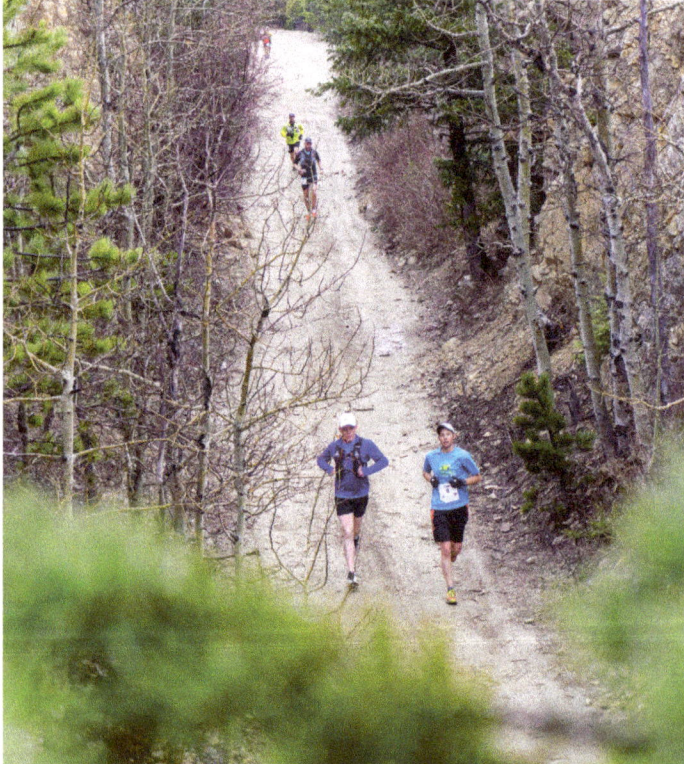

A sweet day of high altitude trails and new/old friends at the Inaugural Boulder Mountain Marathon. Congrats to all who participated and thanks to those who made it happen, fun times were had by all.

While May rain clouds shrouded the Boulder valley just a few miles below, the skies were blue and conditions grew comfortable, perfect for running at the 7:00 am start. A modest field took on the course starting at 8,300' heading west on Gold Hill Road before turning onto the Switzerland Trail which hosted most of the course.

Photos Peter N. Jones, Mike Hugus, Glen Delman

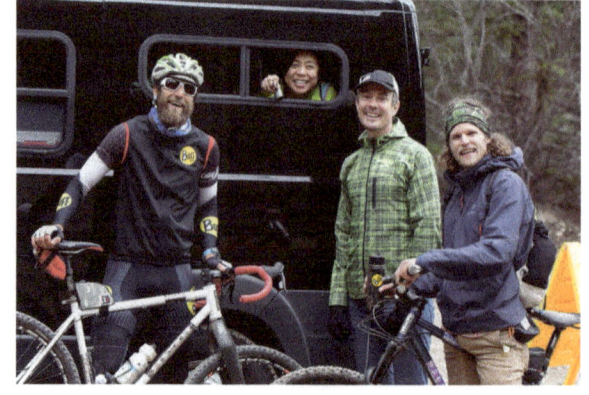

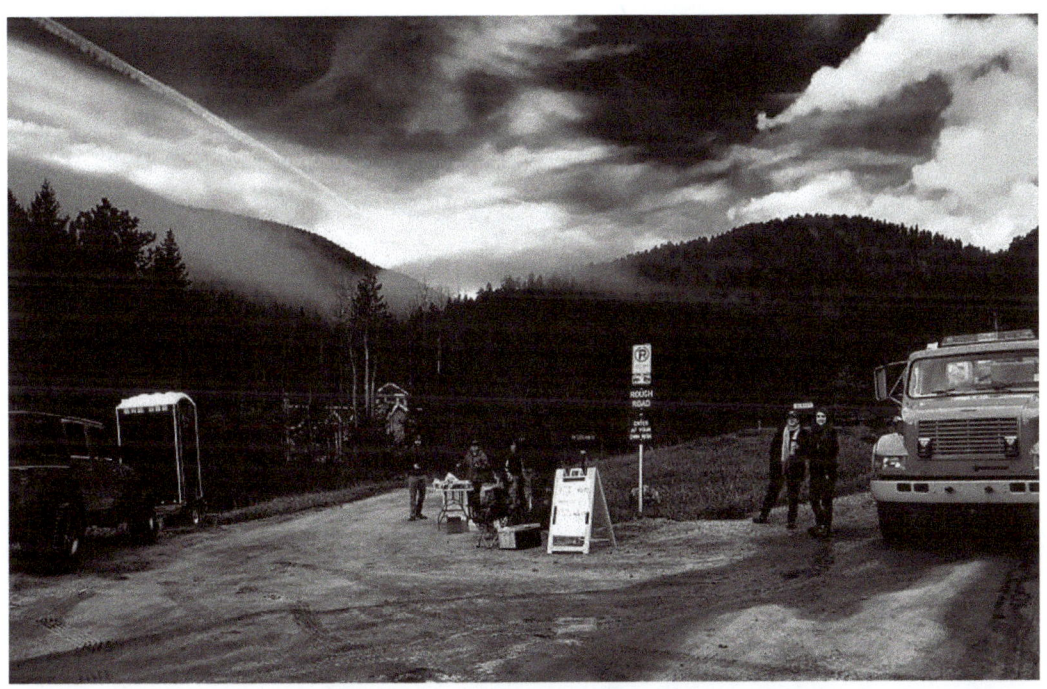

Runners passed through the aid station at the town of Sunset.
Photo Bill Hanson

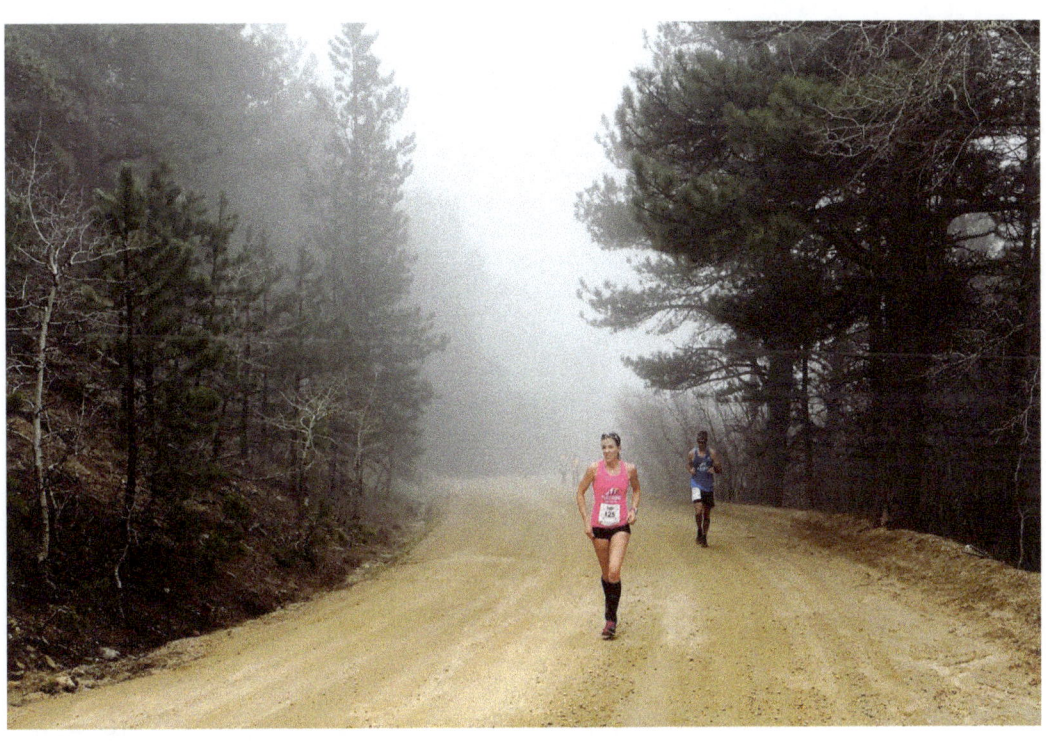

Amanda Lee leads the women's field up Four Mile Canyon for the 10 mile ascent.
Photo Henry Guzman

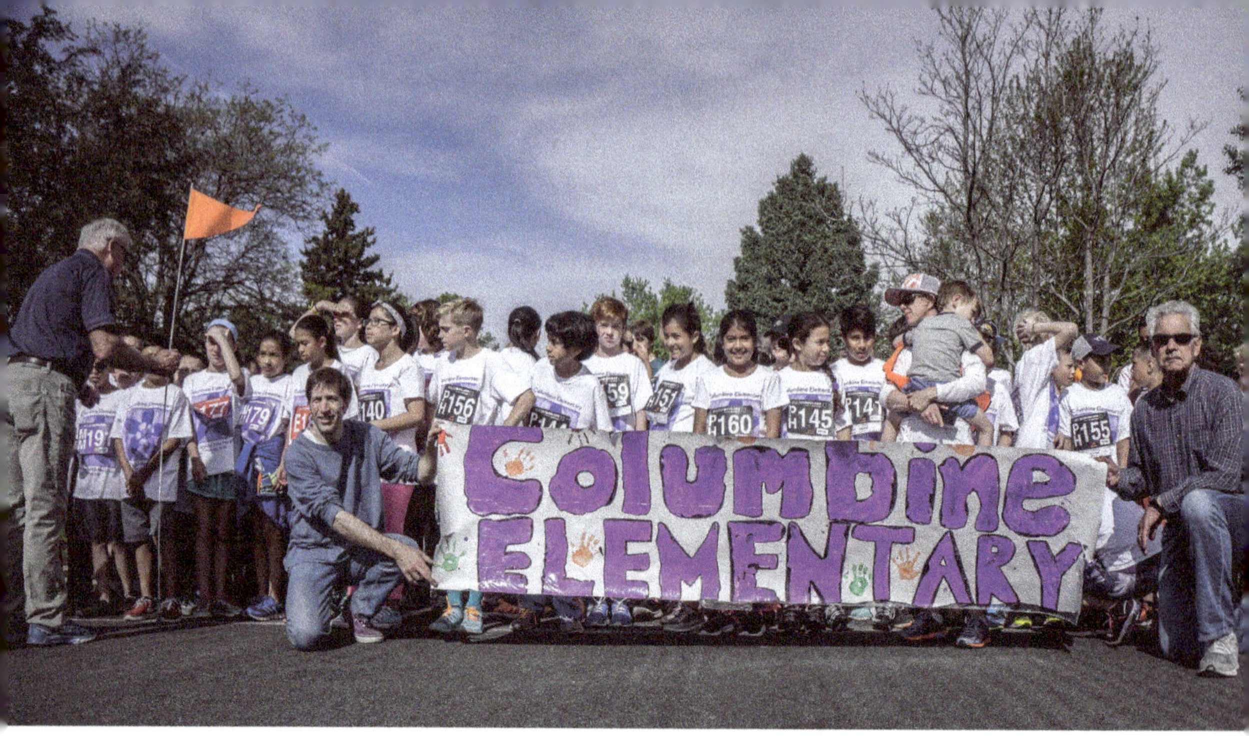

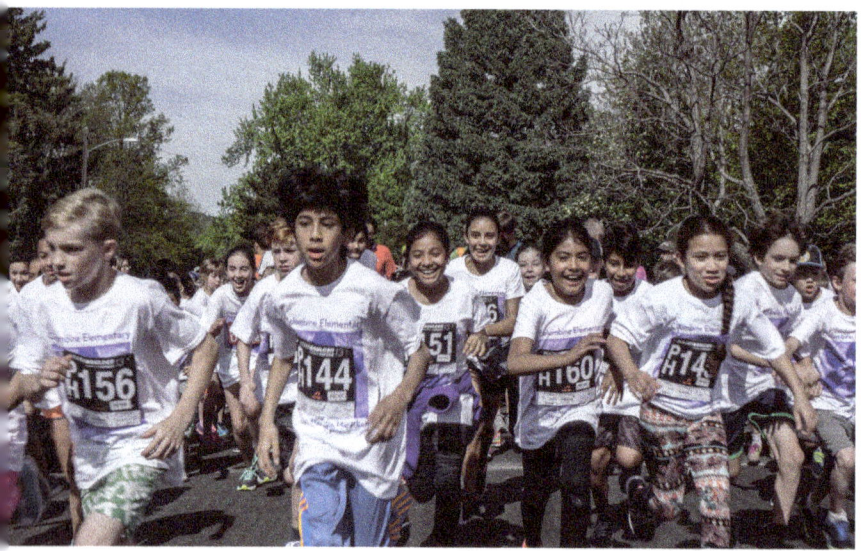
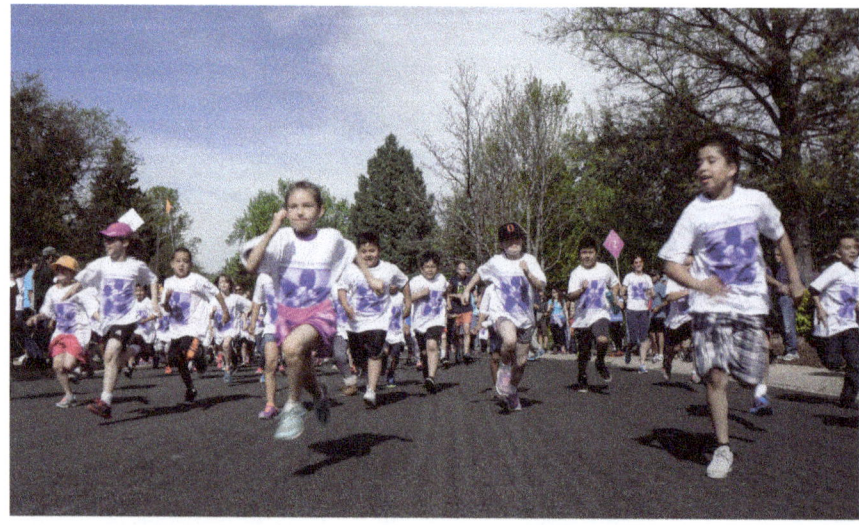

THE COLUMBINE MILE MARATHON

In its 39th year, the Columbine Mile Marathon is a tradition for grade schoolers to get ready for the Bolder Boulder and to promote an active lifestyle. Often supported by recognizable local runners from age groupers to Olympians, Rich Castro's run has created a unique and inspiring event to look forward to each year.

Photos Todd Straka

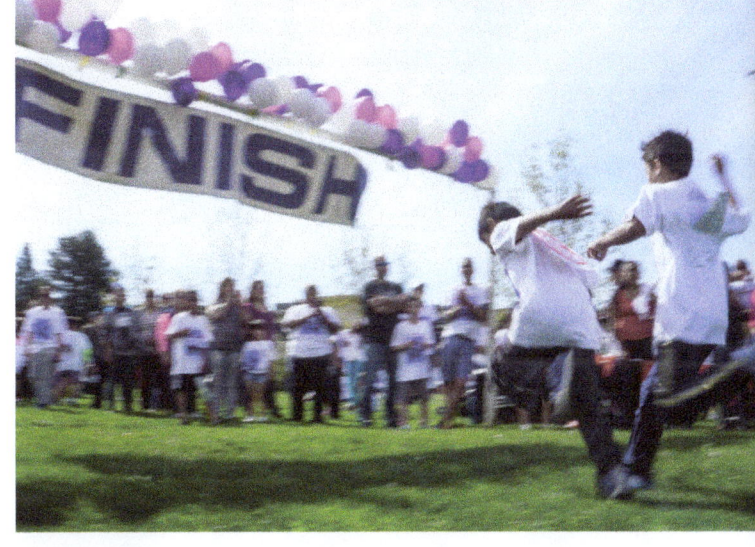

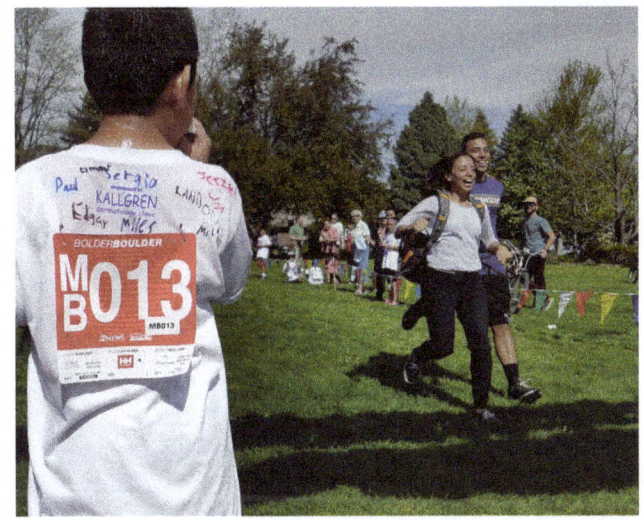

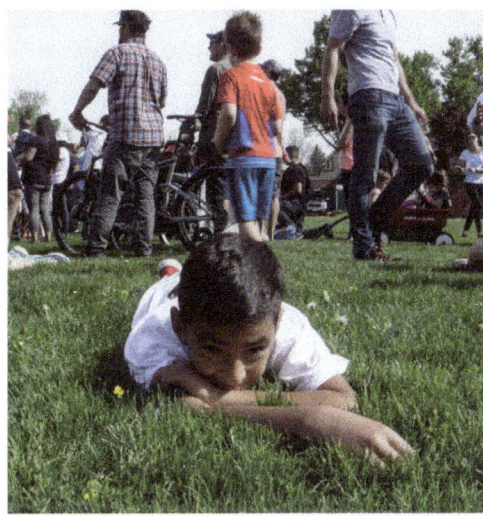

FEAR AND LOATHING ON THE UPPER CREEK PATH

Words by David "Smitty" Smith

I ran easy up to the Red Lion. Enjoying the creek, flowering trees and warm weather. Came back down and as I got on the gravel creek path some guy with gray hair bolted by me just past the outhouse. I sped up and caught him and asked the typical "what are you training for..." He grunted without any eye contact, "Really nothing," and proceeded to drop the pace to 7:30/mile. I hung with him only because it felt kind of easy on the downhill. As we got closer to Elephant Rock he threw in a couple surges. I decided to "do no harm" and let him go. I then noticed he backed off the pace once he knew I was off his backside. By this time he was about 30 yards ahead of me. I got feisty and decided I would give him a "go" again. I reeled him back in and blew by him with authority (something my coach ALWAYS insisted on when racing) at a 7:40 pace. He stayed with me for ten yards and then stalked me at 20 yards all the way back to University Ave. and then disappeared.

There is still a little spunk in the Smitty of 60!

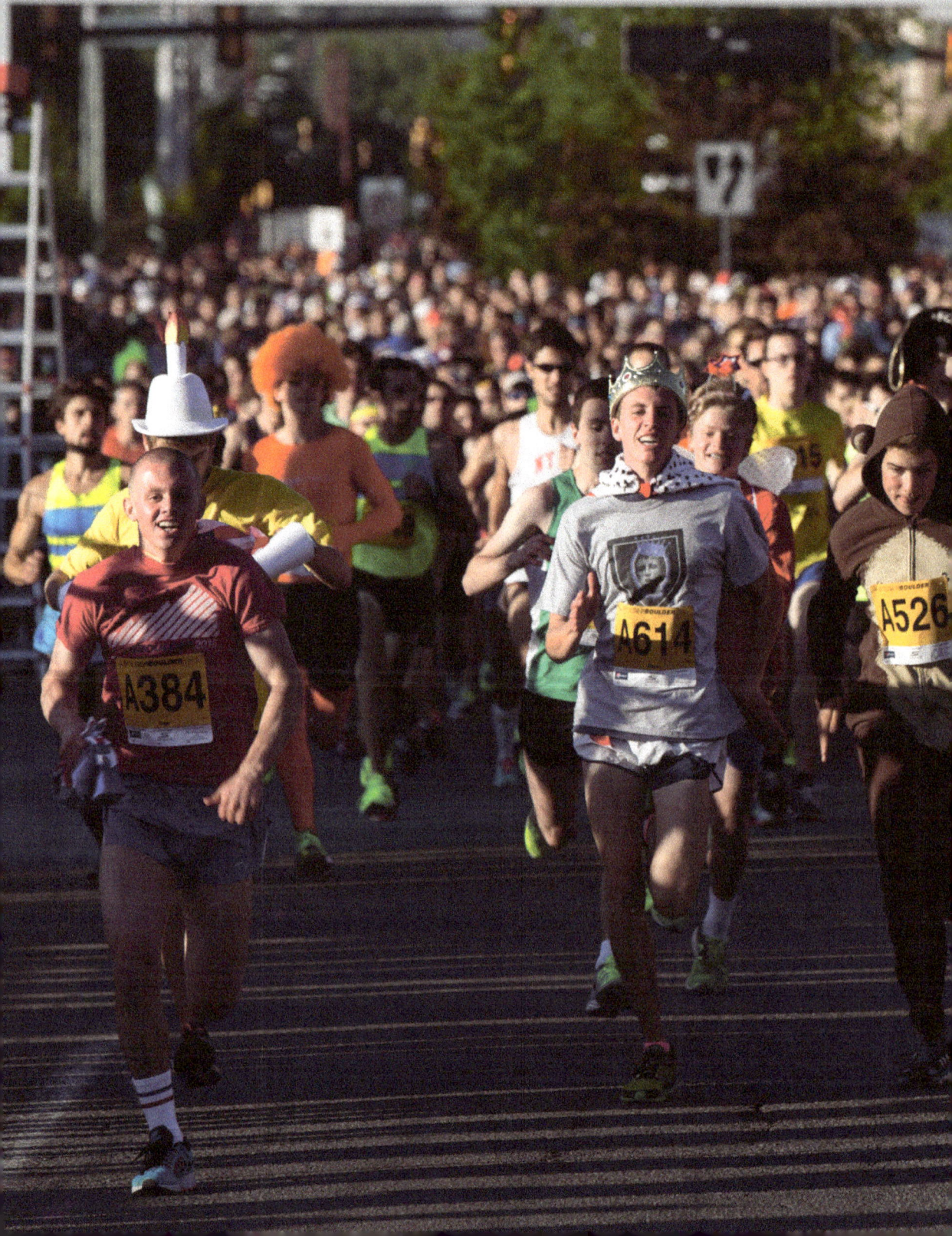

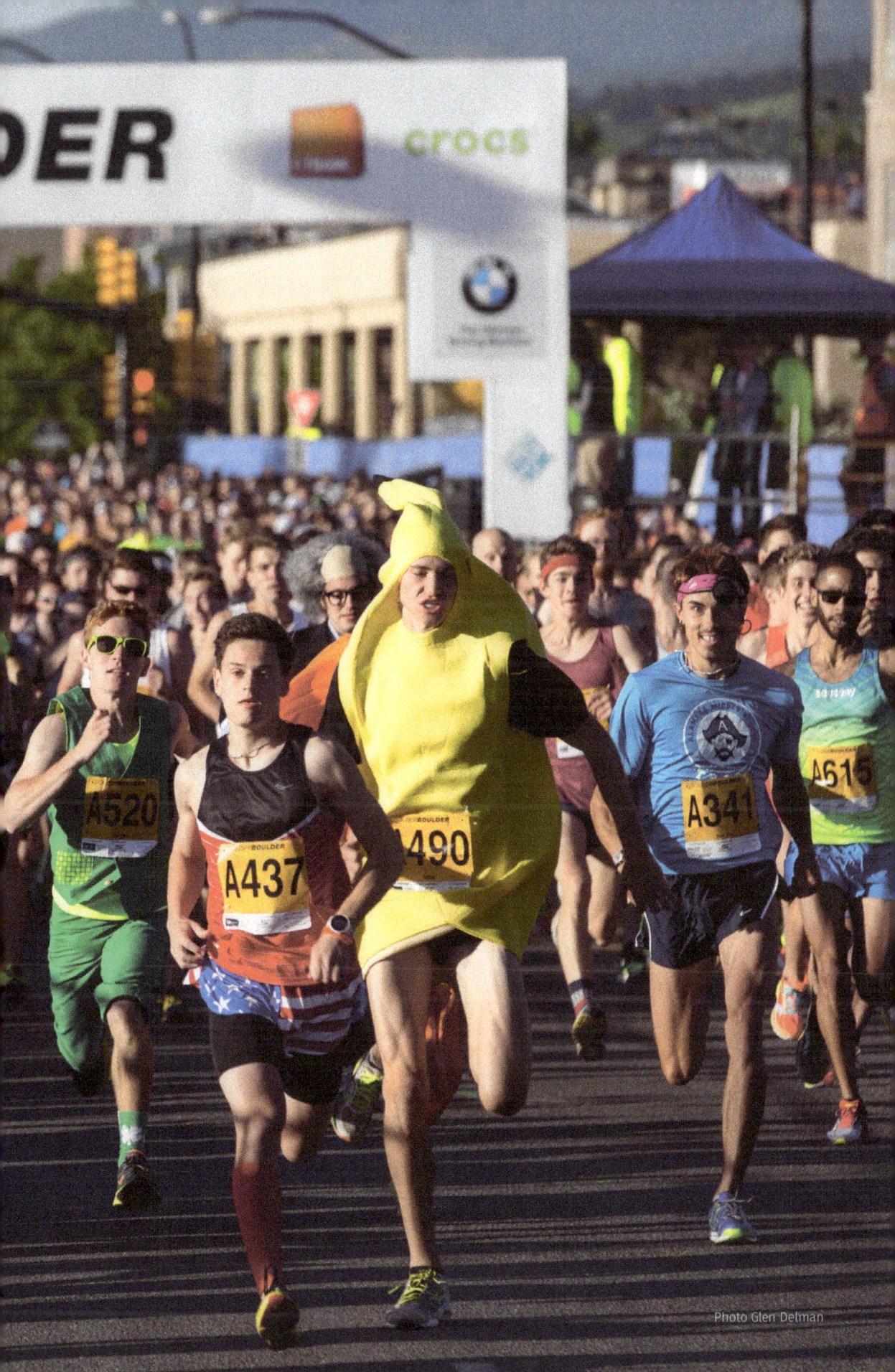

Photo Glen Delman

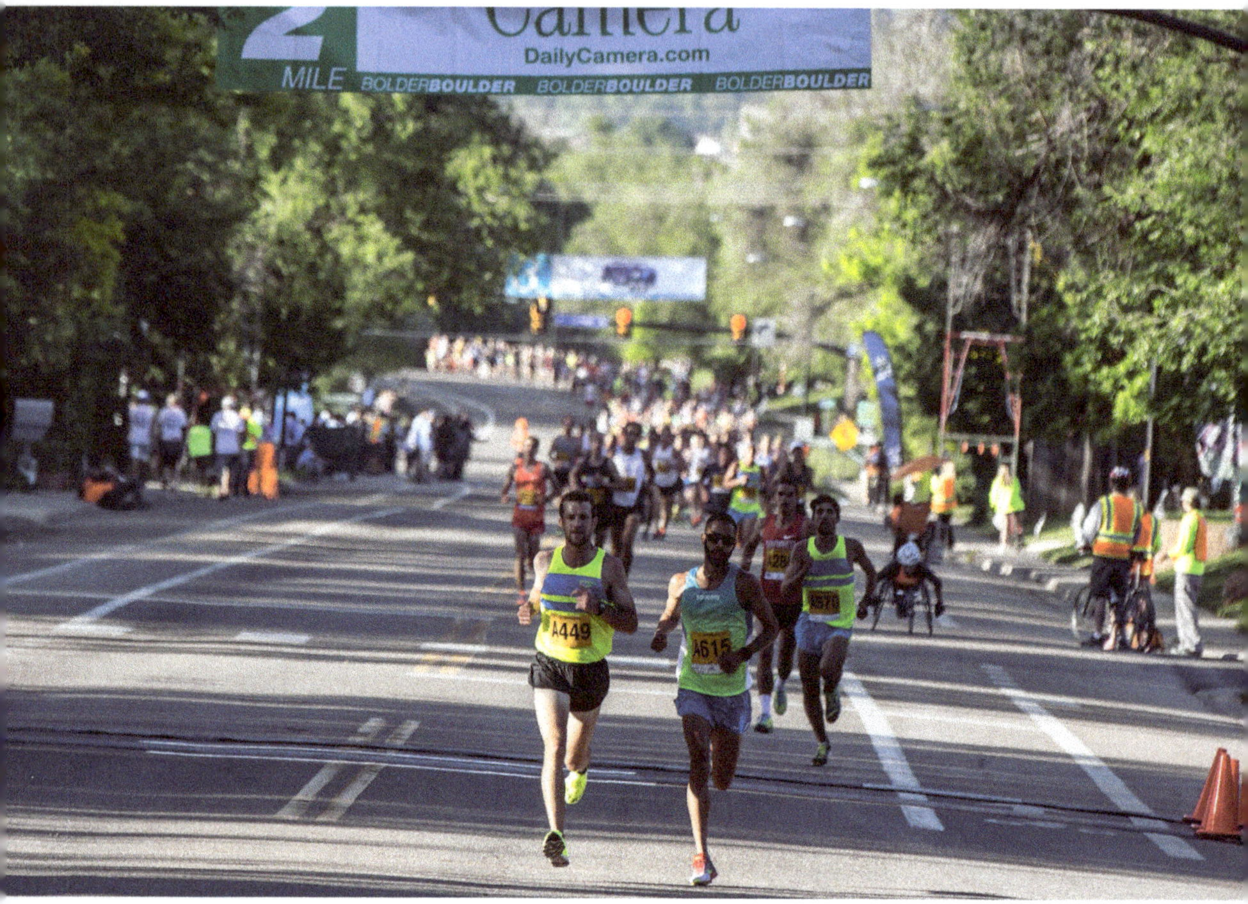

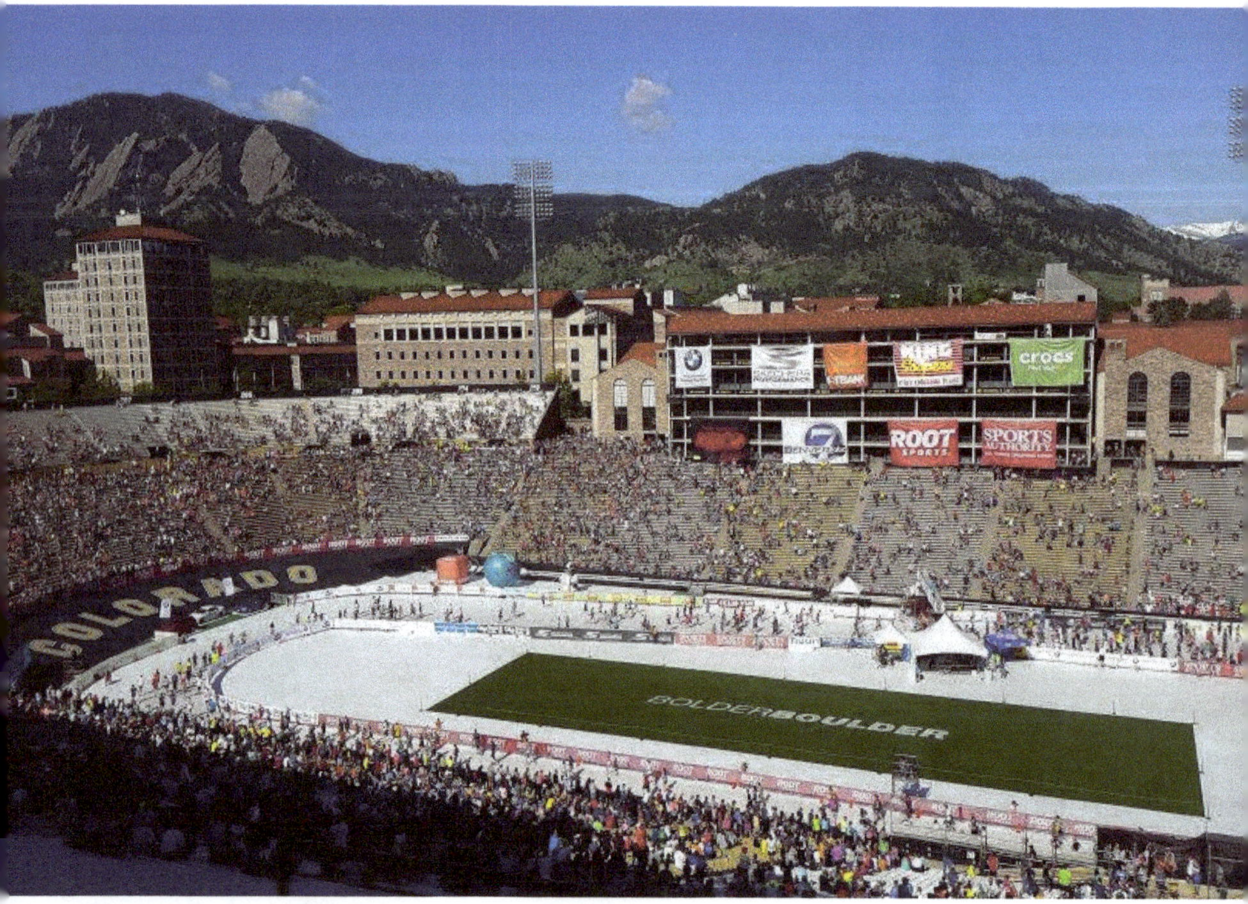

Your race has become our family race. Thanks Boulder. Thanks #BoldNation

Martha Staten @Sauconyandsuds

Photos Glen Delman, Peter N. Jones, Todd Straka

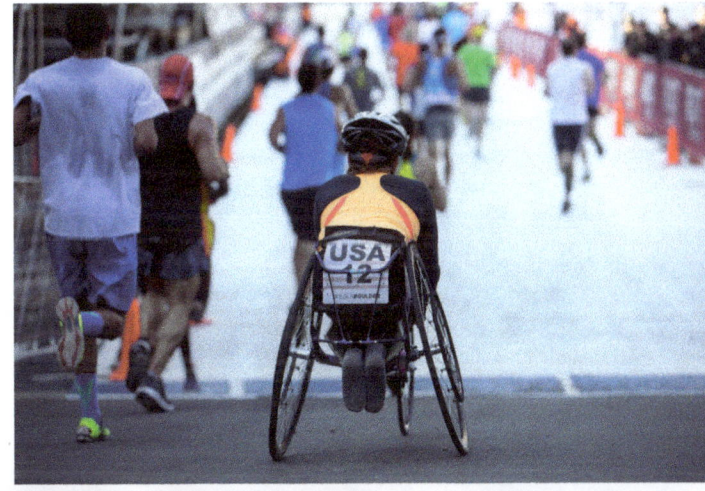

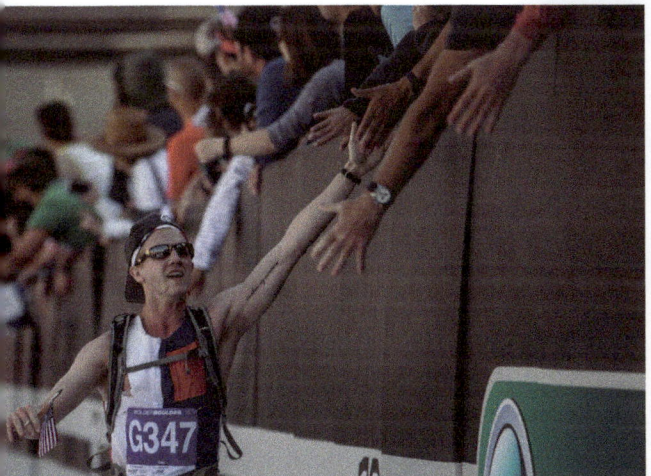

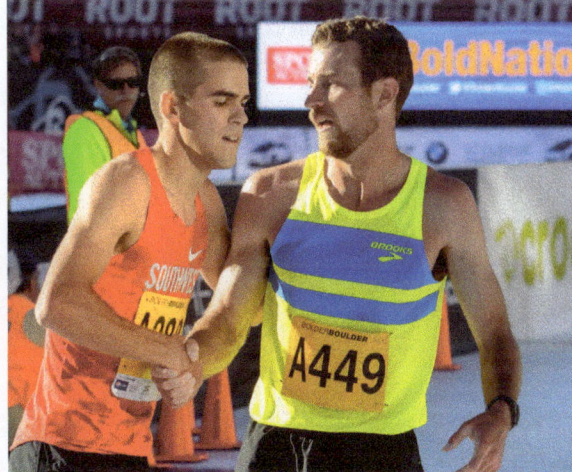

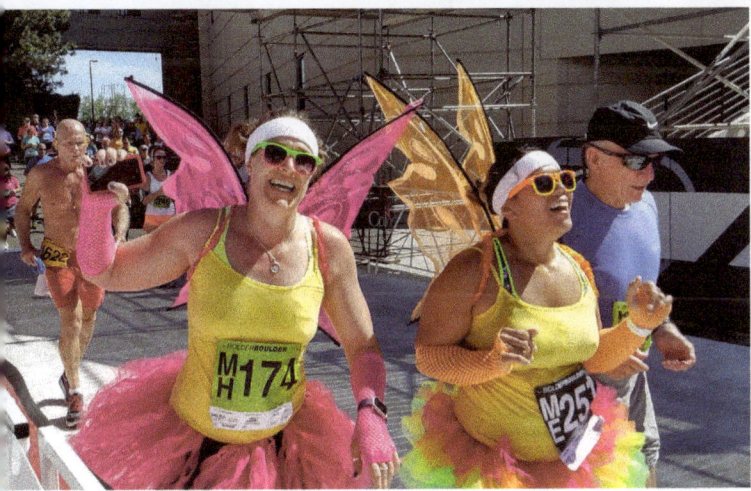

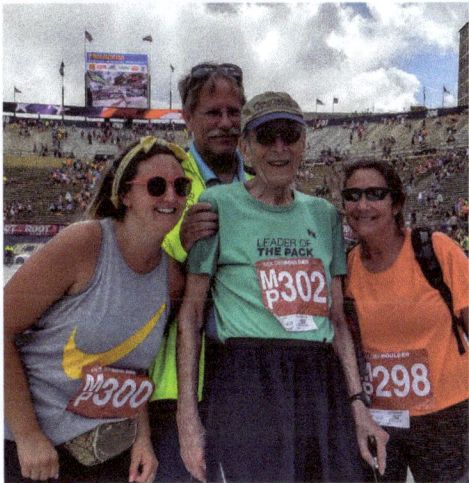

World War II veteran Jim McConnon was the last finisher and drew a wild cheer from the crowd.

#fistpumps for the #bolderboulder! Running is always more fun in a #tutu

Susan Nicole @SuzzEva

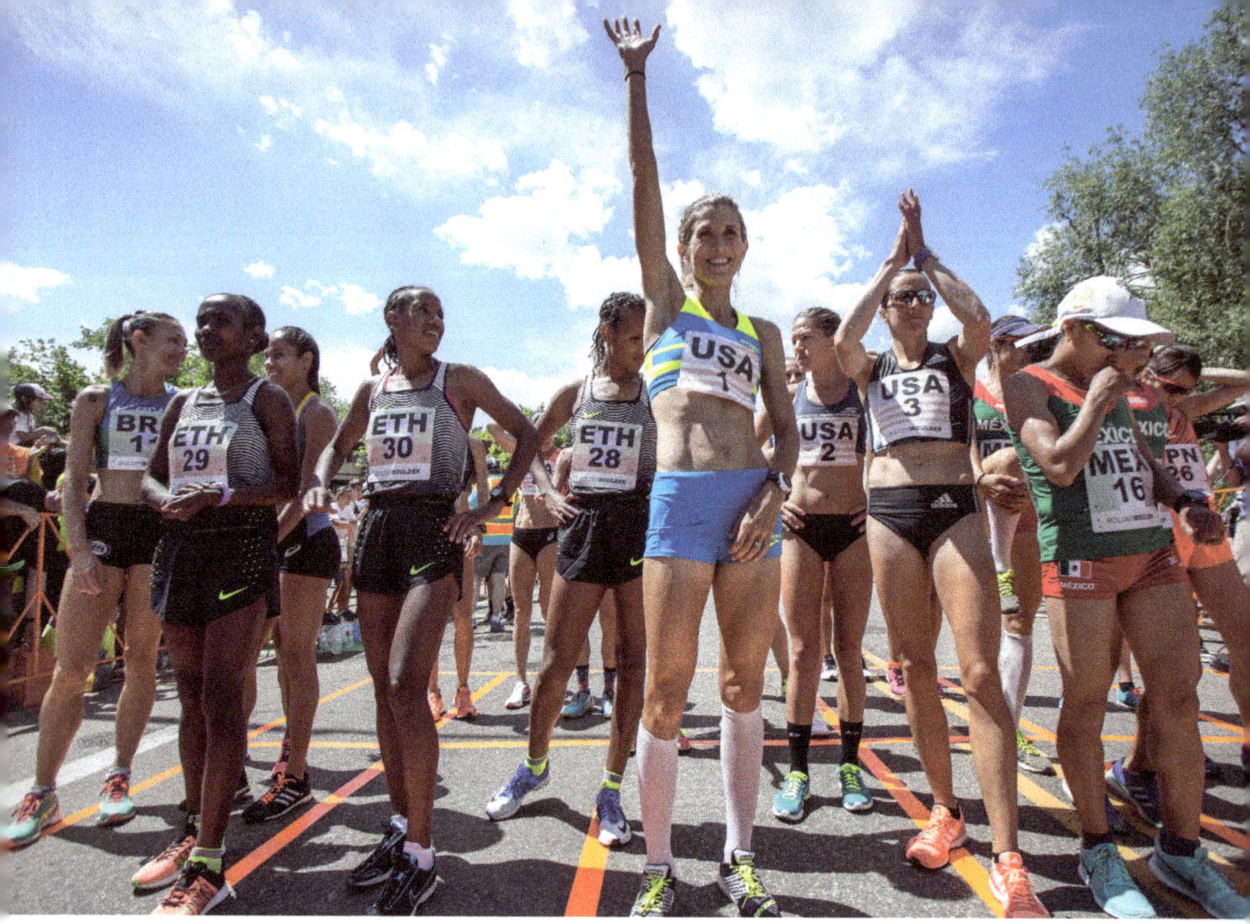

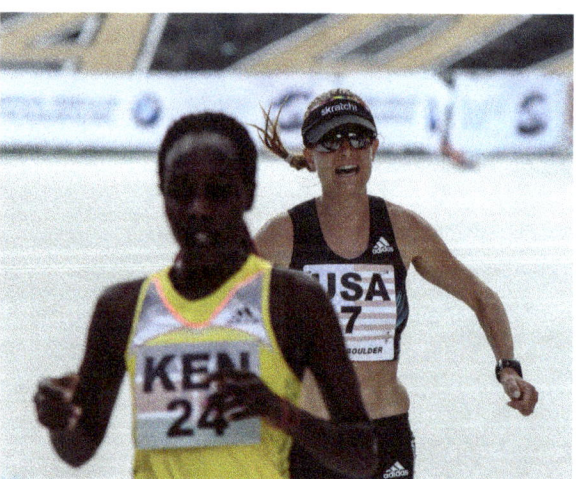

Athletes are introduced at the start of the Women's International Team Challenge. CU Buff Alumn Sara Slattery returns after 10 years as the last American to win the race.

Alicia Williams was first American in the field and lead Team USA Red to silver. It was the first time for Boulder's Alia Gray hot off her Olympic Trials Marathon 9th place finish.

Photos Glen Delman, Peter N. Jones, Todd Straka.

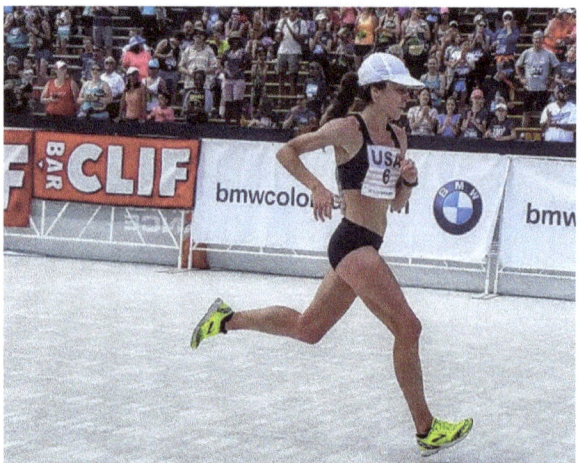

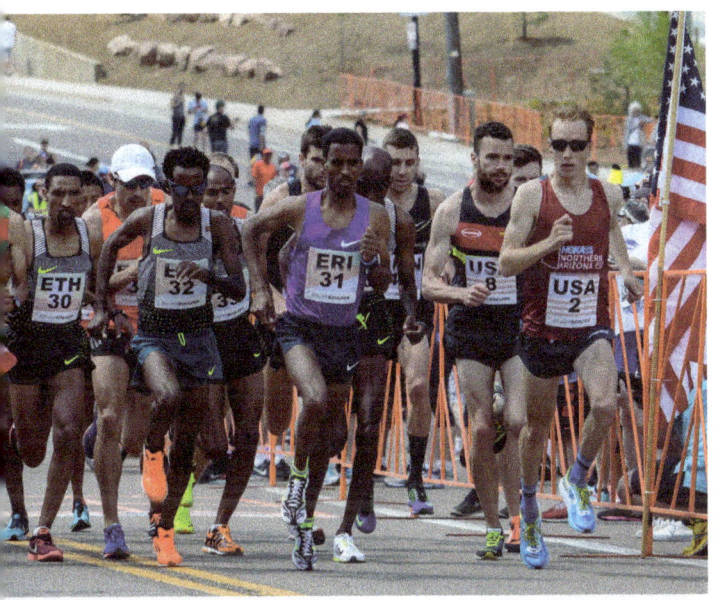
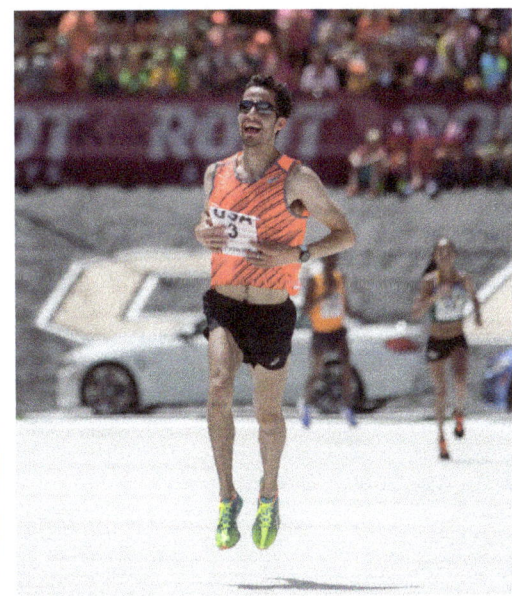
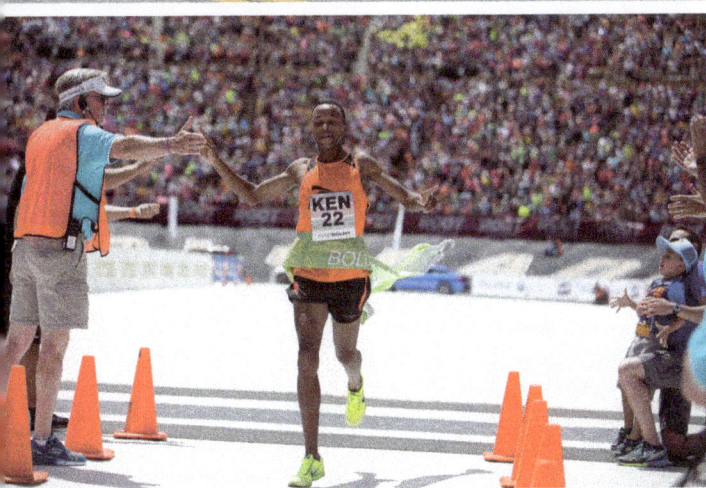

The Men's International Team Challenge gets off to a start at its new start line on Folsom Ave. Just north of Folsom Field.

Isaac Mukundi of Kenya takes the win, Diego Estrada is third overall and the first American leading Team USA Red to silver.

Andy Wacker and Adrianna Nelson watch the sky divers drop the American flag in an emotional post-race ceremony.

Photos Peter N. Jones, Glen Delman, Todd Straka.

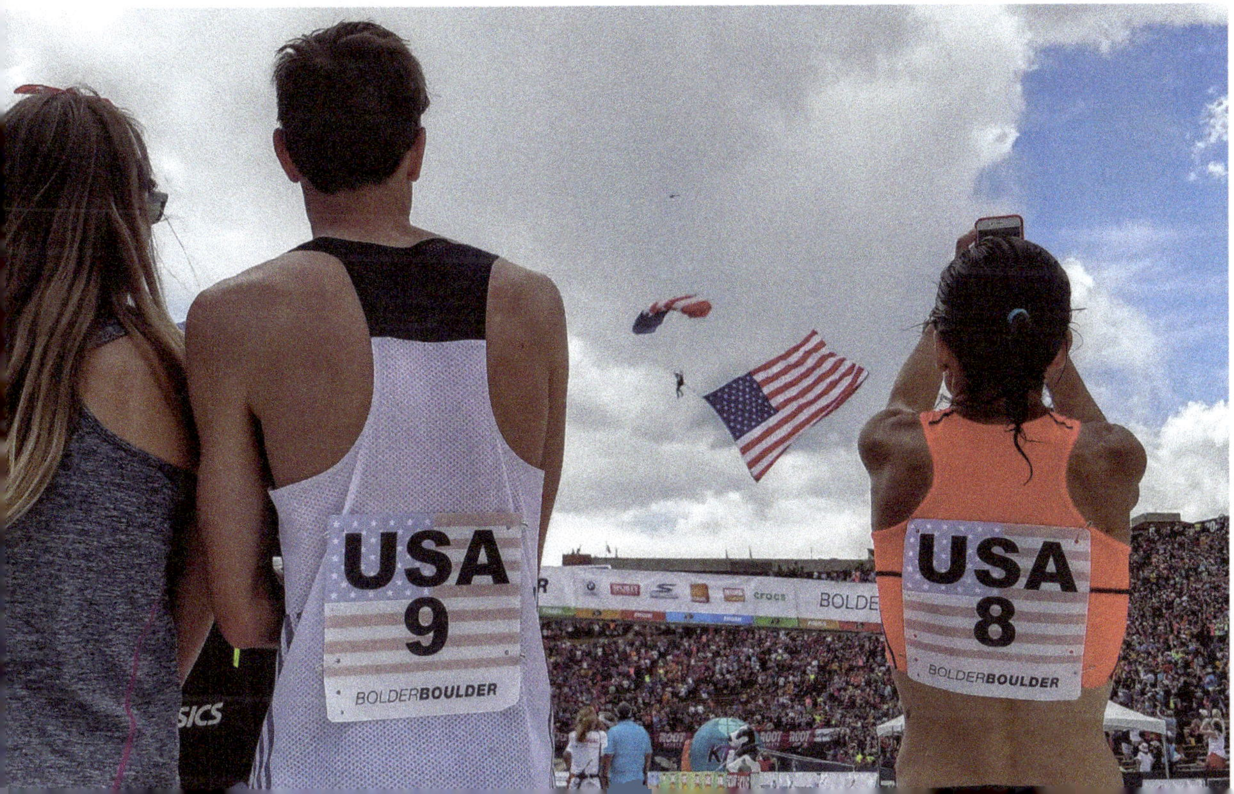

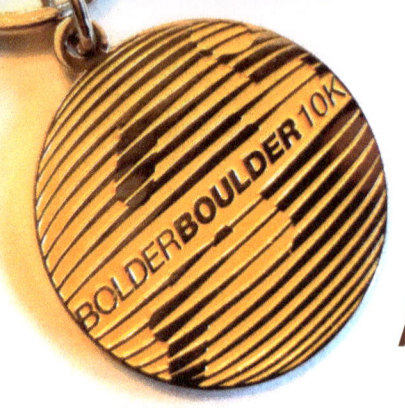

Celebrating the everyday athlete, the BolderBoulder is the only race in the nation to recognize the top winners in each age bracket. Not age group, but age. Here are your 2016 Age Champions.

AGE CHAMPIONS

Age	Name & Time			
6	David Roberts 54:23	Alaan Foster 1:09:54	50 Tom Norris 37:16	Kris Leader 42:15
7	Kendrick Parrill 50:50	MacKenzie McIntosh **47:56 ***	51 Jerry Rief 37:13	Dianne Gates 44:42
8	Logan Coughlin 47:08	Anna Cobb 49:03	52 Peter Tel 39:27	Lin Lascelles 42:03
9	Keegan Geldean **41:17 ***	Bethany Michalak 51:01	53 Rob Runkel 39:32	Mary Alico **40:47 ***
10	Jackson Parrill 40:19	Madison Shults 48:39	54 Thomas Lund 41:52	Terri Cassel 43:20
11	Bradley Troyer 42:08	Bryanna Hoffman 43:45	55 Raul Carrizalez 38:43	Laura Bruess **40:39 ***
12	Henry Murphy 39:15	Alayna Szuch **38:51 ***	56 Daniel Greer 39:57	Cora Randall 49:21
13	Robbie Cozean 36:26	Sydney Thorvaldson **38:39 ***	57 Jay Survil 39:55	Judy Chamberlin 45:16
14	Isaac Roberts 36:56	Riley Geldean 40:51	58 Roger Sayre 38:31	Catriona Dowling 47:30
15	Derk Lyford 37:13	Mary Fox 42:04	59 Kyle Hubbart 38:50	Ann Campbell 49:56
16	Brock Dykema 35:15	Addi Iken 40:46	60 Dan Spale 38:41	Linda Ottaviano 49:43
17	Taylor Stack 33:38	Brie Oakley 36:43	61 Martin Lascelles 42:27	Susan Noe 50:39
18	Paul Roberts 31:09	Lexi Reed 38:50	62 Bruce Kirschner 43:42	Mary Ann Moseley 47:45
19	Ashton Grissom 33:49	Jaci Smith 40:29	63 Heath Hibbard 40:49	Mary E Black 51:13
20	Andrew Johnston 32:59	Honna Swanson 45:15	64 Craig Hayes 48:22	Carla Pederson 50:39
21	Ricardo Kaempfen 32:28	Shellene Rains 44:36	65 Doug Bell **40:48 ***	Tina Albert 50:36
22	Daniel Caddigan 32:29	Sylvia Nordskar 38:27	66 Buzz Allen 46:13	Nancy Antos 54:06
23	Conor Wells 33:15	Becky Lynn 38:52	67 Jim Reynolds 46:06	Lorraine Allen 56:24
24	Ian Butler 31:07	Dominique Stasulli 42:08	68 Bill Dunn 45:00	Laurie Rugenstein **48:46 ***
25	Jeremy Drenckhahn 32:11	Anna Hudson 39:12	69 Dave Dooley 45:42	Marilyn Stapleton 48:41
26	Martin Medina 33:30	Lindsey Knast 40:09	70 Elliott Henry 49:08	Karen Karl 1:01:14
27	Tanner Fruit 31:40	Maggie Callahan 36:11	71 Robert Hannah 52:24	Lola Ackerman 56:38
28	Brandon Johnson 30:34	Amanda Scott 37:06	72 Dennis T Bird 51:21	Judy Megibow 1:03:24
29	Tyler McCadless 32:05	Monica Folts 39:46	73 BEd Craighead 47:06	Mary Young 1:11:01
30	Peter Cole 34:40	Krystalanne Curwood 36:13	74 Dan Lincoln 57:02	Dianne Fuller 1:04:26
31	Scott Dahlberg 31:09	Alexis Wilbert 35:57	75 Don Larson 51:01	Valdene Ranum 1:16:50
32	Nicholas Boehlke 32:15	Kristin Dennis 40:55	76 Gene DaGiau 54:17	Constance Ahrnsbrak 1:00:37
33	Tom Nicholas 33:59	Sarah Pizzo 38:03	77 Bill Obert 1:04:23	Ginnie Vaughan 1:14:45
34	Jordan Jones 33:08	Melissa Dock **35:44 ***	78 Lee Bengston 1:07:24	Judy Smythe 1:27:45
35	Paolo Natali 34:41	Rachel Viele 40:28	79 Paul Turley 1:05:13	Libby James **55:06 ***
36	Eric Green 35:05	Gabriela Trana 41:03	80 Richard Quigley 1:00:34	Shirley Lampshire 1:27:52
37	Nathan Hornok 33:31	Kara Ford 38:17	81 Chuck Merry 1:07:52	Dotti Fite 1:30:58
38	Nicholas Cady 35:25	Brandy Erholtz 43:30	82 M. Taki Meghjee 1:21:57	Bethel Mohsei 2:02:09
39	Zach Watson 36:13	Helen Cospolich 42:31	83 Richard Nagler 1:17:56	Alice Lewis 1:31:08
40	Andy Rinne 35:21	Amy Ilfrey 42:19	84 Mike Fenerty 1:05:24	Marjorie Grant 1:40:46
41	Adelaido Najera 36:28	Kulli Must-Saradzic 41:43	85 Jesse Aweida **1:09:05 ***	Betty Payte 1:46:2
42	Campbell Ilfrey 35:34	Bean Wrenn 39:48	86 Rod Smythe 1:29:15	--
43	Bryan Beiner 36:11	Svenja Knappe 43:53	87 --	Audrey MacDonald 1:32:19
44	Jason Butler 36:26	Kami Alessandro 44:13	88 George Downing 1:29:39	--
45	Marty Wacker 35:20	Shannon Husted 42:28	89 Ray Schramm **1:21:02 ***	Jeanne Smiley 2:21:01
46	Franklin Tenorio 33:37	Gail Quinn 42:47	90 Jim McConnon 3:00:19**	Janet Grenda **1:52:13 ***
47	Kevin Konczak 36:36	Sabine Preisinger 45:38	91 --	Shirley Griffin 2:28:22
48	John Probst 36:59	Rochelle Persson 42:50	92 George Pierce 2:40:46	
49	Todd Straka 35:29	Susan Nuzum 41:57		

***New BB Age Record!** ****Last finisher**

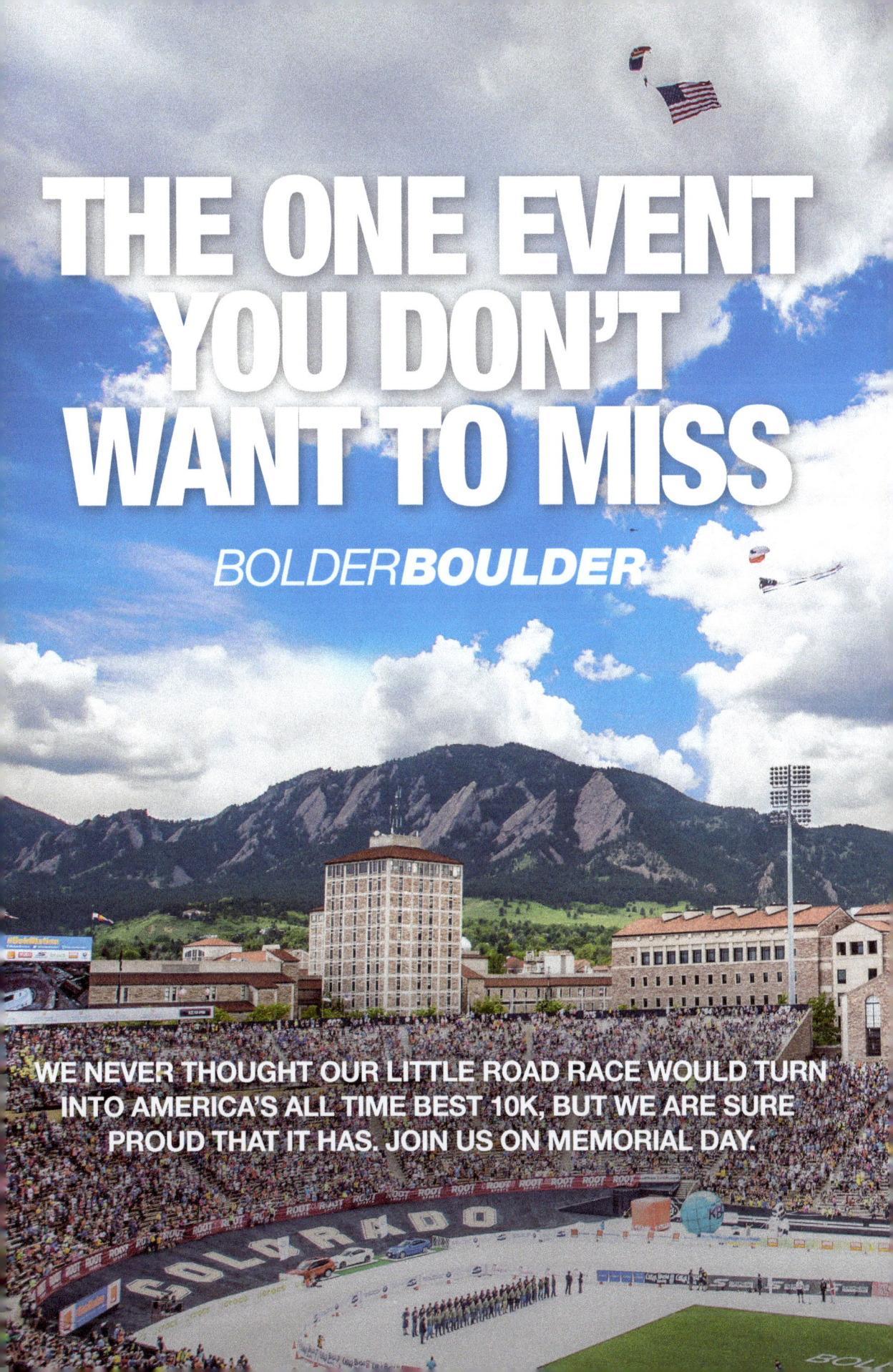

Top Results
April - May

The weekend of April 8-9 was a busy one in Boulder with the hosting of the Colorado Invitational on Potts Field. A summary of the highlights are below:

MEN
800m
1. Zach PERRIN, Colorado 1:49.85
2. Nick HARRIS, Colorado 1:51.33
3. Connor WINTER, Colorado 1:51.91
1500m
1. Morgan PEARSON, Colorado 3:49.29
2. Cole ROCKHOLD, Colorado St. 3:49.96
3. Blake THEROUX, DWCTC 3:51.64
4. Pierce MURPHY, Colorado 3:52.92
3000m
1. Andy WACKER, adidas Rocky Mountain, 8:38.02
2. Ethan GONZALES, Colorado, 8:43.74
3. Christian MARTIN, Colorado, 8:47.25

WOMEN
800m
1. Dani JONES, Colorado, 2:08.97
2. Sara SUTHERLAND, Saucony, 2:09.53
3. Maddie ALM, Colorado, 2:10.38
4. Lindsey PUTMAN, Boulder Track Club, 2:11.44
1500m
1. Sara VAUGHN, Boulder Track Club, 4:24.61

Also that weekend, at the Mad City 50K ultra held in Madison, Wisconsin, Boulder's **Claudia Becque** not only won, but set a new course record with a time of 3:32:26. **Greg Salvesen** also had a good race, finishing 6th in a time of 3:47:07. At the 100K distance, **Cassie Scallon** of Boulder held on for 8th place overall, second female, with a time of 9:12:49.

In Colorado at the 24 Hours of Palmer Lake Run, **Adam McRoberts** of Louisville ran the second farthest, covering a distance of 101.68 miles.

Back on the roads, at the Go! St. Louis Marathon on April 10th, in St. Louis, Missouri, Boulder's **Michael Kettler** missed the course record by only 3 minutes, winning the marathon in a time of 2:23:19.

The Boston Marathon is always a big event, and with the 120th running many Boulder athletes toed the line to test themselves on the streets of Boston. Two Boulder runners with notable times and finishes were: **Clint Wells** of Boulder who not only finished 17th overall, but also was the first Master in the elite field with a time of 2:24:55. In the women's race, Superior's **Neely Spence Gracey**, in her marathon debut, raced to 9th place overall and first US woman in a highly competitive field.

At the Bryan Clay Invitational Meet held at Azusa Pacific University in Los Angeles, California between April 14-15, several Boulder runners had good races. **Sara Vaughn** made her debut at 5,000m and ran awesome for 2nd place running 16:07.22 and **Maor Tiyouri** who was in the middle of marathon training, finished 3rd in 16:16.29. **Jon Grey** had his first rust buster since the marathon trials and ran a great race for 2nd place in 13:48.79 and **Sean Quigley** was 4th in 13:54.85. **Lindsey Putman** then had her shot and she ran the fastest time of her career, running 2:08.46 for 2nd place and 9th overall.

Back in Colorado, at the Cherry Creek Sneak on April 24th, Boulder's Joe **Bosshard** ran away with the win in a time of 25:32. **Nell Rojas**, also of Boulder, came away with the women's win in a time of 29:39.

On May 1st at the Blue Cross Broad Street Run 10 Mile in Philadelphia, PA, **Amanda Scott** of Boulder ran the ten mile course in a speedy 57:59, resulting in a solid 3rd place finish overall.

Also held on May 1st, the Cimarron Endurance 50K took place in Cimarron, CO. Longmont's **Abbie Steinbrueck** came away with the win in a time of 5:47:13, while **Kelsey Swanson** of Erie was 2nd in a time of 6:21:00 and **Lisa Root** of Longmont was 3rd in a time of 7:09:21.

In New York's Central Park on May 14th at the UAE Healthy Kidney 10K, Boulder's **Alex Monroe** was the top American finisher, taking 7th place in a time of 29:54. Just over the Hudson River in Jersey City, New Jersey at the Newport 10,000, which served as the USATF 10K Championships, Golden's **Brianne Nelson** came away with the win in a time of 33:08.99. **Kristen Arendt** of Niwot was 7th in a time of 35:50.42.

On the same day at the 25K US Championships held at the Fifth Third River Bank Run in Grand Rapids, Michigan, Boulder's **Andy Wacker** also came away with a 7th place finish in a time of 1:05:01. **Tyler McCandless** of Boulder was 14th in a time of 1:06:43.

The following day in San Francisco at the 105th Bay to Breakers 12K, **Jeffrey Eggleston** of Boulder finished an impressive 13th place with a time of 32:22.

In the rugged Jemez Mountains of New Mexico, Boulder's **Darcy Piceu** ran away with the win in a time of 10:32:05.

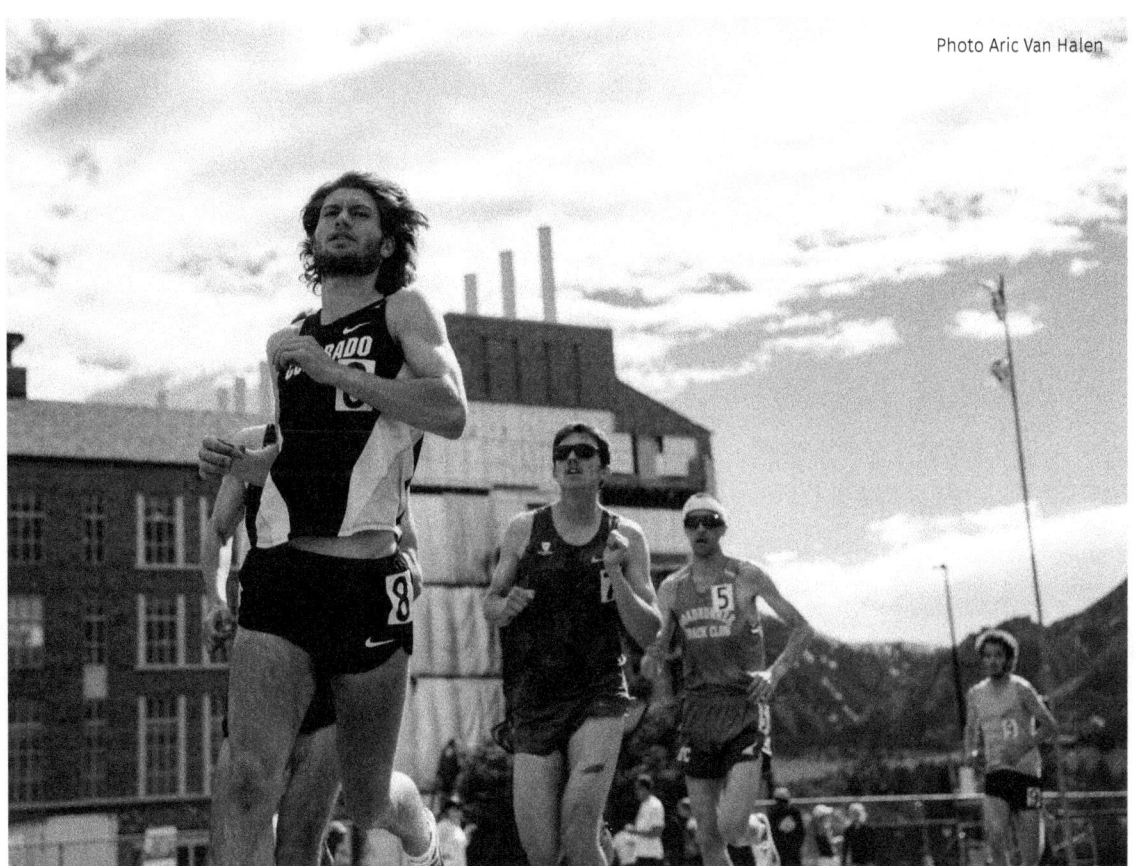

Photo Aric Van Halen

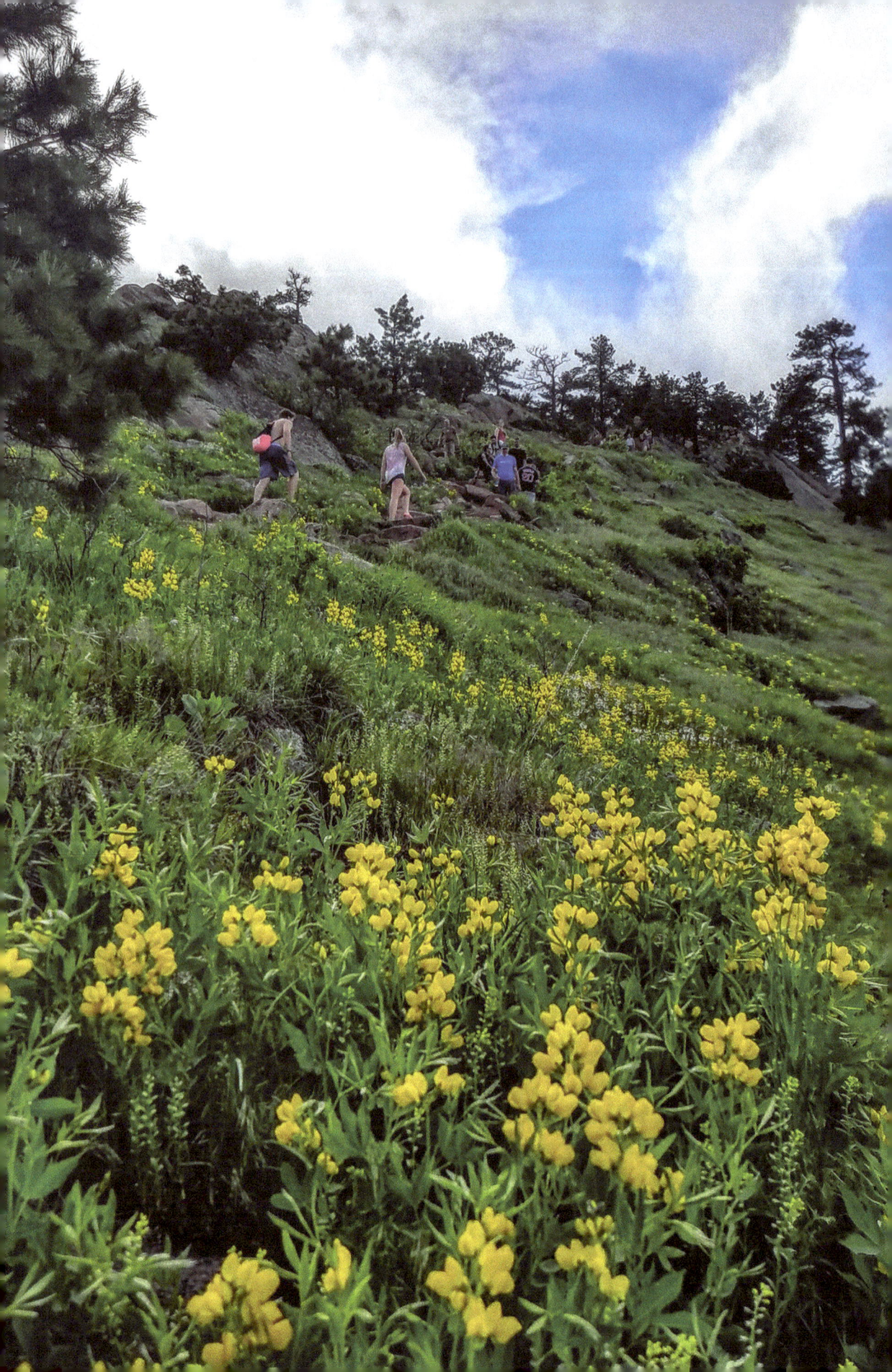

WRITING PROMPT
SPRING
What was your favorite race
memory this season?

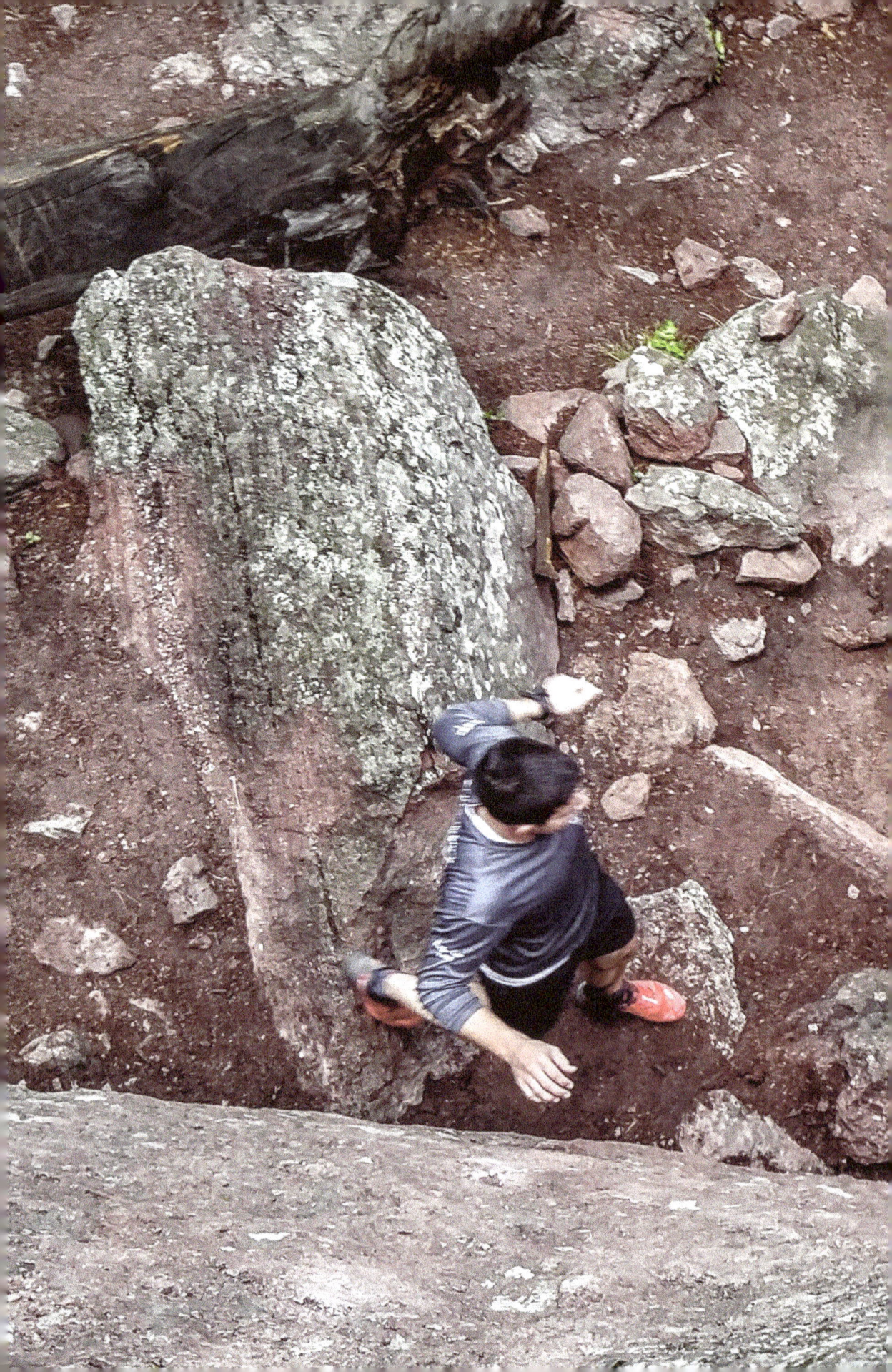

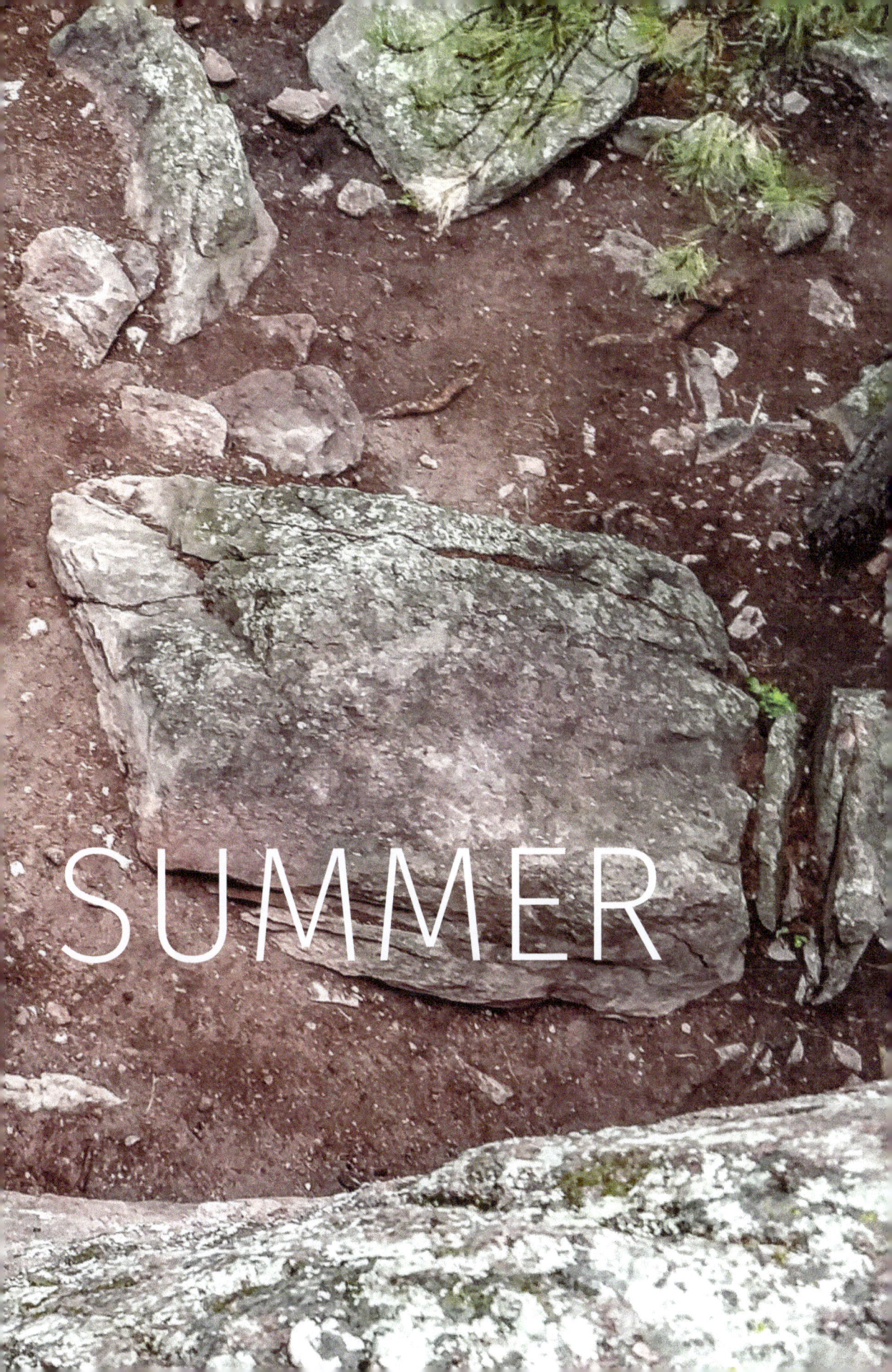

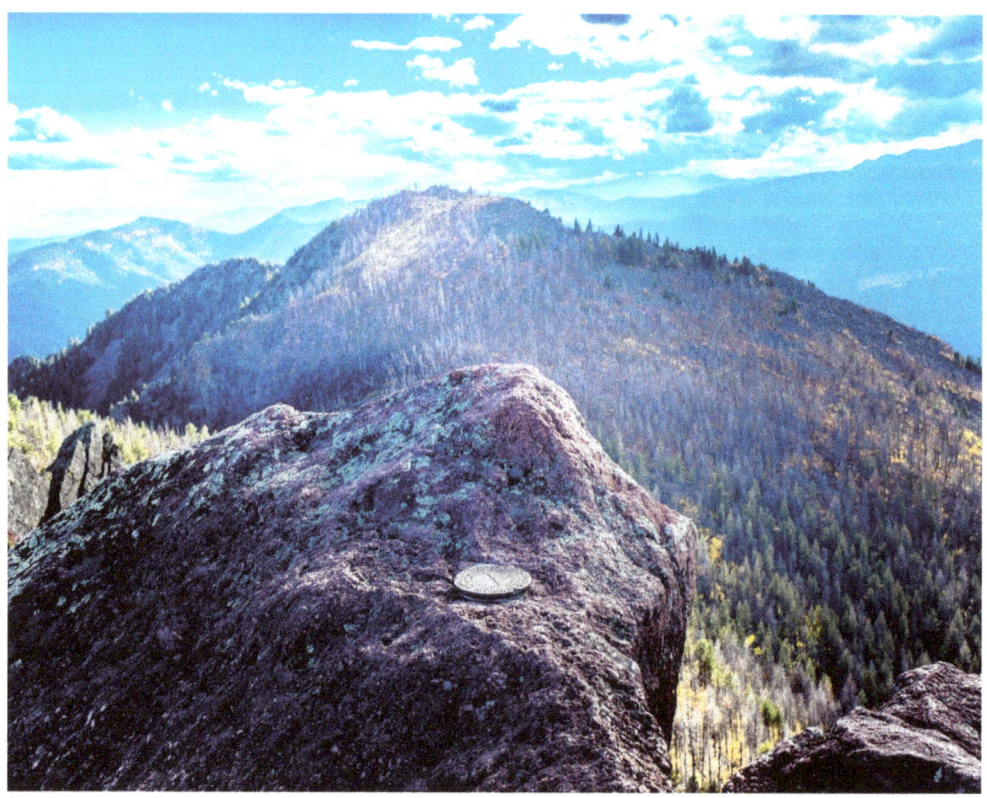
Photo Nick Combs

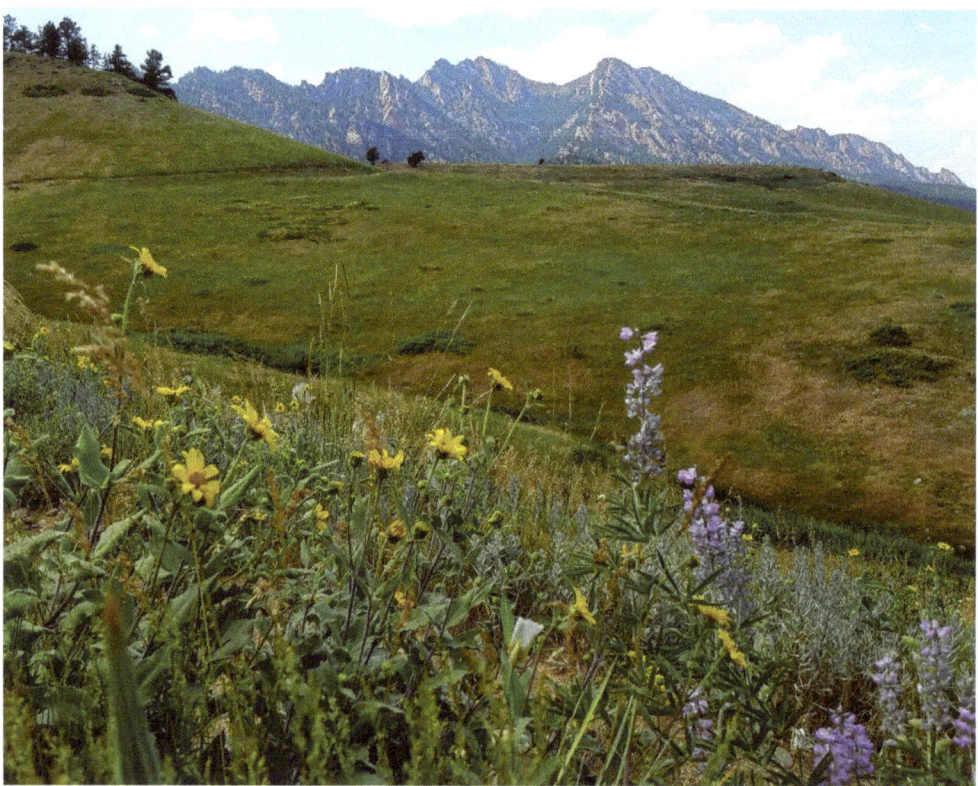
Photo Todd Straka

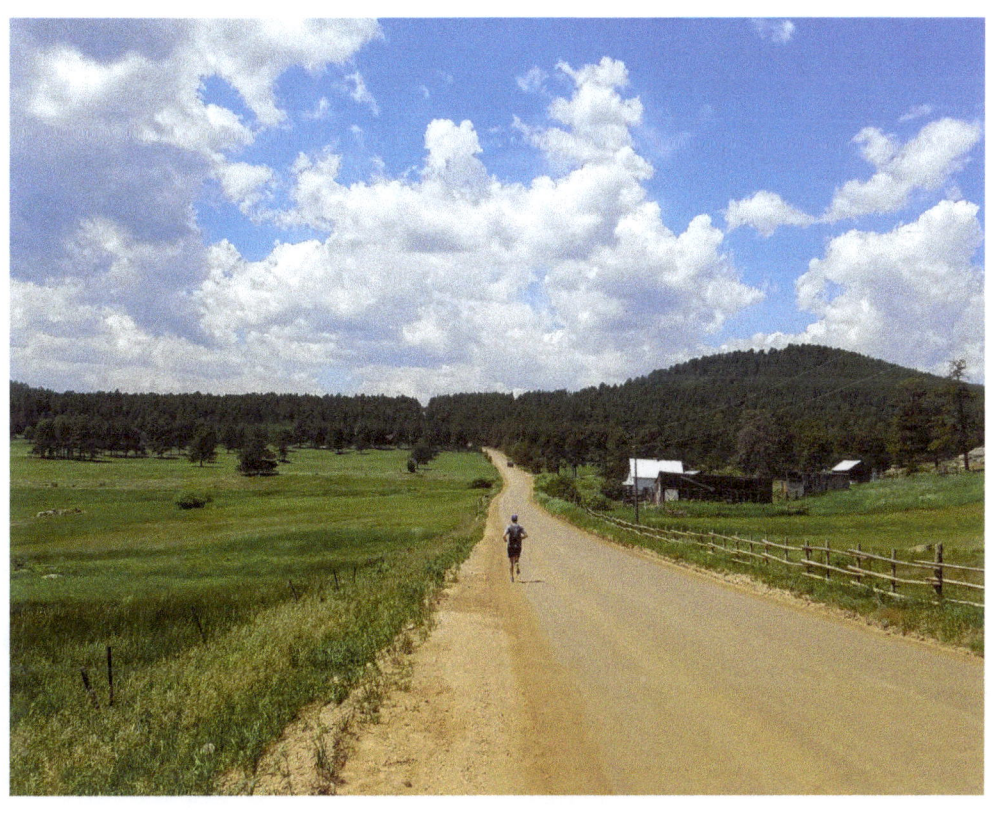

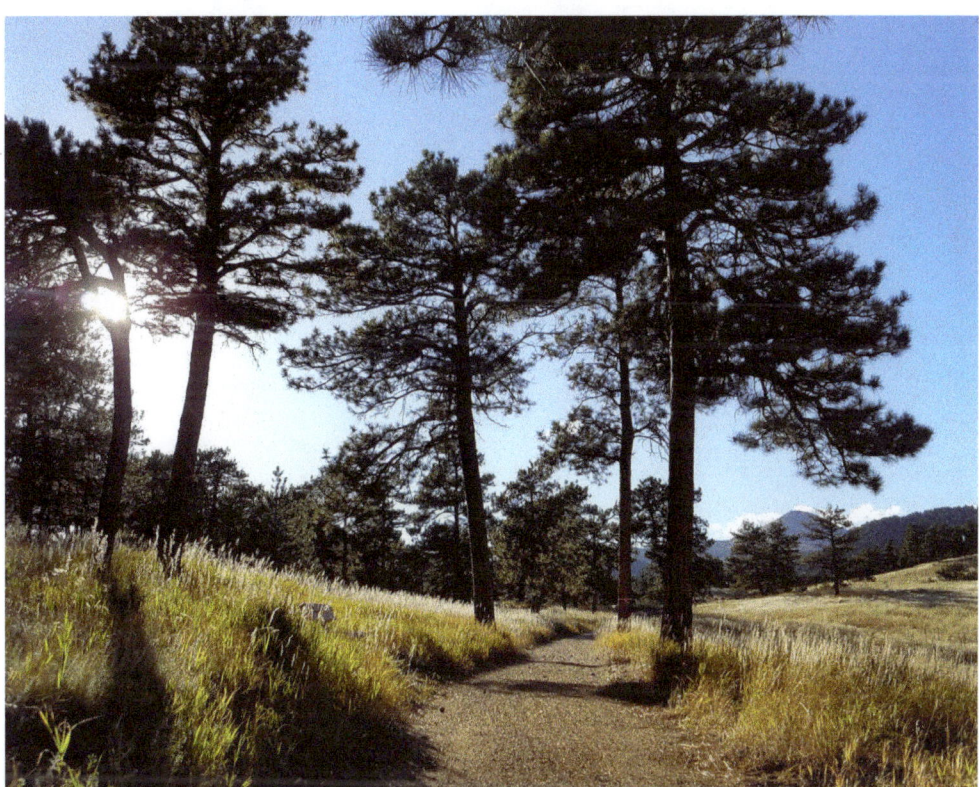

Photos Todd Straka

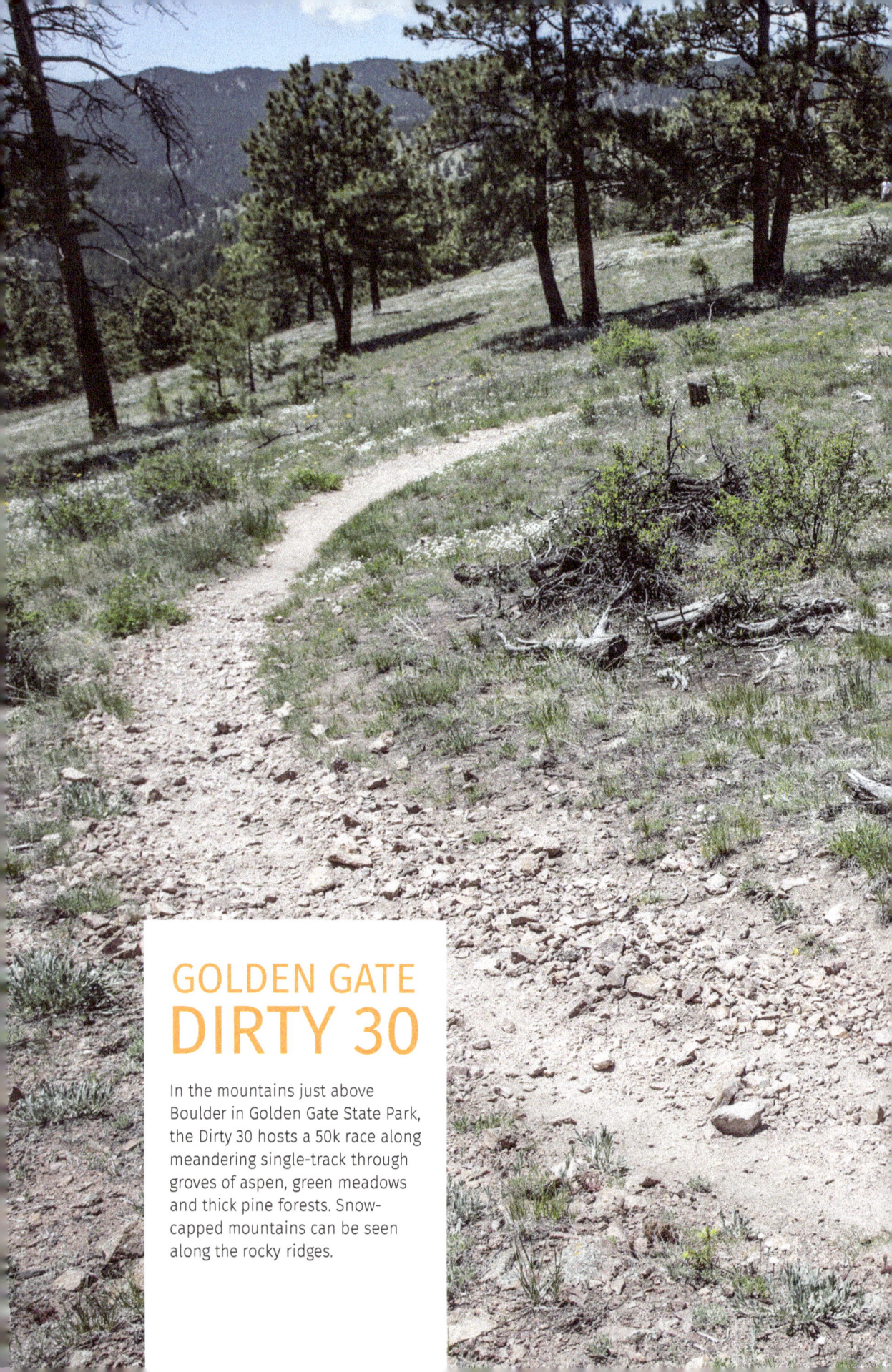

GOLDEN GATE
DIRTY 30

In the mountains just above Boulder in Golden Gate State Park, the Dirty 30 hosts a 50k race along meandering single-track through groves of aspen, green meadows and thick pine forests. Snow-capped mountains can be seen along the rocky ridges.

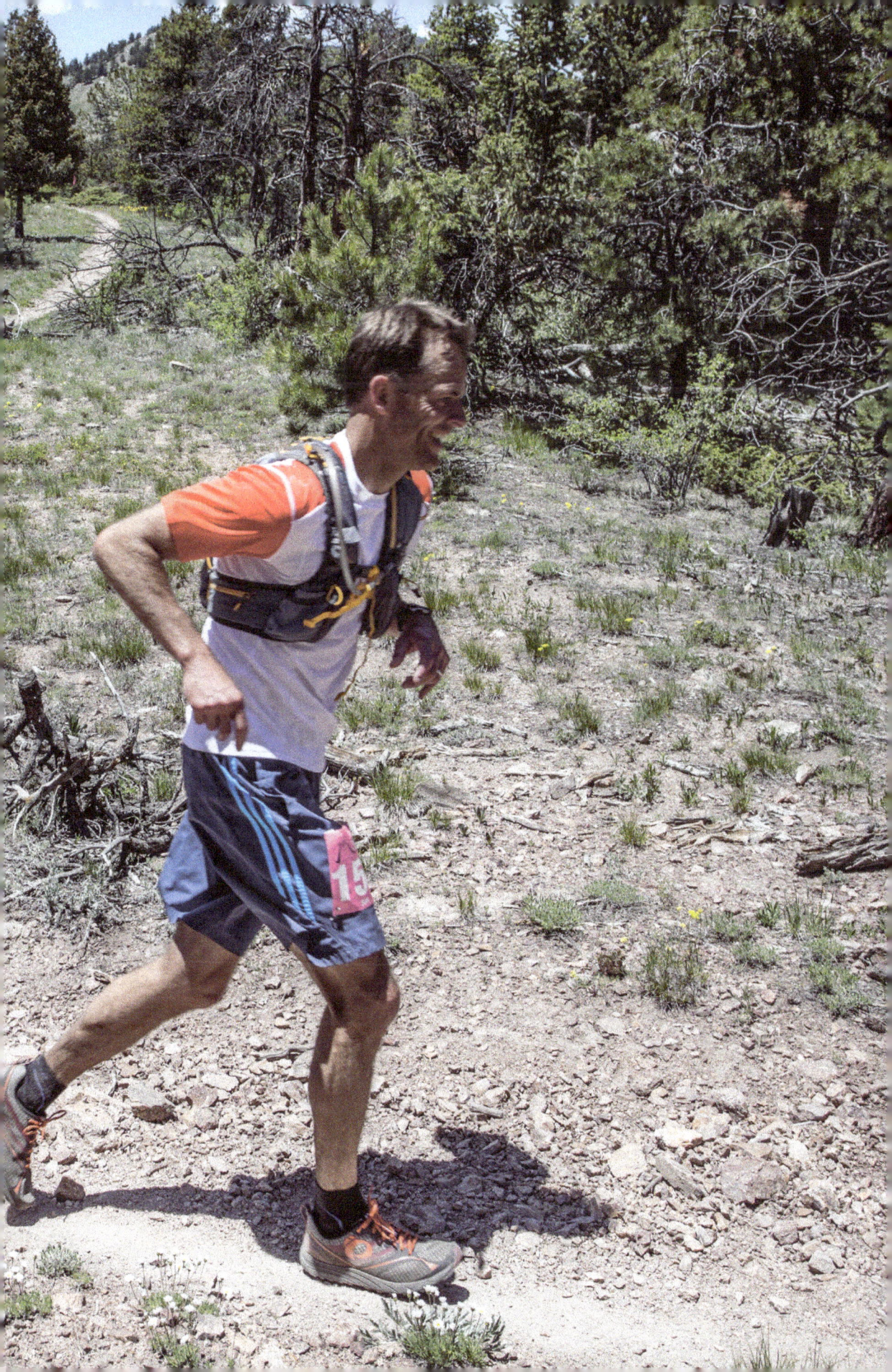

GETTING TO THE START LINE OF THE

TRACK TRIALS

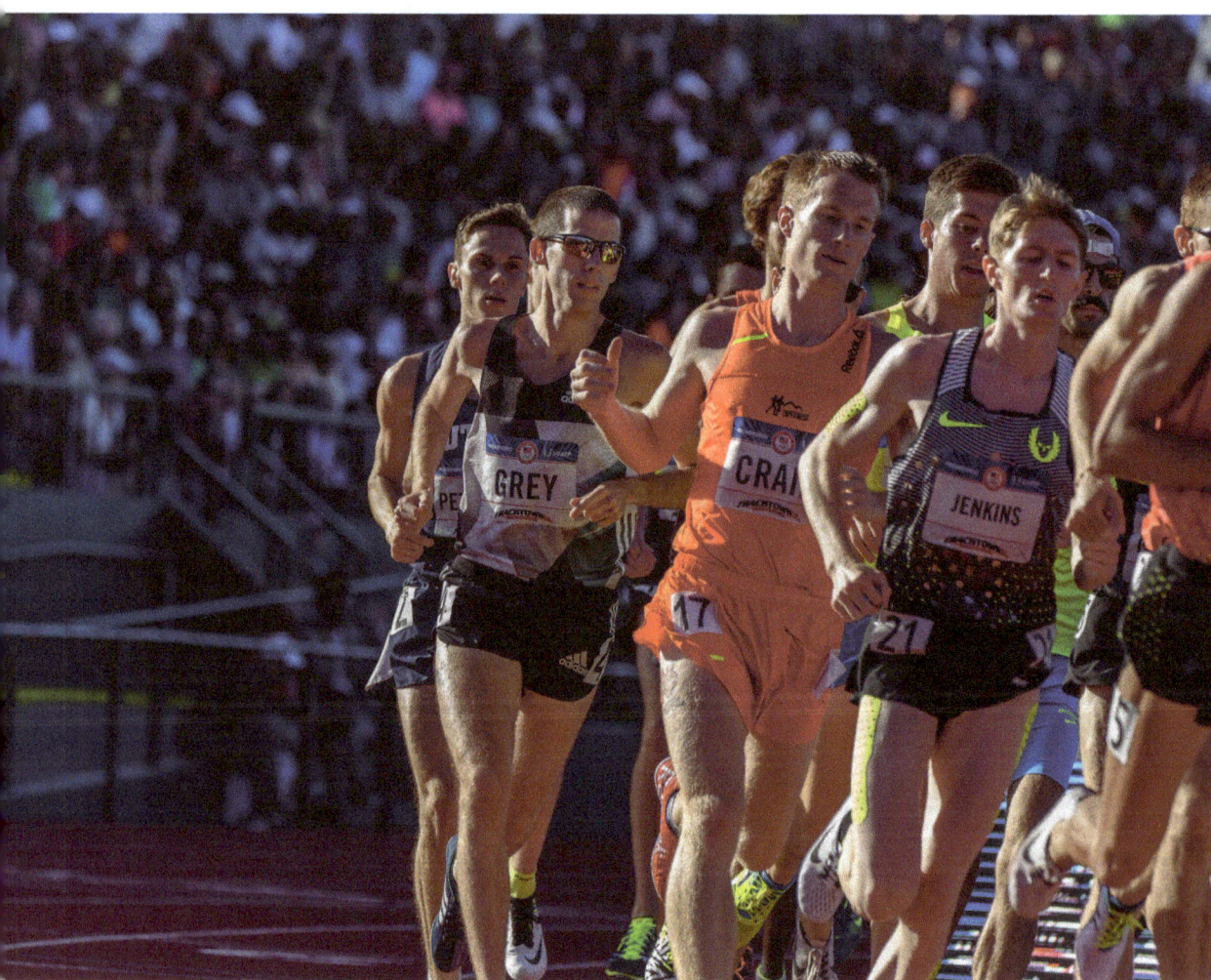

Photo Dave Albo

"Everyone on that start line has a chance, some greater than others, but everyone has a chance. That's why they are there."

Olympian and Coach Lee Troop

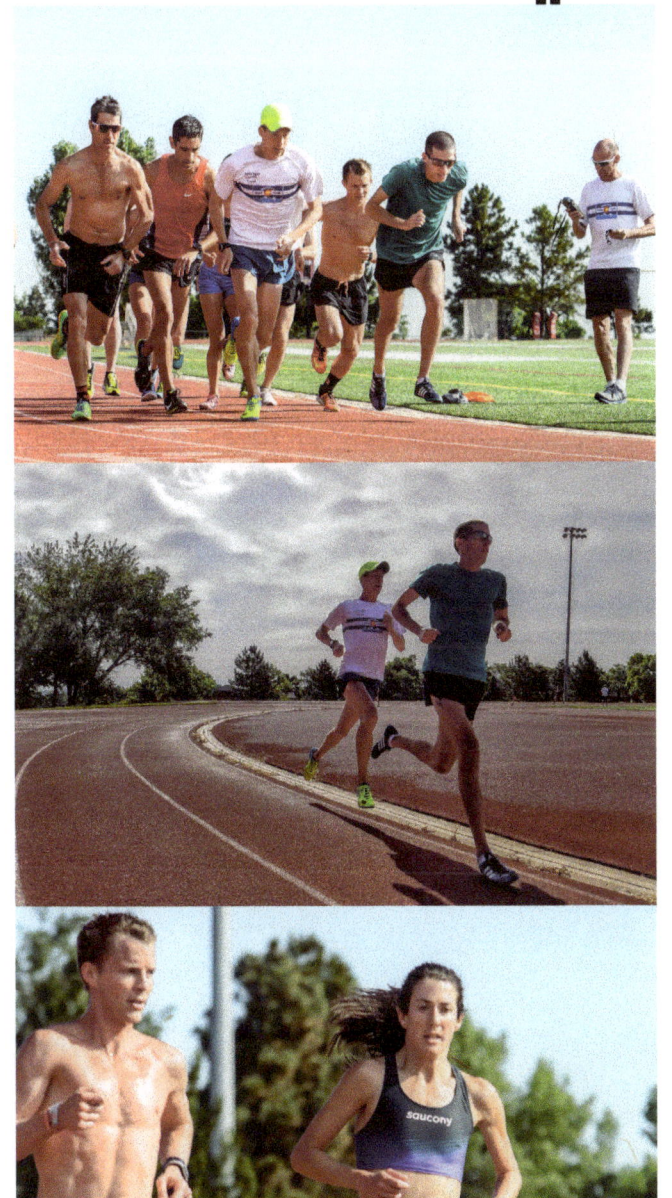

The Boulder Track Club sent four members to the Track & Field Olympic Trials. As a final workout they ran a 3k time trial.

Left: Jon Grey and Alex Monroe alternate pulling through the turns.

Matt Hensley paces Laura Thweatt through the effort.

Two other running groups from Boulder had athletes compete; Roots Running had two members and Mark Wetmore sent six athletes to the trials.

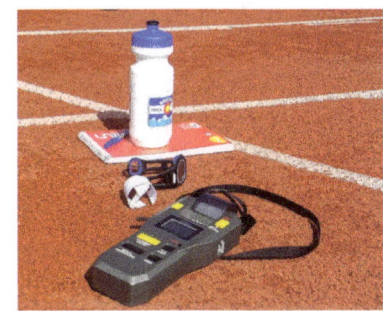

Photos Peter N. Jones, Todd Straka

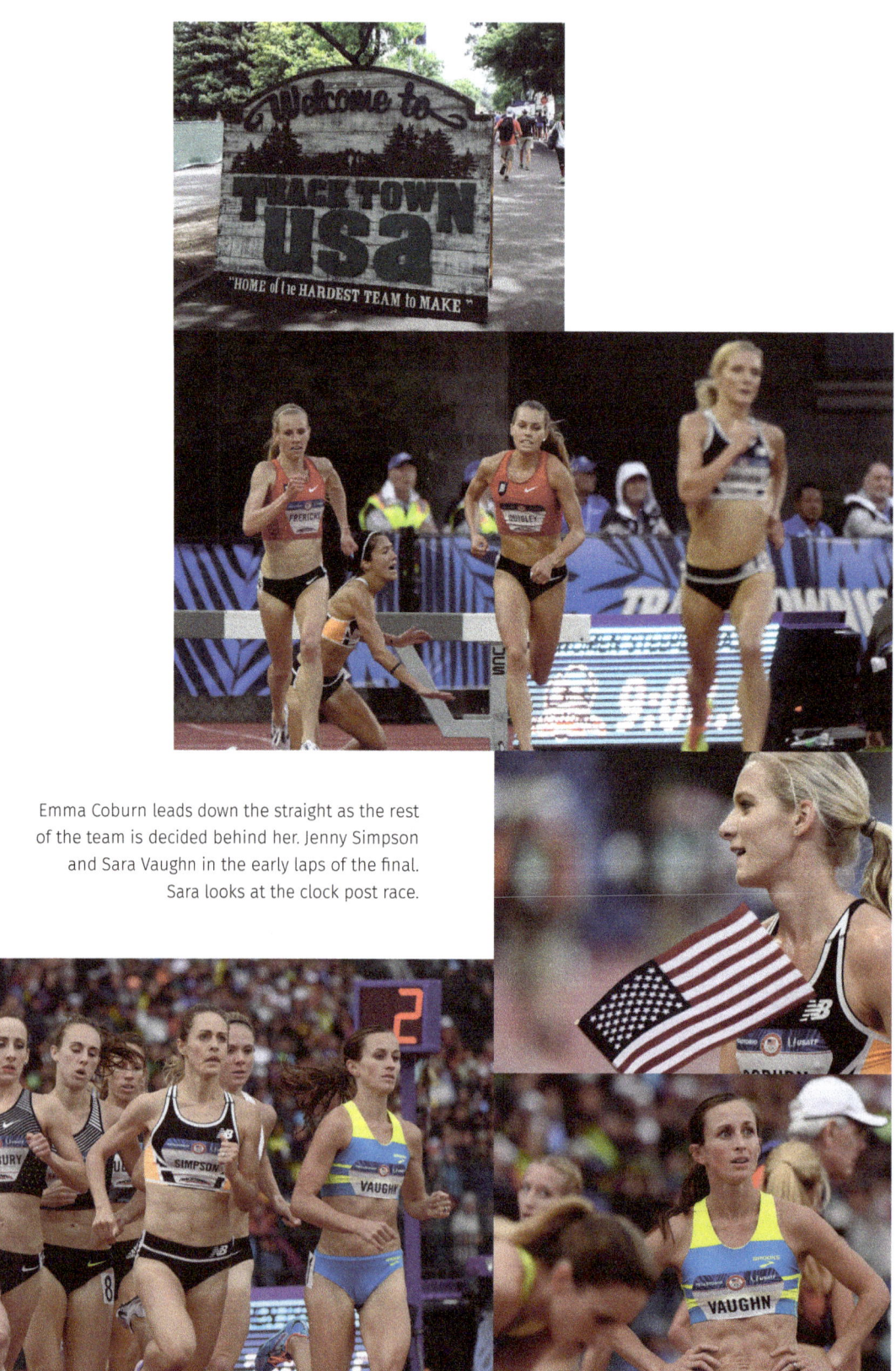

Emma Coburn leads down the straight as the rest of the team is decided behind her. Jenny Simpson and Sara Vaughn in the early laps of the final. Sara looks at the clock post race.

Photos Dave Albo

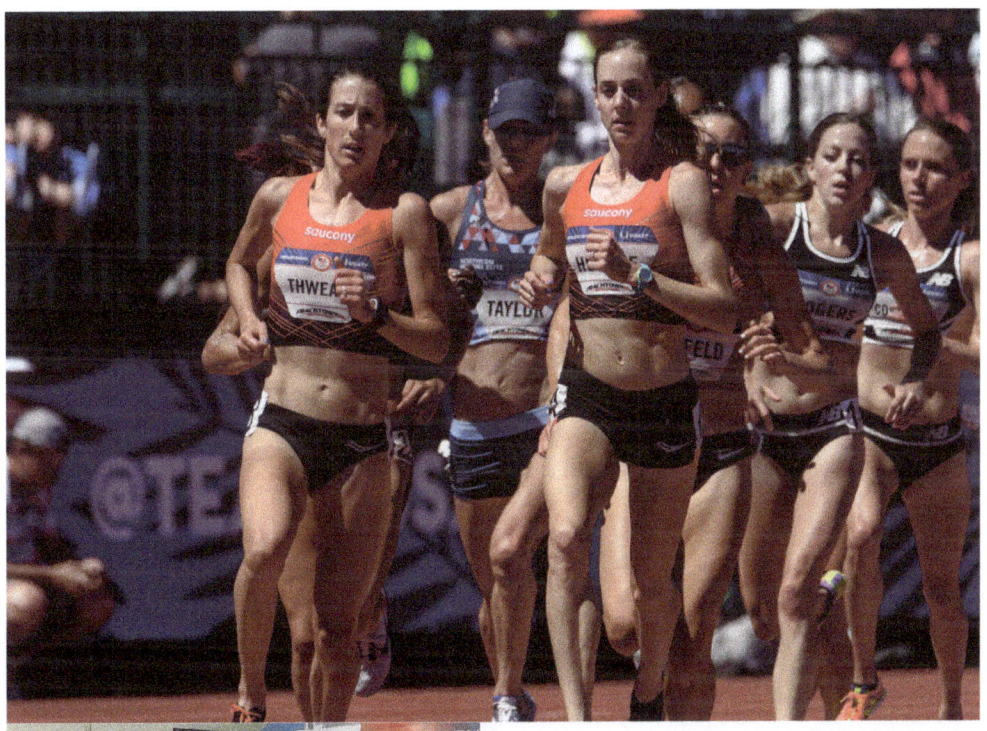

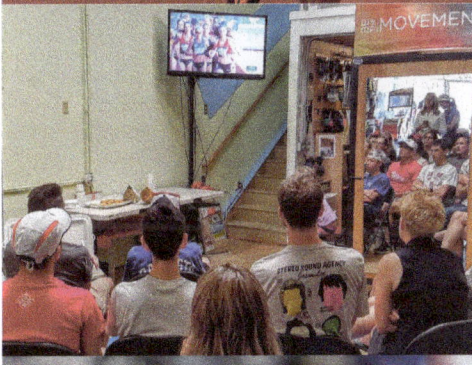

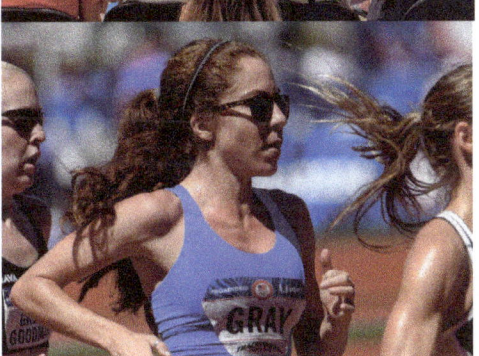

Alia Gray in the 10,000 meters.

10,000-meter contender Laura Thweatt put herself in position around the halfway point of the race, coming up on the shoulder of eventual winner Molly Huddle. But soon after she found herself in the back of the lead pack of five, then lost contact.

"I had a few laps in the middle where I kind of lapsed, and lost contact and thought, 'Oh God am I just going to start going backwards now?' NO, you came here to fight, you came here to leave it all on the track. If you can get back into it mentally, who's to say you can't keep chipping away?' So that's what I did."

Thweatt finished 5th overall with a time of 32:26.21.

"It was hard to step off the track not top three, but the three women who made it definitely deserved to be on that team. They ran phenomenal. So I'm not... stoked, but I'm not totally crushed."

BEHIND THE SCENES

DAVE ALBO

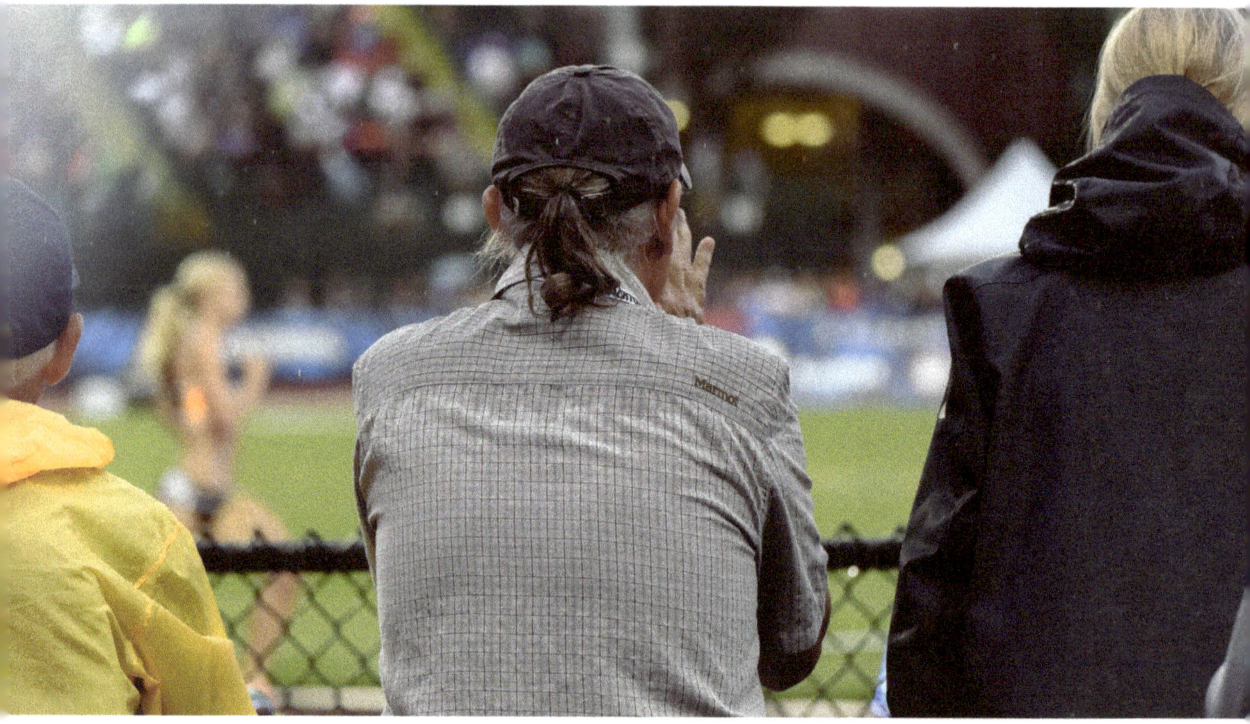

Dave Albo is a track fan. His love of the sport covers events that include athletes of all ages and speeds at the Boulder All Comers meets, high school, at the college level, high achieving masters athletes, as well as those exemplifying the pinnacle of the sport. Fortunately, in Boulder he has a wide range of subjects to study.

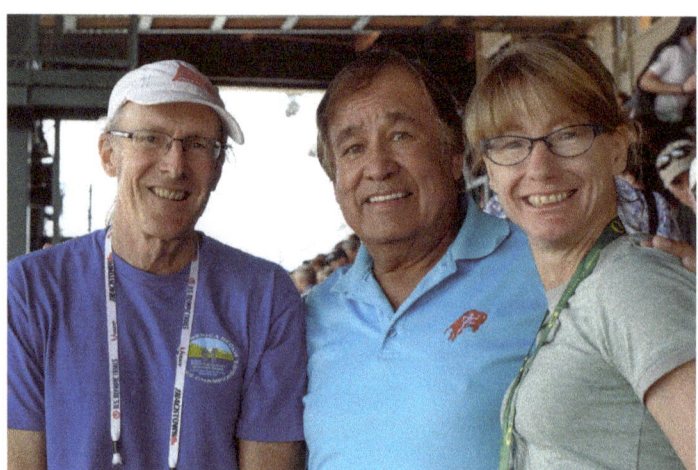

Albo and Murray with Billy Mills.

Opposite:
Alyson Felix
Elise Cranny
Master's 1500m exhibition race from the infield.

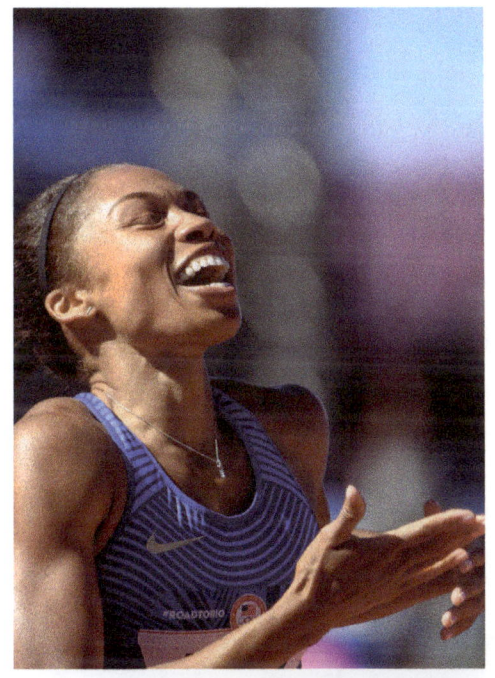

Albo himself still is a high performing athlete as a master spending hours on the track and field focusing on his form and strength. That's the same dedication he brings behind the camera lens looking to capture the most intimate of moments for athletes on the track. Albo's photography "hobby" has taken off over the last few years, as hes honed his skills around the "oval office". And this year it really started to pay off. Albo has been to the last two Olympic Track Trials with his wife Patty Murray, also a huge track fan. In the past he has brought his camera hoping to capture moments from the stands. This year, he obtained a press pass, which placed him in the heat of the action.

With a new larger lens in hand to to really focus in on expressions, he spent the better part of the week bouncing between the field capturing moments and in the stands with wife Murray to observe the meet as a fan.

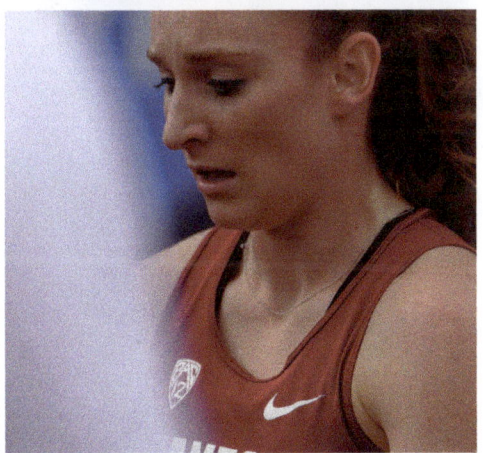

"I am having an amazingly amazing time. Learning a lot, I think I fit right into this scene. My confidence has gone up. I'd be comfortable at ANY track meet now, even the Olympics."

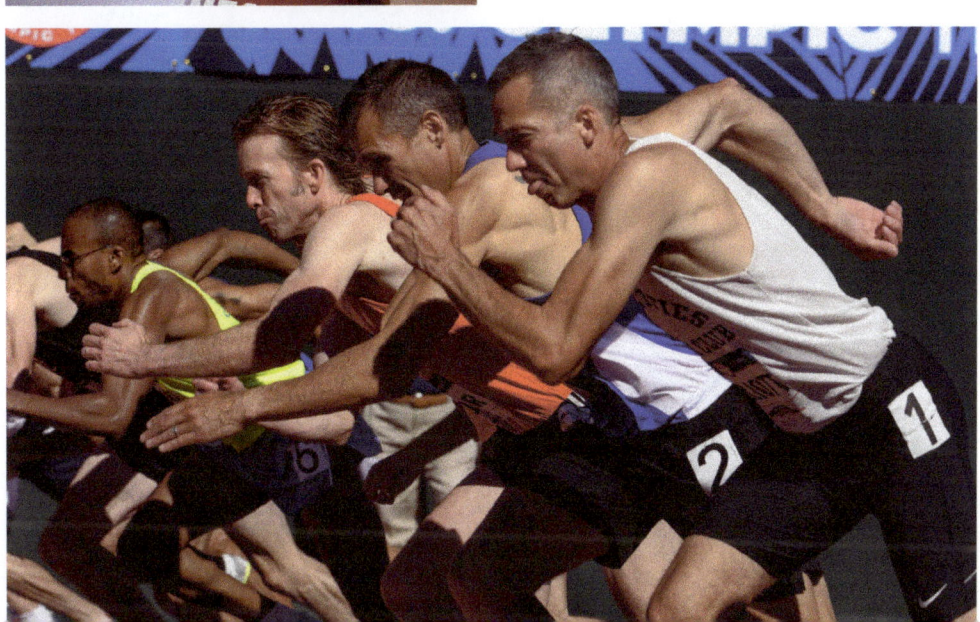

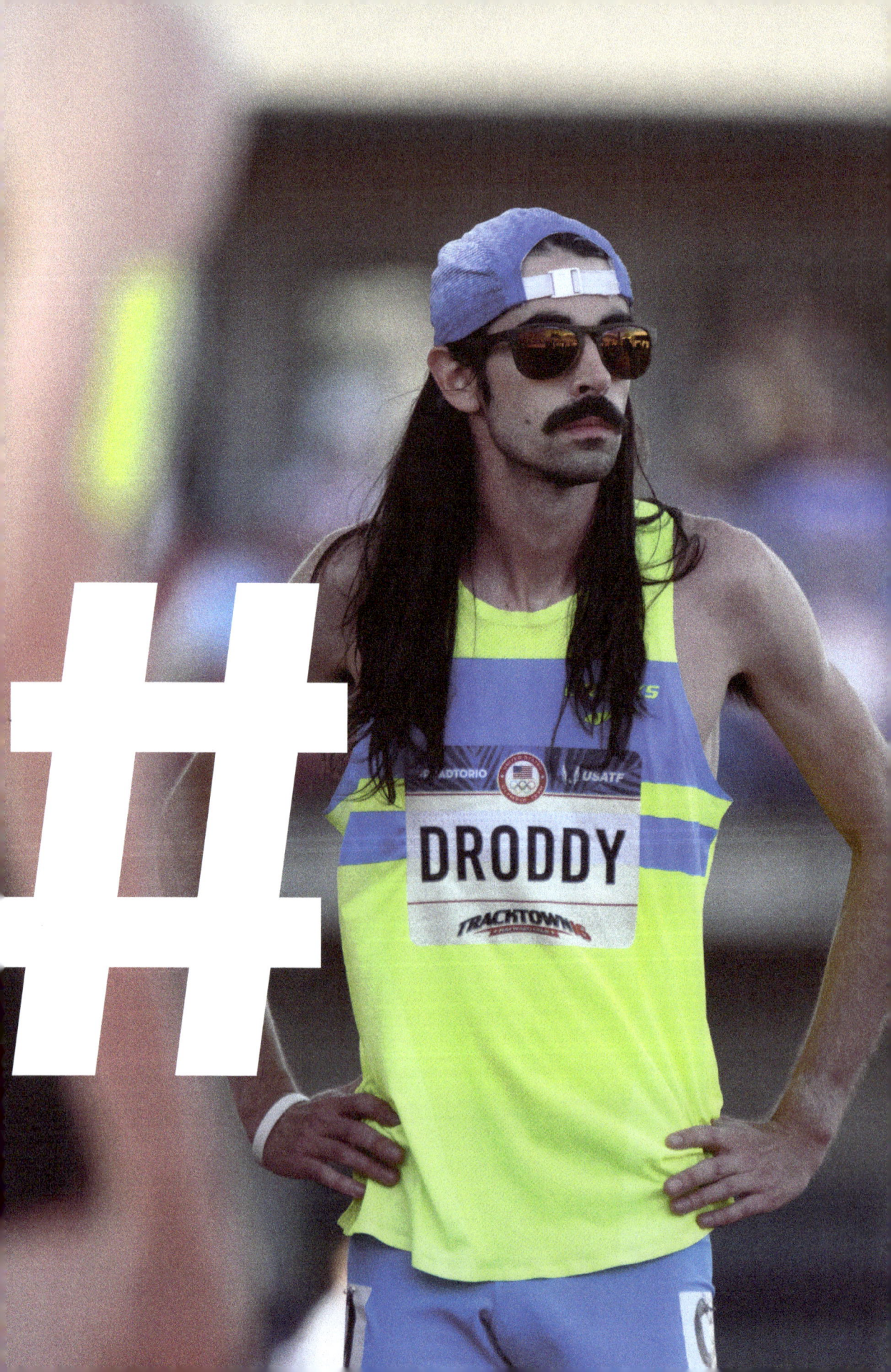

Noah Droddy, sunglasses on, his cap on backwards, with his signature mustache-and-long-hair look, stood unassumingly on the track while the big talent in the 10,000 meters was being announced on the television. That's all it took for the internet to catch fire and create Droddy's own hashtag. Although he finished last in the field (20th at 31:02.99, although ahead of 7 DNFs), he may have just captured America's heart. He got a fair amount of NBC air time, either directly in front of or behind winner Galen Rupp.

Droddy didn't expect to have made the 10,000 qualifying standard that year as he had also run the Olympic Marathon Trials in February and the Bolder Boulder in May.

Since the track trials, though, there has been continued coverage of him through major magazines like Runner's World and his likeness was popular among Halloween costumes this year.

July 1

Give us what we want, Olympic trials announcers! We want the 411 on Droddy! #OlympicTrials #droddy

@therachelkelly

July 1

I feel like Droddy is part of an SNL plant dropped into the field! Go Droddy! #DRODDY

@Madc_1

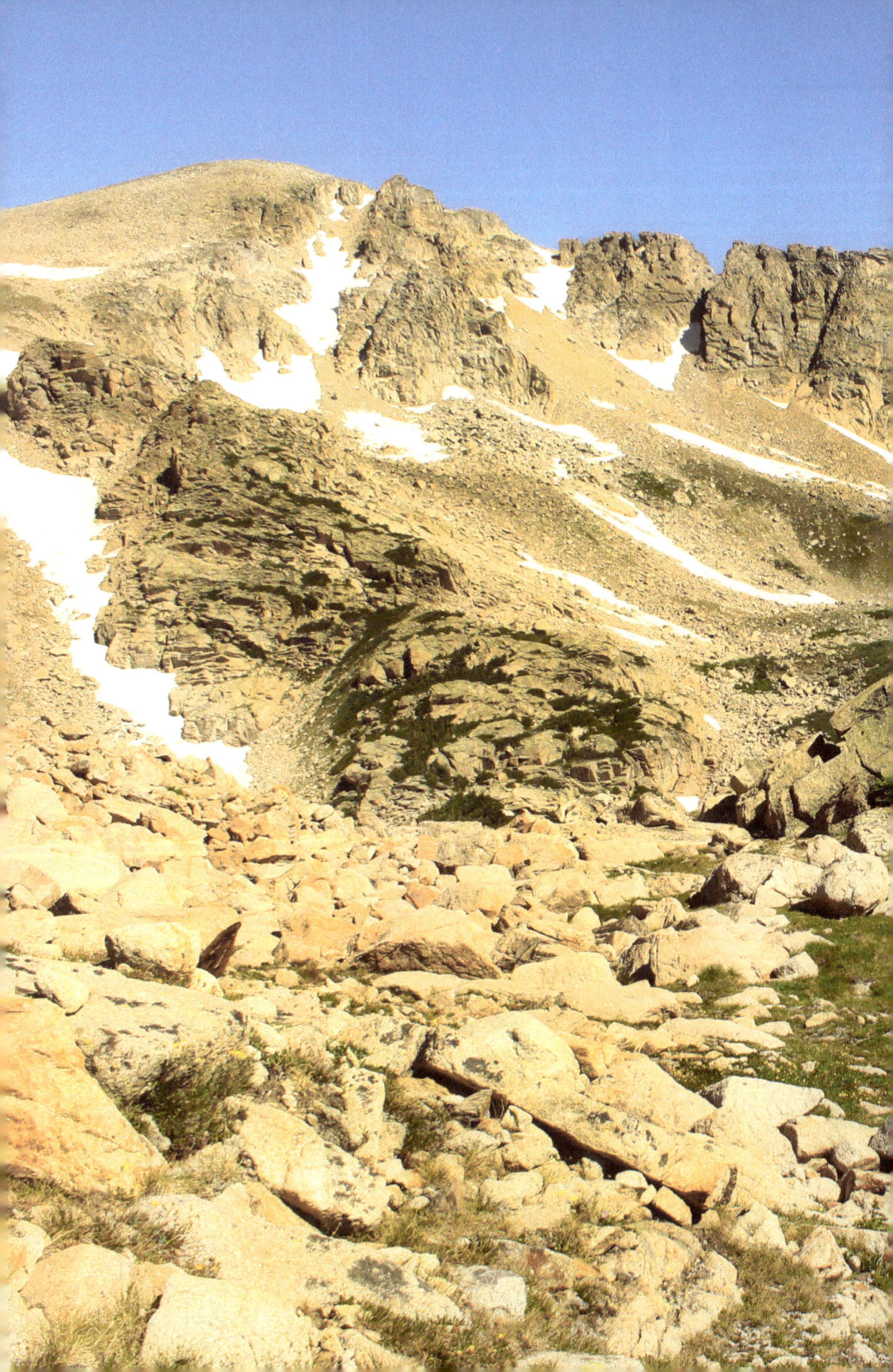

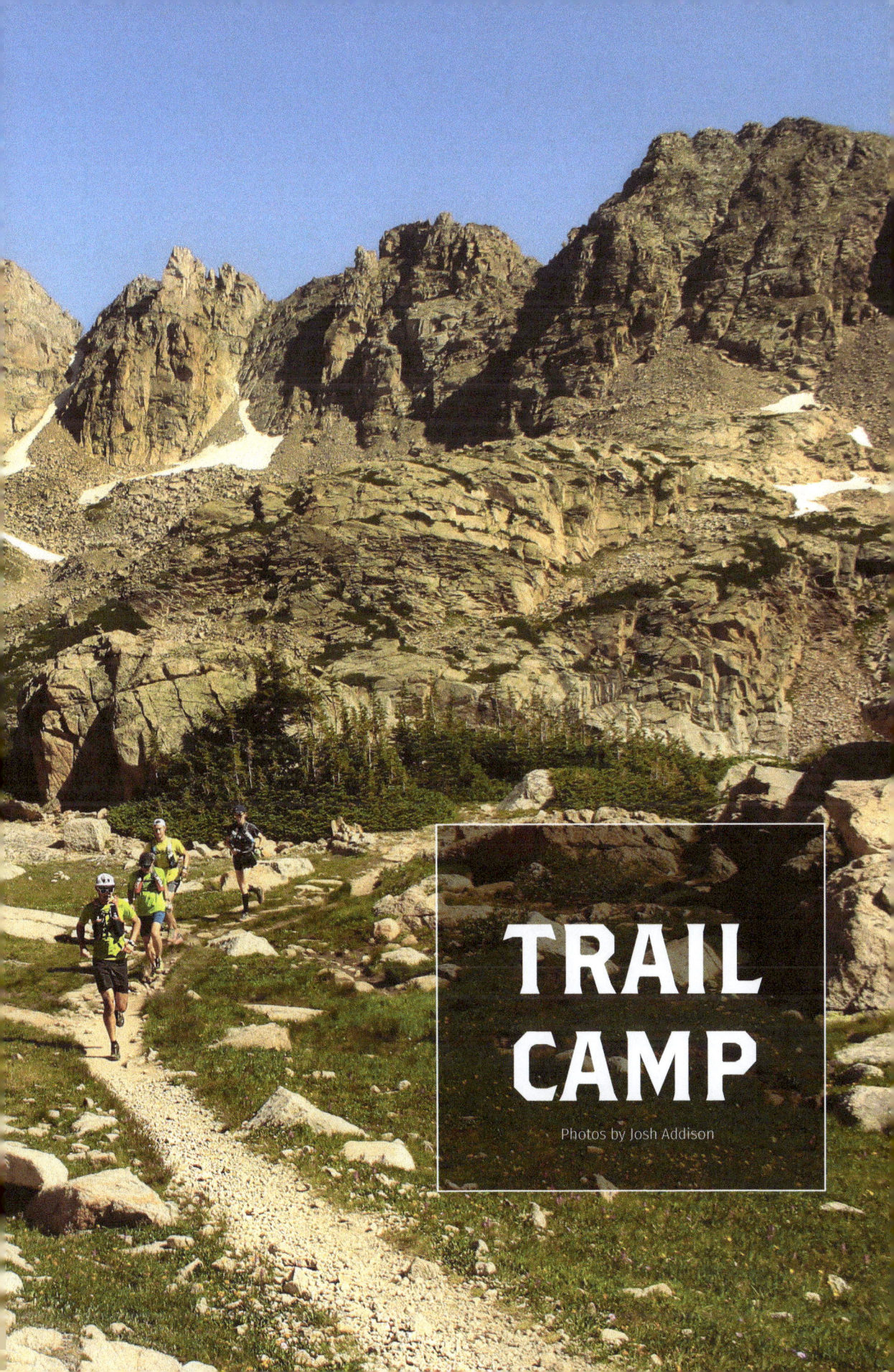

TRAIL CAMP

Photos by Josh Addison

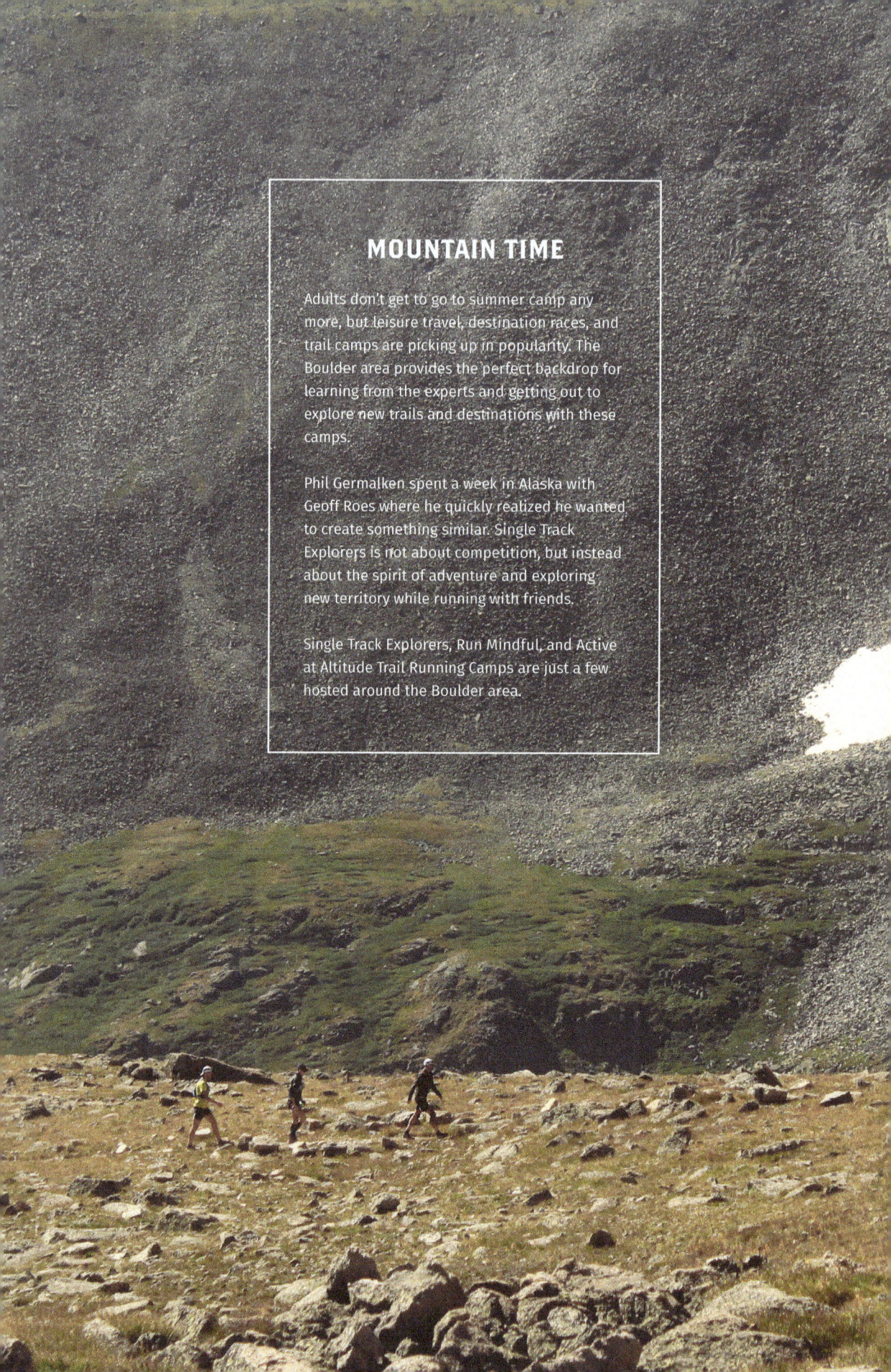

MOUNTAIN TIME

Adults don't get to go to summer camp any more, but leisure travel, destination races, and trail camps are picking up in popularity. The Boulder area provides the perfect backdrop for learning from the experts and getting out to explore new trails and destinations with these camps.

Phil Germalken spent a week in Alaska with Geoff Roes where he quickly realized he wanted to create something similar. Single Track Explorers is not about competition, but instead about the spirit of adventure and exploring new territory while running with friends.

Single Track Explorers, Run Mindful, and Active at Altitude Trail Running Camps are just a few hosted around the Boulder area.

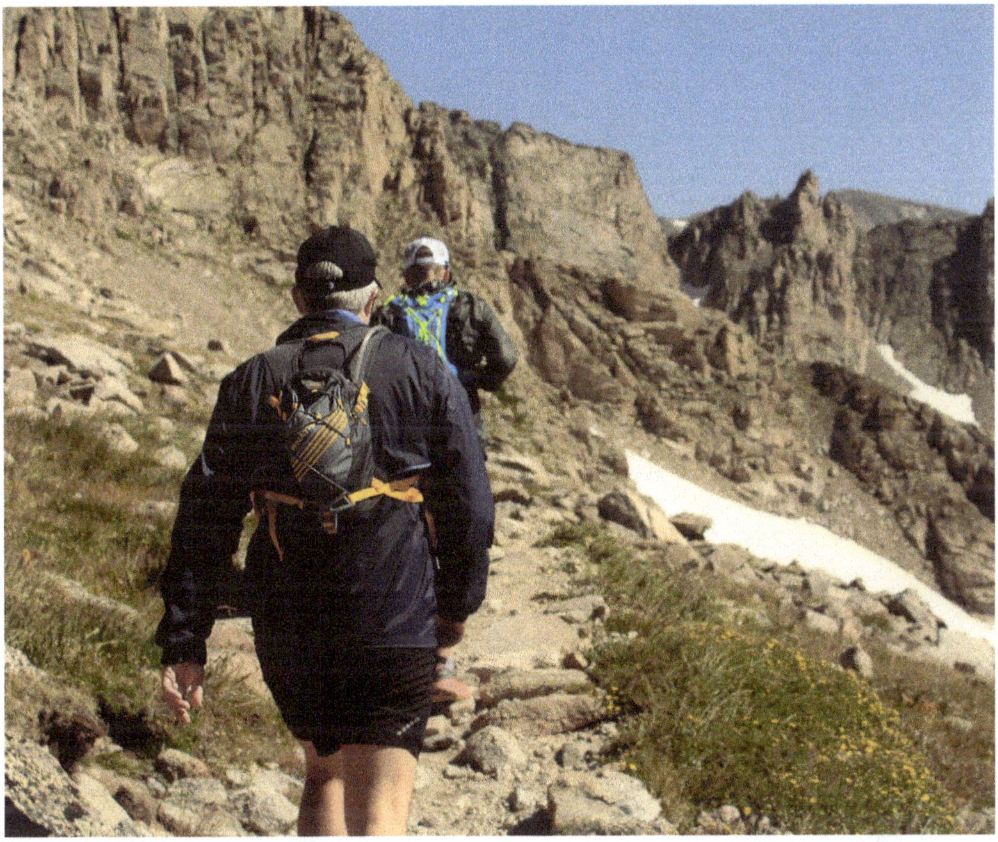

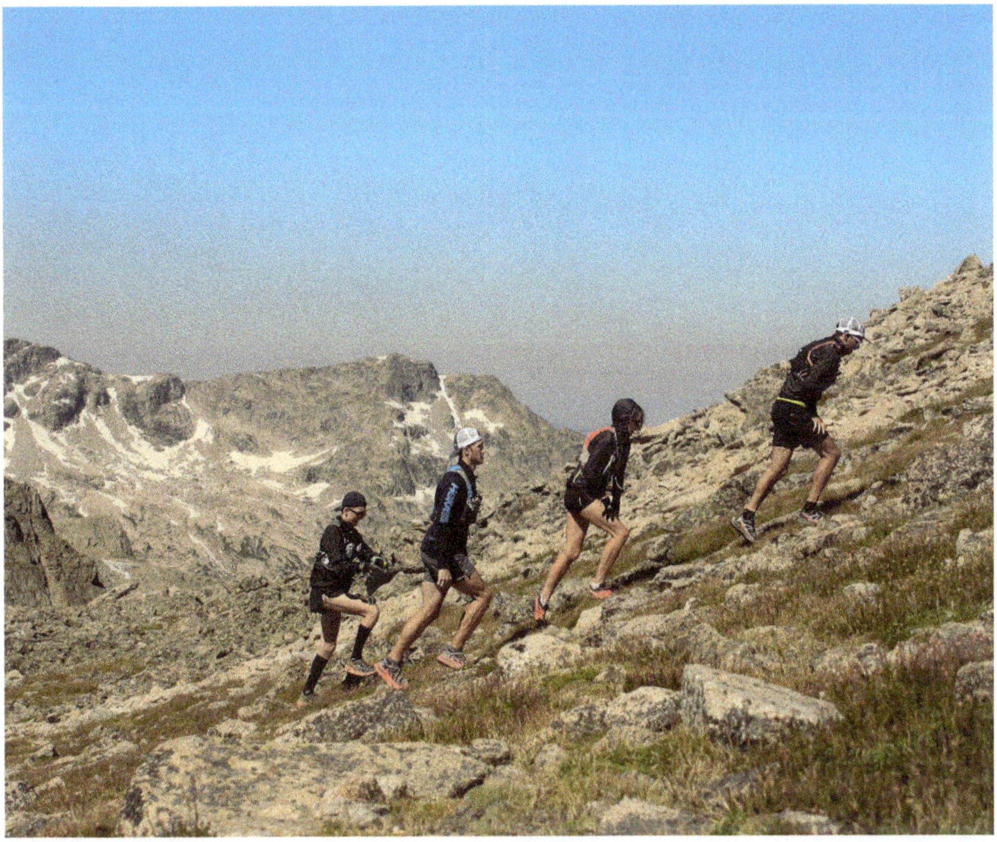

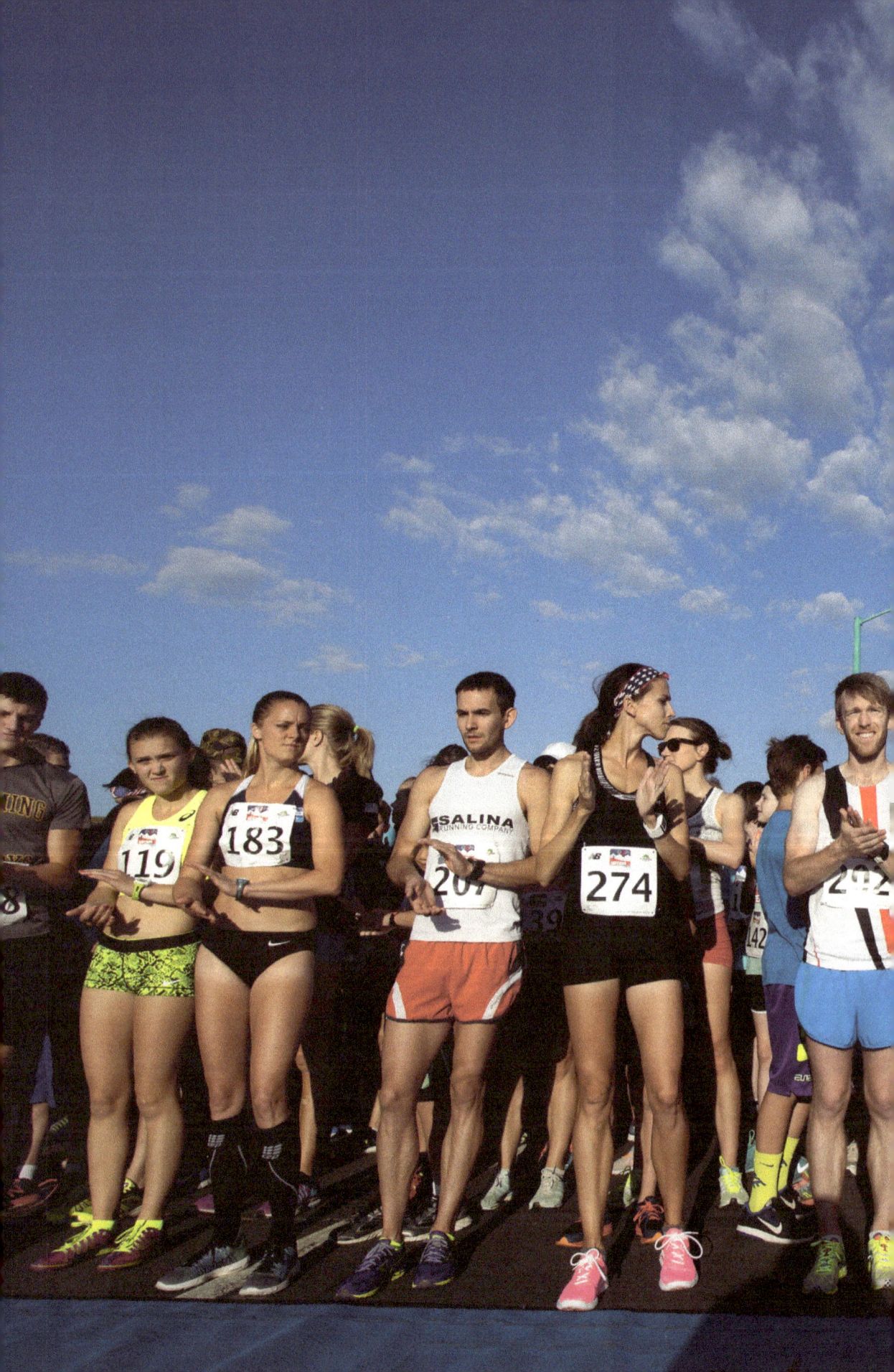

Superior Downhill Mile

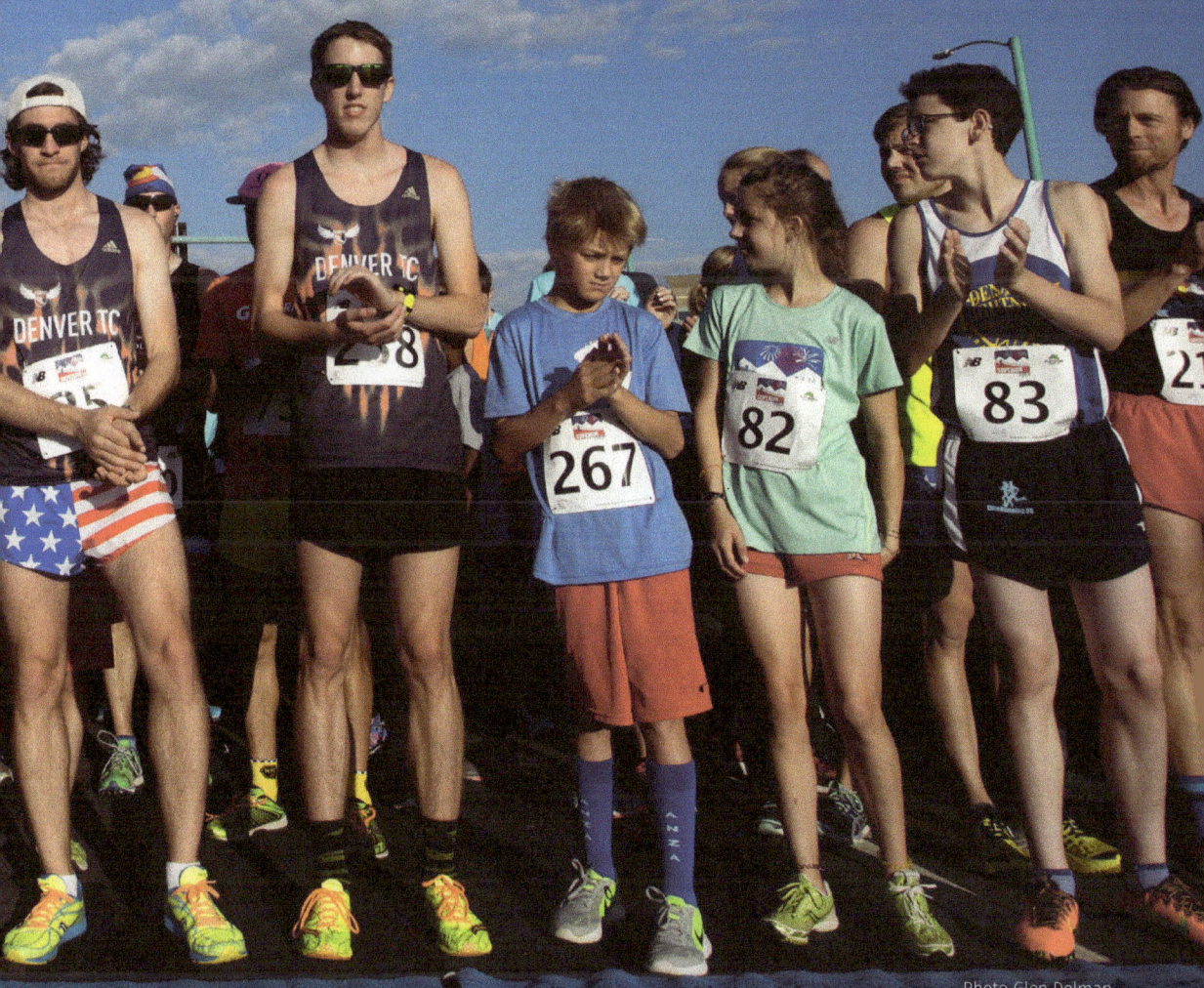

Photo Glen Delman

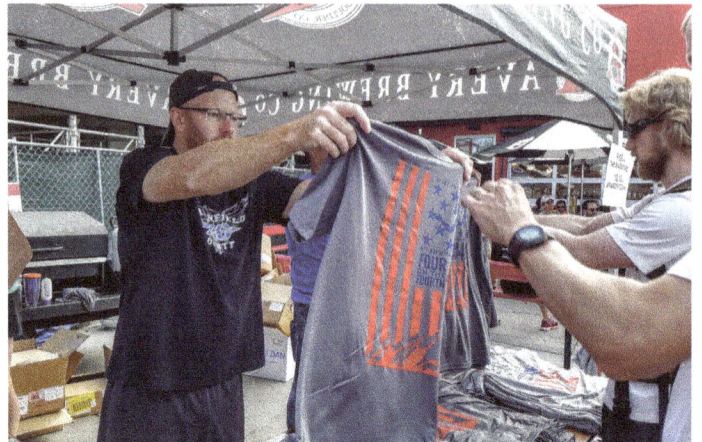
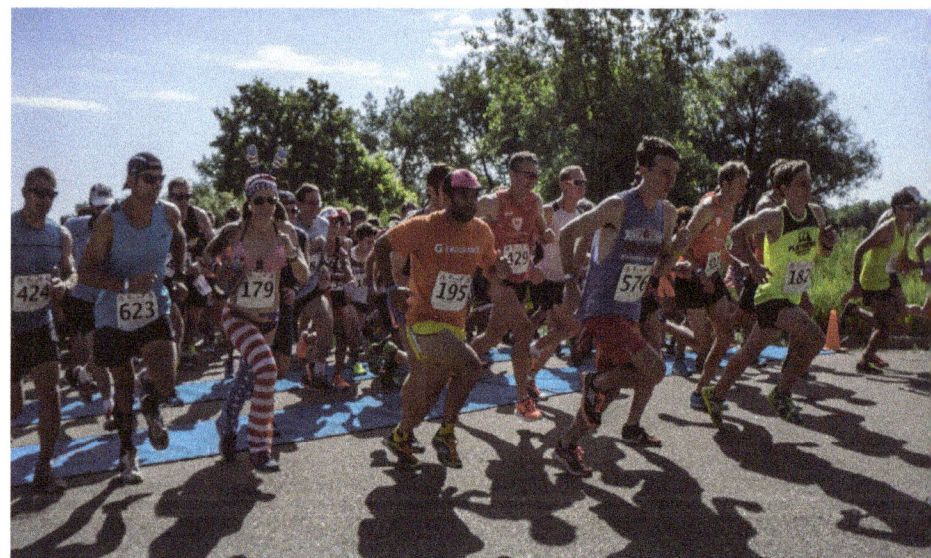
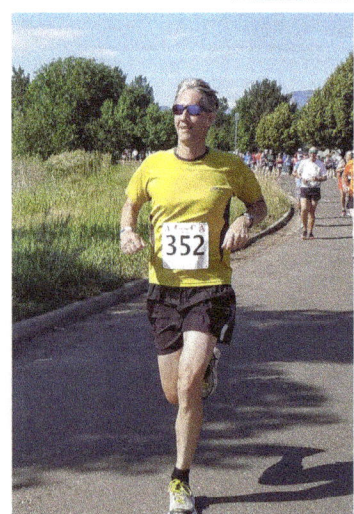
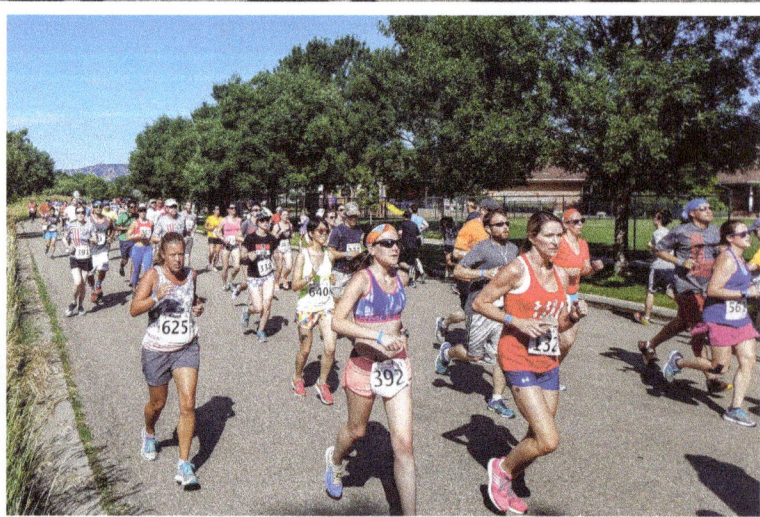

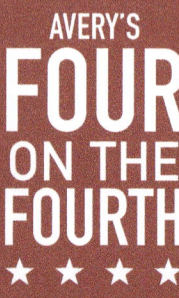

AVERY'S FOUR ON THE FOURTH

★ ★ ★ ★

Photos Todd Straka

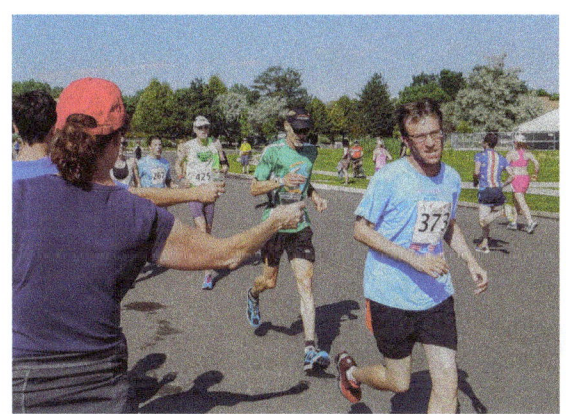
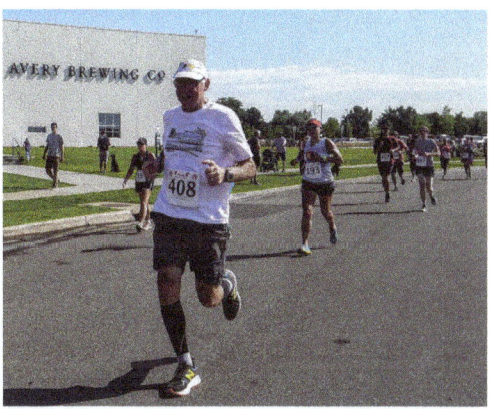
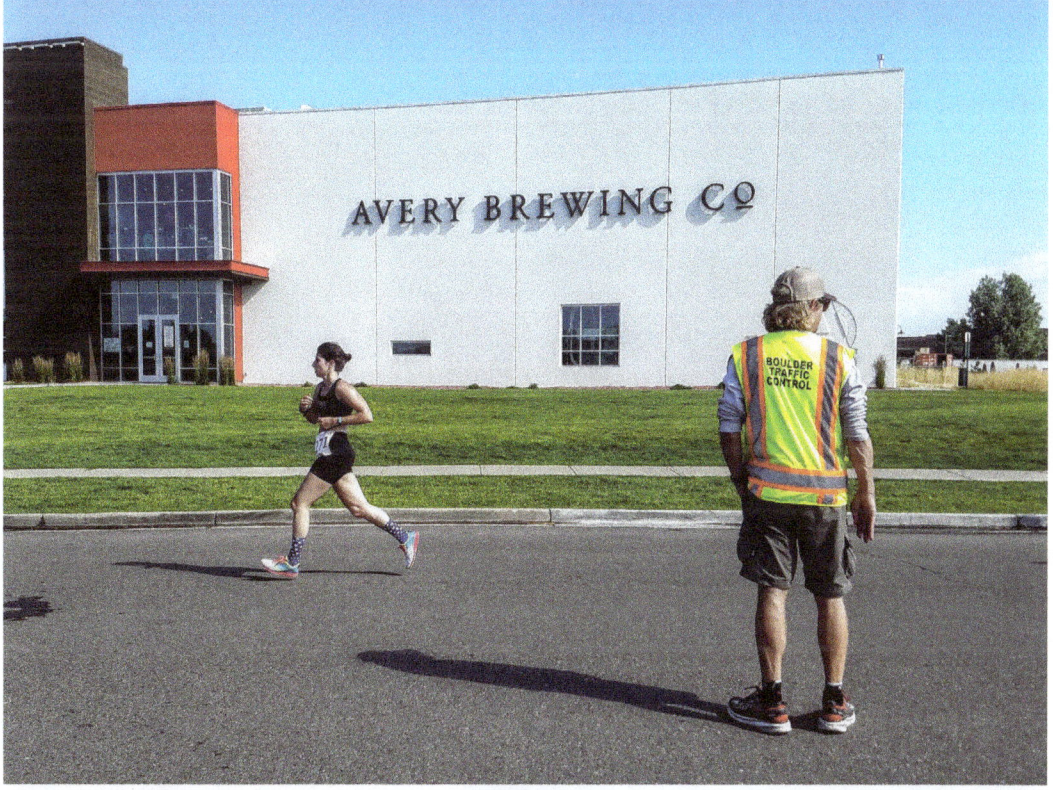
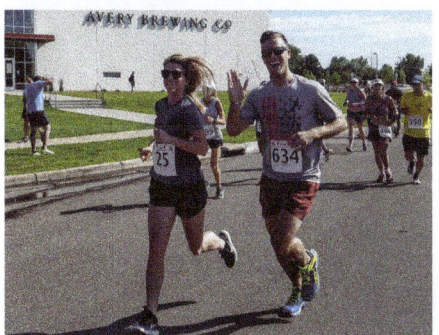
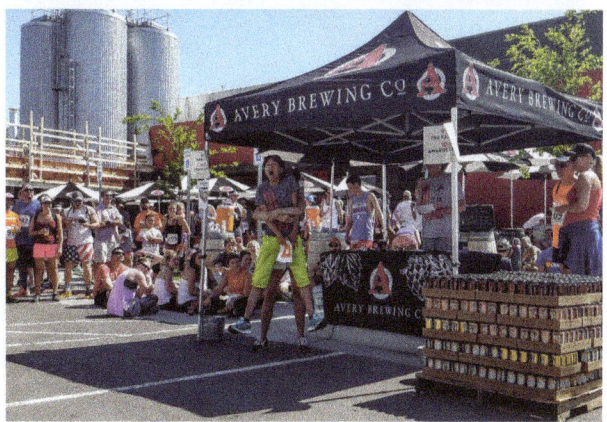
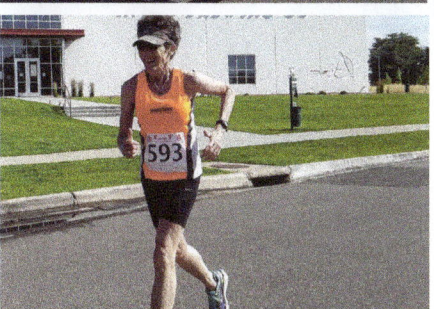

Running TECH

Boulder has been known as a running mecca since the 70s and more recently as a haven for tech start ups and innovation. There has never been a better time to combine those passions. Here are 3 Boulder companies who are making a play at combining tech to make you a more efficient runner, keep you injury free and find new places to explore.

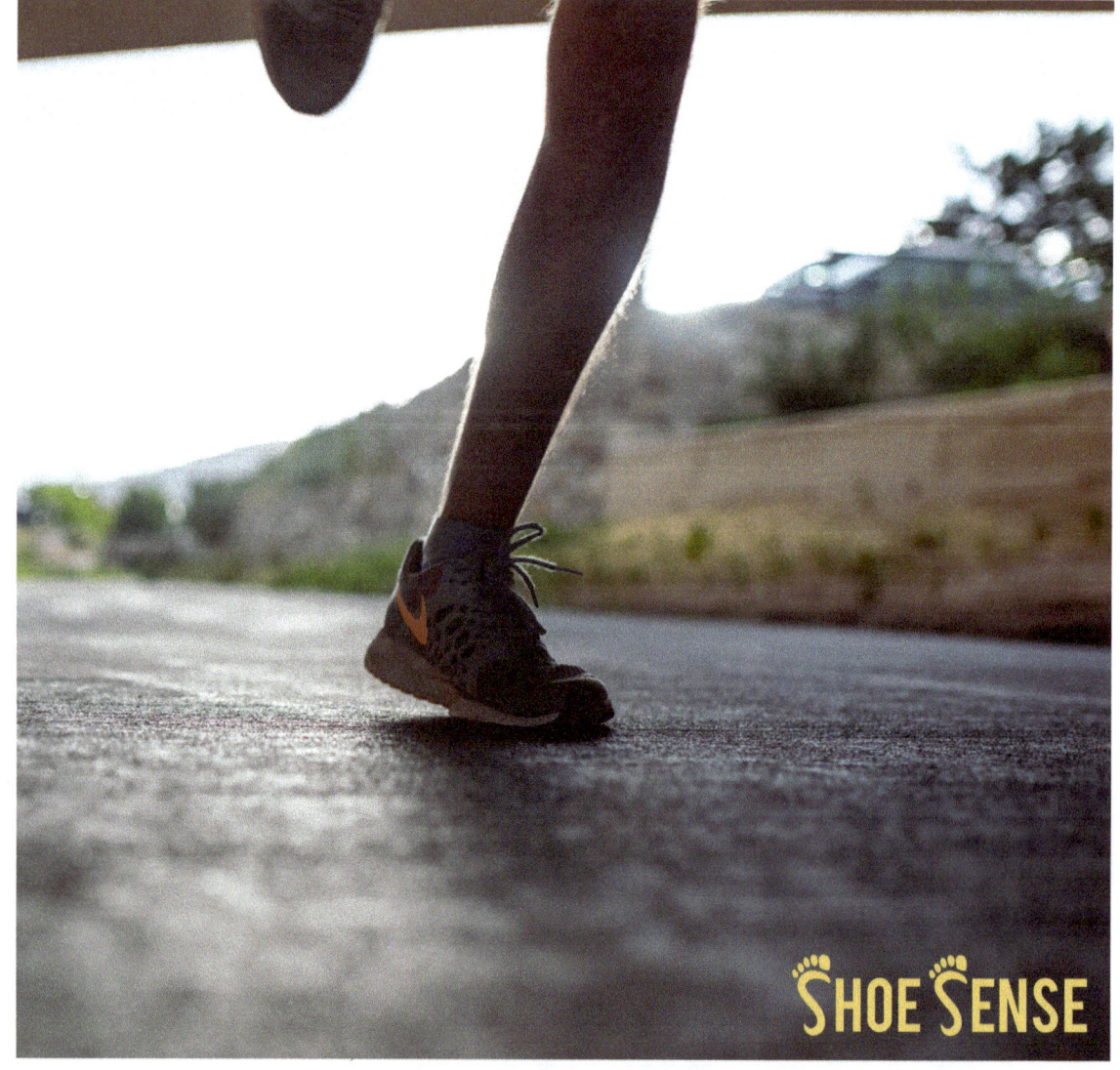

Shoe Sense

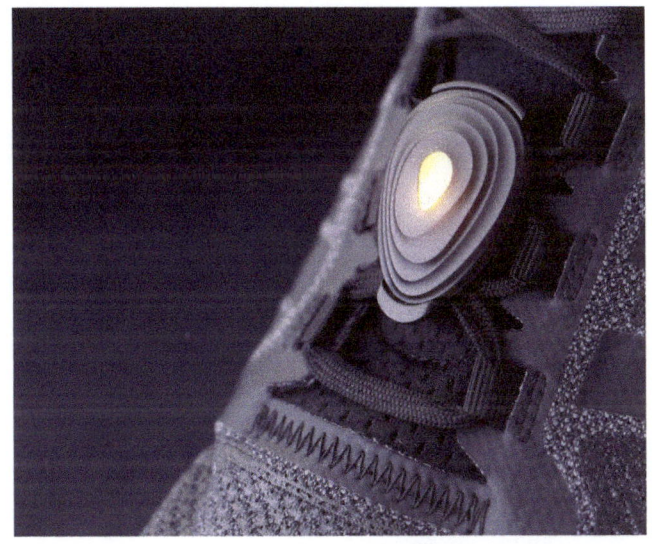

The Stryd Power Meter measures how hard and how efficiently you are running. It calculates this using a power metric which is returned to your watch or smart phone for real-time or future analysis to help you discover your untapped potential. Keeping an eye on stride rate and power output allows you to adjust leg speed and posture to run in the most efficient way possible – and the more efficient you are, the faster you run.

Key concepts are explained and explored along with power based training for races of all distances in the new book from VeloPress "Run with Power: The complete Guide to Power Meters for Runners" by Jim Vance.

Stryd.com

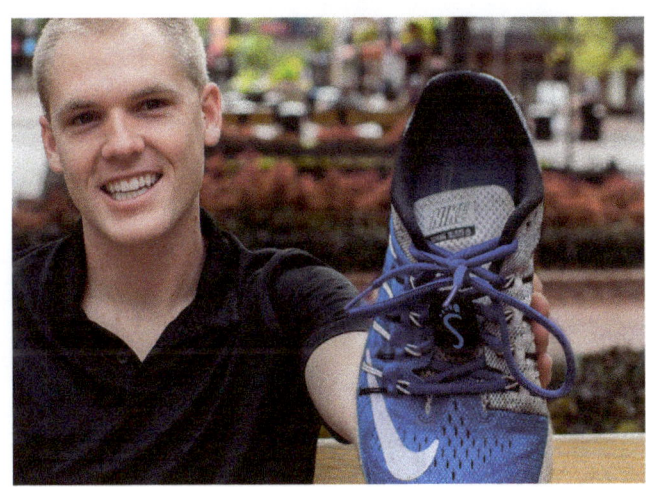

Conner Winter was inspired to help eliminate running injuries when he missed a whole season at CU due to a foot injury caused by wearing worn out shoes. Shoe Sense measures when a shoe's cushioning degrades to the point to where injuries may be a factor, warning the runner when the shoes need to be replaced.

Once running athletes replace their worn shoes, they consistently marvel at how good they feel. I can say with confidence that for many clients, replacing worn shoes is half the injury battle.
- Charlie Merrill of Merrill Performance

ShoeSense.com

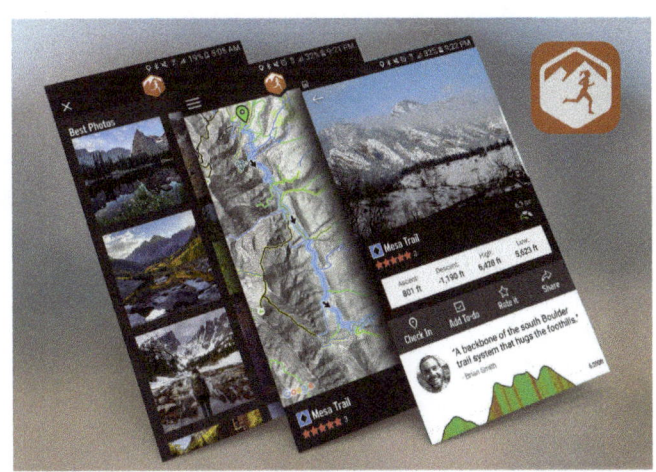

Last year the Trail Run Project and its parent company were funded by REI. Since then, the project has improved with updates to its content, web and mobile app. Trail runners can search for local trails near them, be inspired by new places to run, and get the inside story from locals who have contributed that content. You can check in, add a trail to your to-do list or upload your own photo stoke images.

TrailRunProject.com

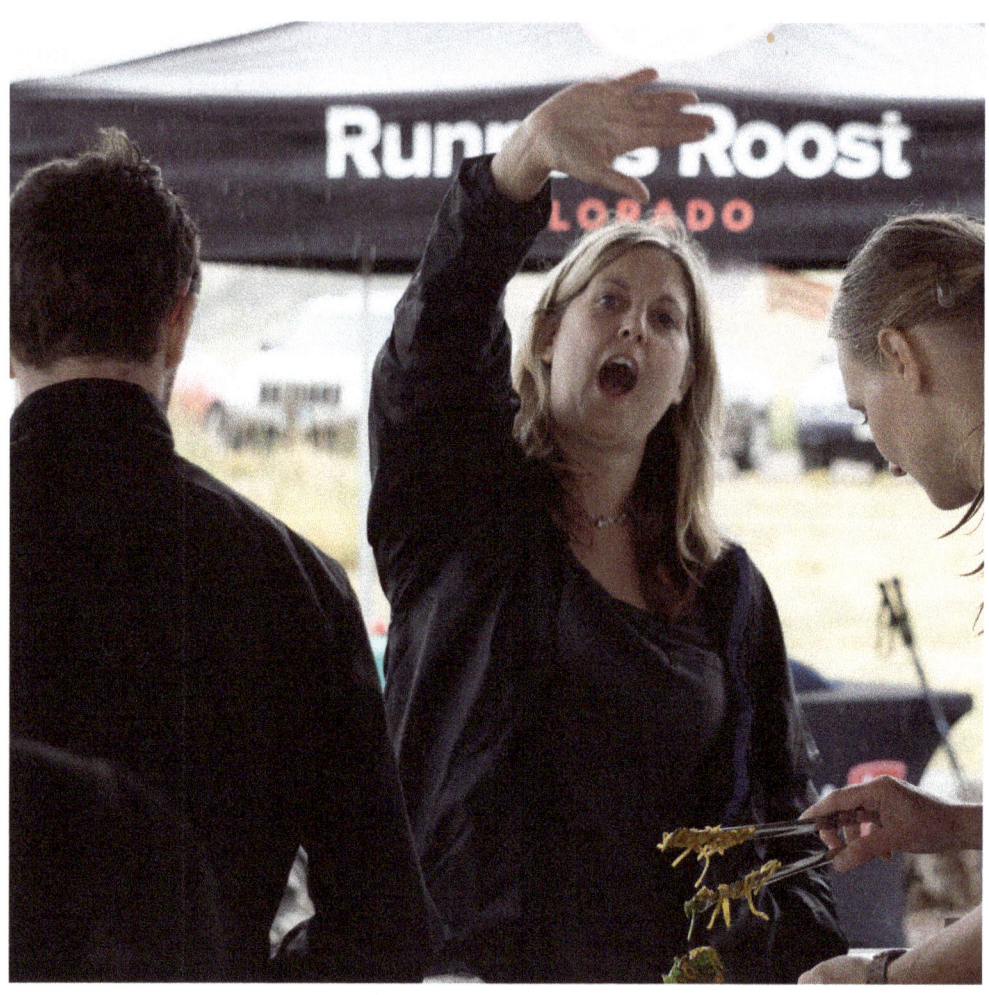

FOOD FOR THE SOUL

Words by Sarah Rebick

It's the second week of July and Kelly and Morgan Newlon are driving their Range Rover loaded without an inch of free space into the heart of the San Juan Mountains for the grueling Hardrock 100. Quite a few people - from Boulder and beyond - are depending on Kelly to feed them with her tasty performance-oriented fare. And I'm not talking just a few racers. In the end, Kelly and Morgan fed more than 5 competitors and their crews, names you know: Killian Jornet, Anna Frost, Timothy Olson, Jason Schlarb, Darcy Piceu. They fed a pre-race party sponsored by Smartwool and a house full of Ultimate Direction athletes and fans. And on the night before the start, once athletes had gone to bed, Kelly invited a filmmaker and the agent of some friends over for dinner at the little house she and Morgan had rented in Silverton. More than 30 people materialized and stayed until midnight.

Eating, after all, and ultras such as Hardrock are about community — and community is what RAD is about.

Kelly and Morgan Newlon are RAD, the husband and wife team behind Real Athlete Diets. Kelly is the chef, while Morgan manages the business and marketing. For them, food is about nourishment and love. It is about fueling people who inspire others. It's about being an essential part of a community of people who take care of each other.

RAD started in 2014 when Kelly was working full time (times 3!) teaching new chefs, mentoring adolescent recovering addicts, and working as a personal chef. Friends asked her to help them with events and parties. She realized that what she really wanted to do was to provide delicious performance-oriented food to busy athletes. The business, which started with individual meals delivered to offices and stores, has grown to providing hundreds of meals to this year's Hardrockers, catering athlete clinics and camps, post-race parties, corporate meetings and more.

Kelly is not new to the racing world. She was a track star in high school in Indiana and started running trails when she was in school at the Culinary Institute of America in Hyde Park, NY. When she moved to Williamsburg, VA she fell in with a great group of runners who were running a lot of fast times on roads and were generally up for adventure. During this time, she read an article about the Boulder-based ultra group Divine Madness and was intrigued, so when someone in her group suggested training for an ultra, she was in. This is when she met Morgan, who was managing an outdoor store in Williamsburg; he sold her the gear she needed to run at night and for longer distances. In 2001, she ran the Hardrock 100. It was her first 100 mile race and she was hooked. The sense of teamwork and community are at the heart of Kelly's love for trail and ultrarunning. This is also what is at the heart of RAD.

This sense of nourishing a community beyond the basics is what propels the Newlons. Not only did Kelly and Morgan provide pre- and post-race food for this year's Hardrock 100 athletes, when Timothy Olson wasn't feeling well late at night, they met him with bone broth to help keep him in the race. Their goal is not just to provide good

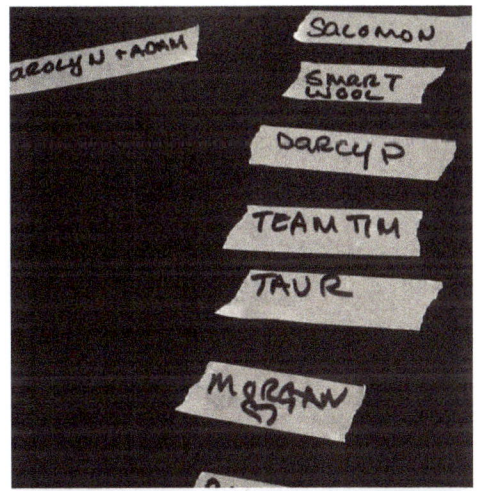

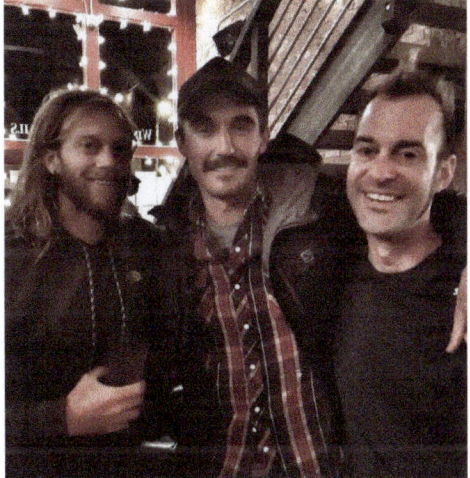

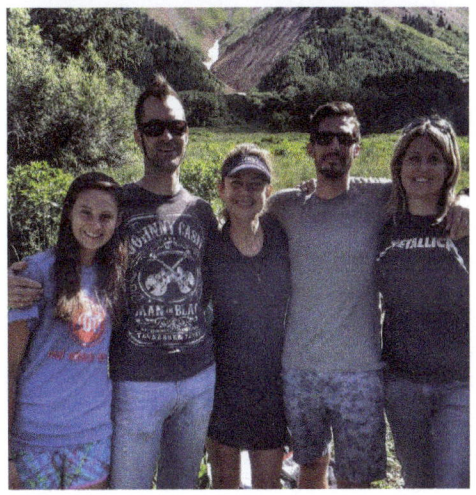

Photos courtesy of Kelly Bailey Newlon

Photos - Todd Straka, RAD Food, Nick Combs

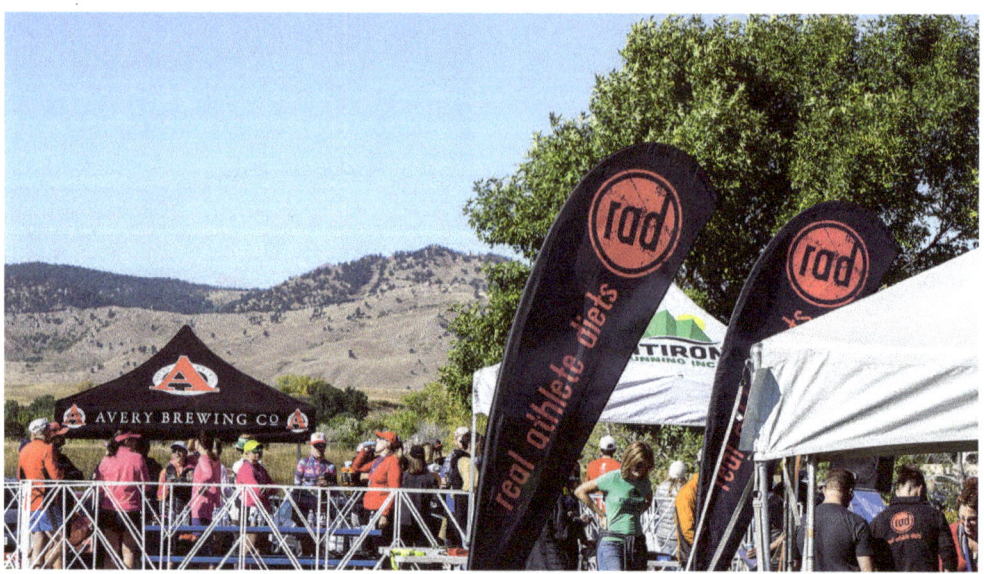

food for people, but to provide it at times when it makes their lives easier. Ryan Lassen, one of RAD's sponsored athletes, speaks to this:

"Every race that I drive to (7 this year), she packs me a cooler with meals for travel, pre-race, and post-race. Complete game changer. When you're driving on I-25 for 7 hours in Wyoming, there is nothing but fast food and truck stops. RAD is the best answer... Unless you're really into eating Big Macs before 100 mile trail races!"

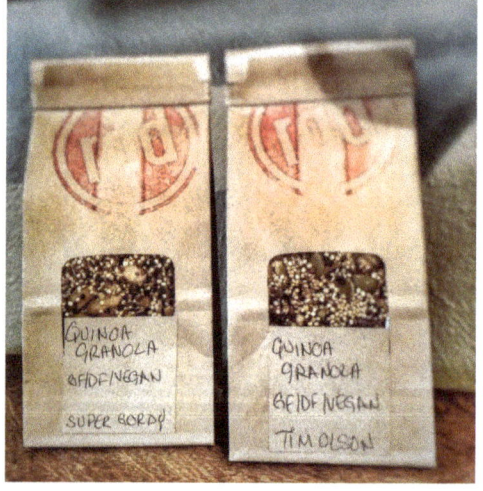

And Kelly doesn't just take care of people while they're racing. When former elite marathoner and Boulder running community stalwart Benji Durden entered the hospital for cancer surgery this summer, Kelly sent his wife, Amie, off with meals for both of them for the hospital stay. She has continued to send them soup during his chemotherapy treatment. "They've helped me get through some difficult times these past few months when eating was not easy," Benji reports. Amie adds that "the sense of community Kelly is fostering means a whole lot to us."

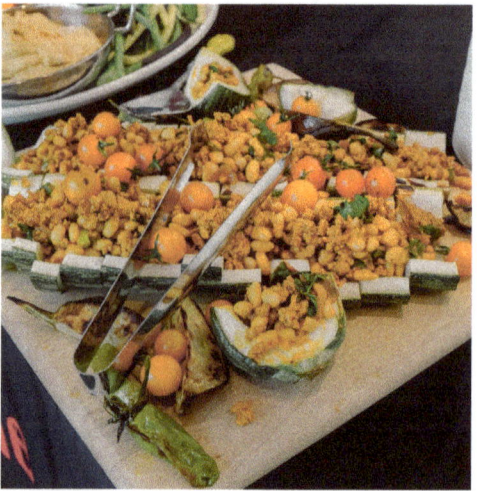

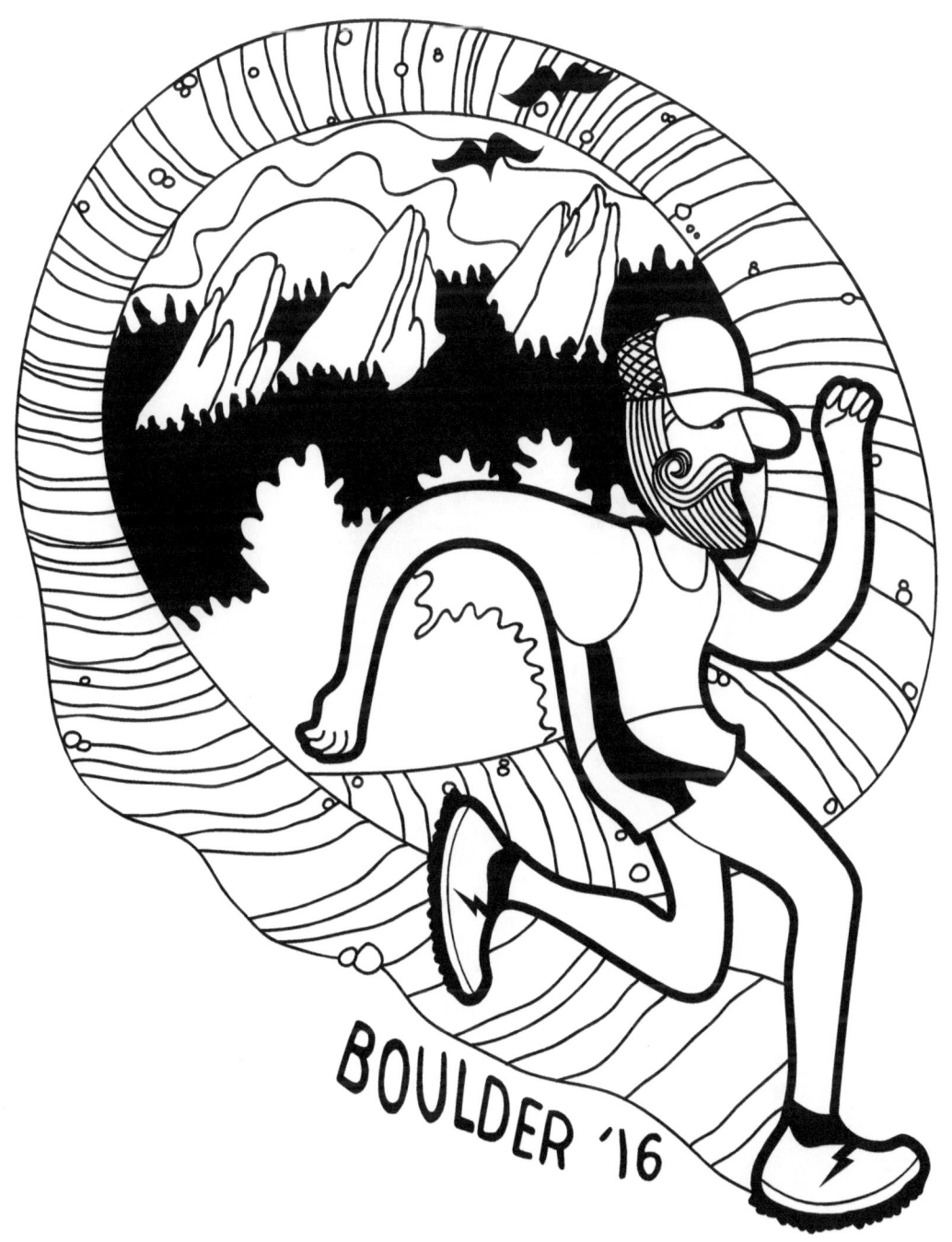

Go ahead, color away.

WEST END

The downtown race series kicked off the summer with the West End 4k, two laps from Downtown to the west on Pearl Street. The race often brings out the best in the area to test their mettle against one another.
Stephen Pifer and Mara Olson grabbed the big W in the elite fields.

Photos by Glen Delman and Peter N. Jones

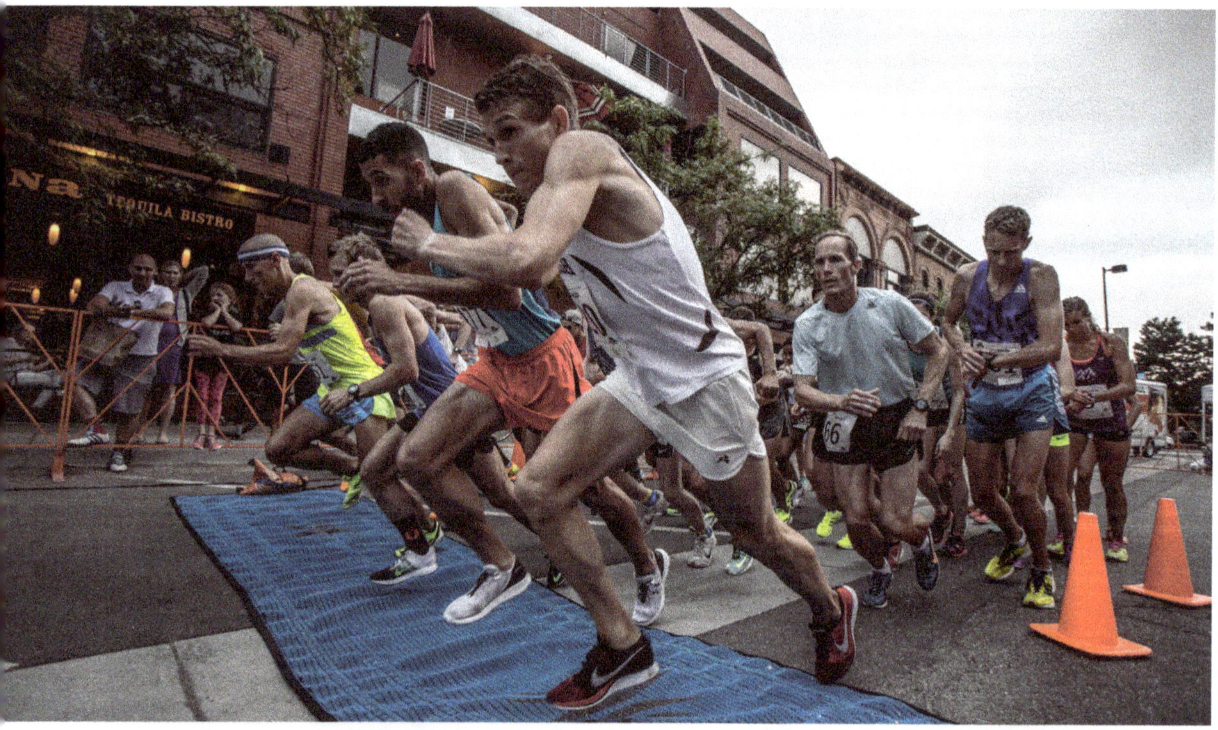

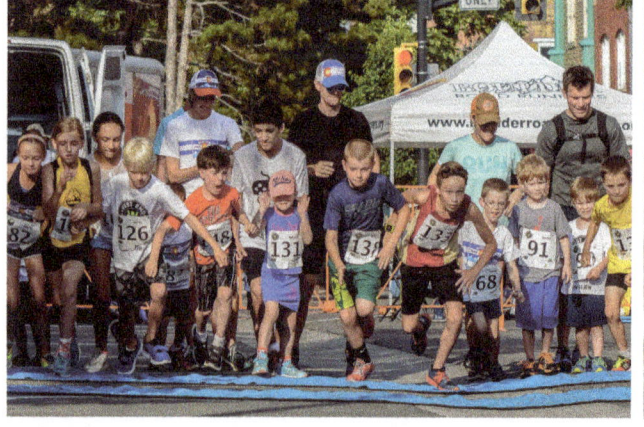
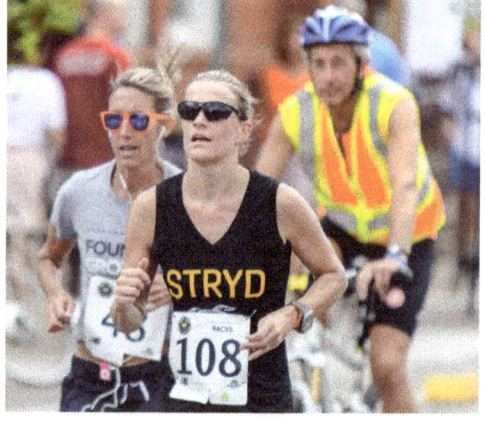

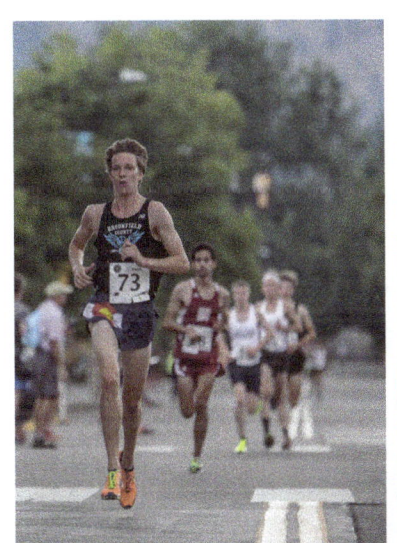
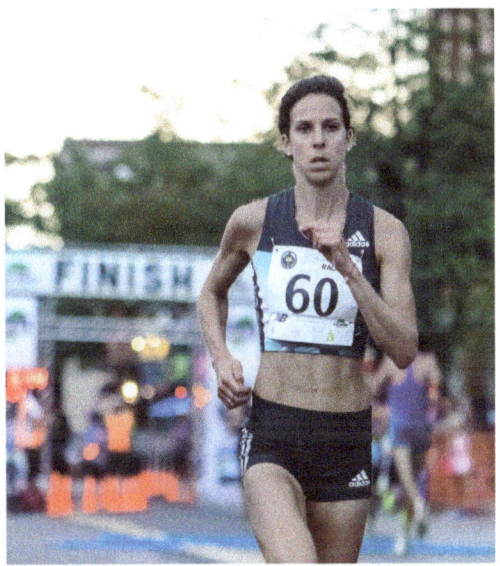

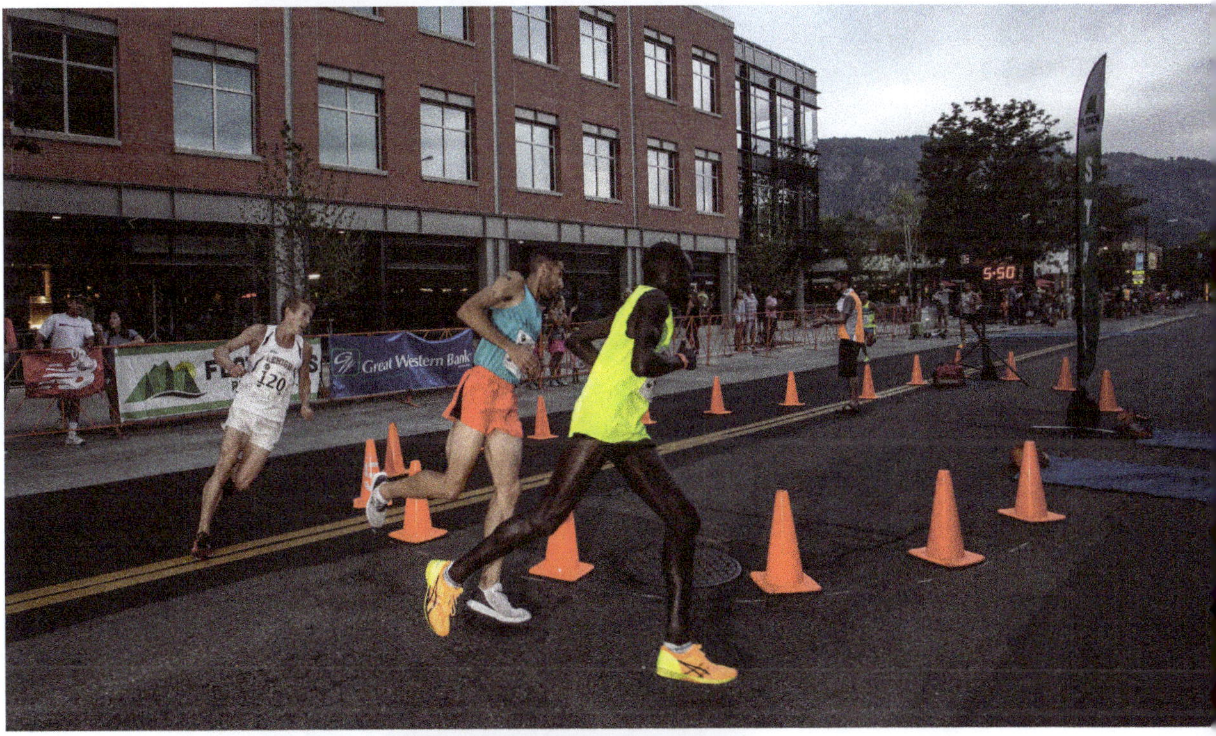

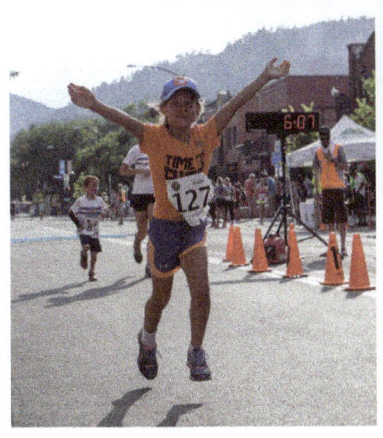
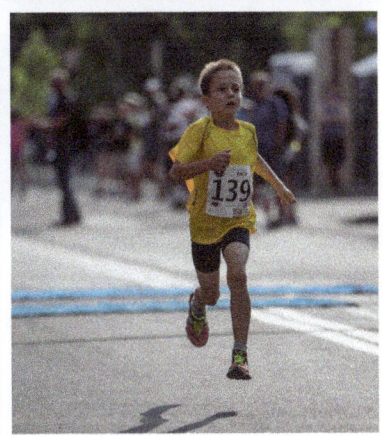
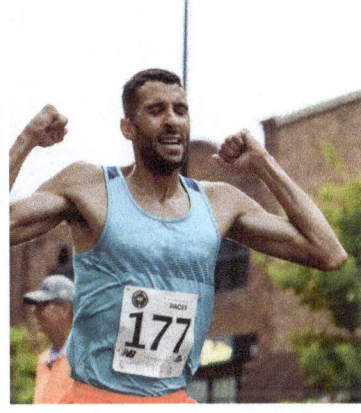

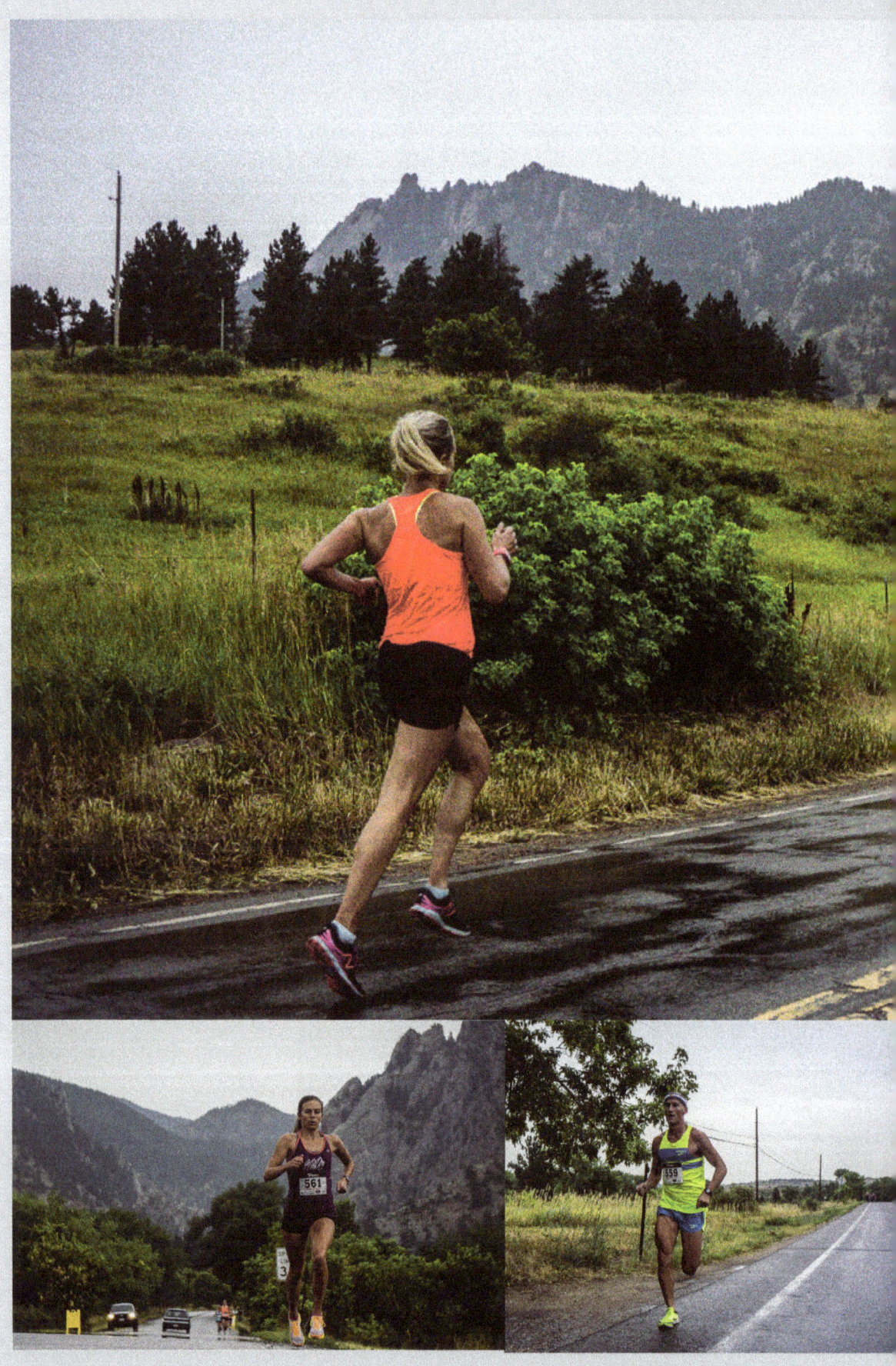

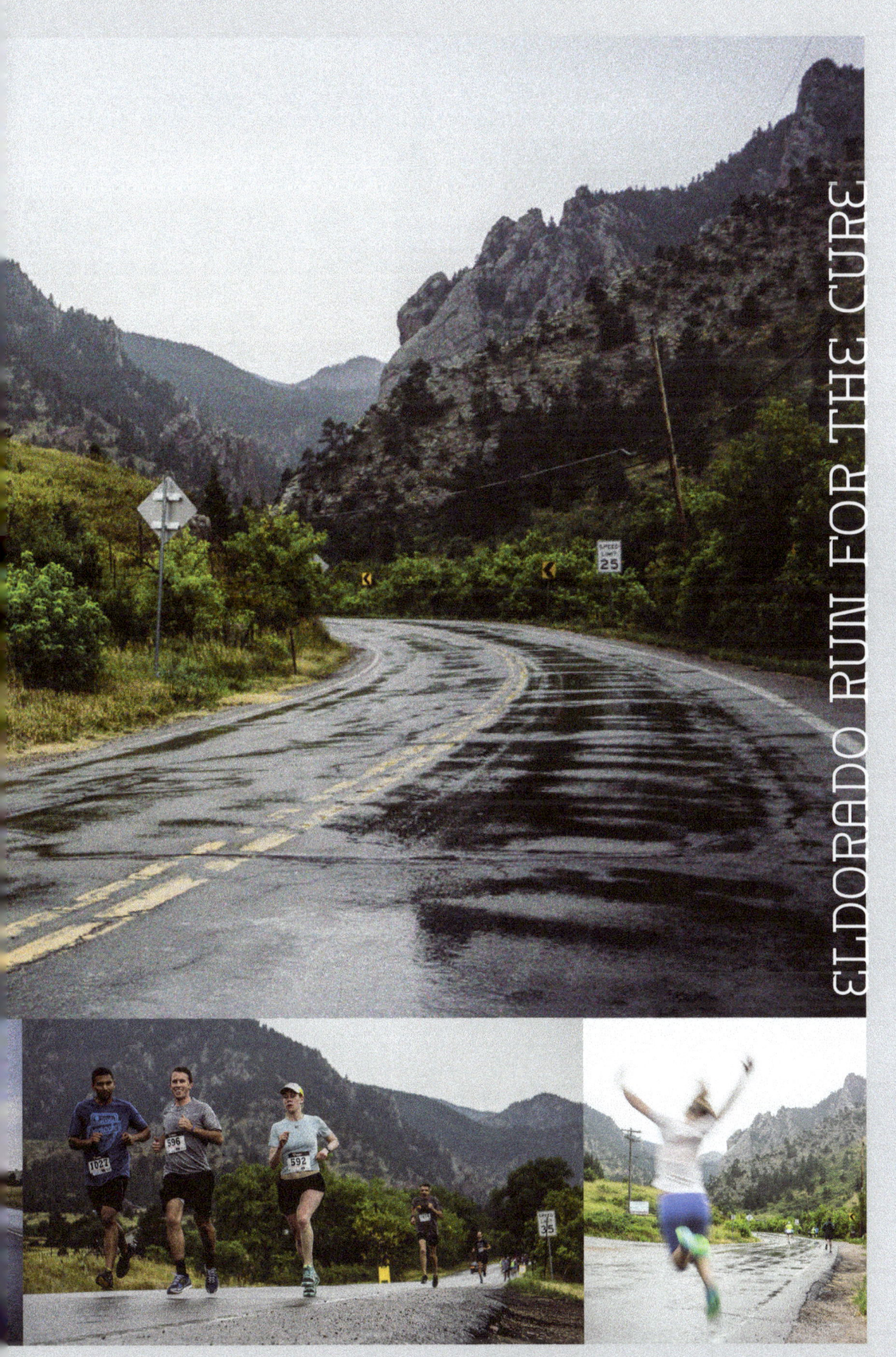

ELDORADO RUN FOR THE CURE

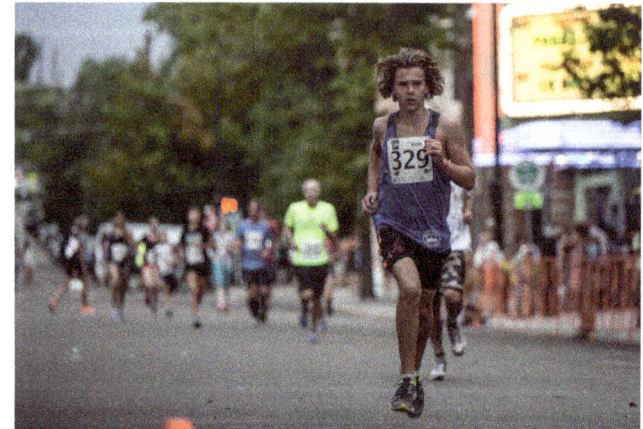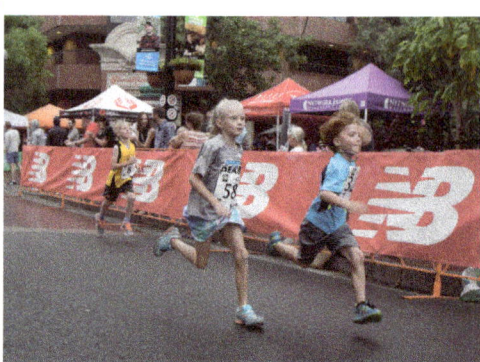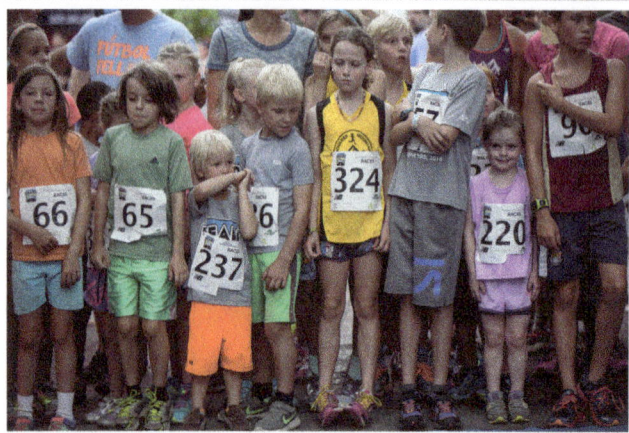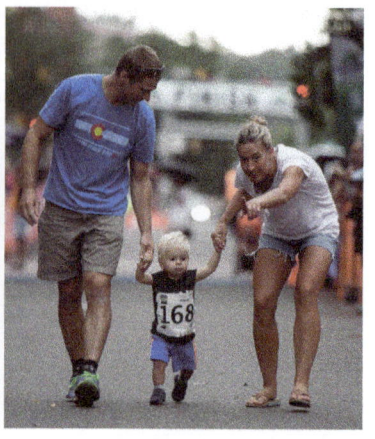

Photos Glen Delman

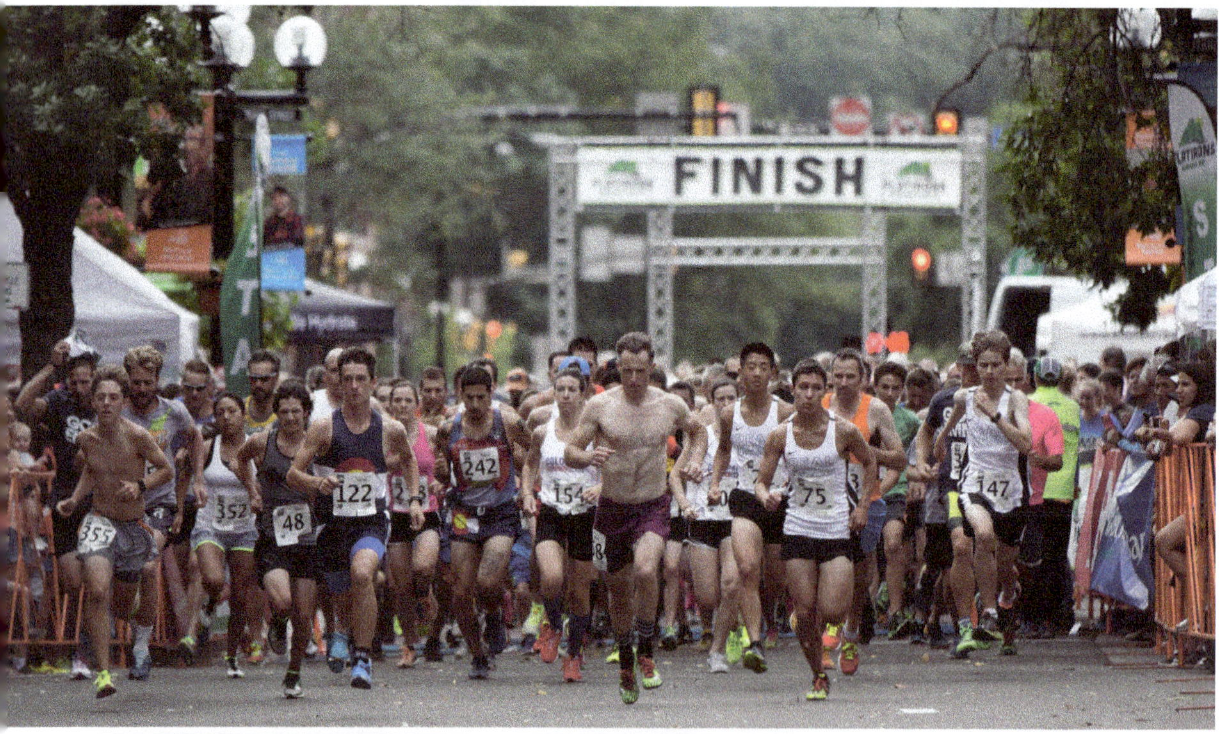

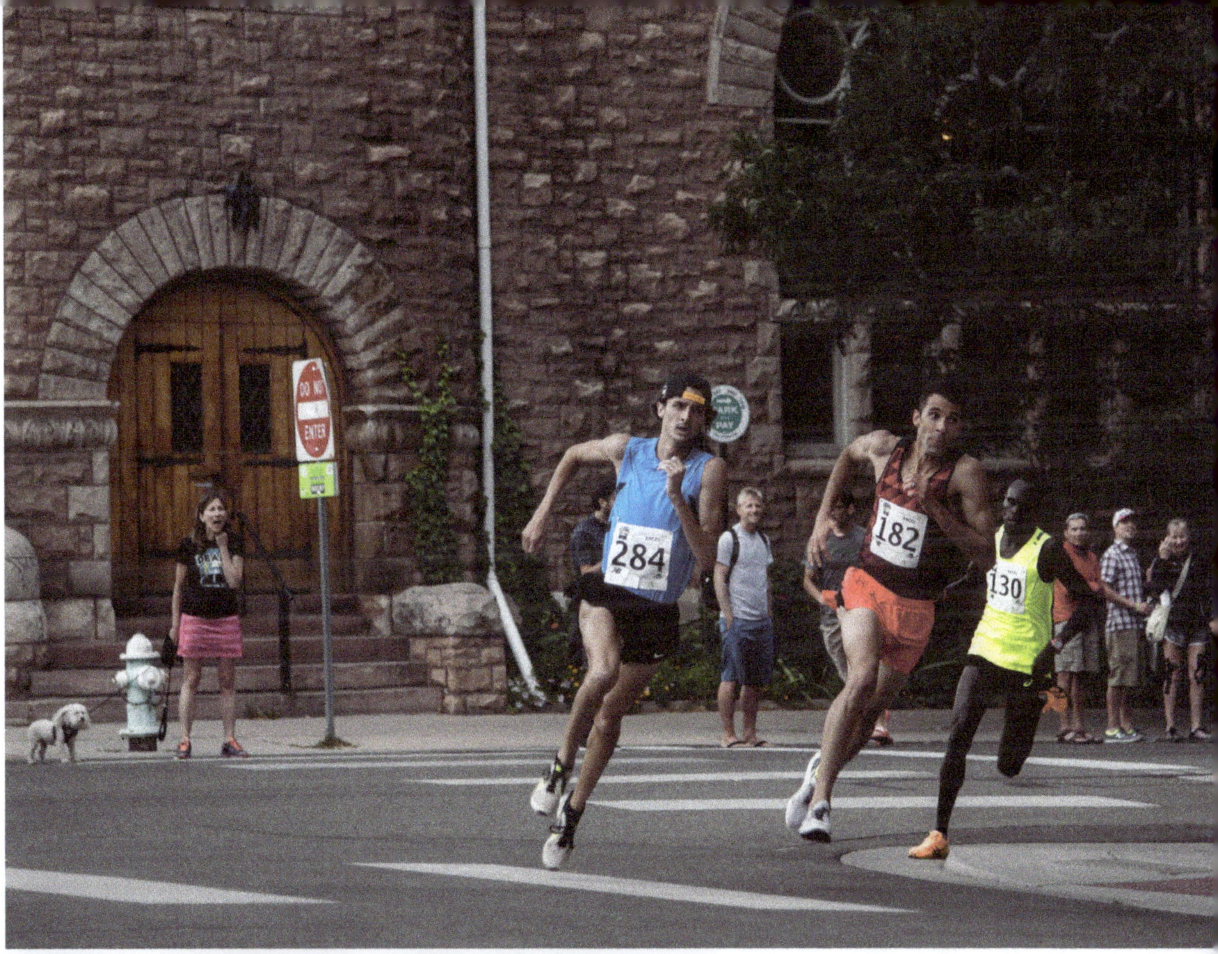

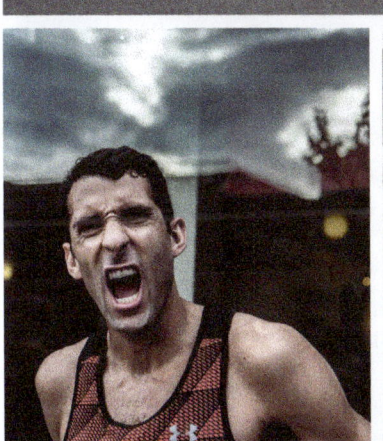
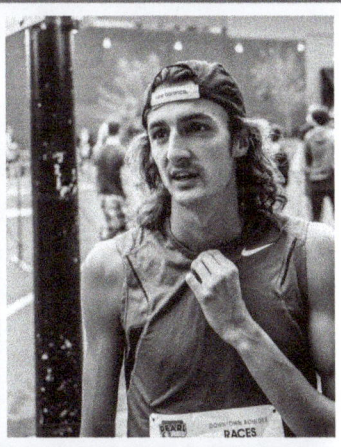

PEARL STREET MILE

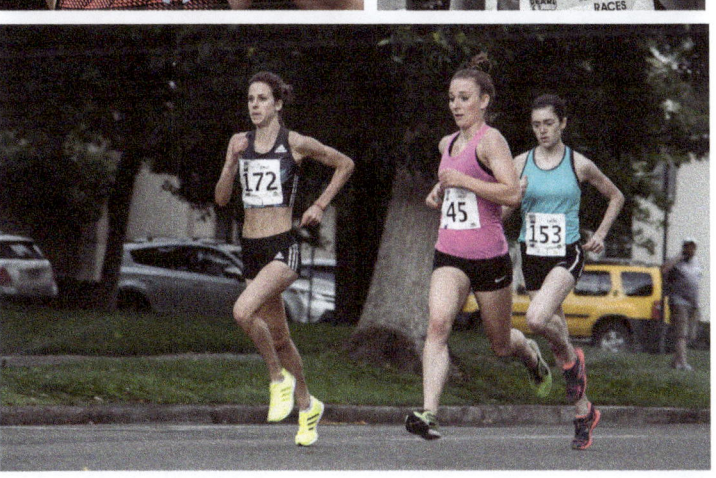

The Pearl Street Mile elite race is always fast and highly contested. This year was no different as former Buffs Blake Theroux and Stephen Pifer faced off. Blake threw down a 4:11 for the win, with Kevin Kochei (130) outleaning Pifer (182) a second later.

Former Niwot HS standout Elise Cranny (45) outkicked Katie McMenamin (153) and Mara Olson (172) for the win in 4:49.

Photos Aric Van Halen

DOUBLE

Photo James Carney

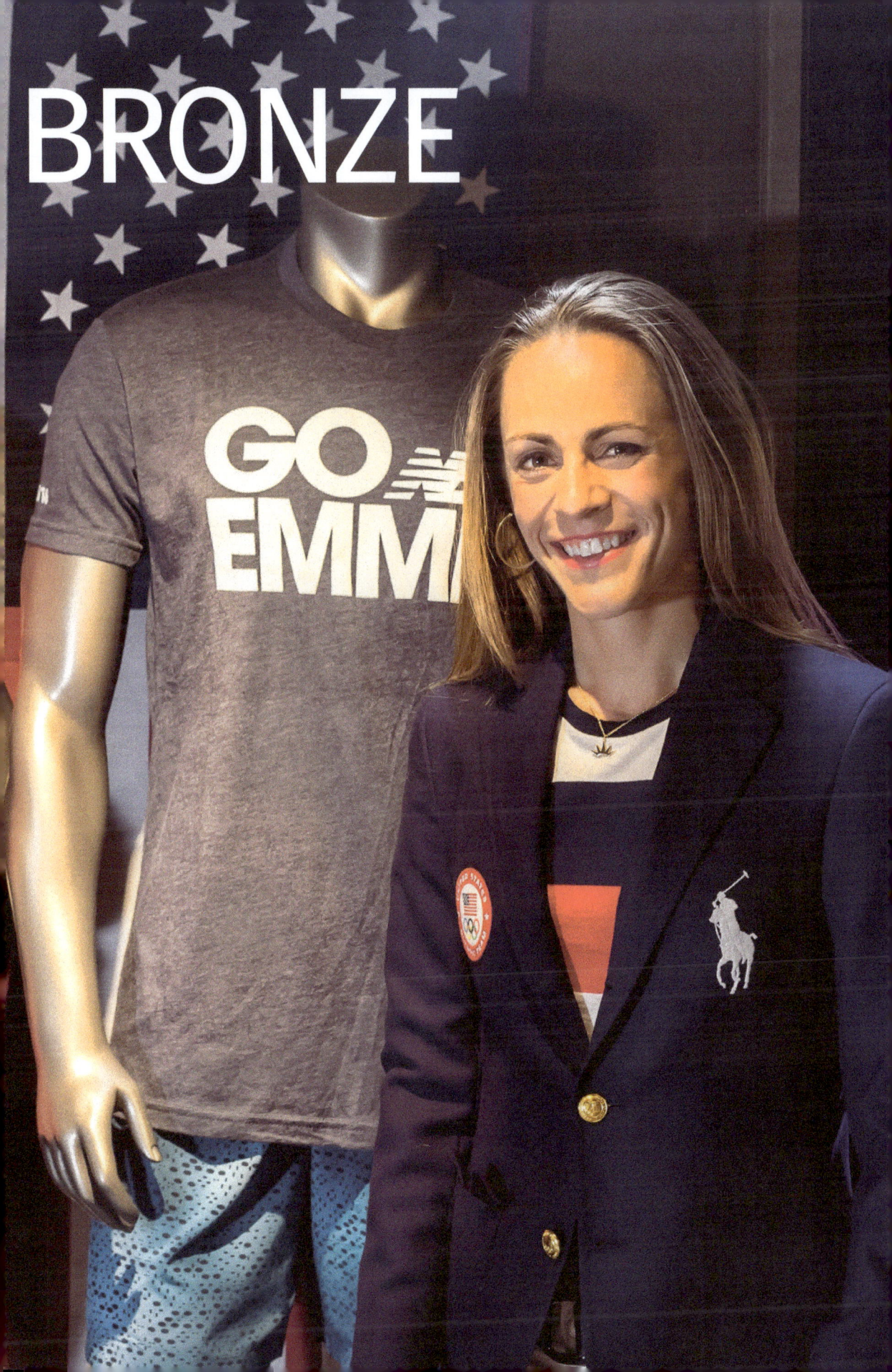

BRONZE

SEND OFF PARTY

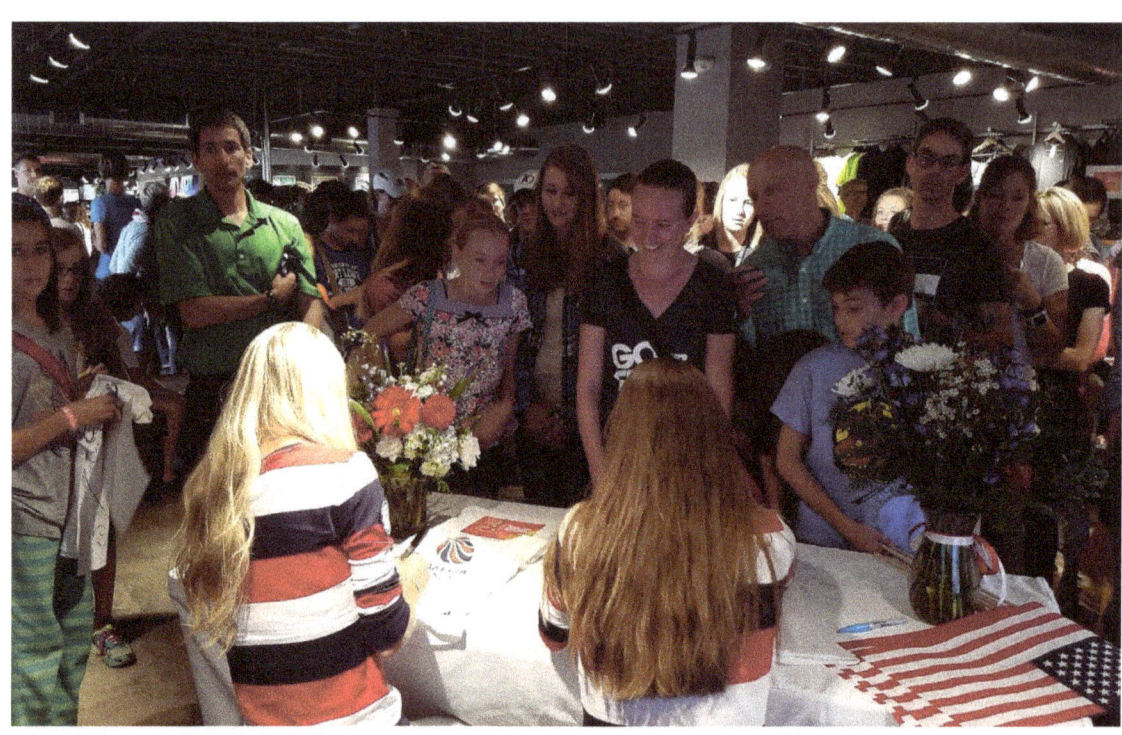

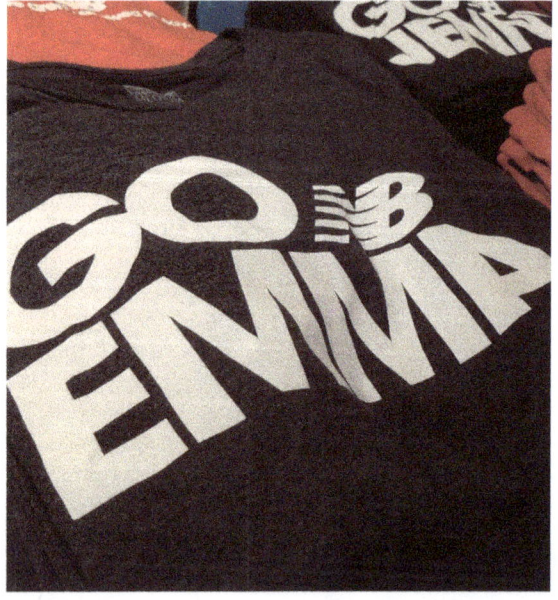

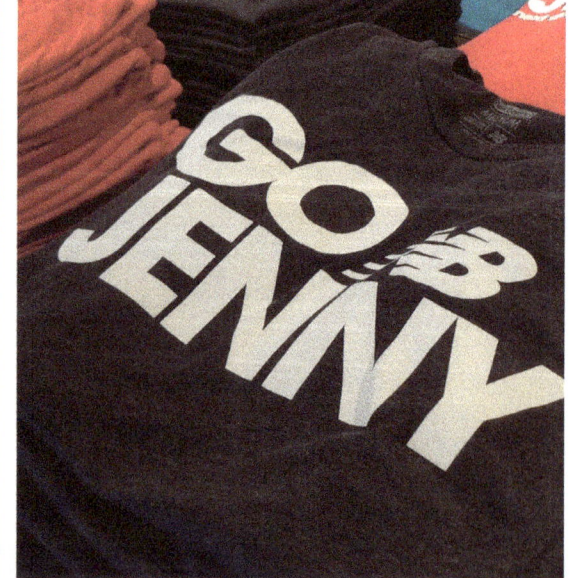

Emma Coburn earned a Bronze Medal in the 3,000-meter steeplechase. A day later Jenny Simpson stepped on the track and and also brought home the Bronze thanks to a furious kick to the finish. At the Welcome Home party hosted at Flatirons Running, Jenny and Emma gave live commentary as a video of their races played.

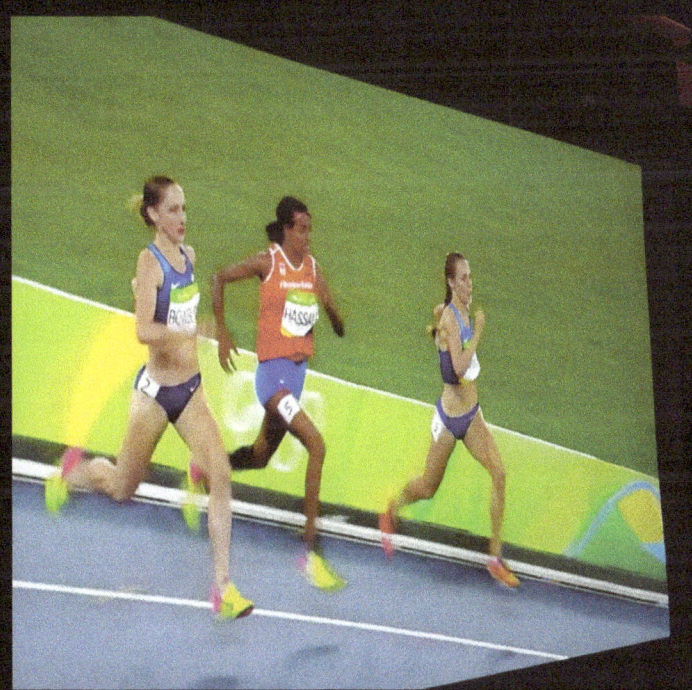

Jenny

What I will tell my kids about this race some day is that when they took off at 800m to go, they got a big gap and I realized that for myself that was too much for me. So I stuck to my race plan. I didn't reach for something and then have my race implode. That comes from running at this level for 10 years.

With 100 meters to go: This part of the race, you can never practice; this is something you have deep inside of you and you hope it comes out that day. I am not thinking about place but just running as hard as I can. If I get to the finish line as fast as possible I will be happy, no matter the results.

Emma

I knew the best chance for me to medal was a quick race, which it played out to be early on. When I race, I analyze the data and I know when I am running fast and know what my limits are. I run the limit but not over it. You have to be patient.

Just after 2k, I remember thinking, oh fourth place in the world, that's not bad. Then the second that thought was complete, I thought "Heck no, that is not ok."

After passing for third place, in my head I was thinking "Don't let her catch you." I was so concerned about not getting fourth that I didn't look up and think, "Oh, I could get second. It wasn't until the bell lap that I realized, "Hey I'm pretty close to her."

WELCOME HOME PARTY

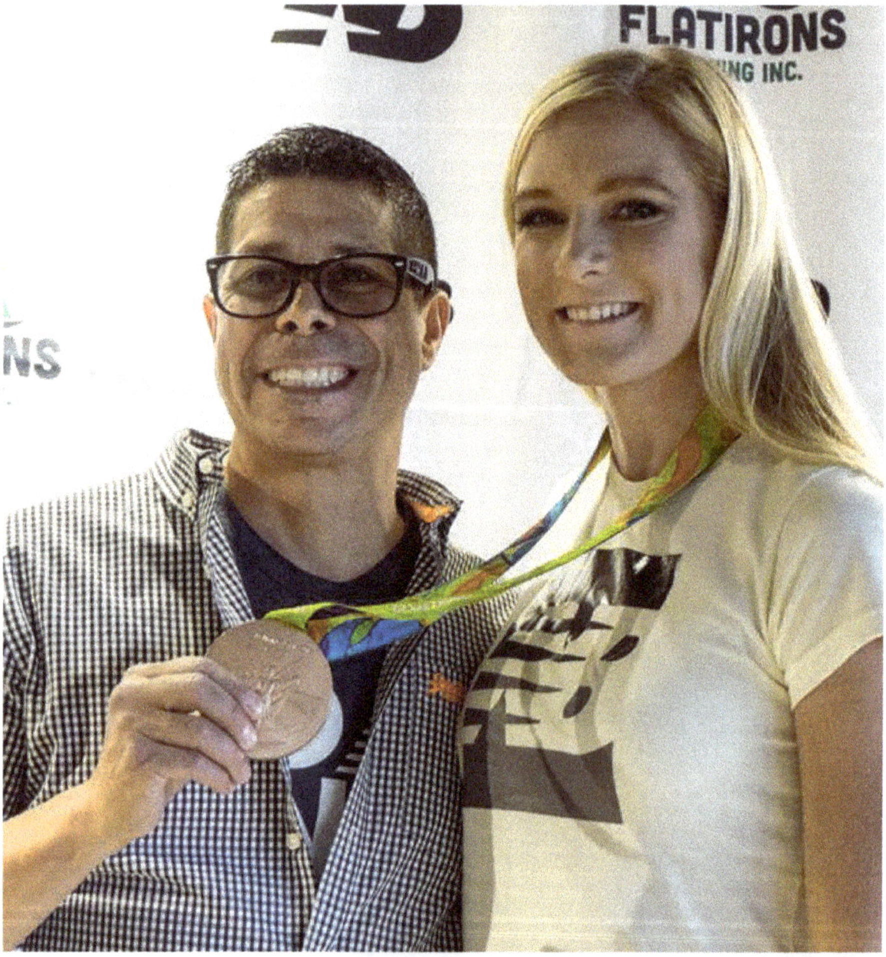

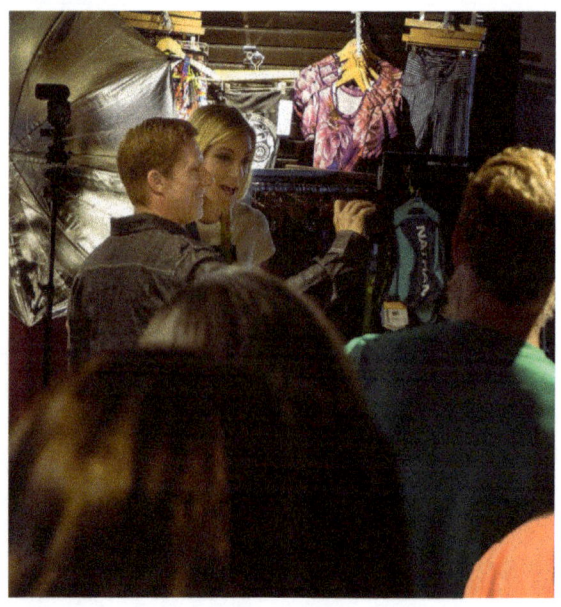

Photos Glen Delman, Todd Straka

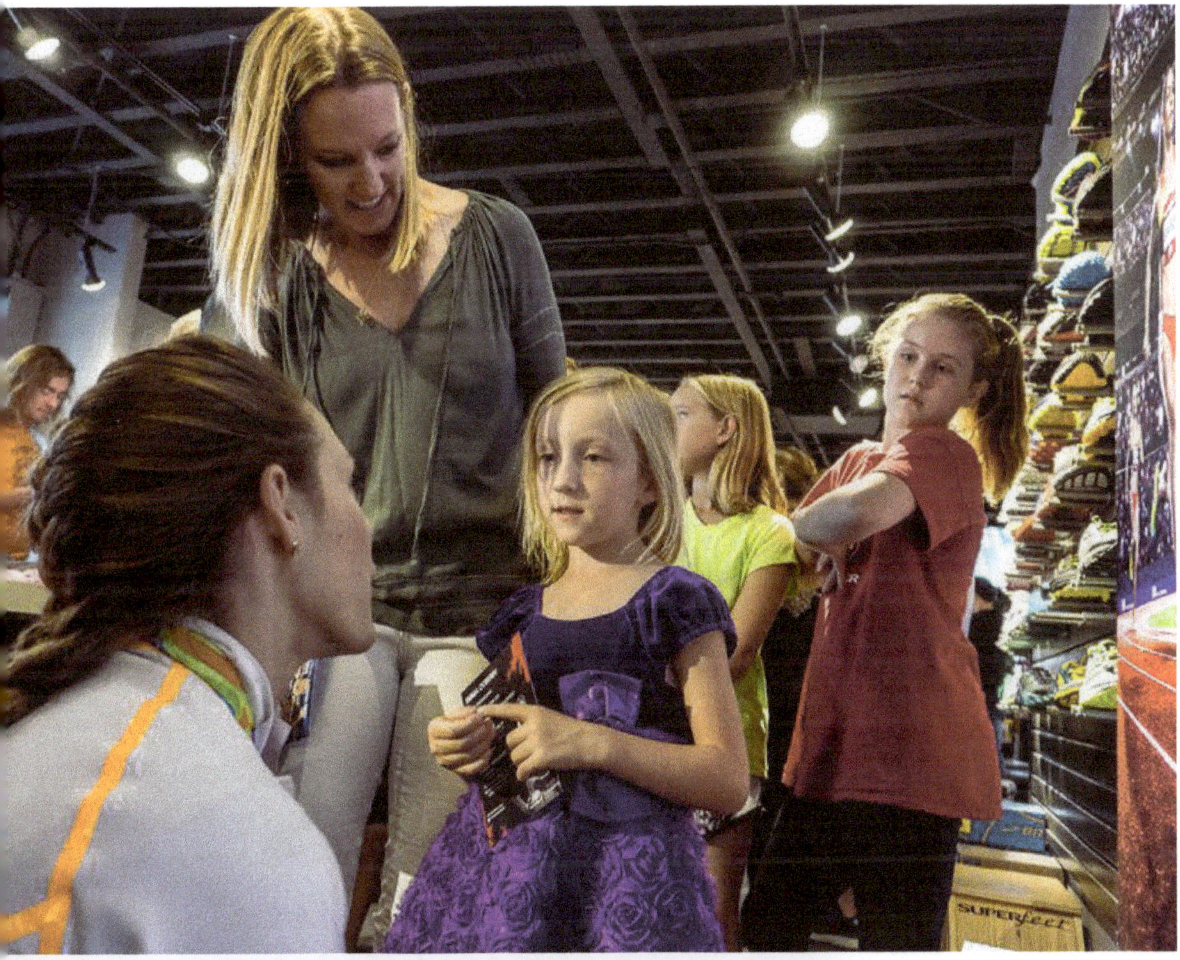

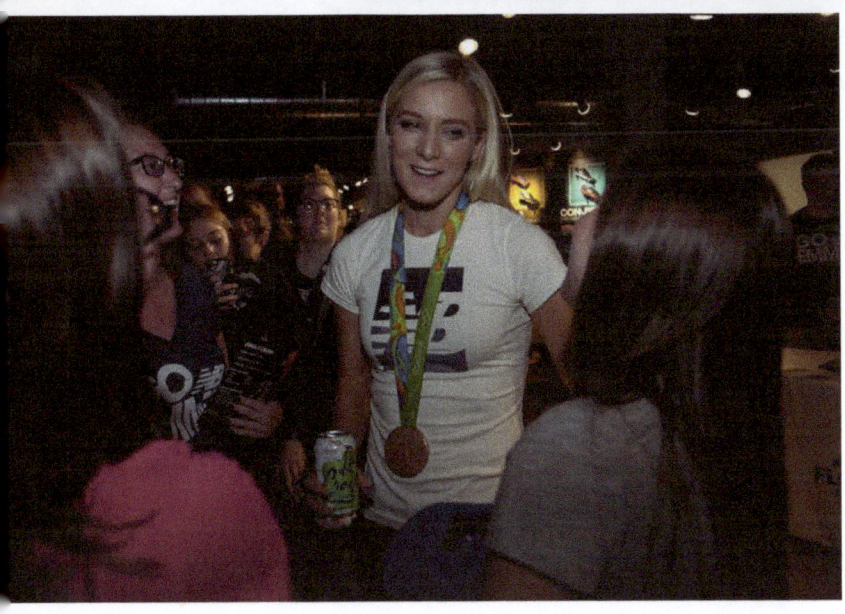

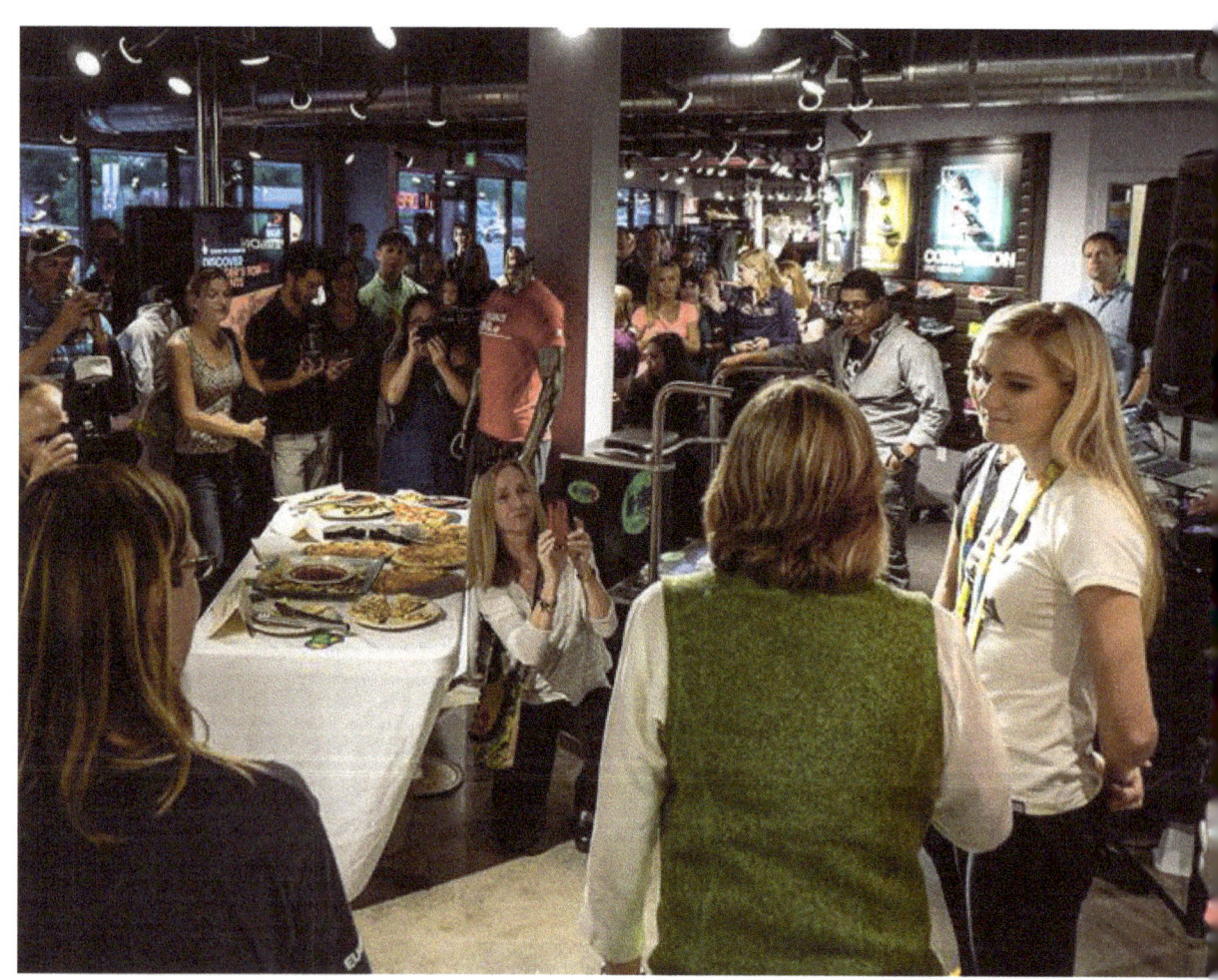
The Mayor of Boulder, Susan Jones, lauds the Olympians in front of a packed house.

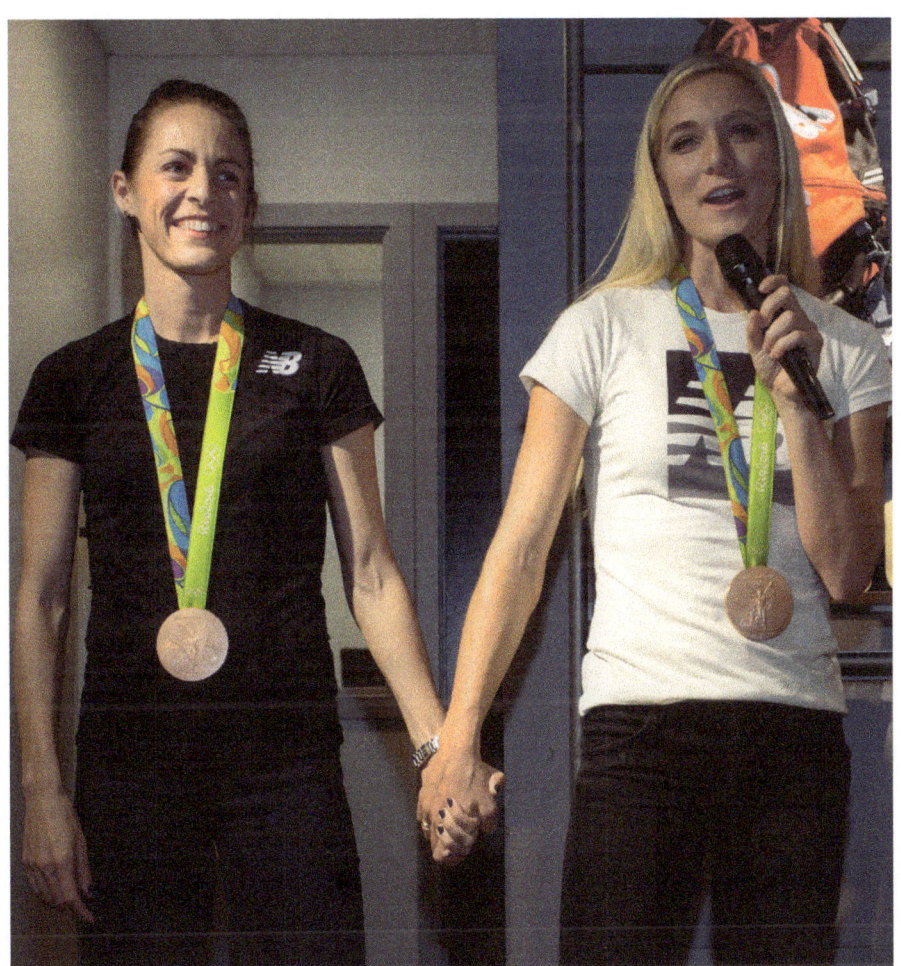

"I didn't realize how special this town is until after traveling around. Thanks for keeping us motivated and not let us slack."

"A big thank you to Jenny, who has been a friend for eight years and whom I have been inspired and motivated by. To stand here together with medals around our necks is just a dream come true."

- Emma Coburn

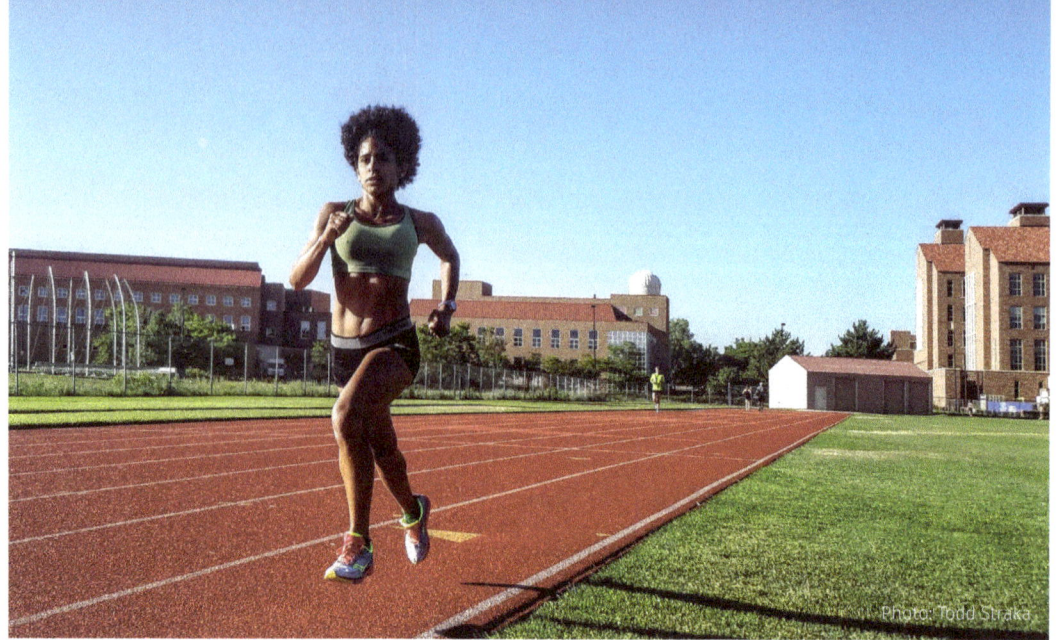

Maor Tiyouri, one of two marathoners to represent the nation of Isreal on a national team of 47 athletes in Rio, moved to Boulder to train with Coach Lee Troop and the Boulder Track Club. The Israeli national record holder in the 5,000 meters (16 minutes, 8 seconds), her aim was to make the Rio Olympics in that event. She just missed the mark, but had one last shot at the Games: run a qualifying time for the marathon, which she did at the Ottawa Marathon in her debut at the distance.

The ROAD TO RIO
is through Boulder

Many athletes and teams often visit Boulder on their way to major championships or the Olympics. Athlete agent Brendan Reilly has been sponsoring Japanese runners for several years. Surrounding Brendan are the distance runners on the Japanese Olympic team including three time Olympian Kayoko Fukushi who was 14th in the marathon in Rio, Yuka Takashima (18th - 10k), Tomomi Tanaka (19th - marathon), and Miyuki Uehara (15th- 5k).

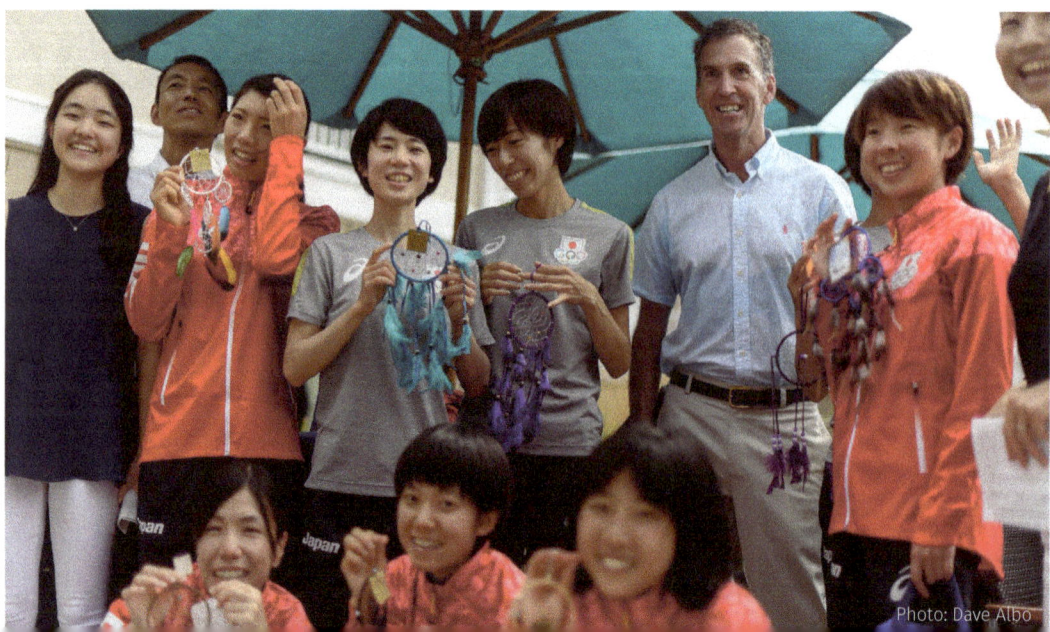

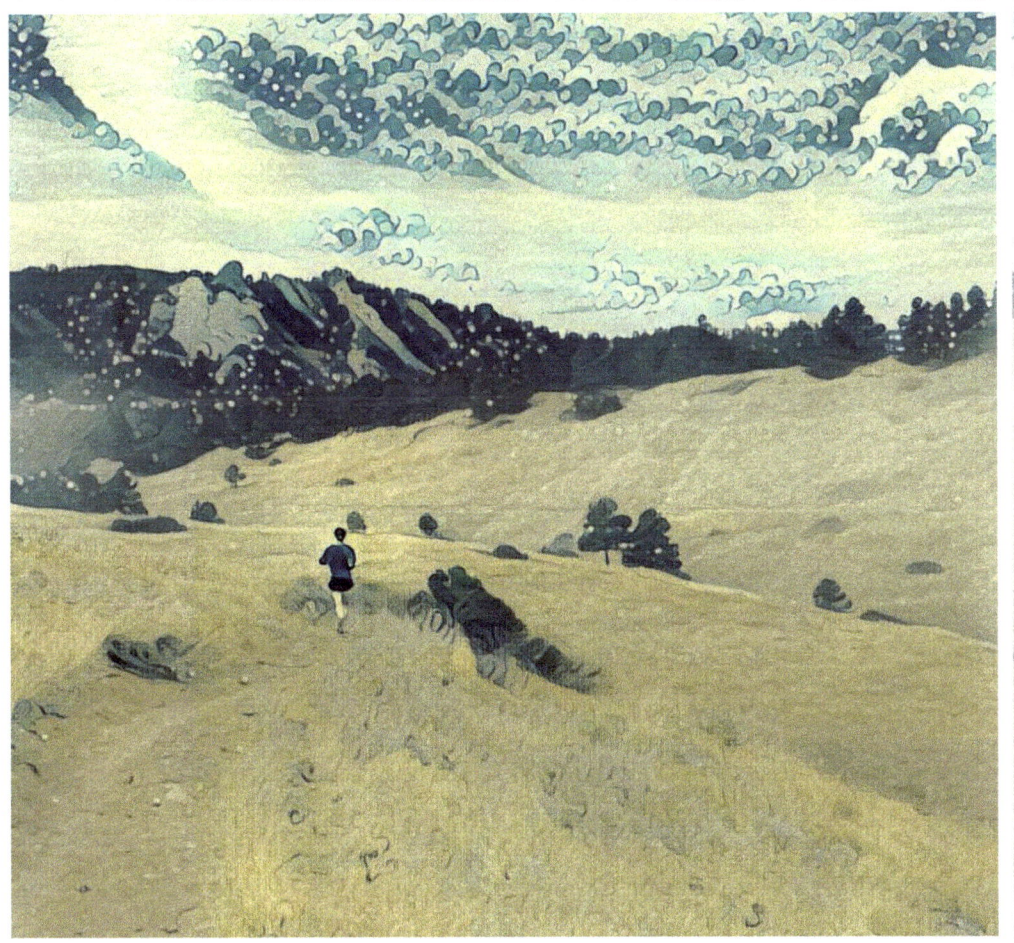

We run because we need to. We crave and rely on the jubilant respite from our sedentary society; from our taxing and mundane occupations, our drama, the world's drama, the world's suffering, our pitiful, but oh-so-powerful personal suffering.

From our worries about the future, about the unknown, about our rent, about our sick family member, about our petty coworker, about our ill-fitting jeans, about our car's impending oil change, about our positive contribution—or lack thereof—to global poverty, about how to improve the world. We yearn to suffer physically, to get away from all of it: the accruing mildew and superfluous grime of our lives. Running is our whole-body version of elbow grease; we've got steel wool on our feet! We drool over being scrubbed clean. We don't care that this 'clean' implies sweat-saturated shirts and shorts, mud caked-calves, and often bloody palms. Running is our innate, instinctive therapy: the un-copyright-able motion of rejuvenation.

Words by Clare Gallagher

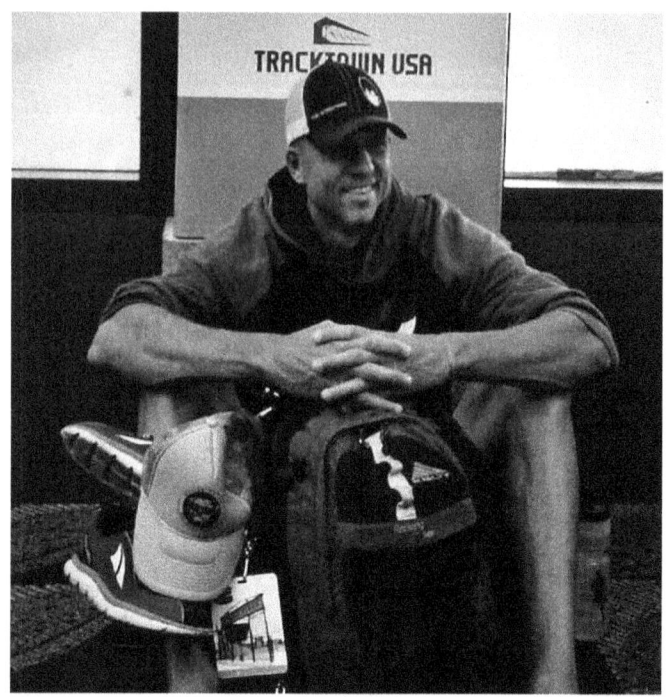

BEHIND THE SCENES
Marcus Allen Hille

Marcus Allen Hille finds many parallels between his day job as a Orthopedic & Sports Massage Therapist at the University of Colorado Sports Medicine and his side gig as the drummer for The Chasing, whose members are all runners.

During the day he works with the highest level athletes to keep their training on point and them healthy. As a drummer he drives the rhythm moving the band and the music forward. In both his body work and with the band, it is all about teamwork, trust, discipline, hard work, and preparation to be ready to perform on the big day.

Leading up to the Olympics his work took him to both the Marathon Trials in Los Angeles and Track & Field Trials in Eugene in support of a large number of local athletes with whom he works privately throughout the year. He also traveled to the Pre Classic in Eugene prior to the Track and Field Trials in support of Emma Coburn and Jenny Simpson and also to work with Ashton Eaton whose regular therapist (Don Butzner) asked him to step in while he was overseas.

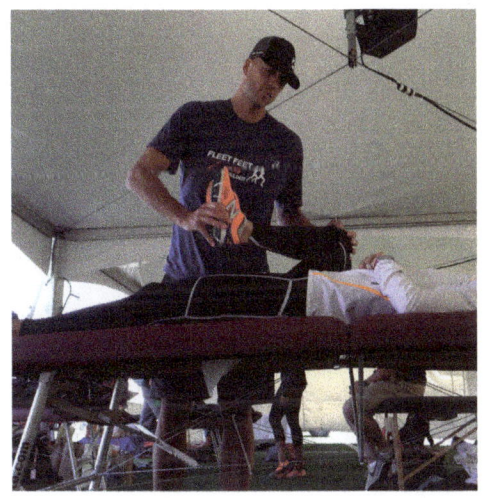 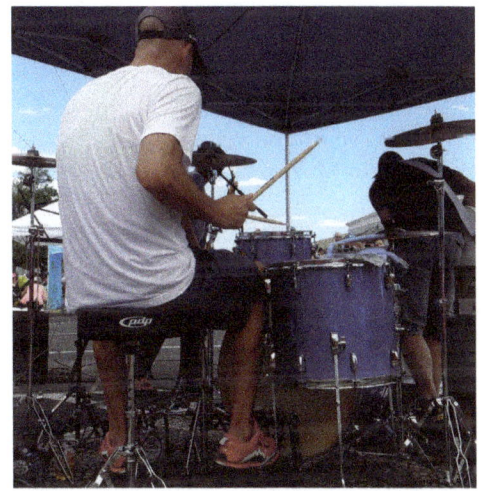

"Given that the Olympics is arguably the biggest stage on which any athlete can compete, the energy, intensity, and magnitude of the event naturally resonates throughout an athlete's support system, affecting everyone involved to some degree. It was definitely an exciting, emotional, and electrifying experience. That said, it is still just a track meet. Our preparation was the same and occupied the same sphere of consistency, trust, and hard work as it did at the office in Boulder throughout the year. Professionally, to be able to see our work through to the end was awesome. We worked incredibly hard to get to this point so to be present and witness the culmination of everything that went into those last few moments meant everything to me as a therapist."

"On a personal level, to have the opportunity help support people for whom I have developed a deep fondness, appreciation, and respect, not just as athletes but also as human beings, ties together so much of why I do this work and what life means to me. Basically, everything meaningful comes down to connection and a commitment to self-improvement. The relationships which naturally develop through this work combined with the purpose-driven aspect of athletics and sport seems to create a prime space to explore, discover, and learn, which is the most valuable aspect of work and play that I can imagine."

"The most significant parallel between my work and music has to do with the internal place from which both disciplines originate. Manual therapy and music, for me, extend from a depth of interest and appreciation for connection and its ability to heal and transform. Both disciplines are an expression of creativity and skill as well as a sensitivity and connection to the world around me, and from this tiny space I occupy and share with others."

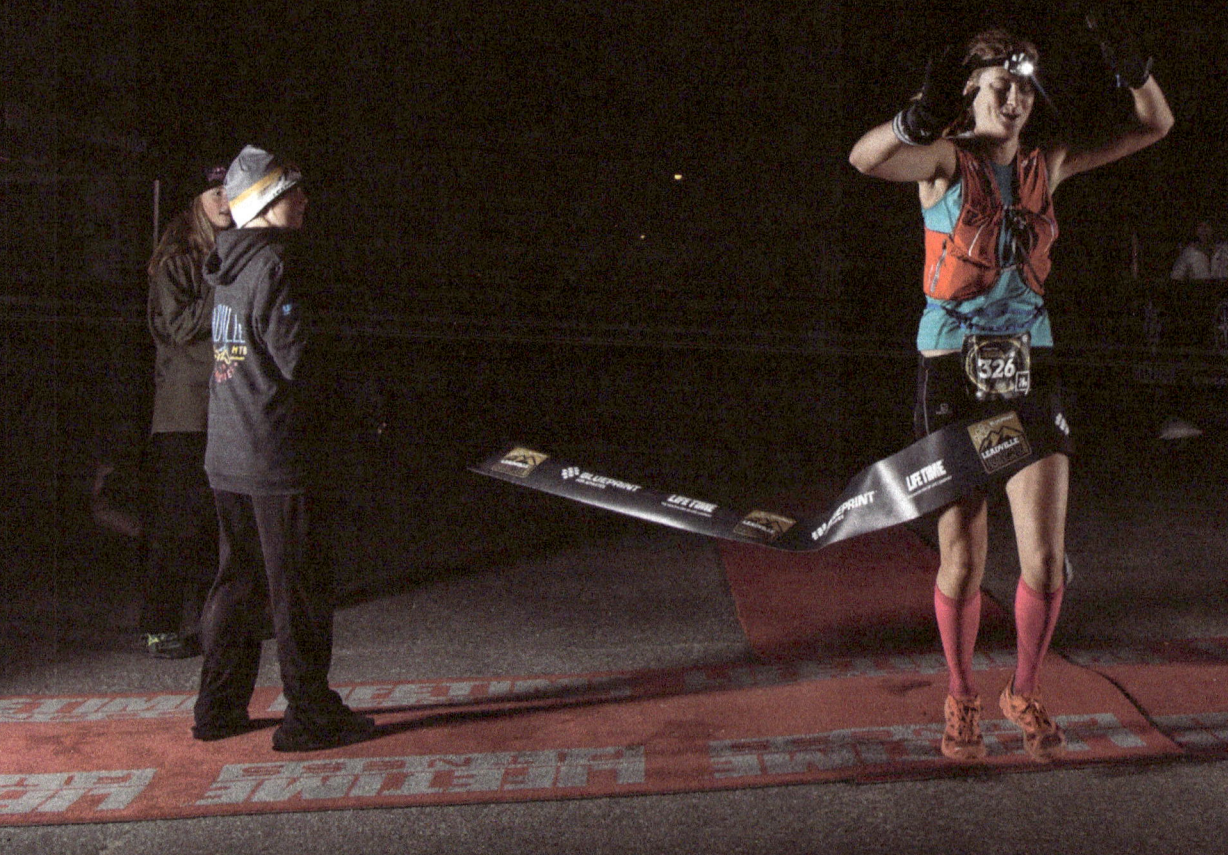

Photos Glen Delman

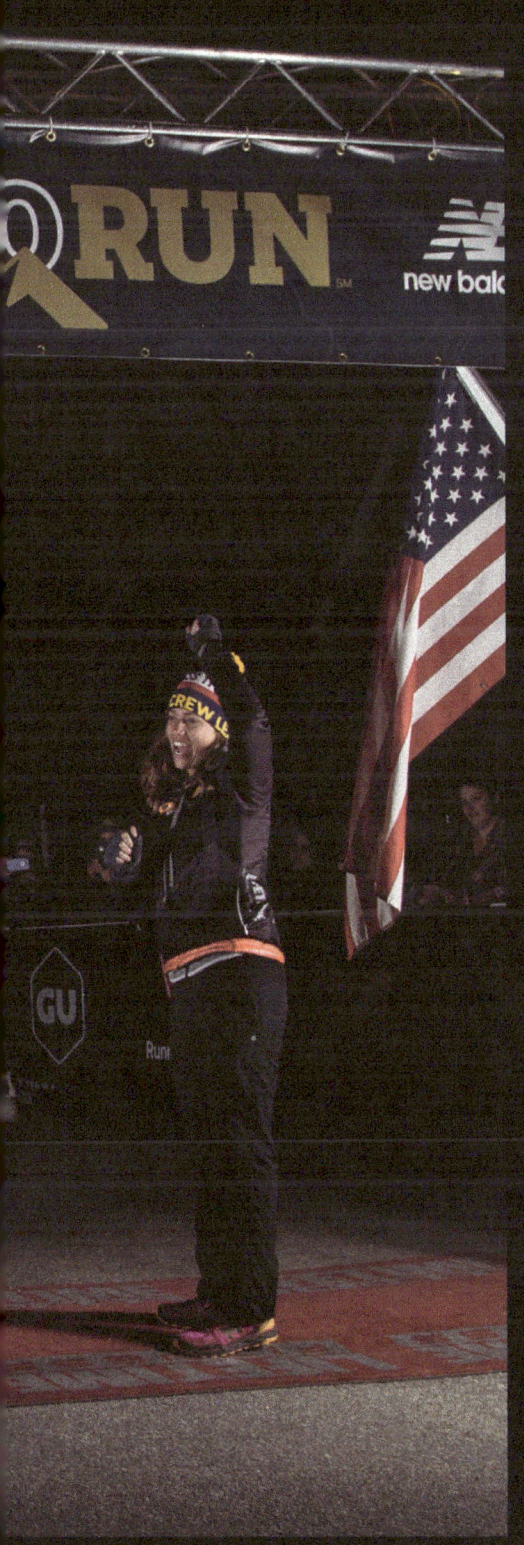

LEADWOMAN

Boulder's Clare Gallagher took the win at this year's Leadville 100 Trail Race. While virtually an unknown earlier in the year, this Colorado raised girl took to ultra running after running at Princeton and a teaching stint in Thailand. Here is what she had to say about her big day.

Since I could read the Denver Post sports section, you just know of Leadville. My family is just involved in 14ers/mountain activities and I just grew up doing those activities all the time.

We would drive through Leadville on the way to the mountains and my dad would be like 'Hey Kids, this is where they do some crazy races.' It never quite clicked that could possibly be me one day.

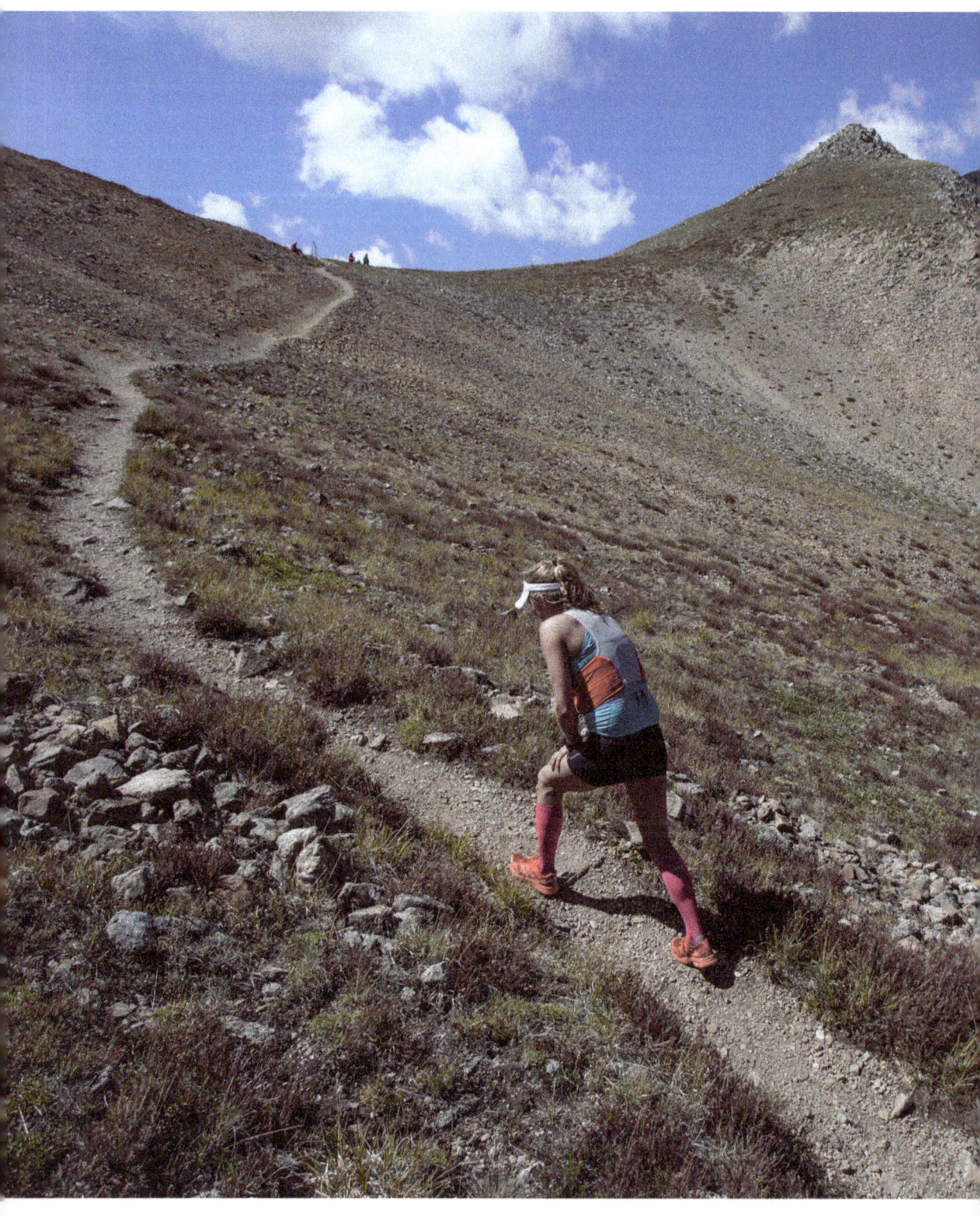

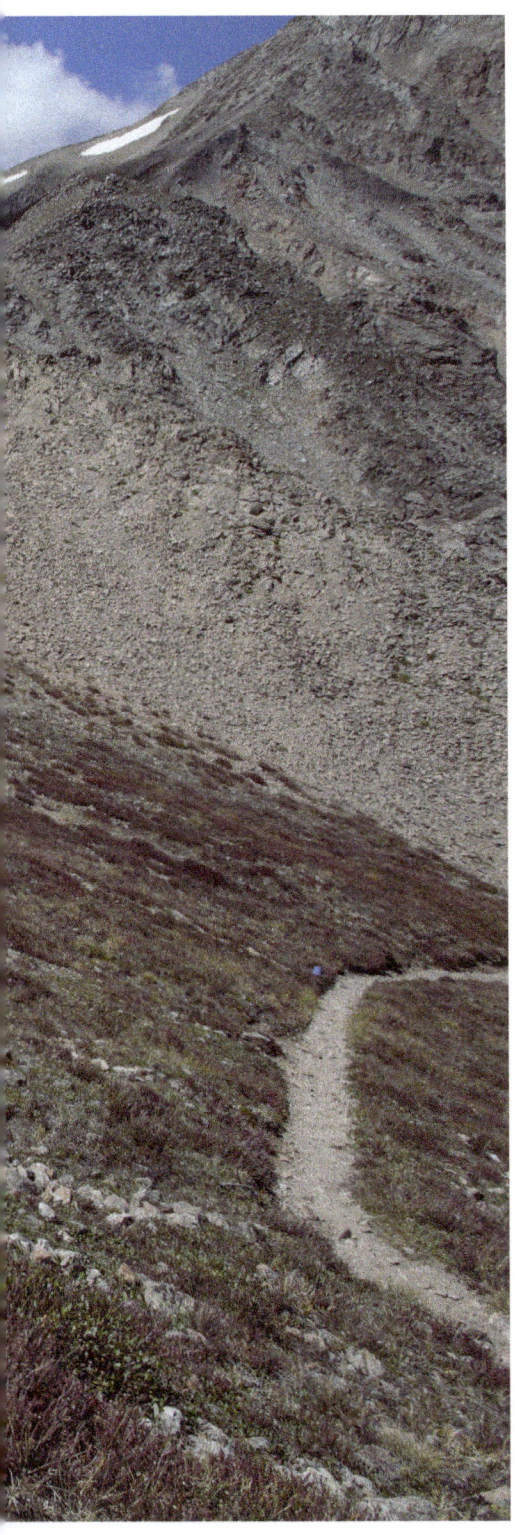

In terms of feasibility, this just made sense. It's local, not trying to buy a plane ticket and to honor the mining history that is so part of Colorado. To have a race have a historical element to it is so nice.

Eating was good. Towards the beginning my fueling was good. I was putting in so many calories. People were disgusted: frosting out of the can, sour patch kids, snickers, a few gels, rice balls. At the end I acquiesced to gels.

Favorite food: I am a celiac. Most of the food is gluten free. Frosting is the best, normally just out of the jar. Rice balls with vanilla frosting, chocolate frosting and peanut butter. Almond butter and Sriracha. At the May Queen Aid Station I had chicken broth. It was clutch. People drink it for a reason.

I only cried once about mile 74. It's almost necessary to check off all the emotions. Overall I tried to stay really, really positive, or else what's the point?

COUNTERPOINT

DEATH BY 100 CUTS

Words by Caolan MacMahon

As I sit at Hopeless, sucking down broth and noodles, shivering in the cutting wind, I know that I am giving up hope of making it through the last aid station cut-off time. The decision, though, is out of my hands. And, importantly, the decision is also made without the information I need. Information I don't ask for because I believe it's already over. The vicious circle of thoughts flush my dreams away.

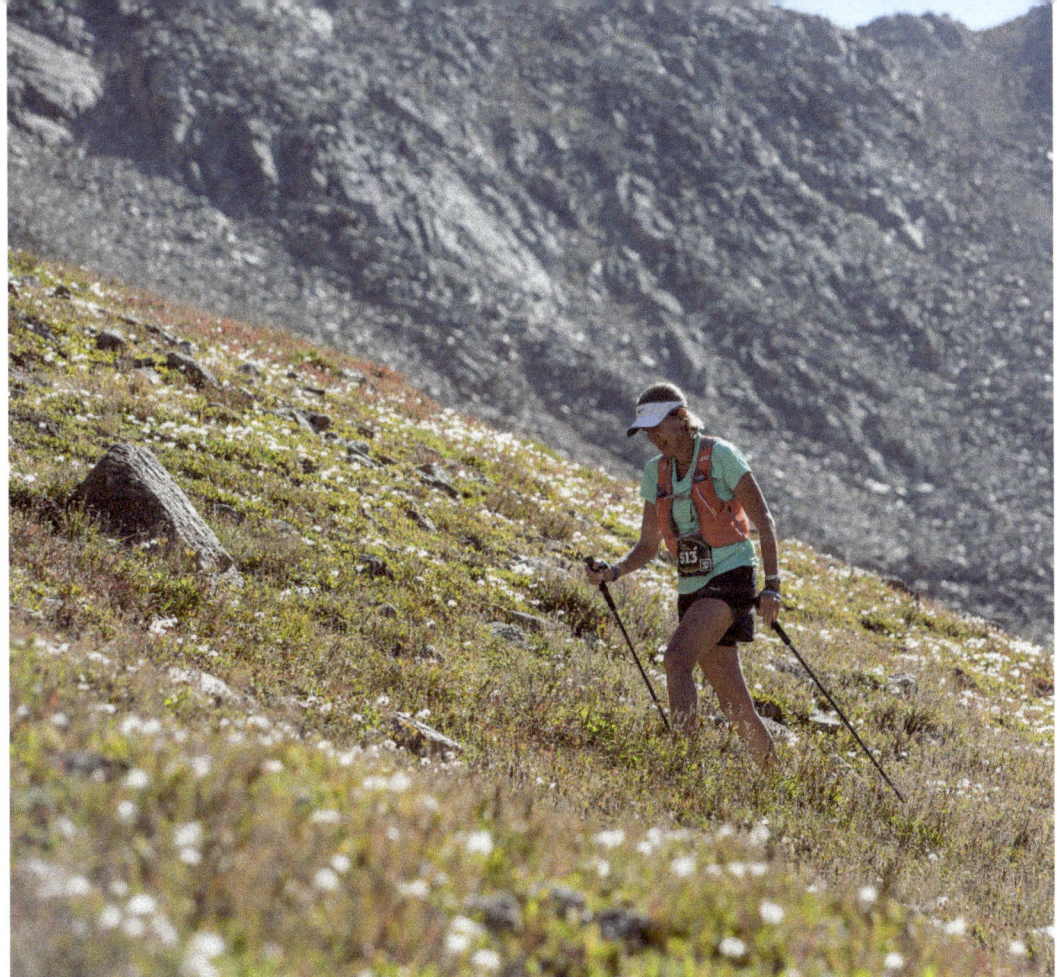

"Only those who will risk going too far can possibly find out how far one can go." ~T.S. Eliot

After the soup settles in I feel better and we make our way down. Now there's no hurry since it's already a done deal. The final insult is that my body, my muscles and tendons, feel better at this point than any of my previous 100s. But the Leadville Trail 100, the "Race Across the Sky", did not go as I hoped it would. After decades of running and racing, I left Leadville with my first DNF instead of a shiny new belt buckle.

After much reflection, I have surmised these to be my three biggest challenges.

1) Aid station management: I took too long and had a hard time adjusting to the set-up that Leadville had.

2) Fueling: I let things slide on my fueling when I shouldn't have. The deficit started early and by the end it was too late to catch up. As I walked down the road to Winfield a woman stood by cheering me on and I bellowed "I'M HUNGRY!!" But the rush and chaos at Winfield was the final nail in my coffin. Because I was already behind on fueling at this point I had to eat here or I had to grab more for the return trip over the pass. I did neither. And as we left Winfield I passed that cheering woman again, and I remember saying "I'm STILL HUNGRY!!"

3) Poor crew and pacer management: If I were to do this again I would give my crew very specific instructions. They did a great job, but again, little things got me. I should have had them collect food and carry for me. Muling is allowed but I carried all my own gear and fluids. I have a hard time asking people to do these things, but it may have made all the difference.

There is the issue of pushing one's limits, but there's also the issue of making the right decisions along the way. Often little decisions do not seem terribly important, but over time they add up. When time is precious, the plan must me tight and solid, while flexible enough to deal with the unforeseen. I had the flexibility but lacked the essentials of the plan. This lesson will not be forgotten.

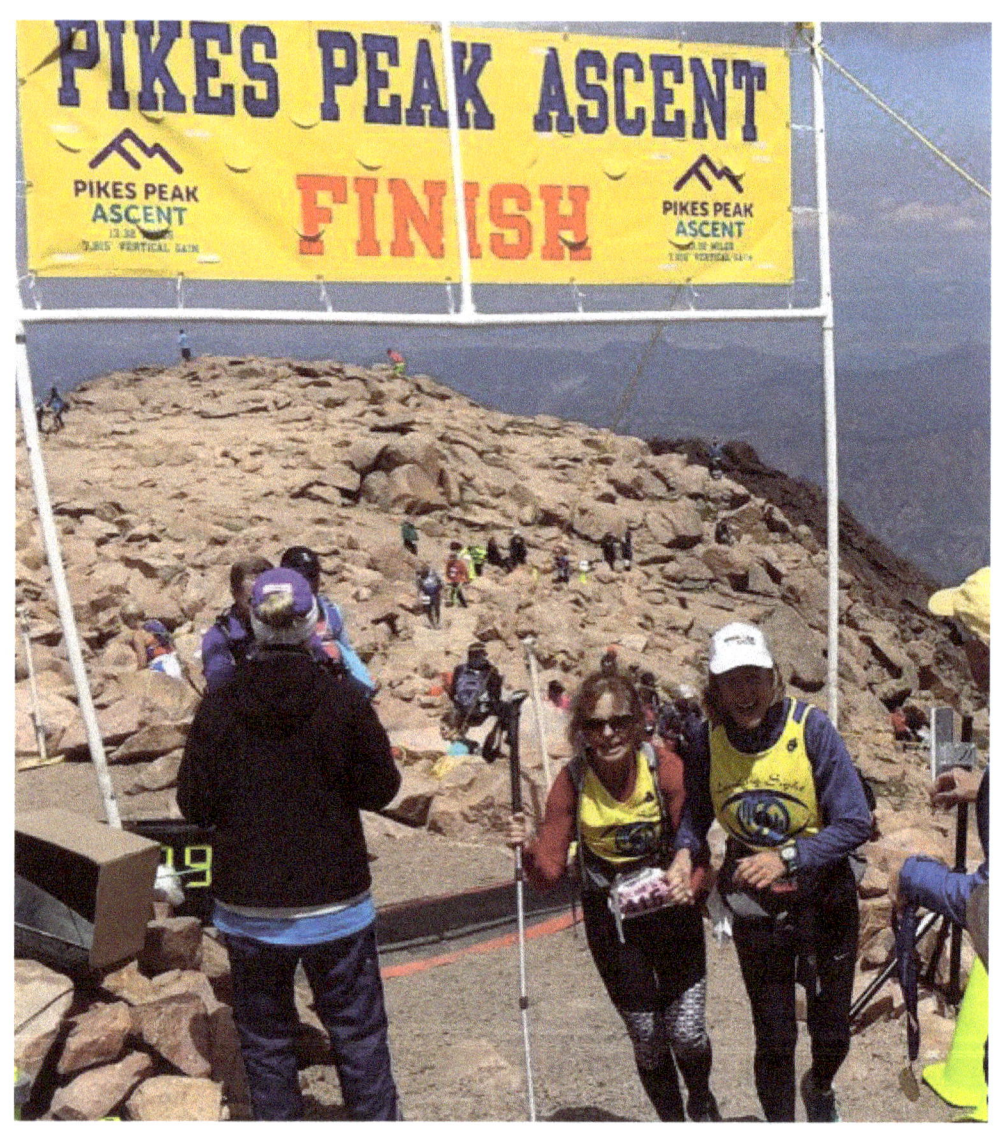

BlindAmbition

On August 20, Boulder's Luanne Burke, with guides J'ne Day-Lucore and Jessica Oldham, became the first blind runner to ever attempt and complete the Pikes Peak Ascent.

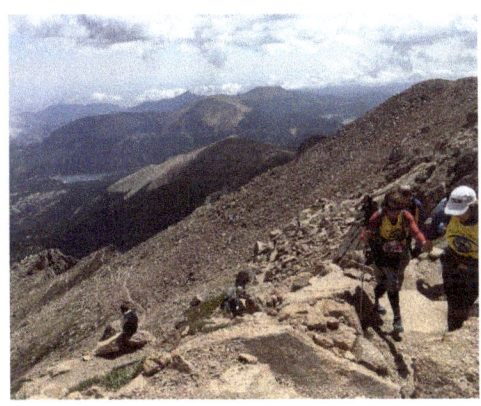 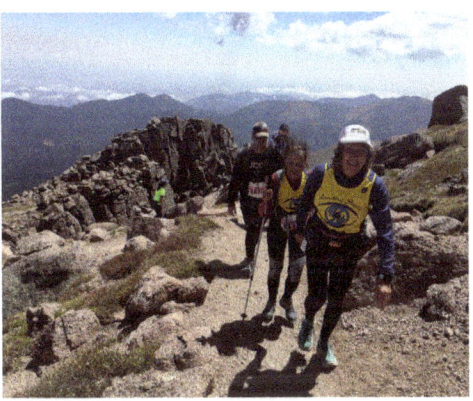

The Pikes Peak races are considered to be the world's most difficult half and full marathon. The Ascent course is a challenging climb with an elevation gain of 7,800 feet over its 13.32 miles. It is a narrow rocky course requiring intervals of climbing, running and bouldering.

Burke, 51, finished the grueling event in 6:12:23. Her successful summit during the Ascent also marked her completion of the Triple Crown of Running, which also includes the Garden of the Gods 10-miler and the Summer Roundup Trail Run. A strong competitor, Burke had finished third in the Garden of the Gods race and won her age group by a ten-minute margin in the Roundup, securing a course record by six minutes. With her Ascent finish, she took third place in her age group in the Triple Crown.

Burke has a degenerative eye condition called retinitis pigmentosa. She had little to no night vision at a very early age. By nineteen she could no longer drive a car. But she has been a runner since she was fourteen years of age and remained one through each of the stages of her condition.

Despite her demonstrated strength in the prior two Triple Crown races, going into the Pikes Peak ascent, Burke realized her competitive edge would wane as she climbed the rocky face. "Being blind slows the process of climbing and navigating," she said. She listened to cues from Day-Lucore and Oldham, climbing over rocks, around and through streams and along root-filled trails.

She closed her eyes and focused on the listening.

"I did not want to be distracted by bits of light shooting through the forest, or light landing on a rock that might make me hesitate. I just listened and felt my way up the mountain."

"I kind of looked at this race as my Camino [de Santiago, a famous pilgrimage route in Spain]," Burke recalled. "I even cried a little as the crowd cheered me in. It is not my nature to be team-oriented. I am an introvert by nature, and it is only athletics that brings out the extroversion in me. I did Pikes Peak with a team of incredibly athletic women who were willing to help me get to the top.

"It was my Camino because I had never been on this mountain until two weeks before the race, and I had never done the whole thing until race day. I am forced to accept my blindness in times like this. I can prepare for a race as much as time, guides and circumstance will allow. To me it was a race that forced me to embrace my total blindness that has been slowly coming and has finally arrived. Of course this is bittersweet, and it was the first time I ever embraced a crowd cheering for me. It feels so exposing but it is the truth.

"What is also true is that I love to run. I love the feeling of legs and arms moving in a rhythm. I love getting in that groove and lifting away to a higher place," she said, adding with a smile, "That is why I don't like my guides to talk too much."

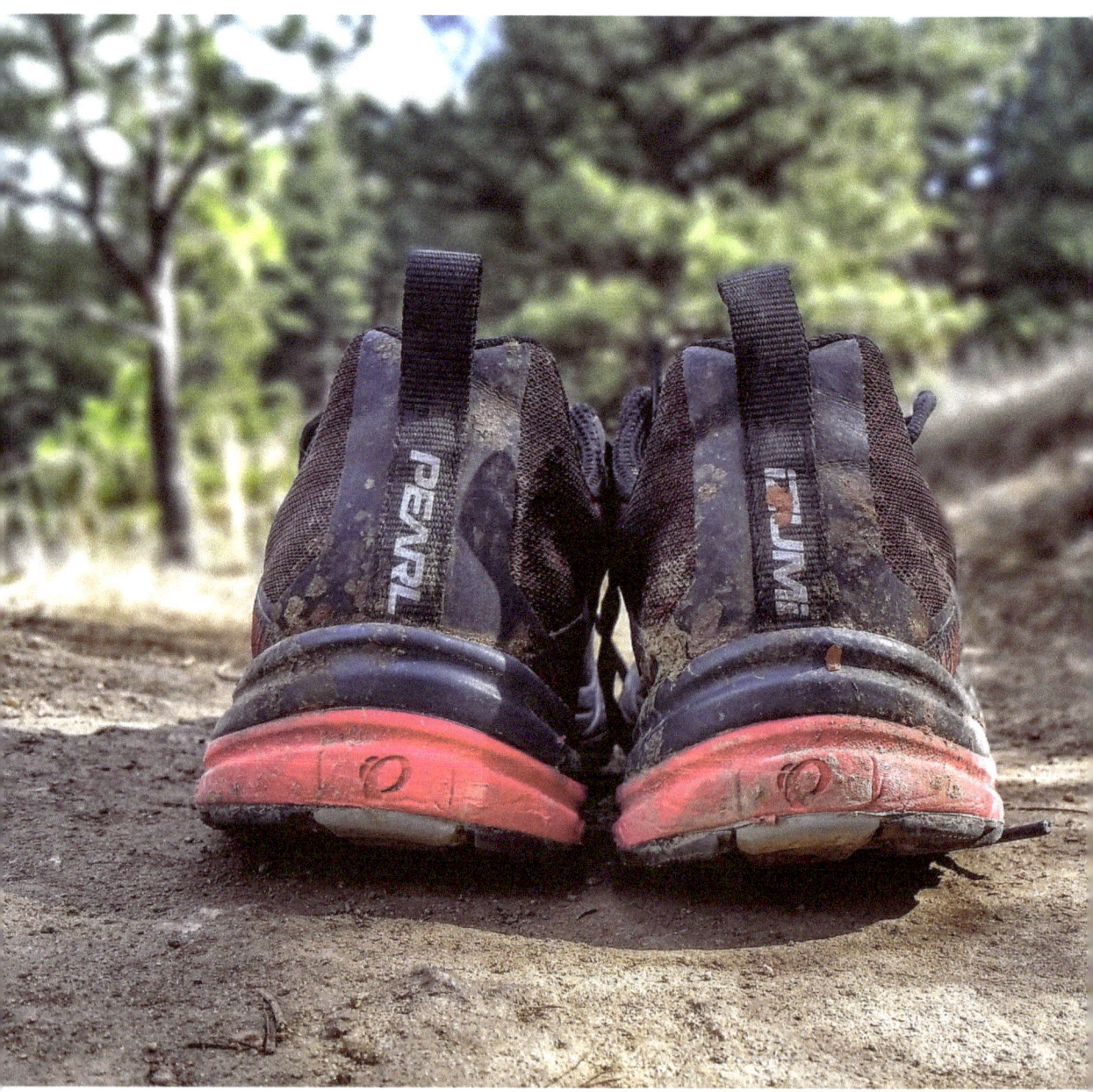

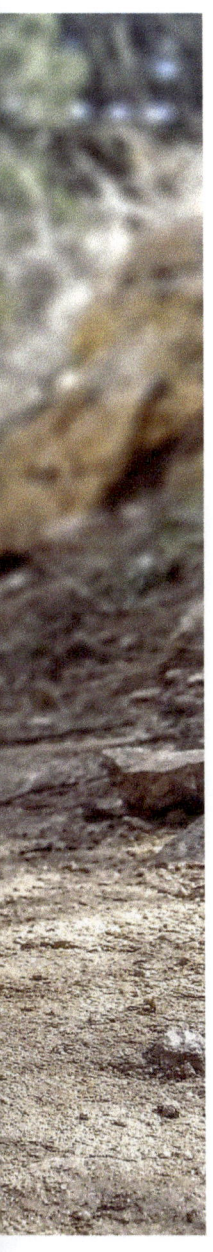

Bye - Bye Pearl

In August Pearl Izumi of Louisville, CO announced it would be pulling out of the running market in Jan. 2017 in order focus on its core cycling business.

"Over the past 13 years, our Run team has designed award-winning product and gained a loyal consumer following. This is a tough decision, but it's time to recommit to our core."

- Mike O'Connor, Pearl Izumi's President

"We want to sincerely thank our Run customers, sales reps, retailers, distributors, and Champion Team who have not only helped shape the Pearl Izumi brand but have been vocal ambassadors for our gear."

- Chuck Sanson, Director of Run for Pearl Izumi

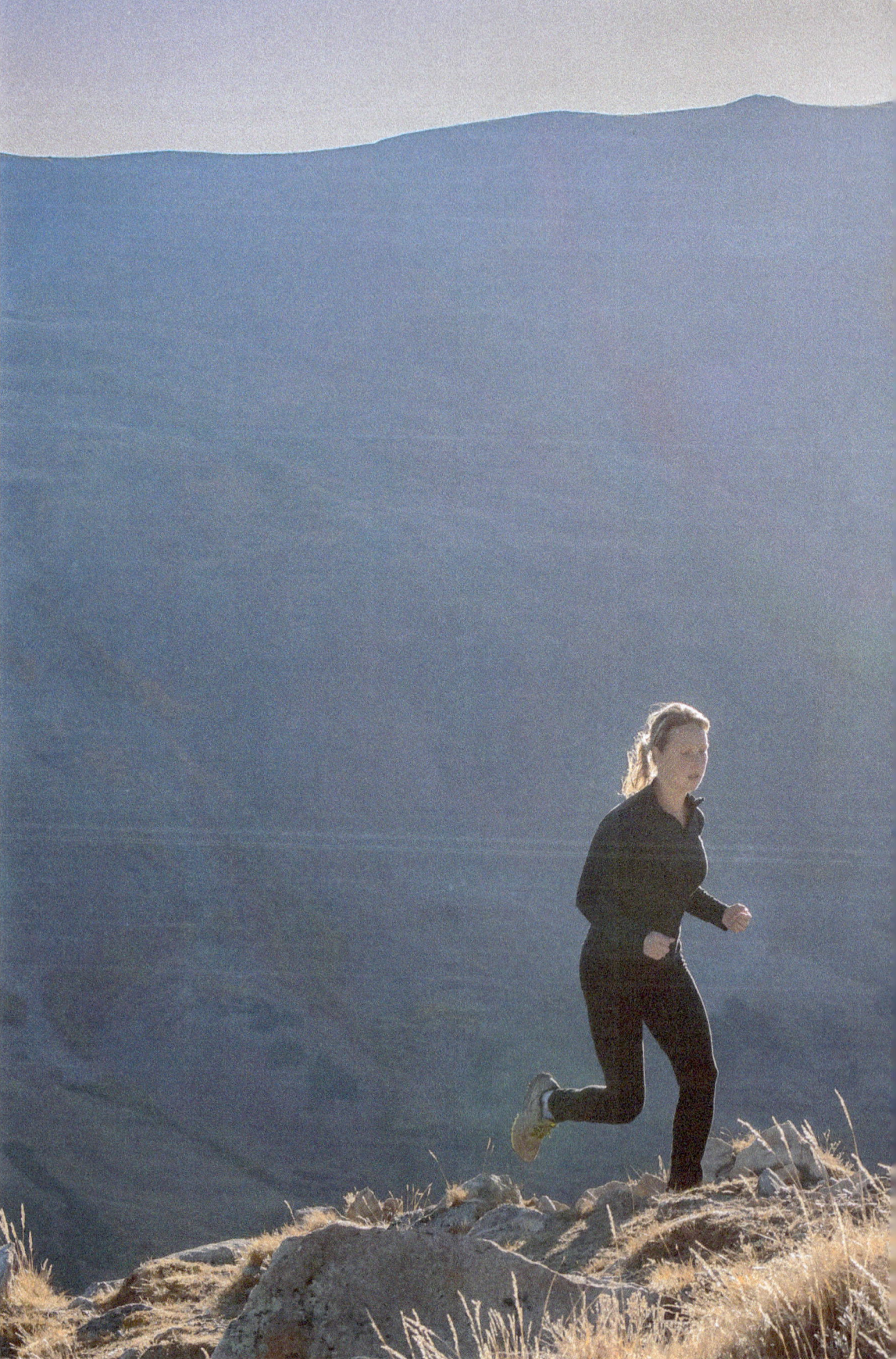

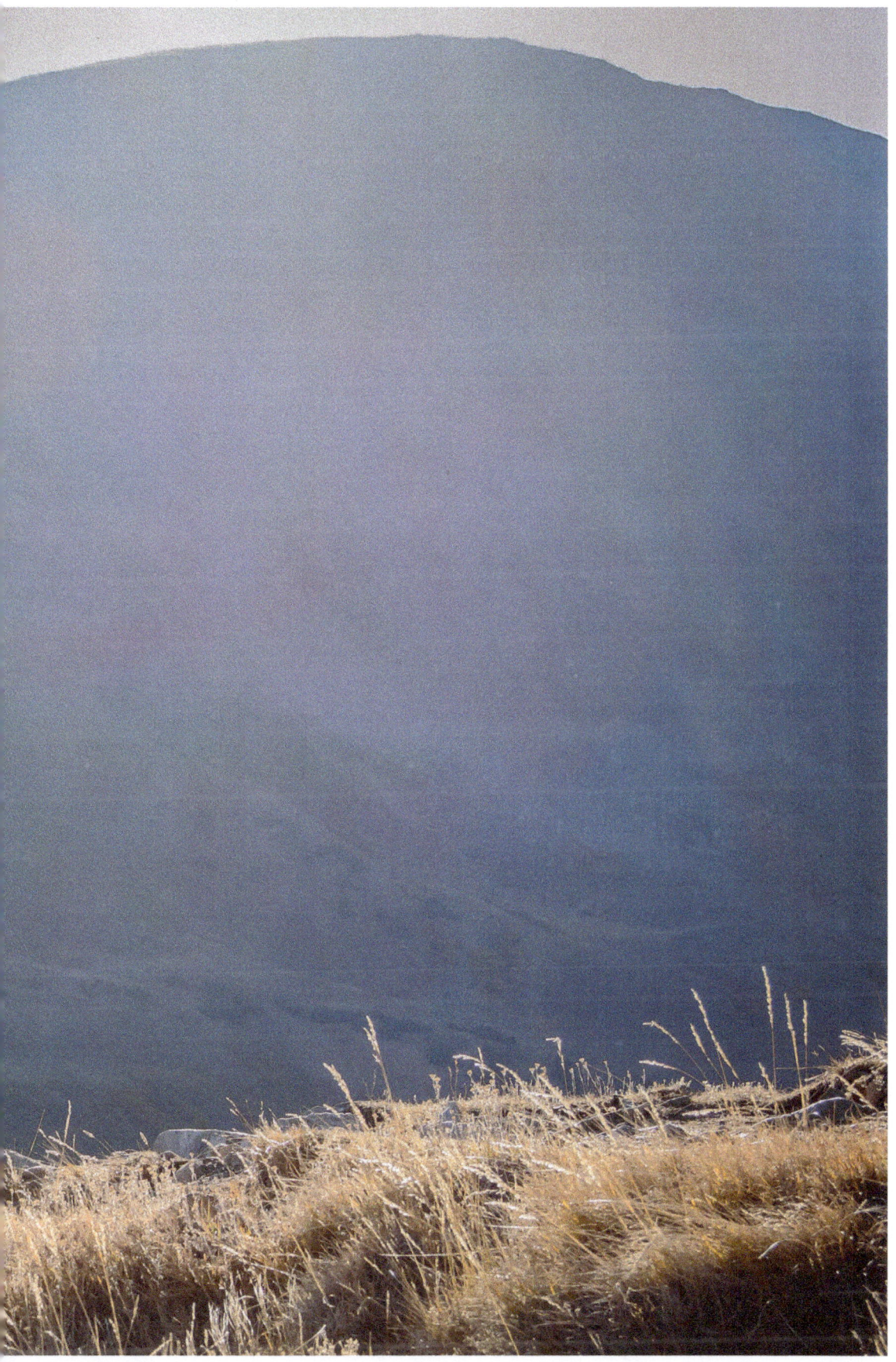

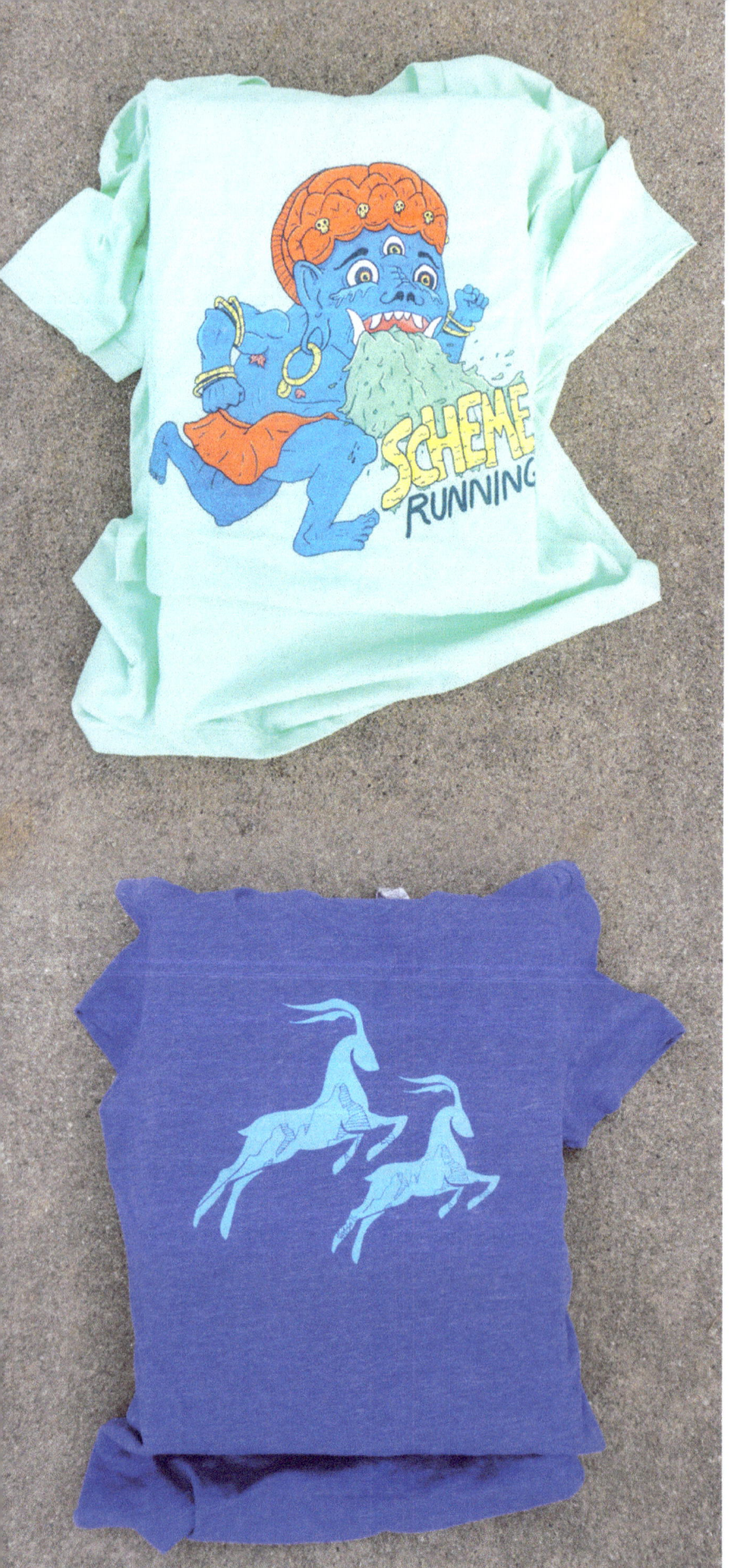

Scheme Running
Mara
SchemeRunning.bigcartel.com

Trail Sisters
Gazelle
TrailSisters.net

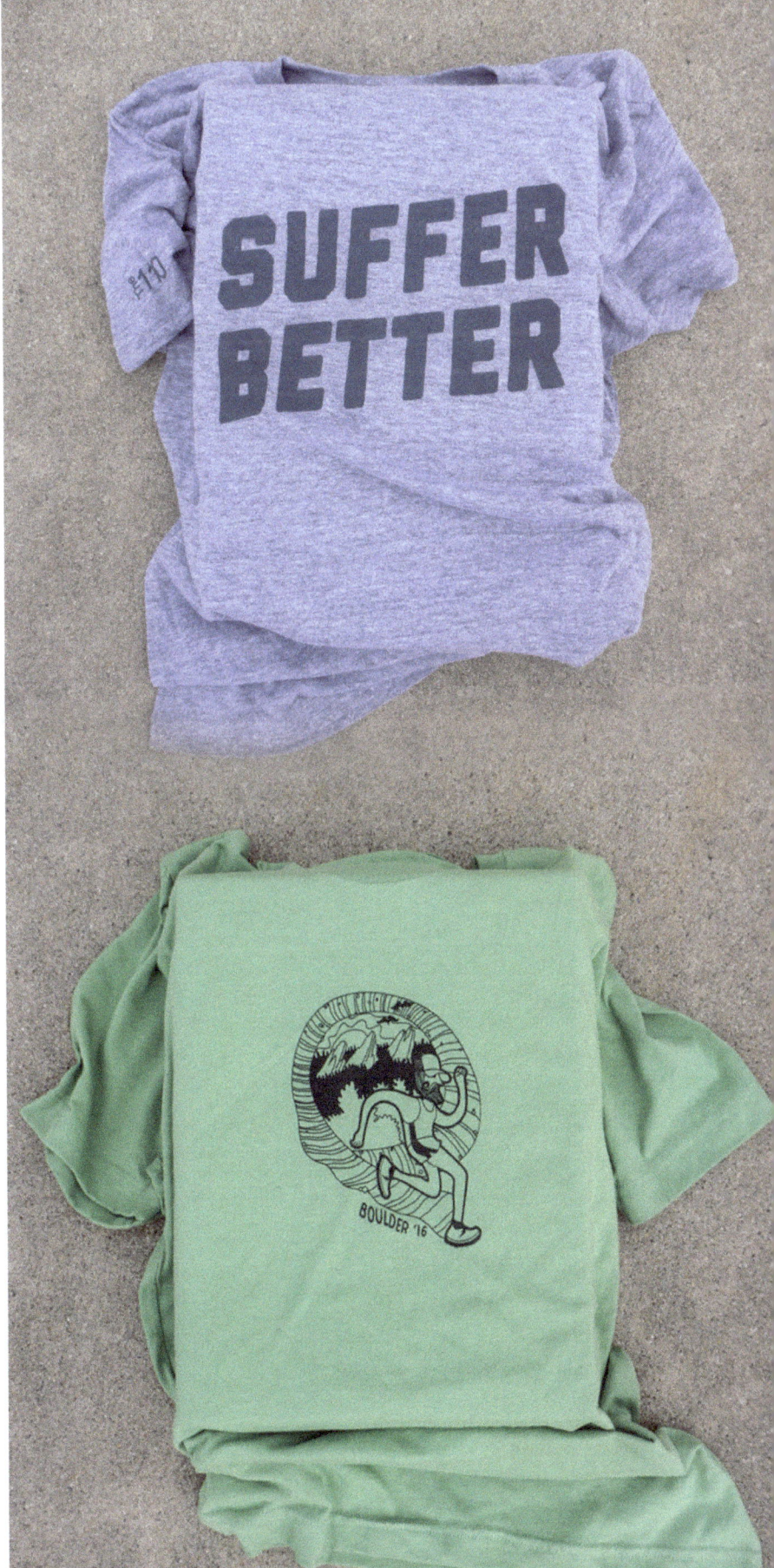

Suffer Better
New Look
SufferBetter.com

Boulder Running
Trails in Motion
BoulderRunning.com

MASTER'S CLASS

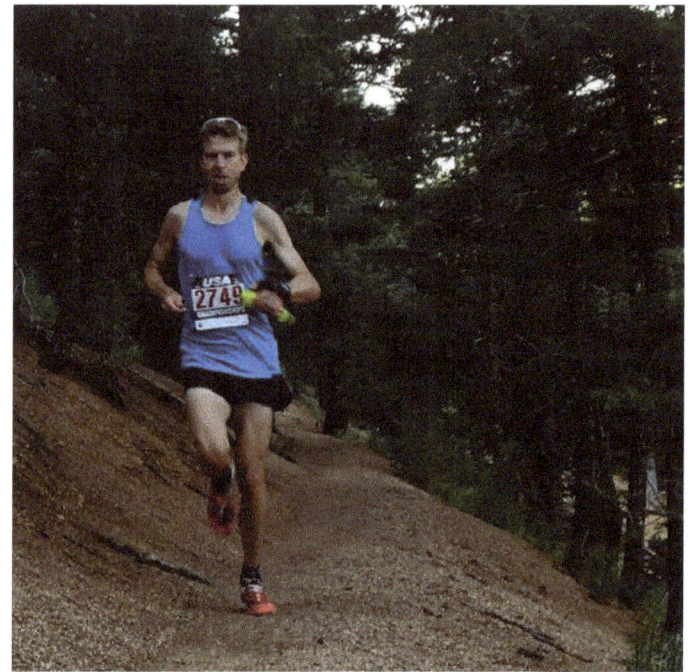

Photo Nancy Hobbs

Chris Grauch

Chris Grauch of Nederland has quietly been dominating the trail and mountain running scene locally, nationally, and even internationally for several years. With little fanfare or social media bragging, Chris has come to be one of the top Master runners in the country – a true Master Class. In 2015 Chris was named **Master's Mountain Runner of the Year** by the USTAF. Coming off of that 2015 title, Chris won the Master's Title at the USATF Mountain Running Championships held at Loon Mountain Resort in New Hampshire. Then, in August at the World Masters Mountain Running Championships held in Susa, Italy, Chris once again demonstrated his master class skills, finishing 29th overall and 7th in his age group.

"It was a seriously tough field. I was hoping for a higher age group placement and maybe could have gone a touch harder the first half, but I was a little nervous of completely popping and loosing big chunks on the second half. Four or five 50+ guys handed me my ass. Seriously tough mountain runners over there, but a great race!"

Finally, this fall at the USATF Half Marathon Championships held at the Lake Padden Trail Half in Bellingham, Washington, Chris won the Master's Title while finishing 12th overall. It's this continued excellence – year after year – that places Chris in a Master Class of his own. He won't tell you that, and it's hard to know that based on what's hot on social media or in the news, but local runners know when a tall, blonde haired runner starts to catch up with them on a local trail, it's almost futile to try and stay ahead – it's probably Chris and he will pass you.

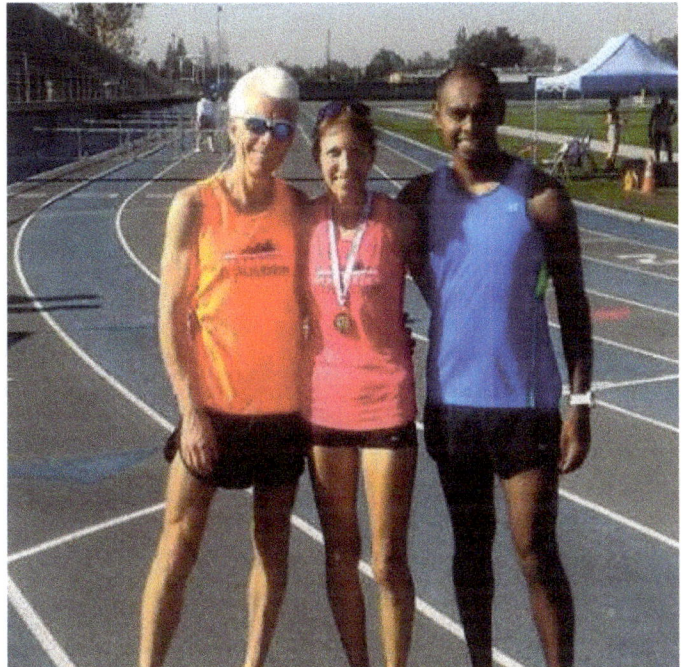

Photo courtesy of Laura Bruess

Laura Bruess

This summer, Laura Bruess took over the title of American Record Holder in the 10k for the women's 55-59 age group on June 18 at the West Region Masters Championships at Cerritos College. But achieving the mark didn't come easy, she said, recalling how the race unfolded.

"My plan was to go out at 6:20 pace and pick it up at 4 miles. I started out at 6:18 pace and it seemed really comfortable until 4 miles when instead of feeling good, I felt really tired," she said. "Then I started losing seconds and I was trying to just hang on. With one lap to go, I saw that I was really close to the record and I went as fast as I possibly could. Later the race director told me he thought I was going to fall down. We waited an anxious few minutes before we got the official time."

That time: a swift 39:37.05. The previous W55-59 record was 39:37.78, set by Kathryn Martin in 2007.

Always a strong runner, Laura has lately found even more success in her training and racing. She attributes this to her recent retirement, the support and encouragement of her teammates, her vegan diet and her coach and husband, Rick. Also the coach of Athletics Boulder, he designs workouts specifically for her. "They are hard but mentally doable," she said. "I look forward to them! I feel like I had a big breakthrough this year."

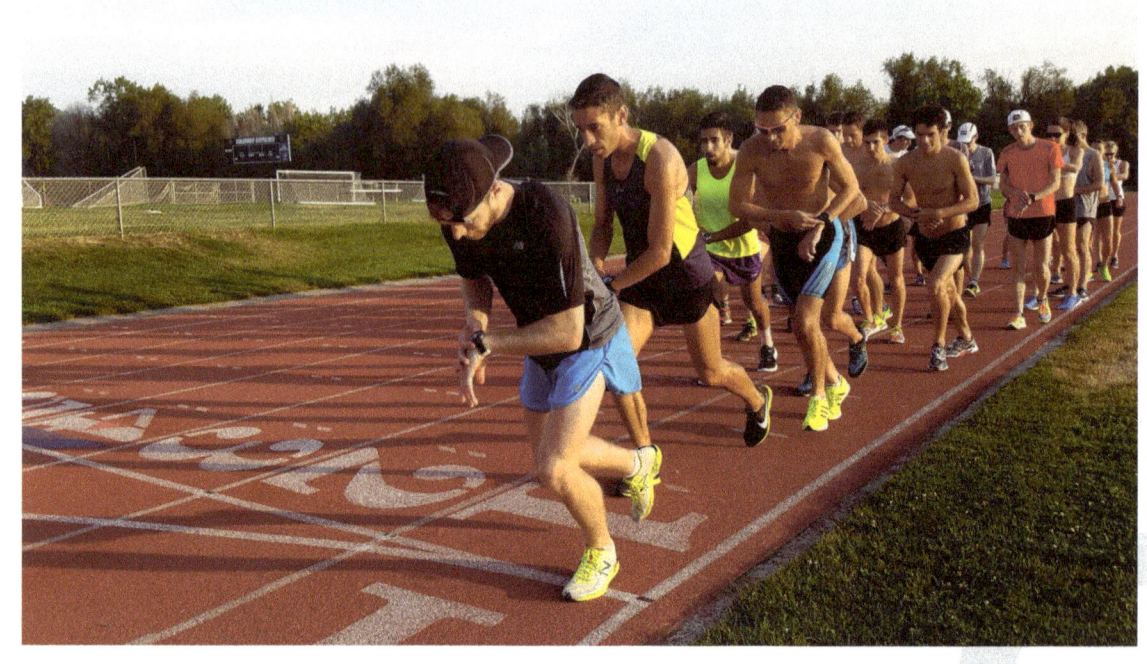

TRAINING GROUPS

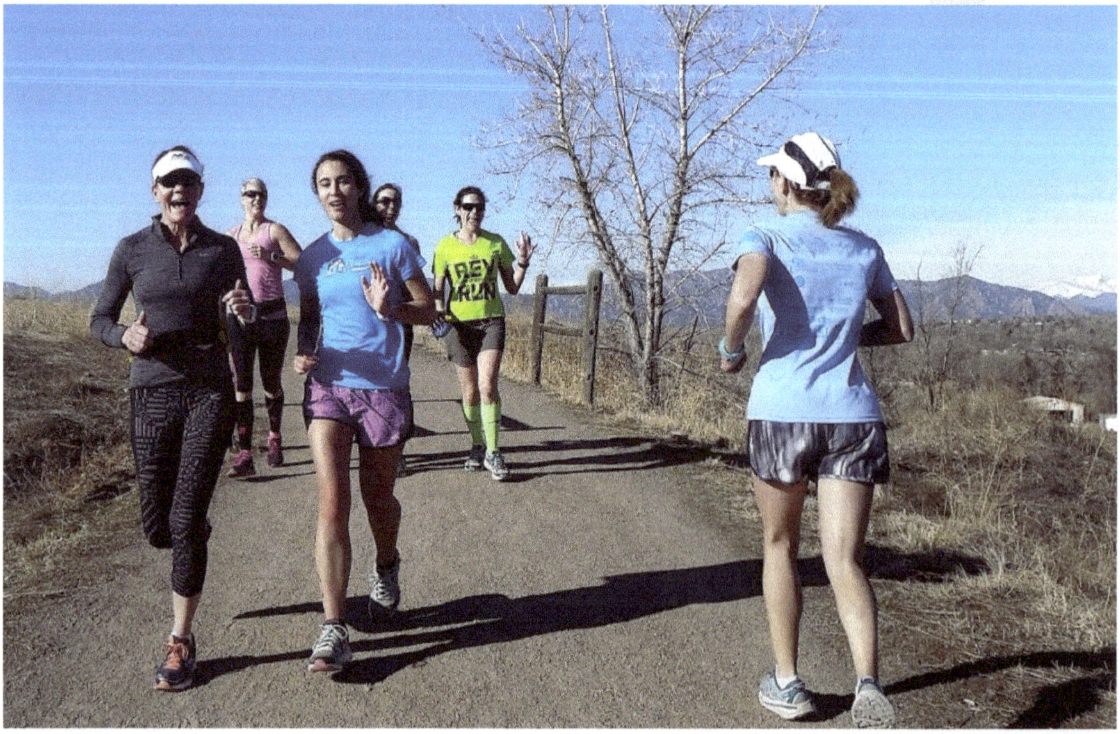

Photo Nick Combs

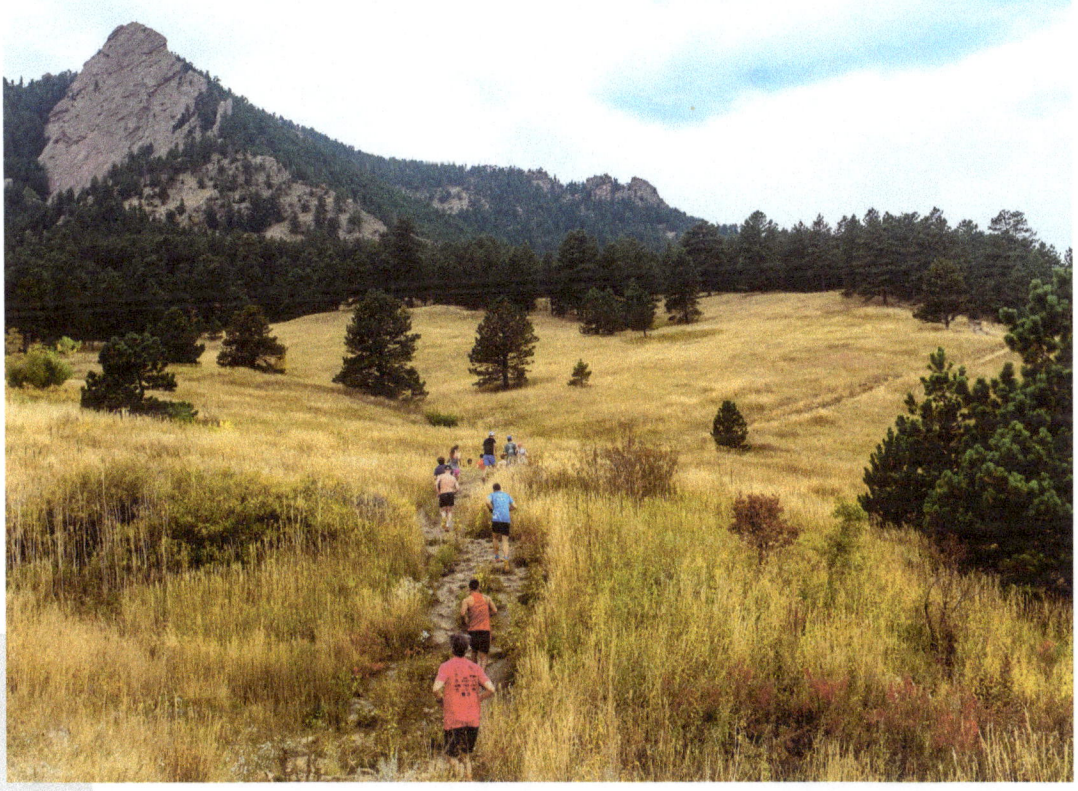

FUN RUNS

It's no secret that running with others can help motivate you and add extra enjoyment to your workouts, long runs or any time you're just wanting to enjoy the outdoors. There are a wide variety of group options in Boulder County, from elite level training and coaching groups for running enthusiasts to weekly fun runs at one of the local running stores. Often stores will support the run with shoe demos, food, drink, giveaways, and speakers or celebrities who have included Olympians Jenny Simpson, Emma Coburn, and Kara Goucher; trail runners Scott Jurek, Sage Canaday, Zach Miller, Silke Koester, and Jason Koop; Trail Sisters and many more. It's a great opportunity to be a part of the community and meet new people who have just moved to town, are visiting or have been here for a long time.

Boulderrunning.com/resources/run-clubs_training-groups

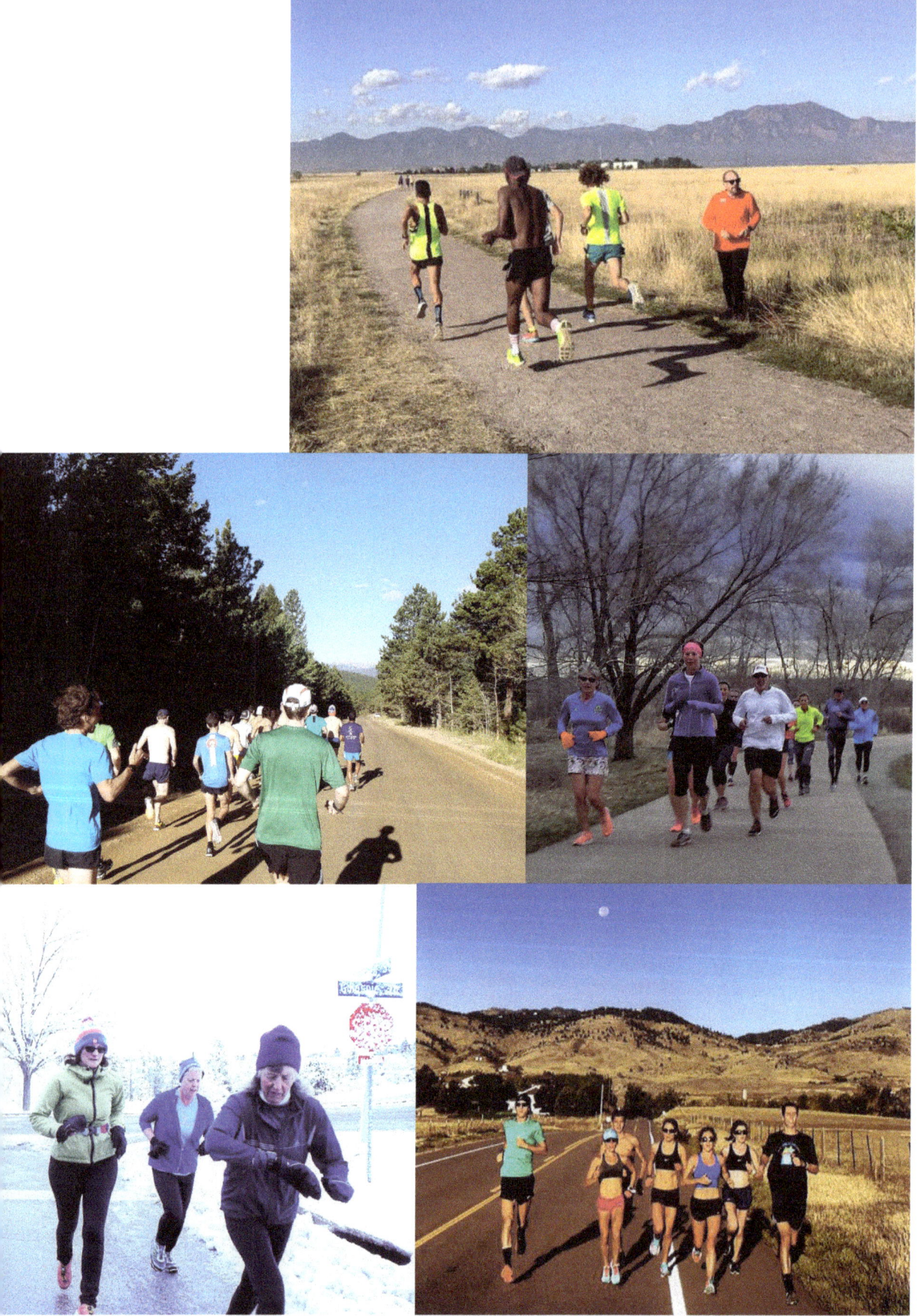

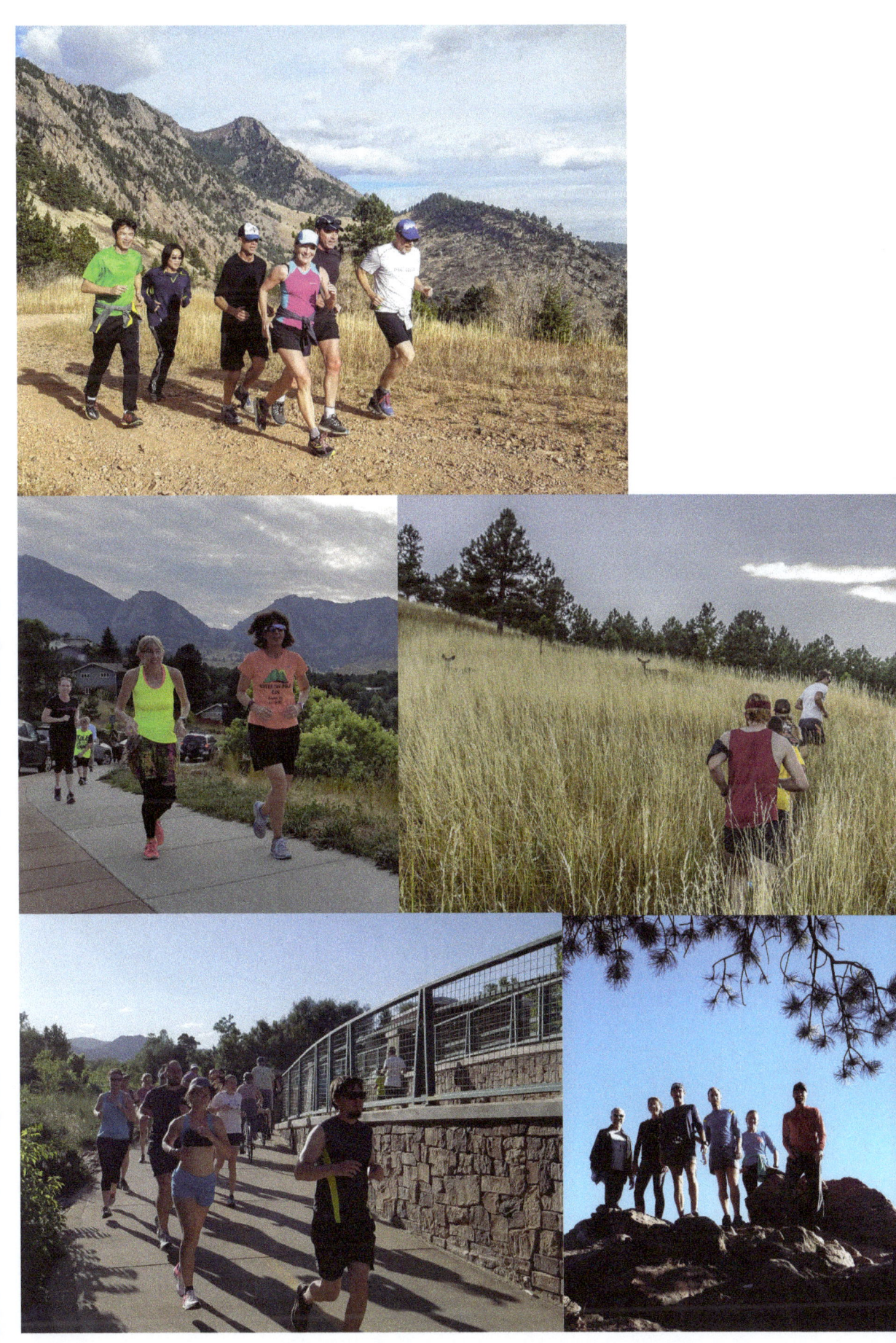

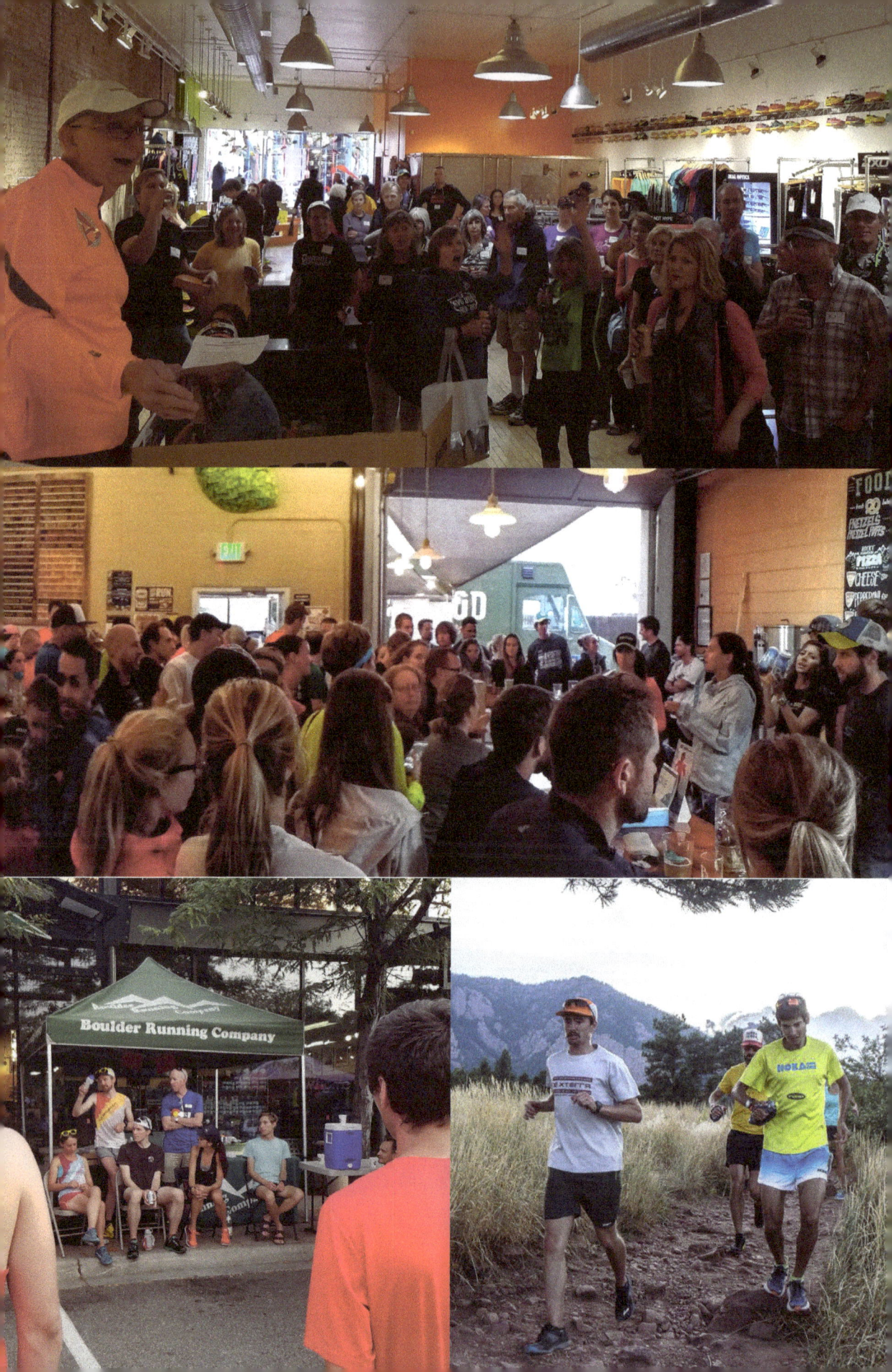

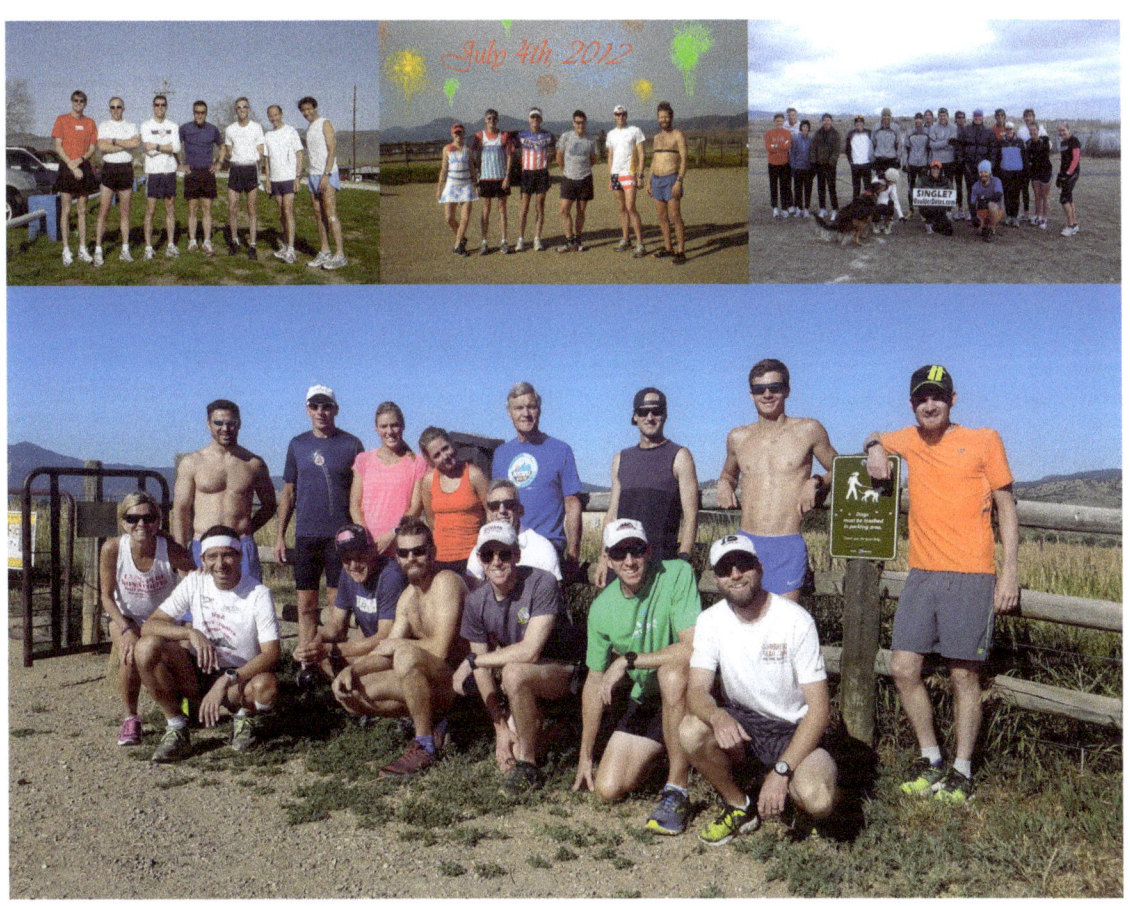

WEDNESDAYS

At the Eagle Trailhead closing in on 8:30 am cars start to pull into the parking lot and runners sleepily gather around, greeting each other with tidings of how they are feeling this morning. "How are you?" "Out of shape." "Join the club."

Matt Hill quips, "I got a baby sitter this morning. This is going to be an expensive run. It better be a good one."

The Wednesday Rez Run is one of the longer standing traditions in Boulder. This free run seems to have started back in October of 2004, just after restauranteur Bobby Stuckey moved to town and was looking for people to run with. Its founders are Paige Bodine and Bill Lawrence. They do the same 10 mile course around the Eagle trail then the Boulder Reservoir. It's an eclectic mix of runners: trail runners, elites, members of different formal training groups, some looking to achieve personal goals, others just out to enjoy the company.

"We've had the likes of James Carney, Benita Willis, Kenyon Newman, and even Steve Jones came out to shuffle with us. For a brief stretch years ago, we had the duo of Tyler Hamilton and Cameron Widoff joining us for some very respectable, post retirement efforts," Bodine recalls.

Each week they grab a picture of the group before heading off; at the end of the year they make a calendar.

Running Philanthropy Missions in Cuba

Words by Brian Metzler

While Americans are just now getting the chance to visit Cuba again, Boulder journalist Michael Sandrock has been making regular trips there for more than 25 years. While his initial interest was exploring Ernest Hemingway's long-ago connection to the island nation, he's primarily gone to Cuba on running philanthropy missions through the One World Running non-profit organization he co-founded in the late 1980s.

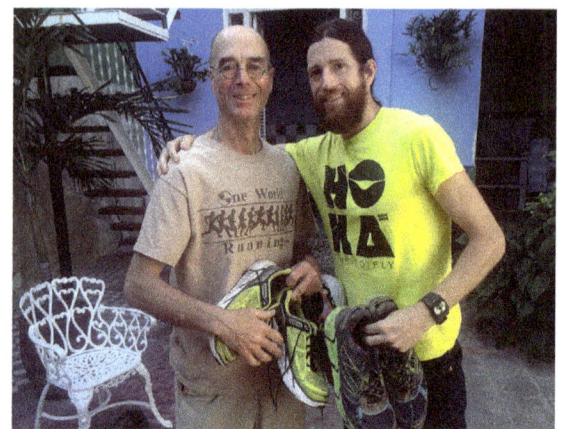

With the help of Boulder nurse Ana Weir, Sandrock has been taking used running shoes to Cuba for years and also played a big role in organizing running races and kids events. The photos here are from Sandrock's trip in March, where he delivered more than 150 pairs of running shoes to runners and triathletes in Santiago and Baracoa and helped organize a track and field meet for kids from five schools. The kids wore Boulder Running Company race bibs and received school supplies as prizes.

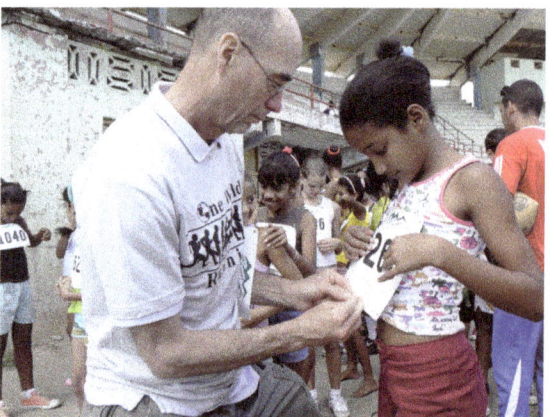

Sandrock continues to go to Cuba because of the bonds he has made and the lifelong friendships that have developed.

"It starts by sharing a bond with running and shoes, but many times it develops into much deeper, lasting friendships," Sandrock said. "That's what running is all about, and that's why I still enjoy it. We're all one world and everything is connected. Everyone is connected to each other and you can really feel that through running and the people you run with, and that's why it's so satisfying."

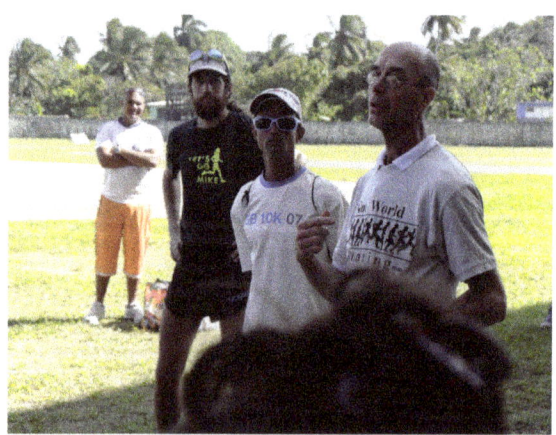

For more about One World Running's service missions to Cuba, visit oneworldrunning.com.

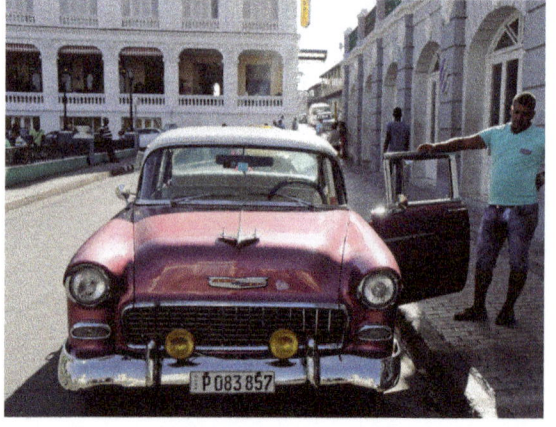

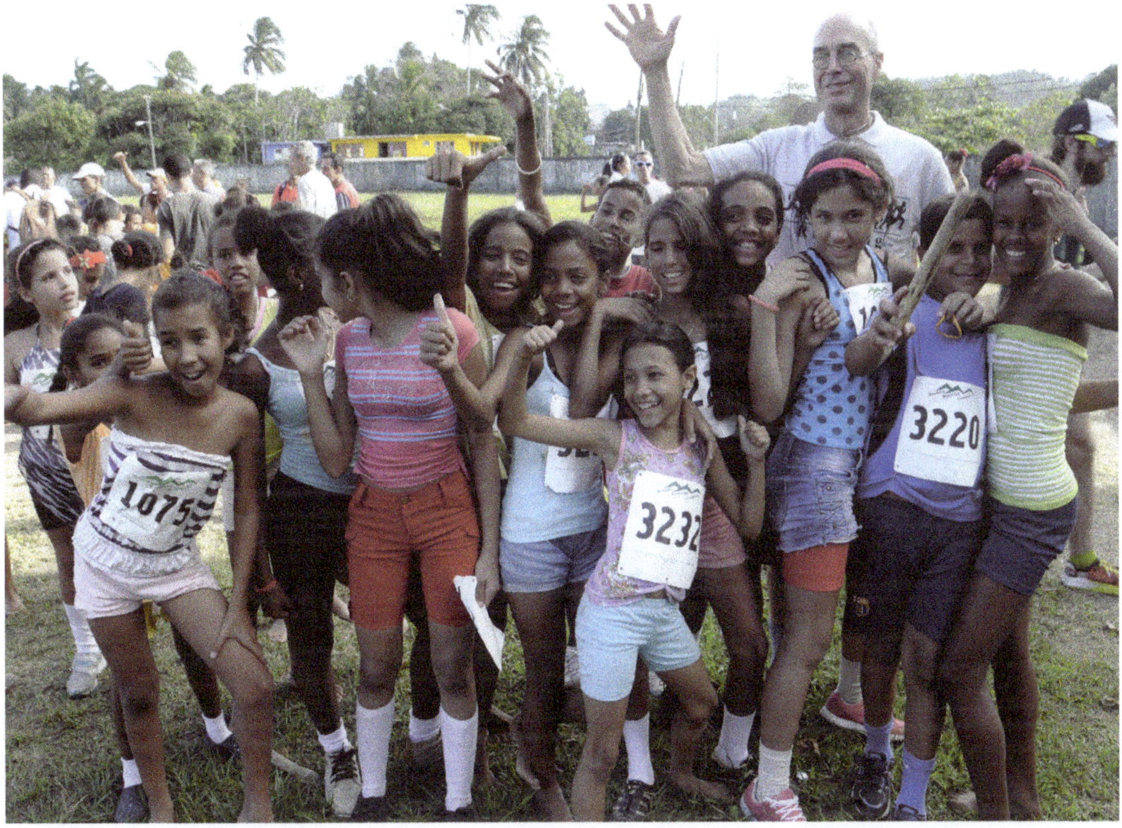

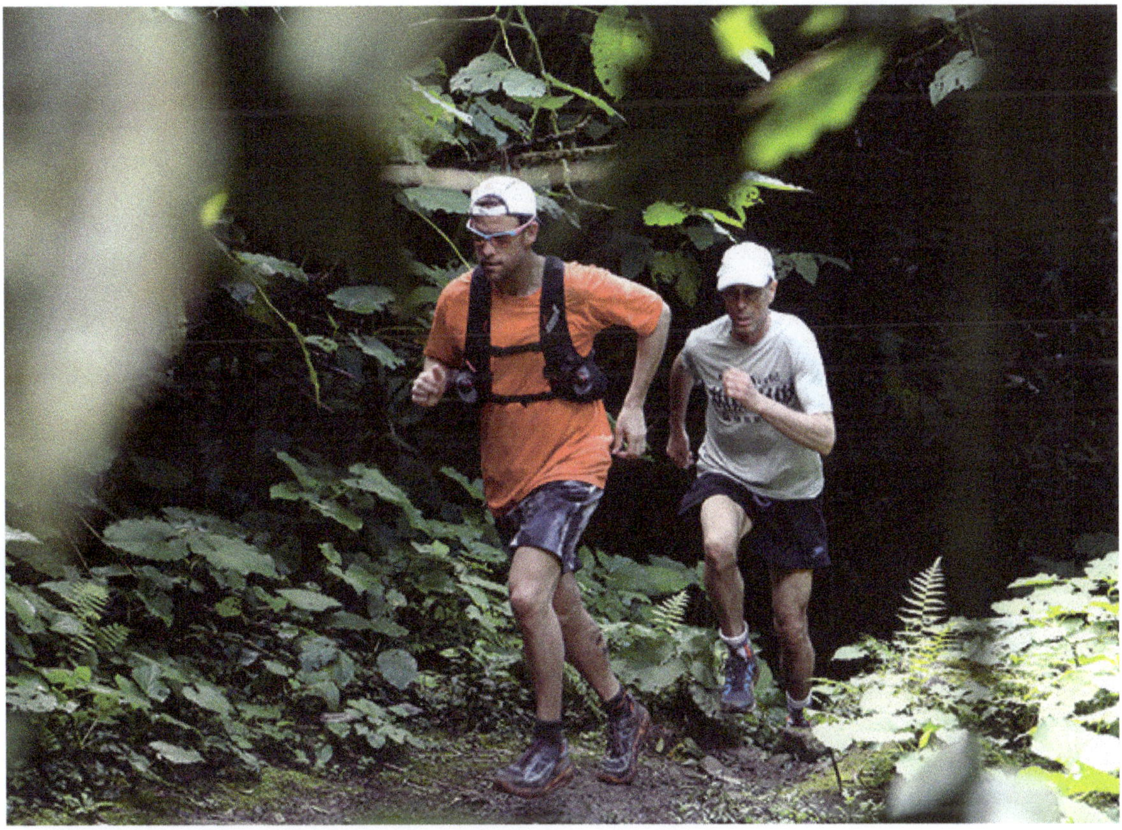

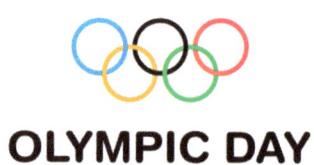

OLYMPIC DAY

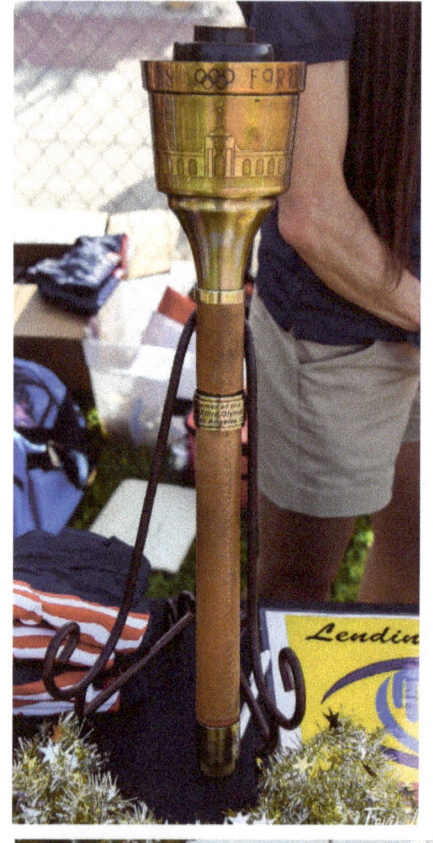

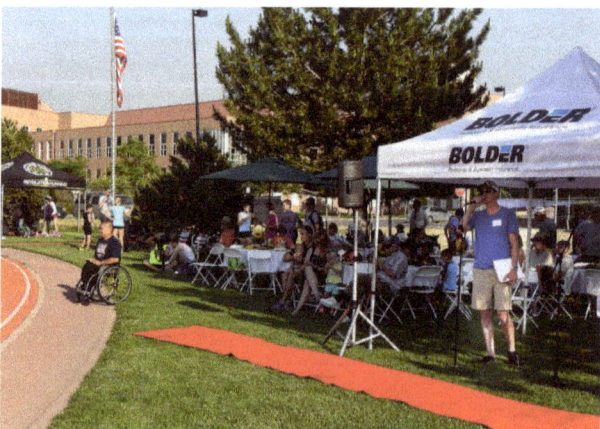

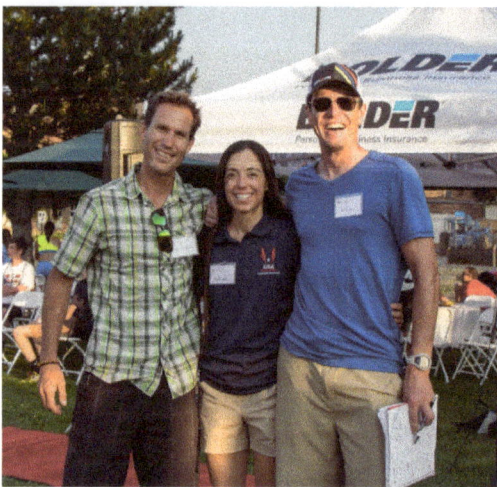

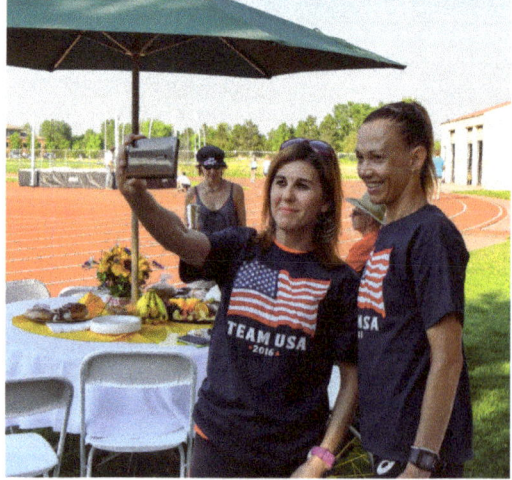

Olympians across many sports were recognized on Olympic Day on June 16th. The celebration coincided with the Boulder Road Runner's Summer Track Meets. - The Olympic Relay Torch which was carried by Amie Durden leading up to the 1984 Olympics in Los Angeles. - Ryan Van Duzer, Organizer Deb Conley, and meet announer Will Kelsey - Nuţa Olaru capturing a selfie. Photos by Tevis Morrow

CLEAN SPORTS

The OLYMPIC OATHS

In the name of all competitors, I promise that we will take part in these Olympic Games, respecting and abiding by the rules which govern them. Committing ourselves to a sport without doping and without drugs, in the true spirit of Sportsmanship, for the glory of the sport and the honour of our teams.

Athletes' oath is a rutual during the opening ceremony - Olympic Charter 2003.

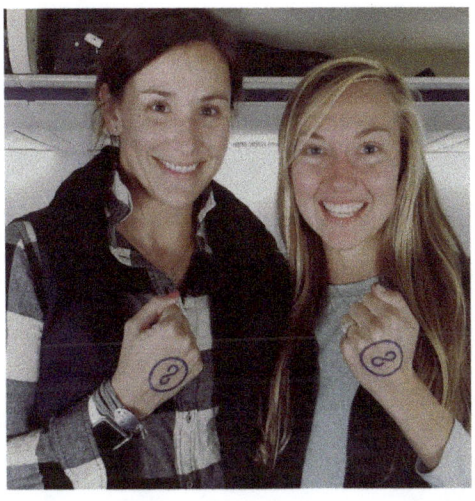

Photo Kara Goucher

The **Clean Sport Collective** is a non-profit 501c-3, launched on November 2nd with the mission of "United together for honesty, integrity and transparency in sport."

Shanna and Kevin Burnette of ModCraft Studio looked for a positive way to raise awareness through the celebration and recognition of the clean athletes and brands doing it the right way.

"I pledge to honor myself, competitors, sponsors, sport and society by choosing to stay clean of performance enhancing drugs. Choosing to not play by the rules steals from hard working athletes who choose to do the right thing and challenges the health and integrity of sport. I will be a positive example in the community as an advocate and ambassador for clean sport. I pledge that I have and will always train clean, compete clean and live clean."

Follow the movement on social channels wtih #CleanSportCO - cleansport.org

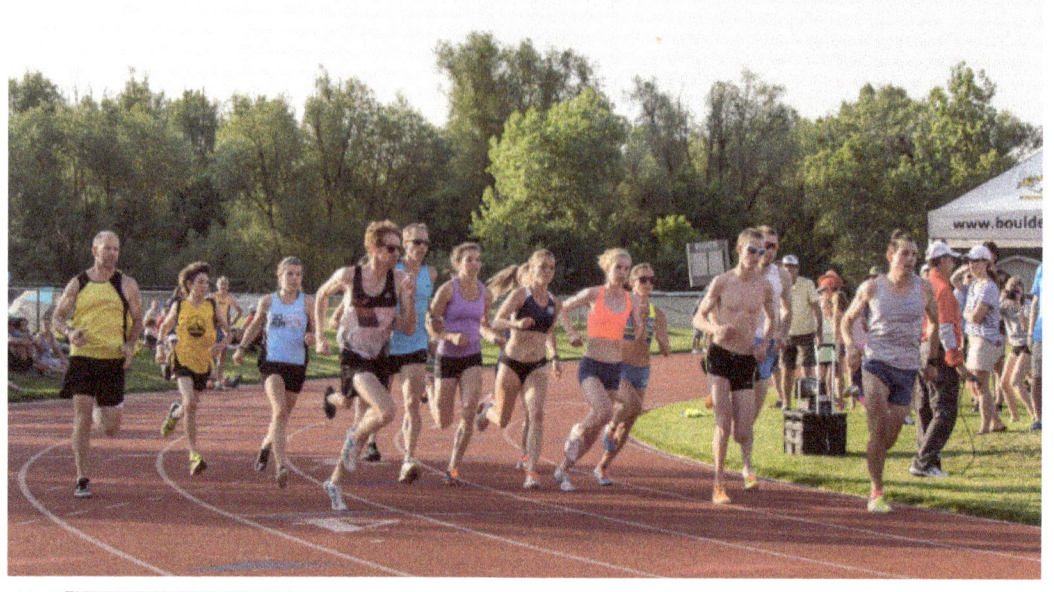

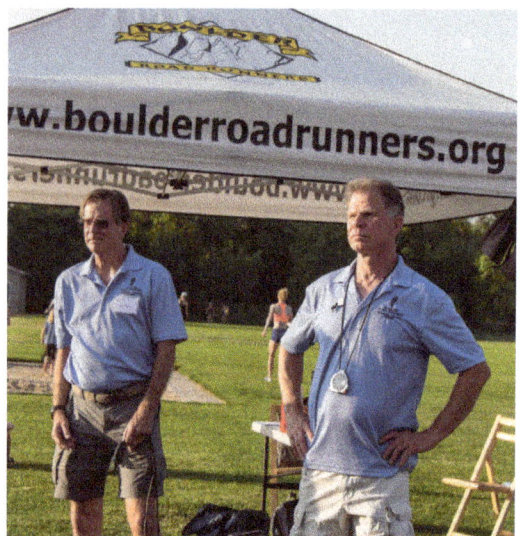

Boulder Road Runners
Summer Track Meets

Photos Tevis Morrow

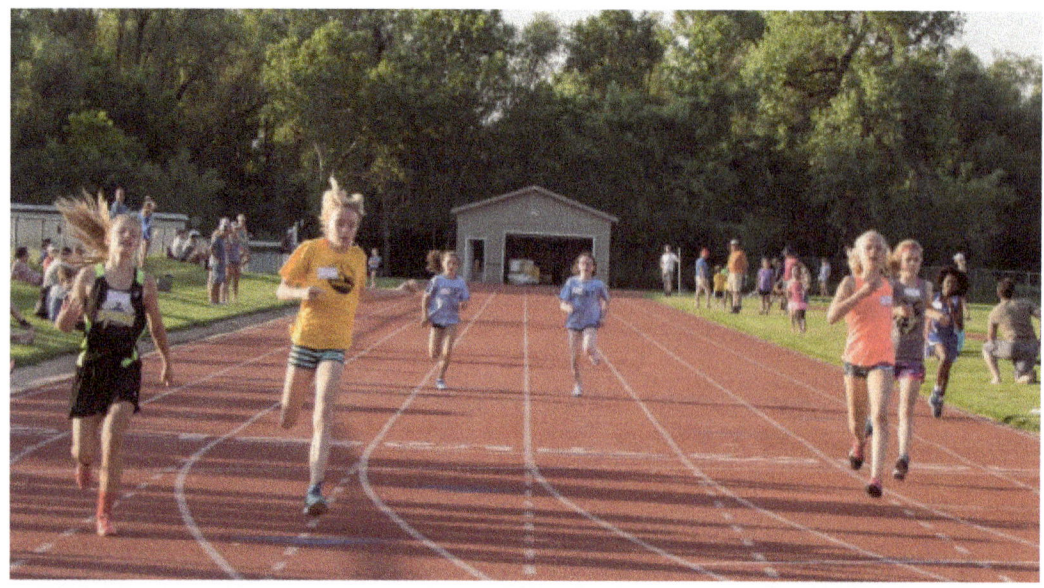

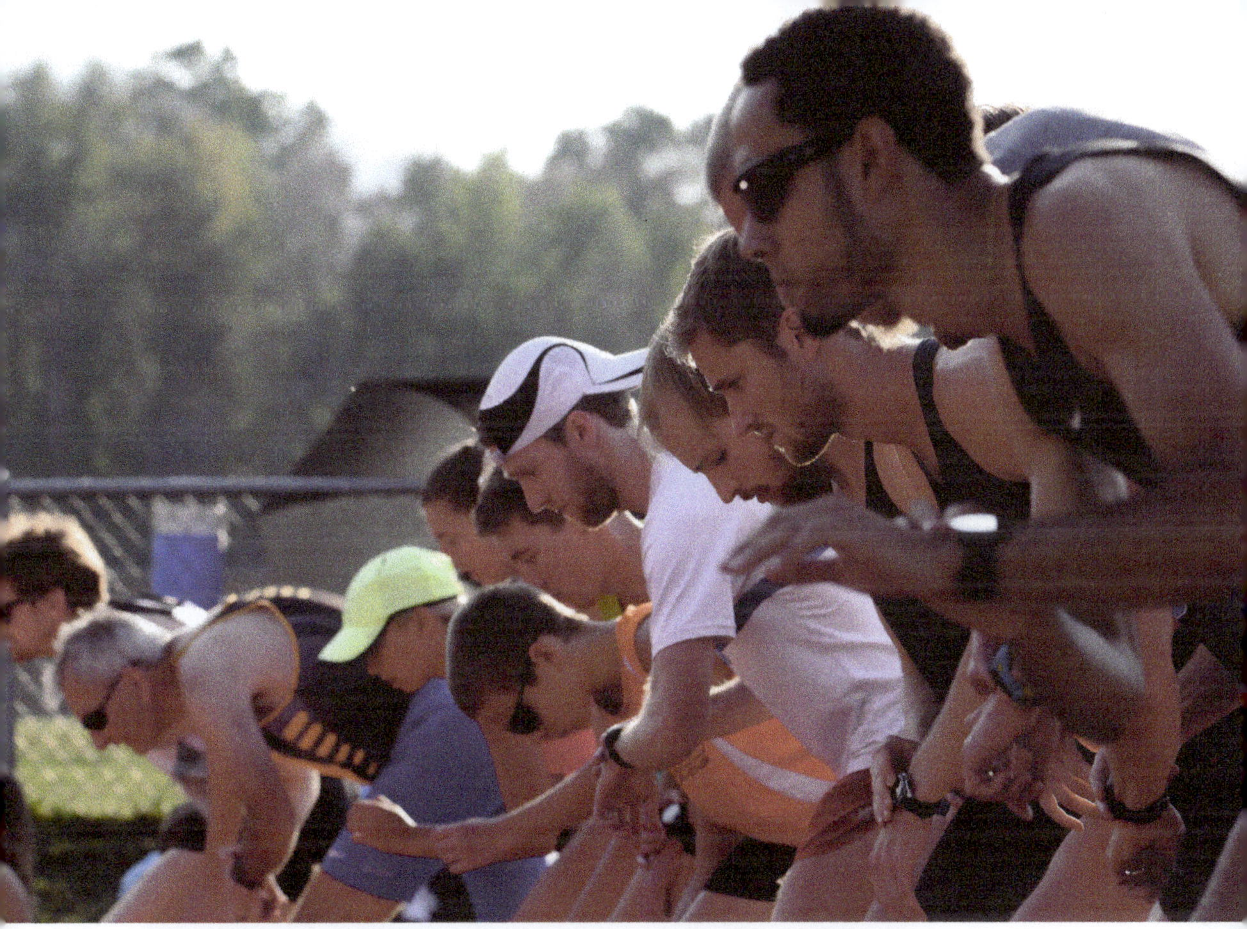

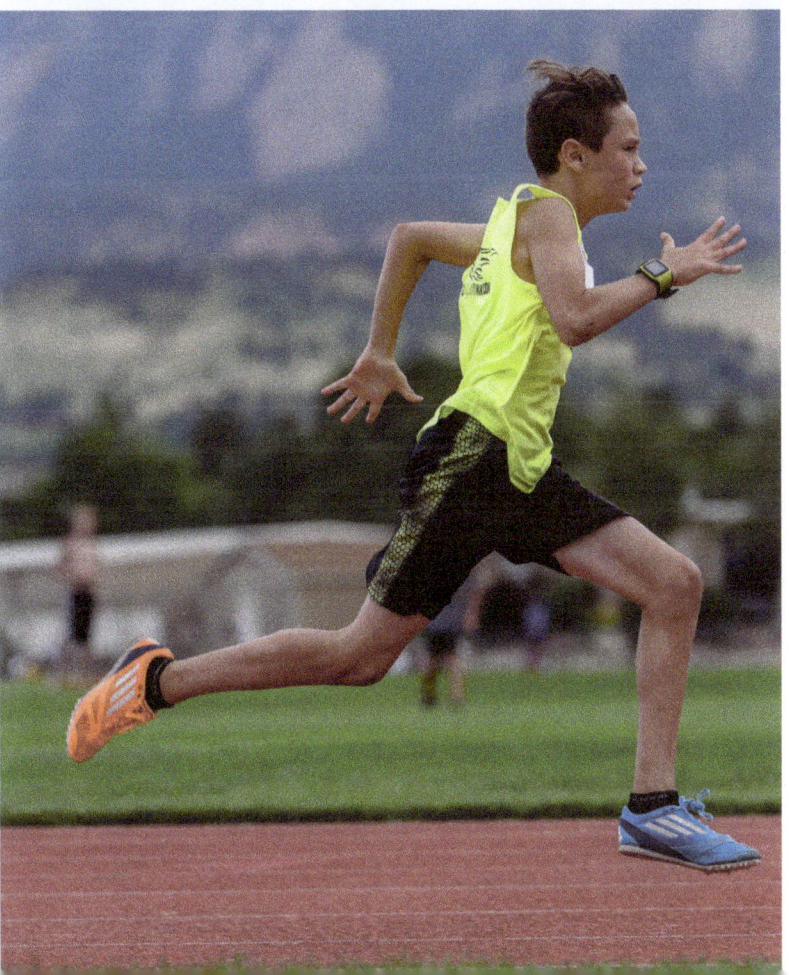

Photos by Dave Albo

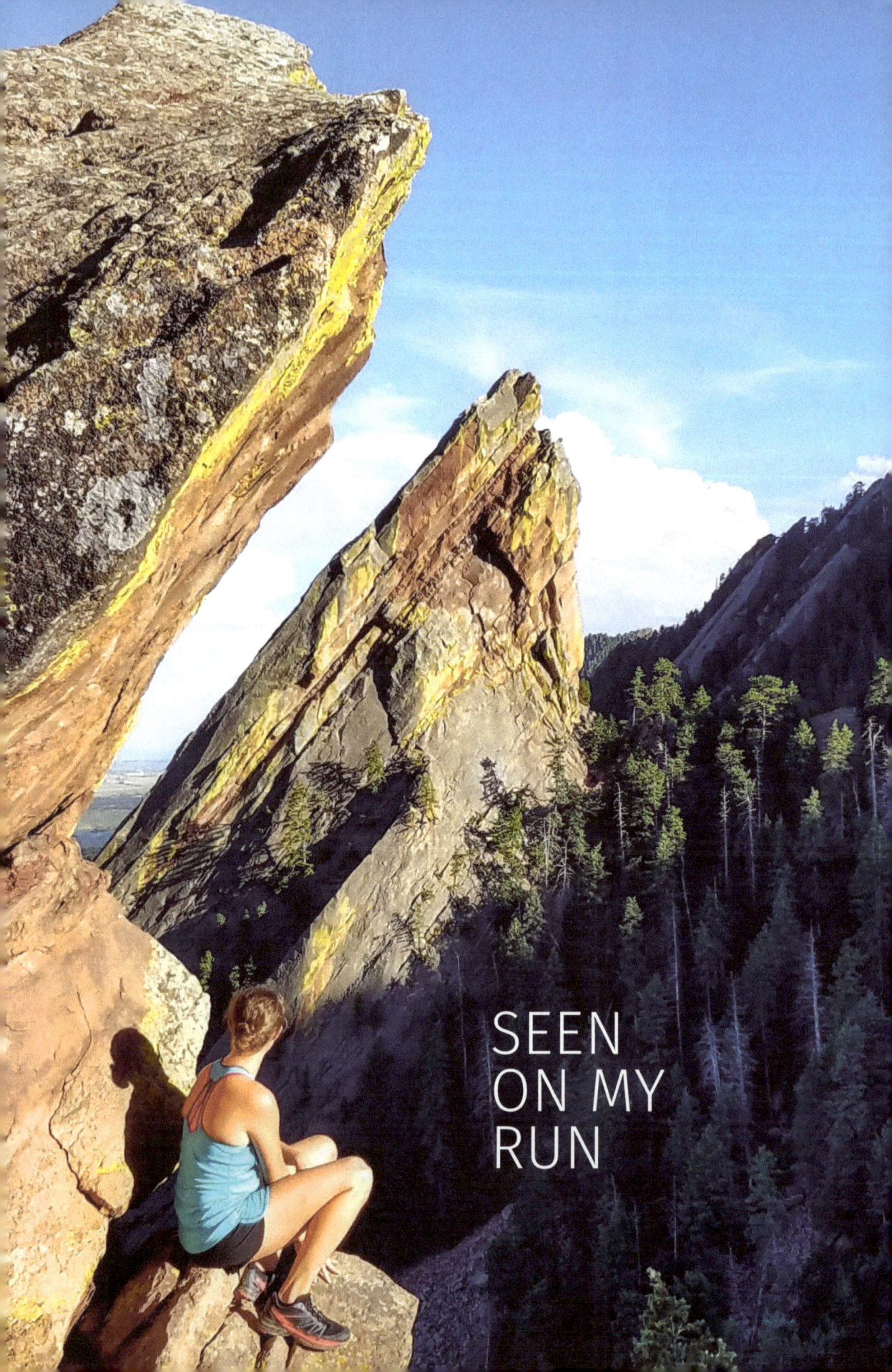

SEEN ON MY RUN

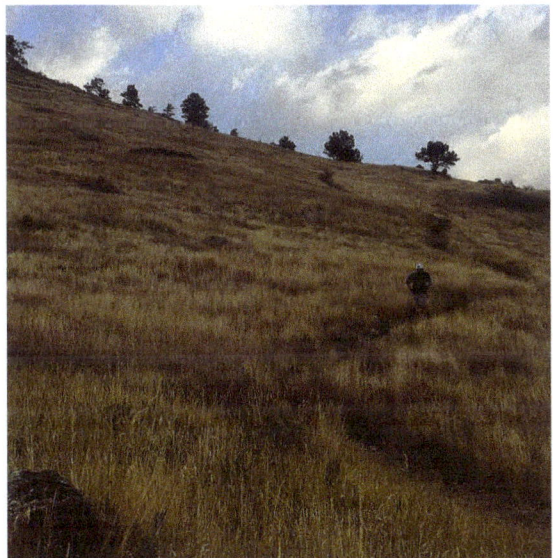

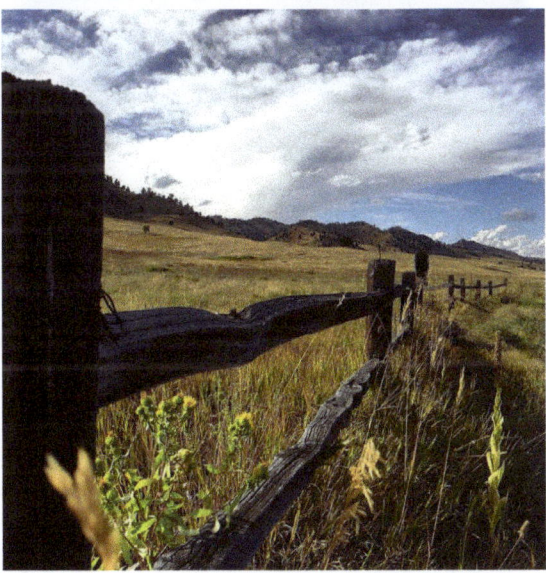

Being out on a run allows you to take in the scenery in a whole new way. Many of us carry our smart phone cameras, a GoPro, or even a sleek SLR. No matter your capturing tool of choice sharing what we see when we run is just another way for us to connect as a community. Here is a small collection of recent favorites from the feed.

If you would like to contribute, make sure you tag **#SeenOnMyRun** and **#BoCo_Trails.**

@germakian - @distilledCoaching

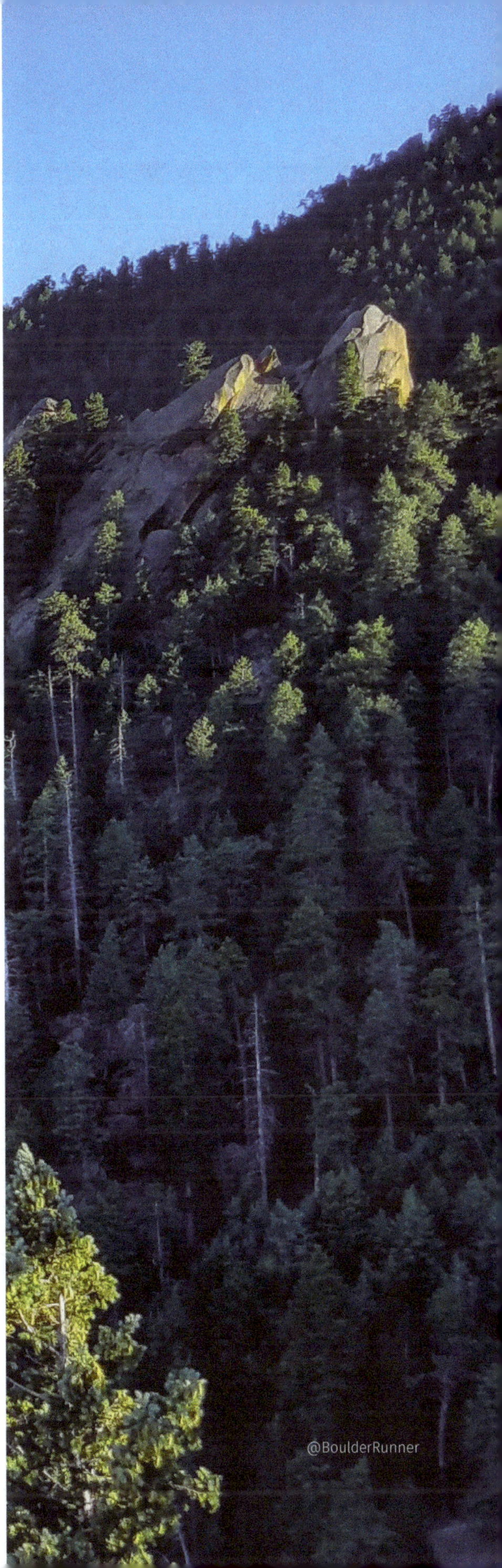

@BoulderRunner

#SeenOnMyRun

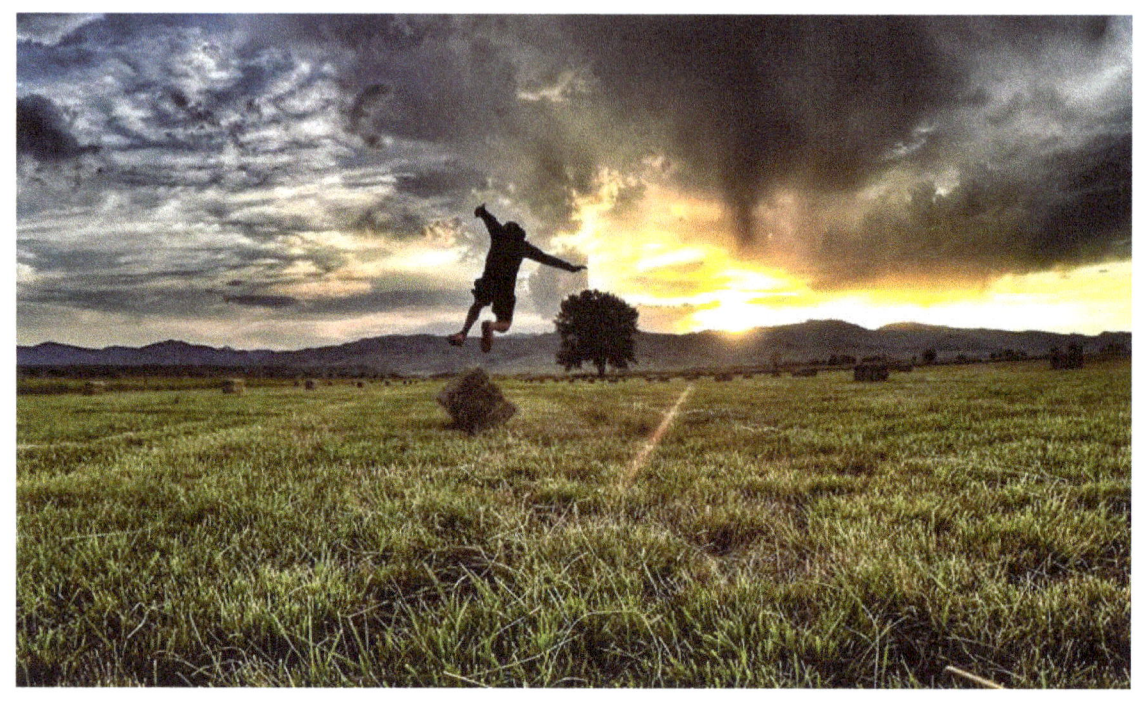

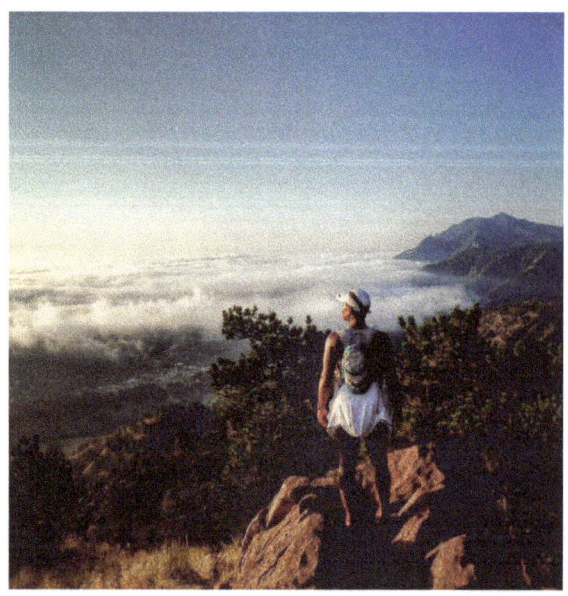
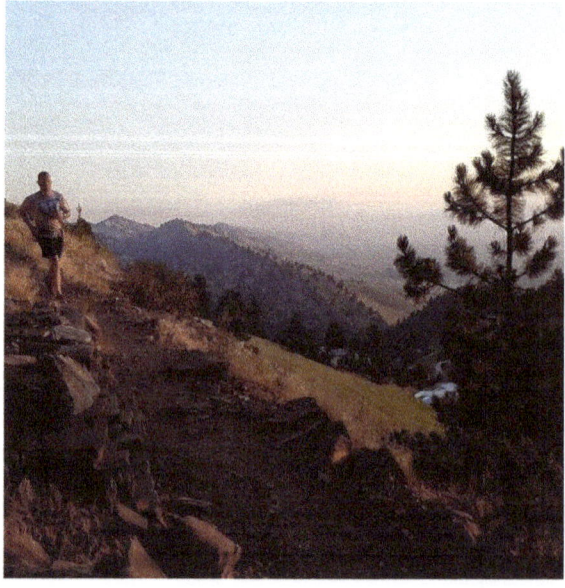

@traveledeyes
@skamm11 - @BoulderRunner

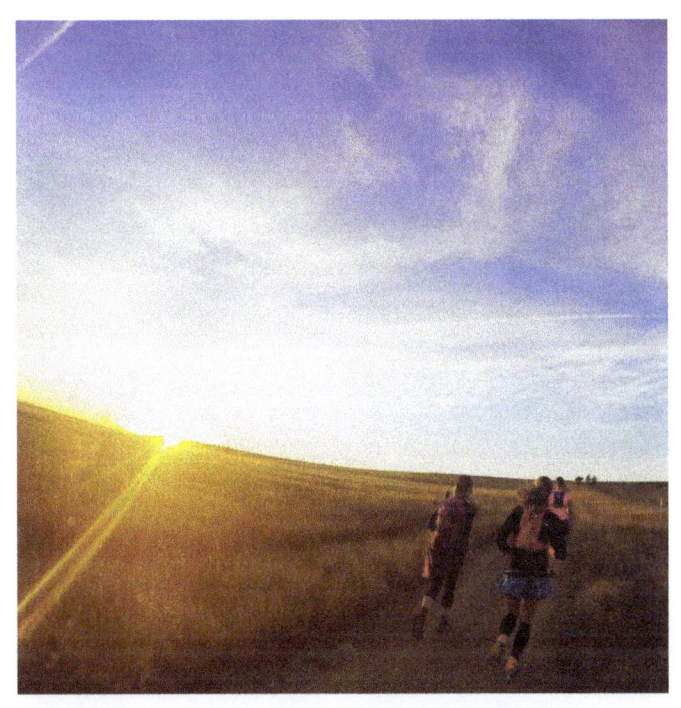

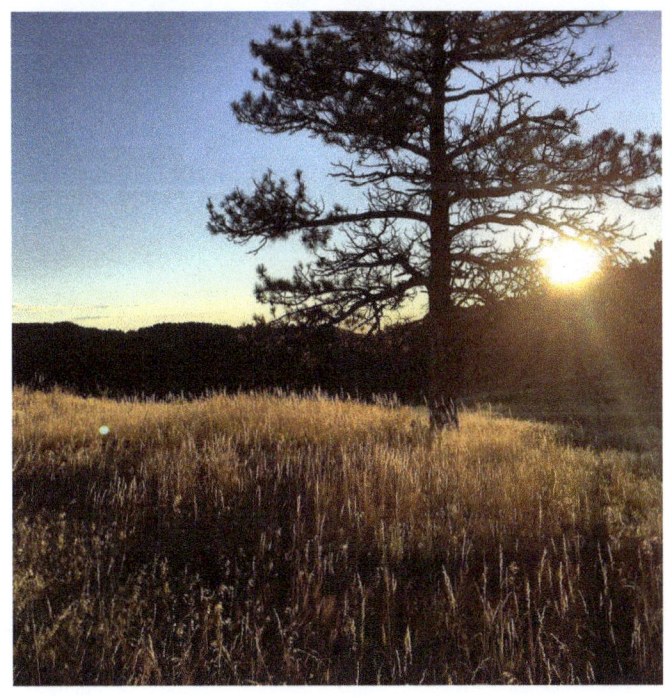

@amachael
@distilledCoaching

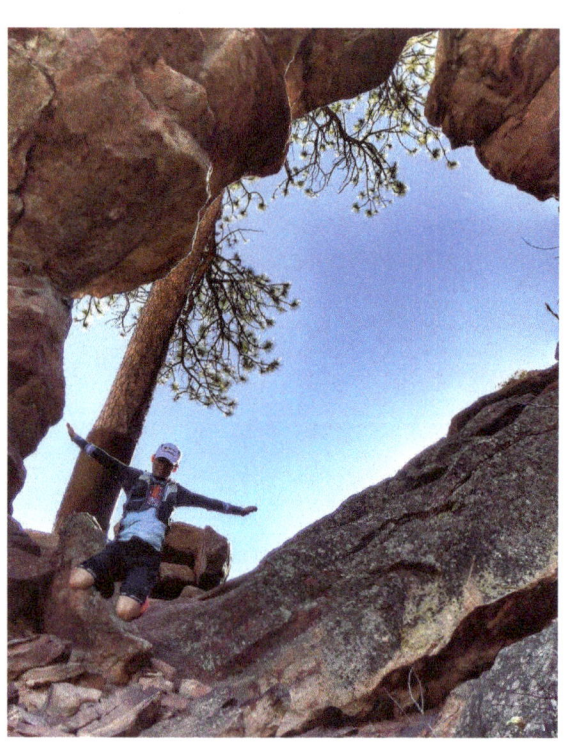
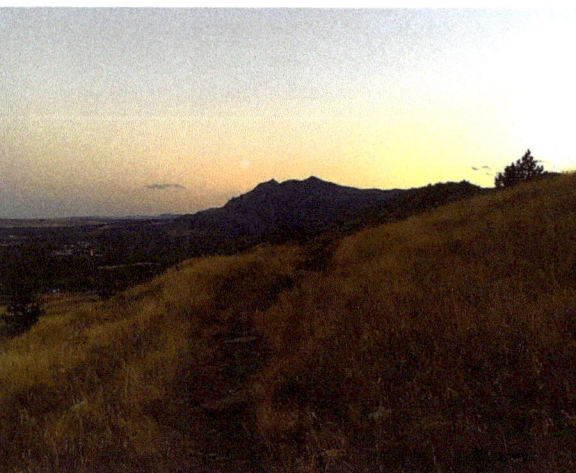

@runwithpatrick - @massimoalps
@colotrailrunner - @bobcat_onu

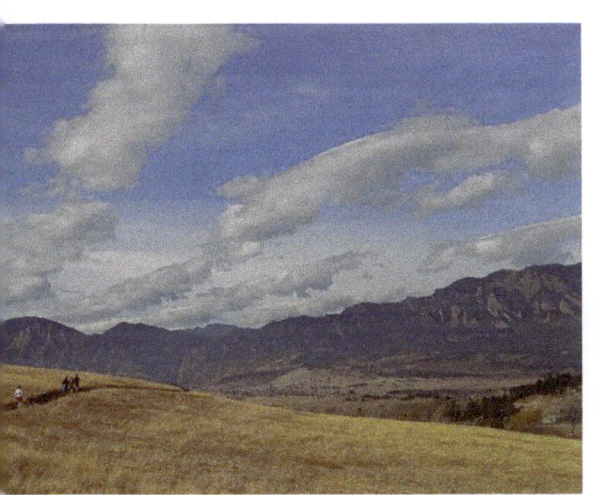
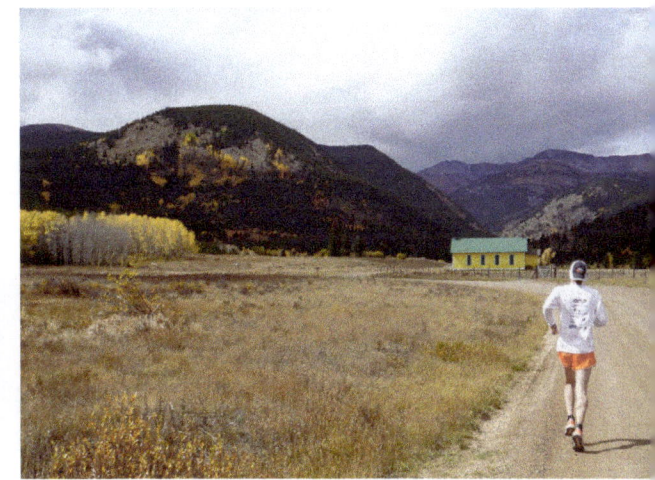

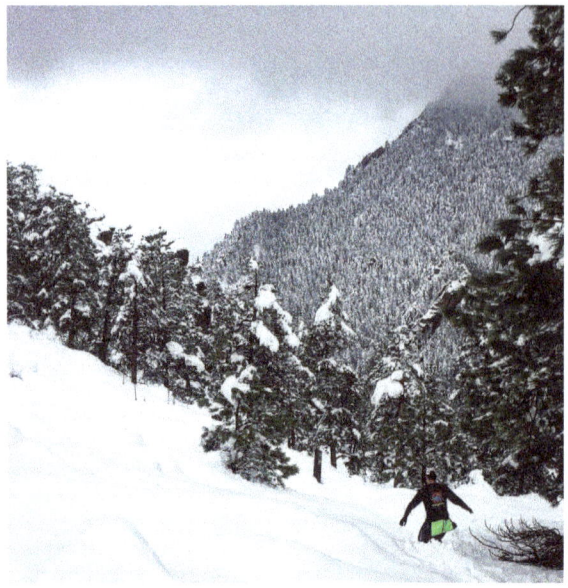
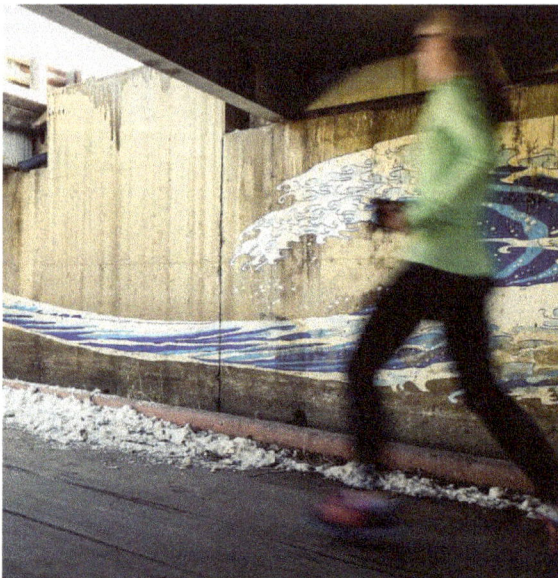
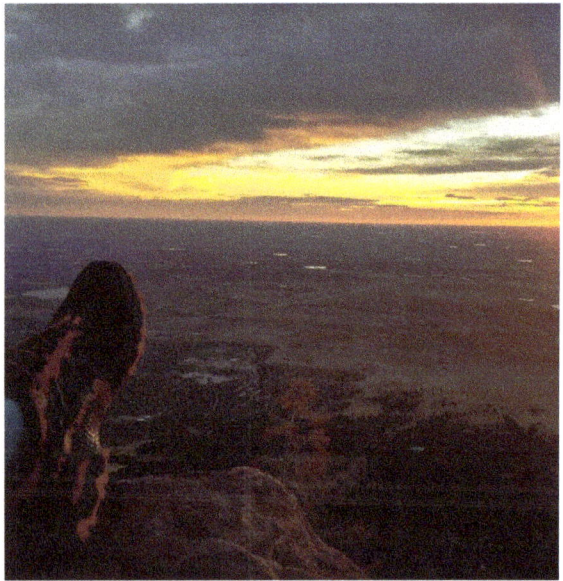
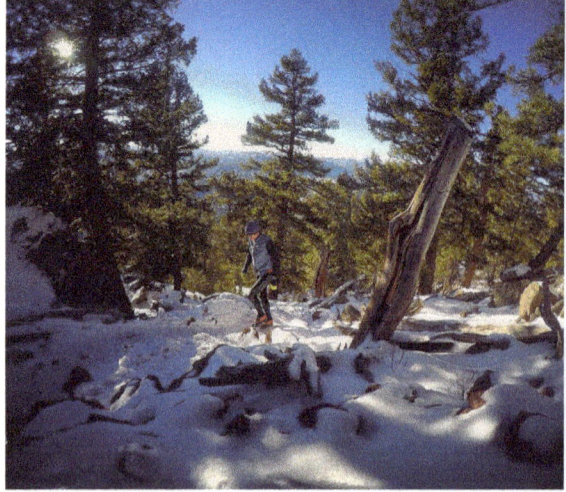

@_toofast - @mikehugus
@colotrailrunner - @traveledeyes
@BoulderRunner

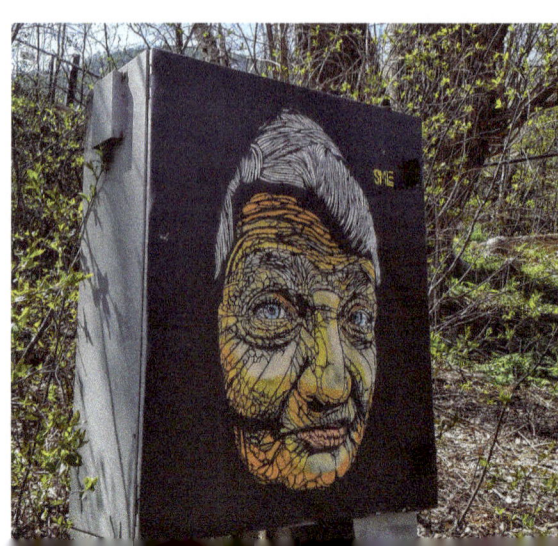

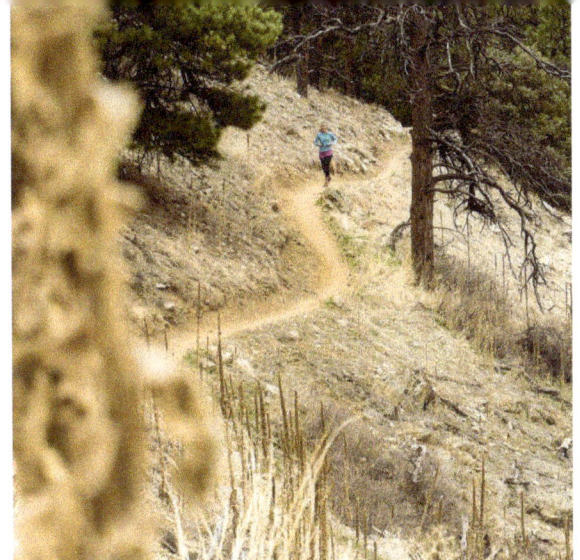
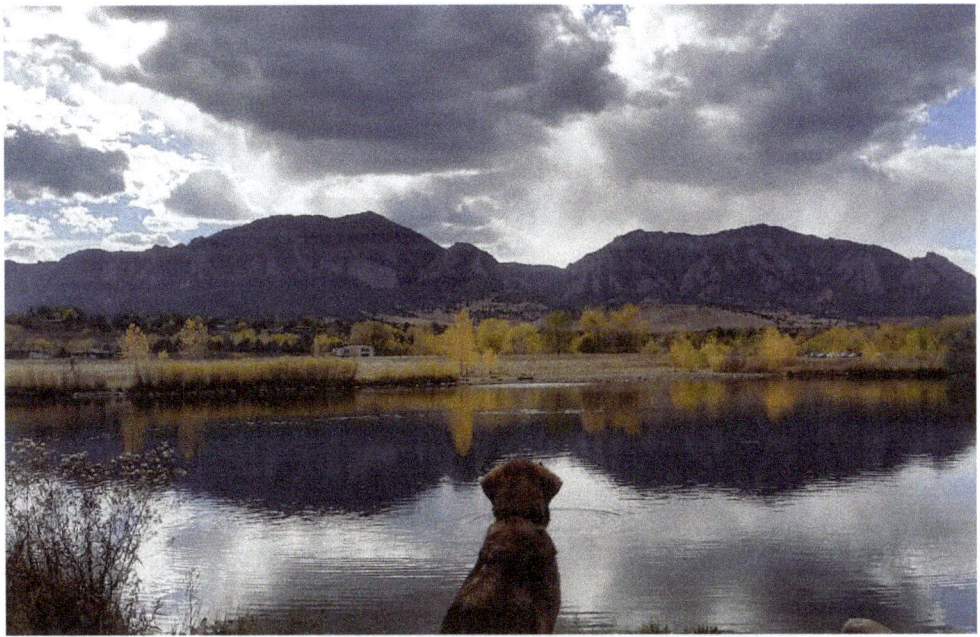
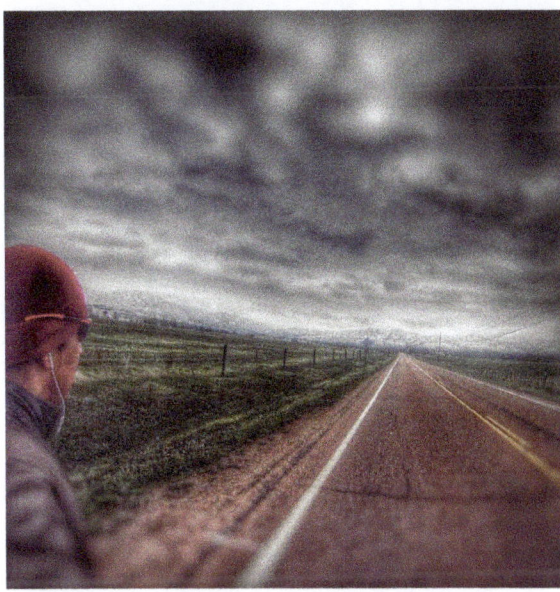

@mikehugus
@peak.running
@BoulderTrainingMecca

The Allure of Boulder's Backroads

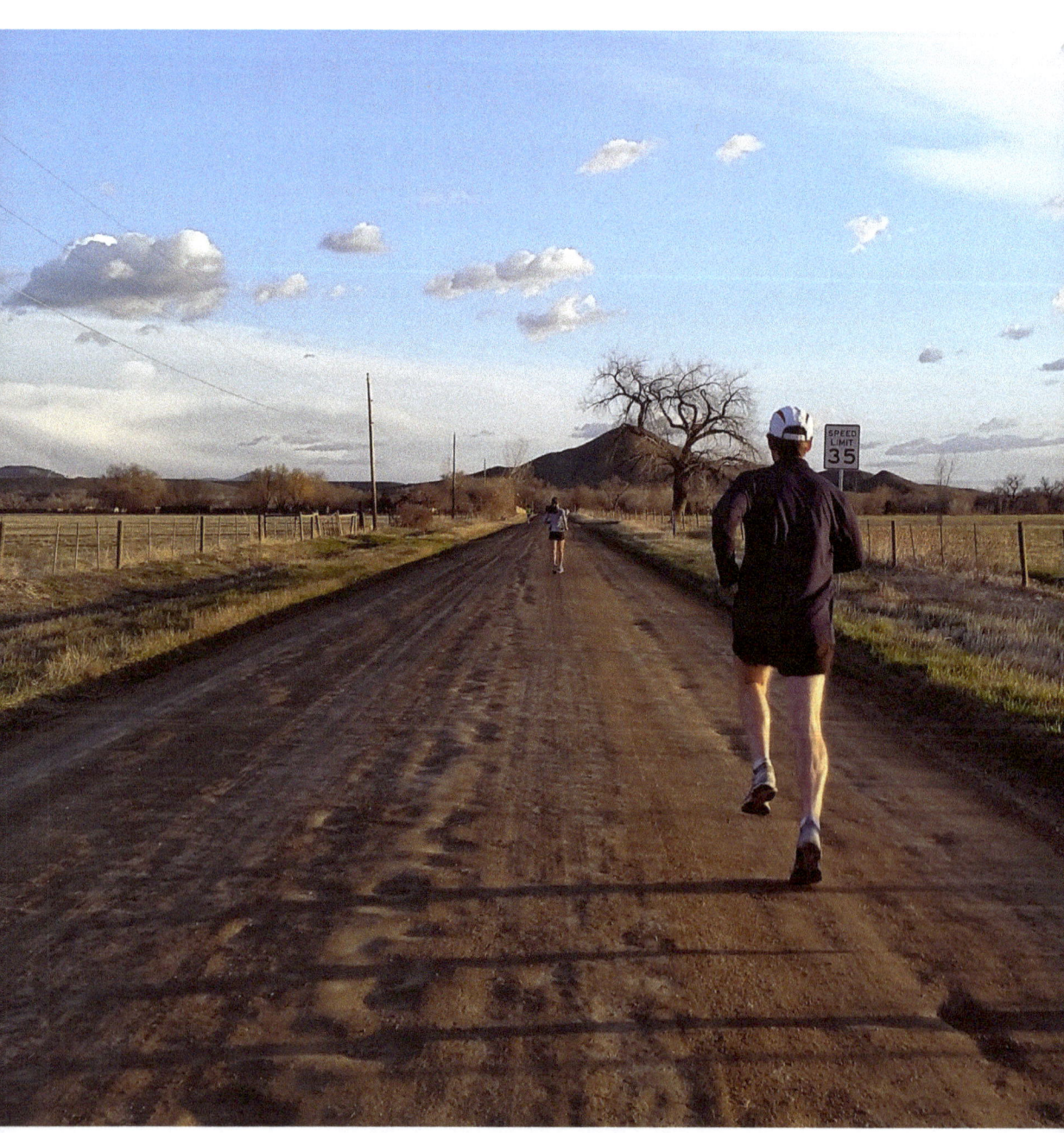

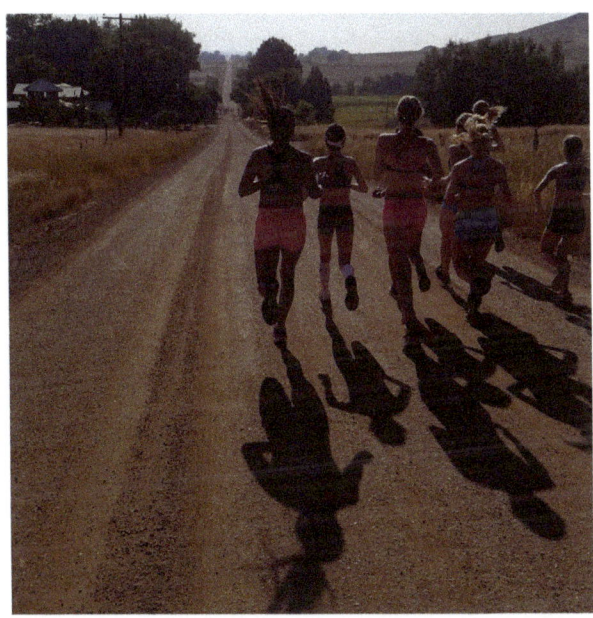

Boulder's running pioneers discovered the county's backroads early on, spending endless hours toiling on their softer surfaces and rolling hills to prepare for the biggest races around the world. Since then, Olympians and near-Olympians, CU harriers, and countless weekend warriors have watched the sun rise doing repeats on Monarch Rd., taking on "the Grange", or slogging out long runs with Haystack Mountain to the north and the Flatirons to the west.

As you run these storied roads, you too can draw upon their strength.

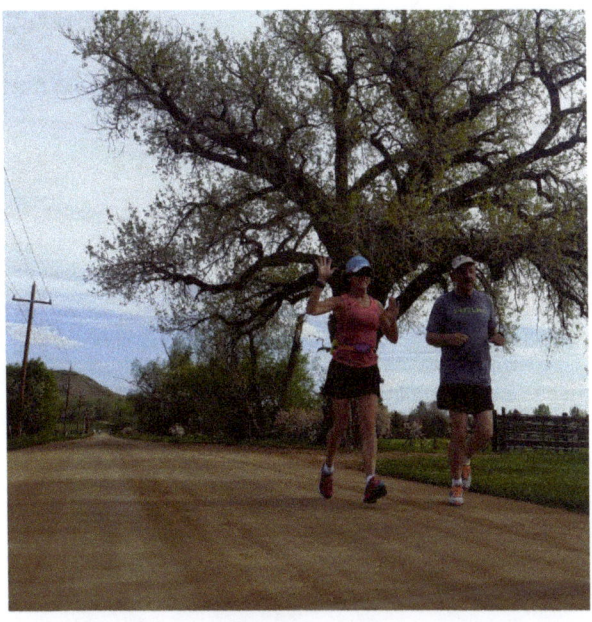

Top Results
June - August

On June 4 at the Freihofer's Run for Women 5K, which was also the USATF Road Championships, Golden's **Brianne Nelson** ran away with the win, completing the course in a fast 15:46.

Also on June 4 up in Leadville, Boulder's L**auren Laskowski** had a strong run at the Turquoise Lake Half-Marathon, finishing 2nd in a time of 1:47:08.

Also on June 4, the North Fork 50 Mile and 50K races located just outside Pine, CO, had a competitive field as always. In the 50 mile, Superior's **Evan Kimber** came away with a solid 3rd place in a time of 7:51:21, while Longmont's **Scott Howell** was just behind for 4th place in a time of 7:55:22. In the 50K race, it was Boulder's **Marianne Hogan** who dominated the field, winning outright with a time of 4:41:03. **Leila Degrave** was 2nd in a time of 5:21:59 while **Laura Capps** of Golden was 3rd in a time of 5:34:53.

Closer to home, in Golden Gate Canyon State Park at the Ultimate Direction Dirty 30, Boulder's **Joshua Arthur** came in 2nd with a time of 4:54:07. **Clare Gallagher** of Boulder ran to a second place finish for the women in a time of 5:46:10.

At the 14th Music City Distance Carnival on June 5th, **Jordan Jennings** of Boulder Track Club ran a 1:56.67 in the 800m. **Lindsey Putman**, also of Boulder Track Club, also had a solid race in the 800m with a time of 2:09.58.

In San Diego at the Suja Rock 'n' Roll Half Marathon on June 6, Boulder's **Jeffrey Eggleston** had a strong run, finishing in a time of 1:03:44 for 3rd place.

In New York on June 11 at the 45th running of the NYRR New York Mini 10K, **Brianne Nelson** took home 5th place with a time of 33:02.

Locally, on June 12 at the Garden of the Gods 10 Mile Run in Manitou Springs, **Tyler McCandless** came away with a third place showing in a time of 52:49 while **Mario Macias** placed 5th with a time of 53:37. **Amanda Lee** of Boulder had an excellent race, running a time of 1:08:08 for 2nd place.

At the ever competitive Garry Bjorklund Half-Marathon on June 18th, **Ashley Brasovan** of Golden came away with a 8th place finish in a time of 1:18:05. **Matt Hensley** of Superior also had a good race, finishing 16th with a time of 1:08:53.

Up in Seattle, WA, at the Alaska Airlines Rock 'n' Roll Seattle Half-Marathon on June 18, **Kara Ford** of Broomfield came away with the win in a time of 1:20:00.

On the same day in Peoria, IL, at the Steamboat Classic 4 Mile, **Jeffrey Eggleston** ran a time of 19:14, good for 7th place.

Just outside of Lake City, CO, the San Juan Solstice 50 Mile, always a tough race, was held on June 25. Boulder's **Andrew Skurka** came away with a solid 4th place finish in a time of 9:11:57. **Courtney Dauwalter** of Golden also had a great race, finishing 2nd with a time of 10:52:02.

On June 26 at the Scotiabank Vancouver Half-Marathon, **Adriana Nelson** of Boulder ran away from the field for a dominating win in a time of 1:14:35.

In Chicago, at the Humana Rock 'n' Roll Chicago Half-Marathon, **Neely Gracey** of Louisville put down a fast time, running away with the win in a time of 1:12:26.

On July 16 just outside of Fairplay, Colorado, the Sheep Mountain 50 Mile Endurance Run took place. Boulder's **Abby Mitchell** came away with 3rd place in a time of 12:11:00.

Just outside of the hamlet of Gould, CO, on July 23, the Never Summer 100K once again drew a strong field. **Christopher Schurk** of Boulder ran to a second place finish in a time of 12:30:33, missing the top spot by less than a minute. **Nick Pedatella** of Boulder was 4th in a time of 12:54:31. **Keira McMahon** of Nederland was 2nd in a time of 16:18:57, while **Cindy Stonesmith** of Louisville was 3rd with a time of 16:25:51.

At the USATF 30K Trail Championships on July 29, hosted at the Pikes Peak Ultra 30K, **Matt Daniels** of Boulder had a solid race, finishing the tough course in 1:53:26 for 2nd place while **Chris Grauch** finished 6th in a time of 2:00:23. **Clare Gallagher** came away with a 2nd place finish with a time of 2:10:21 while **Amanda Lee** finished 5th in a time of 2:24:11.

At the Sir Walter Miler held Aug. 5 at Meredith College, **Sara Vaughn** ran a solid time of 4:35.52 for 11th place in a highly competitive field.

On Aug. 6 at the TD Beach to Beacon 10K held in Cape Elizabeth, ME, Boulder's **Joe Bosshard** had a solid race, finishing 10th with a time of 29:27.

Also on Aug. 6 at the Telluride Mountain Run 38 Miler, Boulder's **Jason Killgore** came away with a 3rd place finish, completing the difficult course in 7:20:57.

Locally, at the always fun and competitive Pearl Street Mile, held on Aug. 10, **Blake Theroux** came away with the win in a time of 4:11, while **Stephen Pifer** came in 3rd with a time of 4:12. **Elise Cranny** of Niwot won for the women in a time of 4:49, while **Katie McMenamin** was 2nd in 4:49 and **Mara Olson** was 3rd in 4:51.

At the Mt. Sneffels Marathon just outside of Ouray, **Vincent Dorzweiler** of Boulder came away with the overall win in a time of 3:13:19, while **Jamie Pfahl** of Boulder won for the women with a time of 3:44:45.

On the same day at the Longmont Sunrise Stampede 10K, **Kevin Kochei** of Boulder came home with the win in a time of 33:04, while **Joe Zamadics** of Boulder came in 2nd in a time of 34:12. **Kristin Johansen** of Longmont won for the women with a time of 36:48 while **Kristin Arendt** came in 2nd in a time of 37:26 and **Becky Lynn** was 3rd in a time of 38:17.

On August 14, **Andy Wacker** runs the Fastest Known Times (FKT) on both the North to South (43:22) and round-trip (1:28:52) routes on the Mesa Trail. The North to South route starts from the ranger cottage at Chautauqua to to parking lot at the South Mesa Trailhead.

Dave Mackey had the previous FKTs, N to S in about 47:00 and round-trip in 1:34:29s, June 3, 2003.

On Aug. 20 at the Leadville Trail 100 Mile Endurance Run, **Clare Gallagher** blew away the women's field, crossing the finish line in 19 hours and 27 seconds for the win. **Erich Wegscheider** of Boulder finished 12th with a time of 20:25:24 in the men's field.

In Manitou Springs at the Pikes Peak Ascent, held on Aug. 20, Boulder's **Andy Wacker** came away with 2nd place in a time of 2:13:59. **Addie Bracy** of Longmont also finished 2nd for the women with a time of 2:46:44, while **Monica Folts** of Golden finished 5th in a time of 2:55:18.

The following day at the Pikes Peak Marathon, **Galen Burrell** of Boulder had a strong race, finishing 4th in a time of 3:56:05.

At the Hideaway Hundred 100K race held in Winter Park, CO, **Scott Sundahl** of Boulder pulled off a 3rd place finish in a time of 18:00:26. Meanwhile, in the 50K event, **Courtney Dauwalter** of Golden took home 2nd place overall in a time of 5:02:30.

What were your top results?

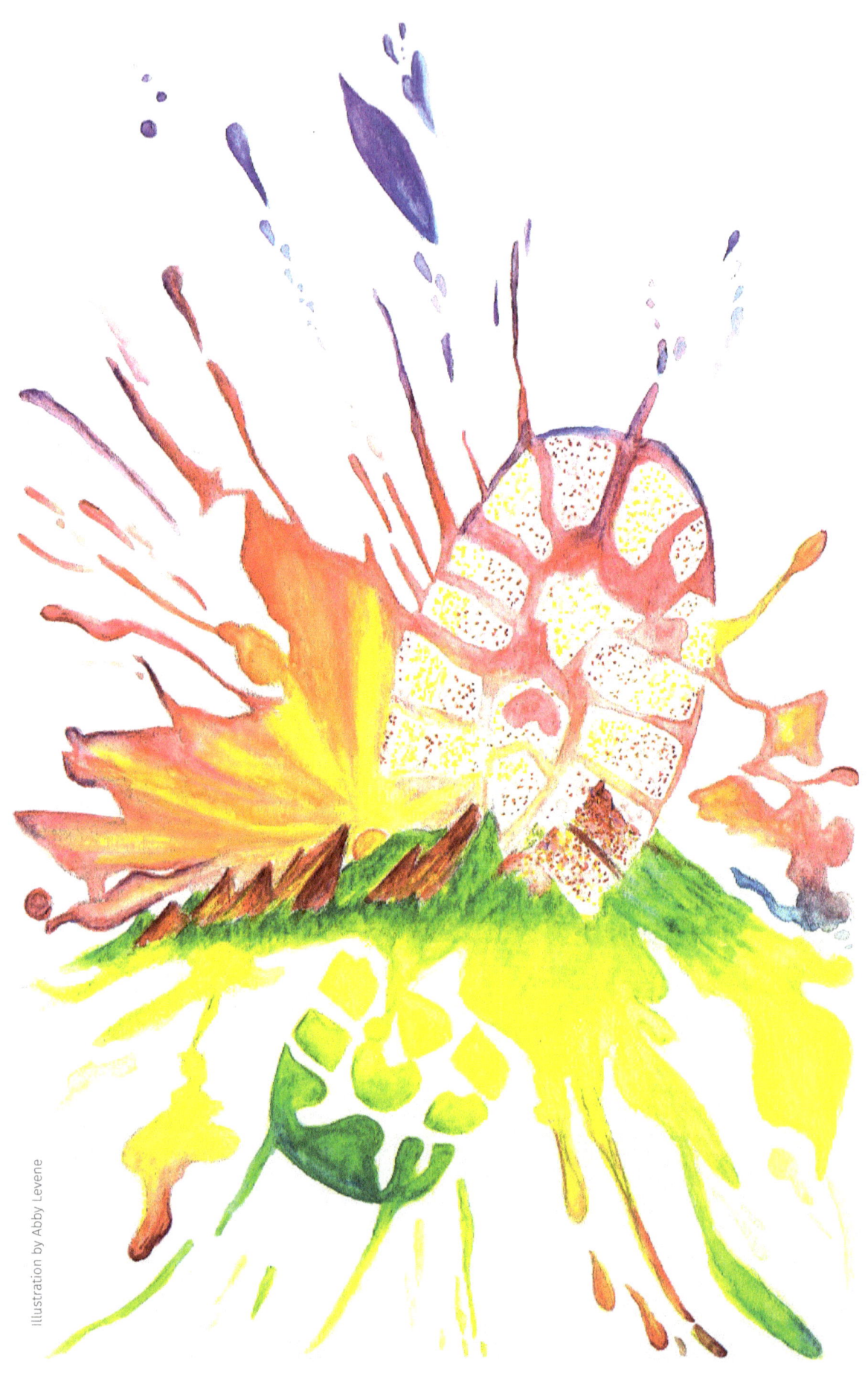

Illustration by Abby Levene

WRITING PROMPT
SUMMER
Where was the most inspired place you explored?

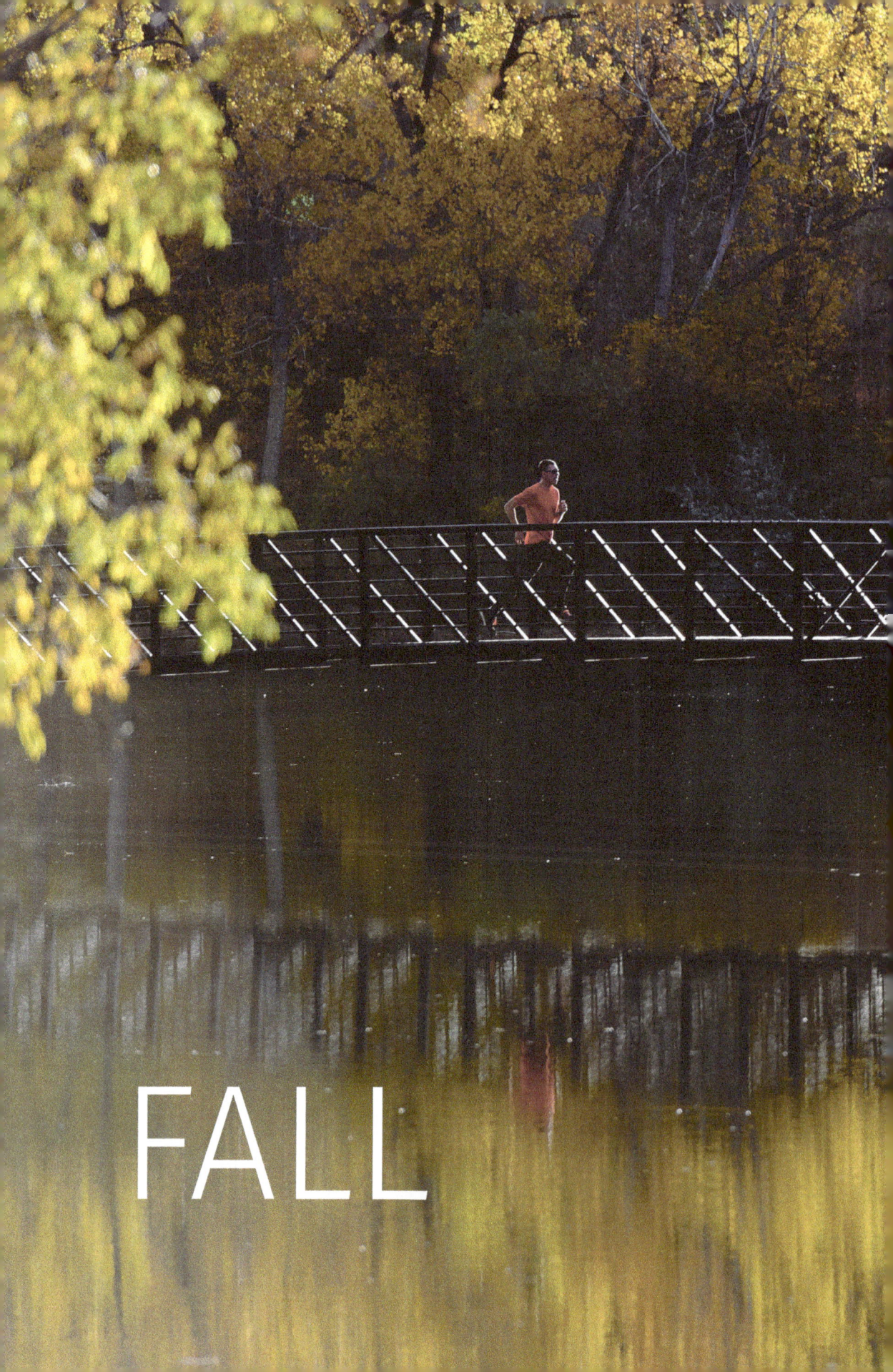

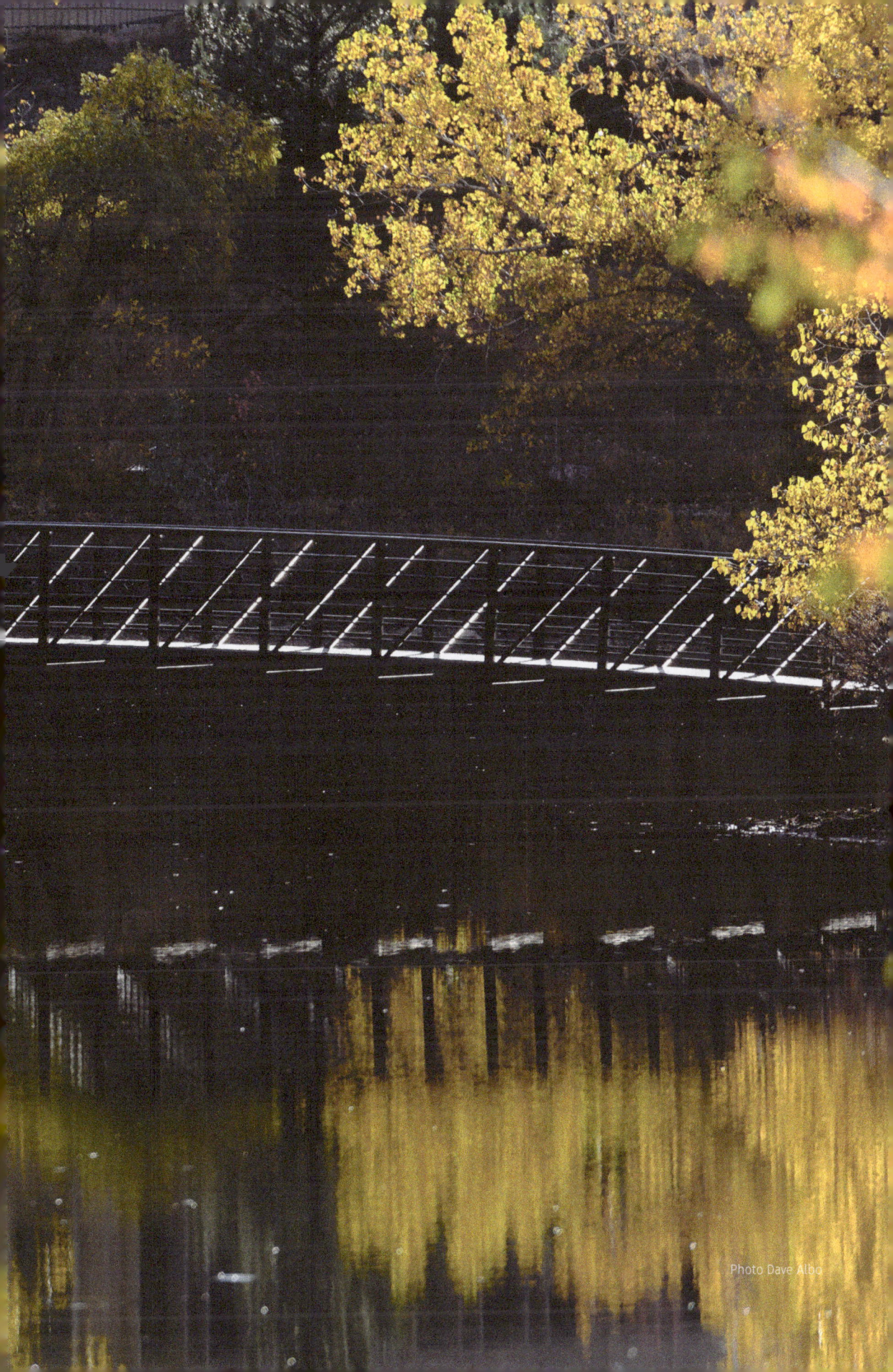
Photo Dave Albo

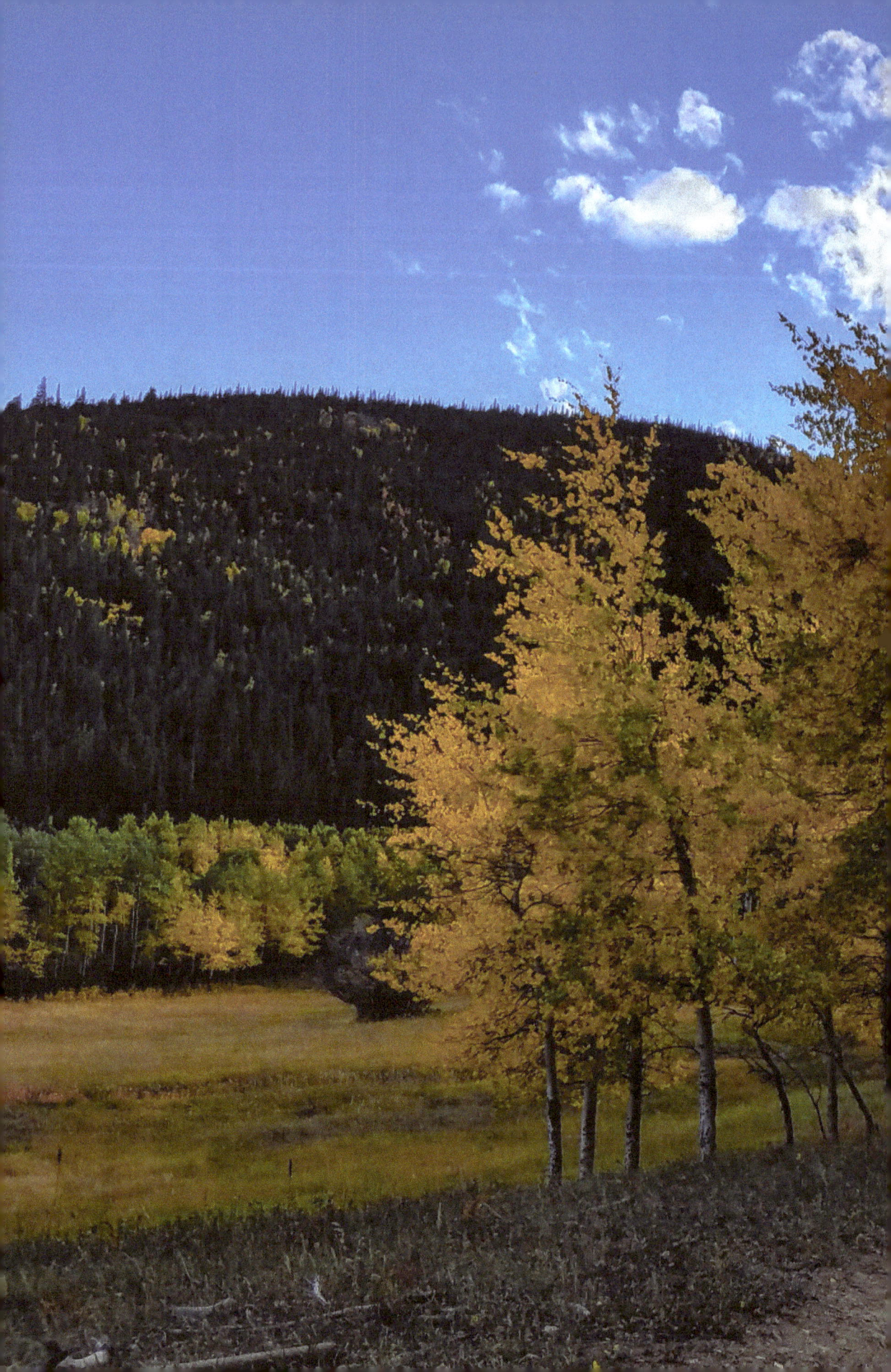

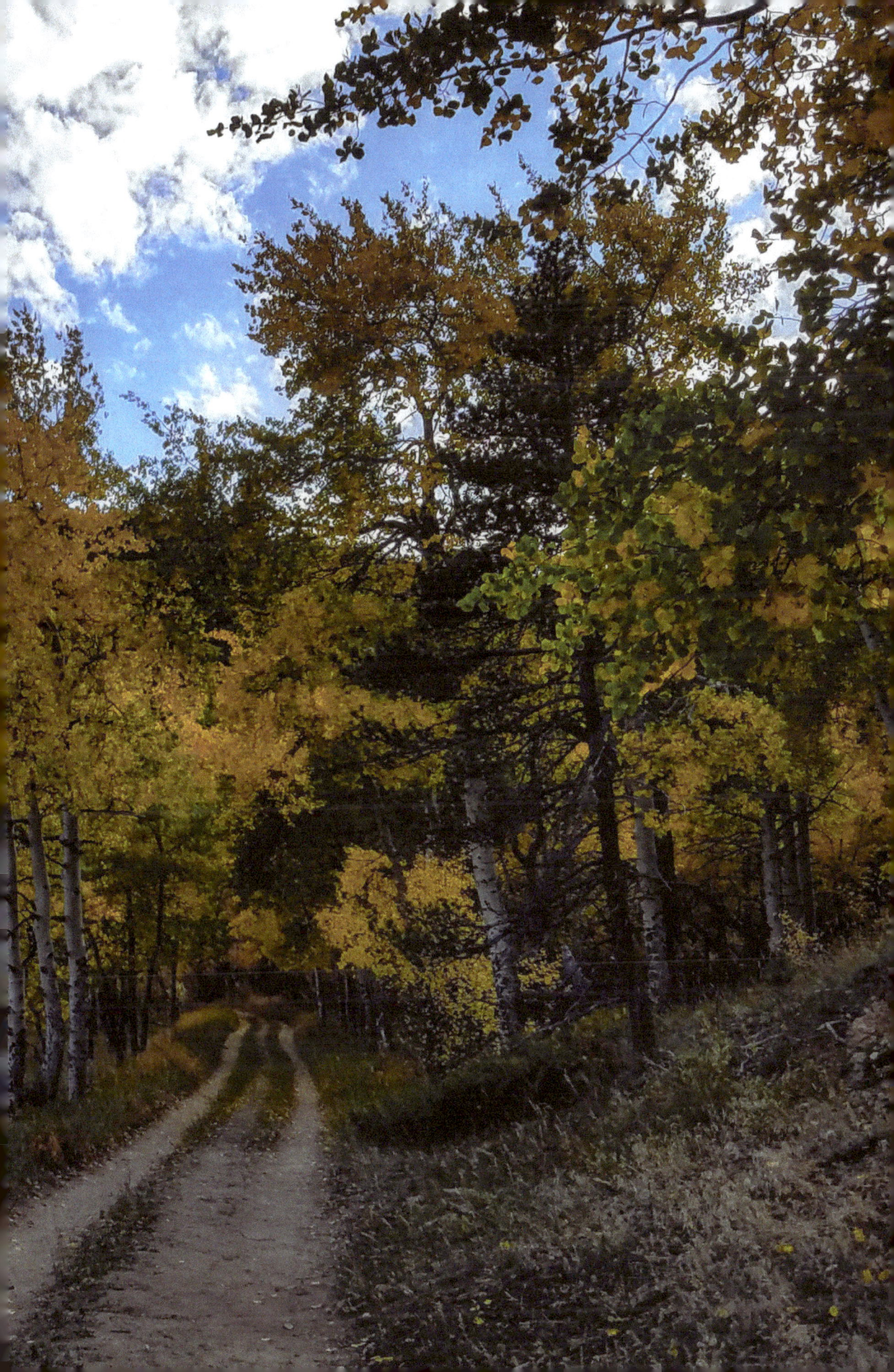

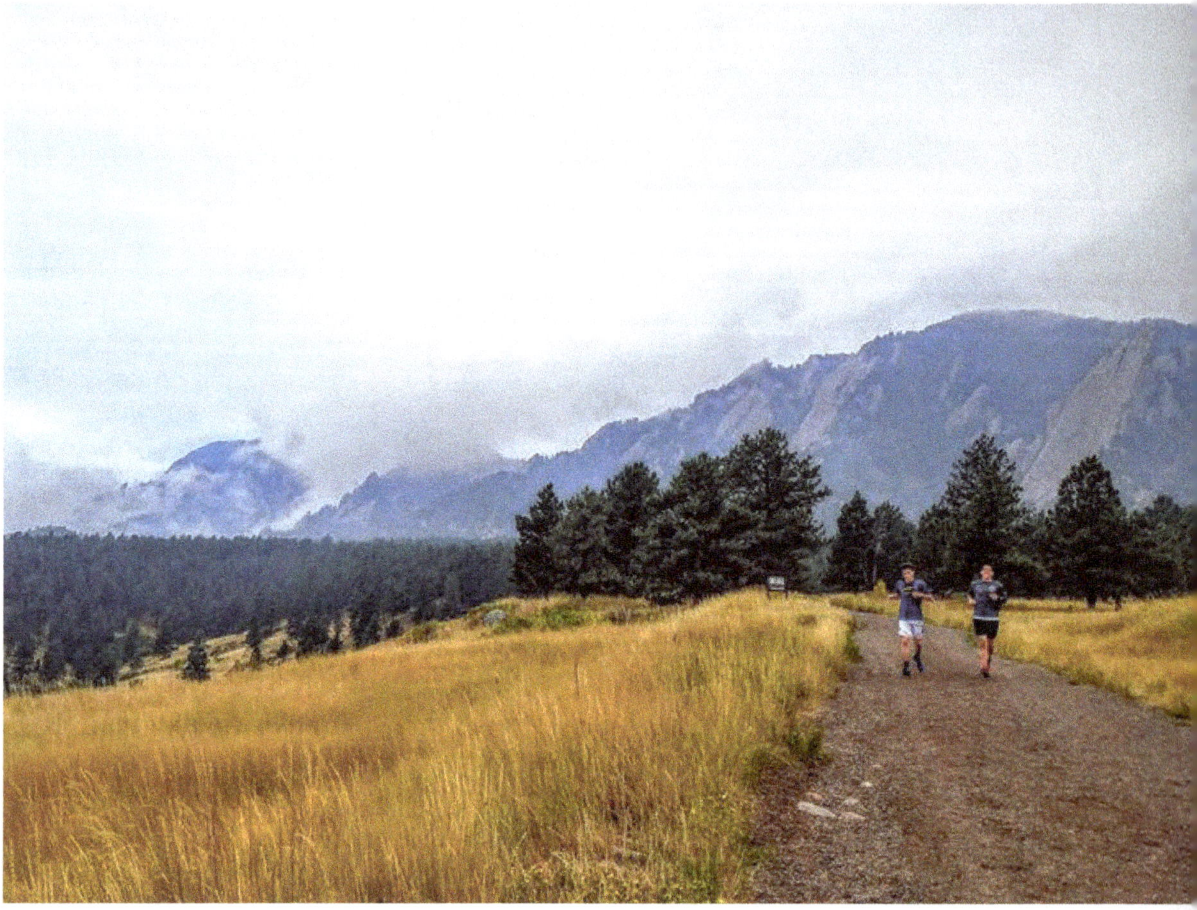

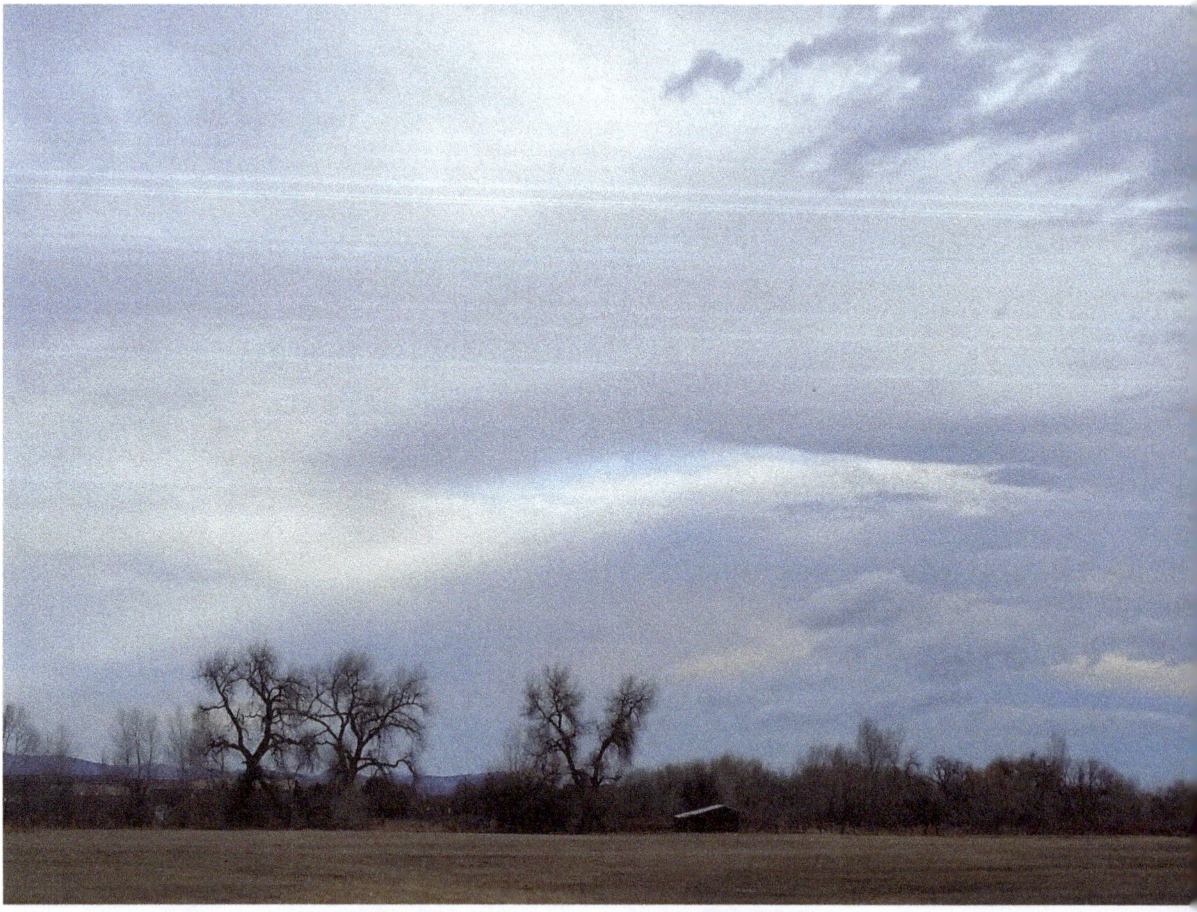

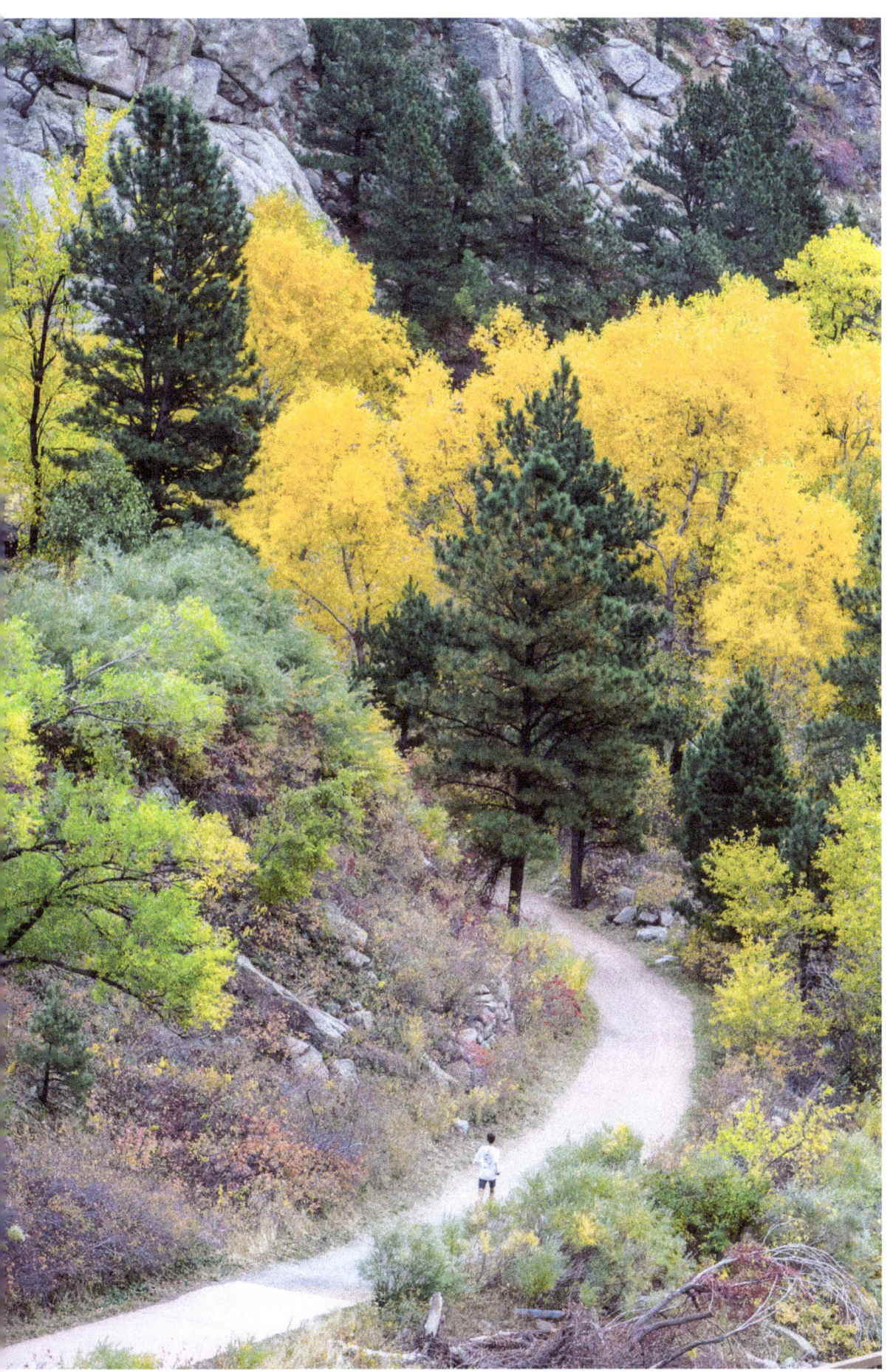

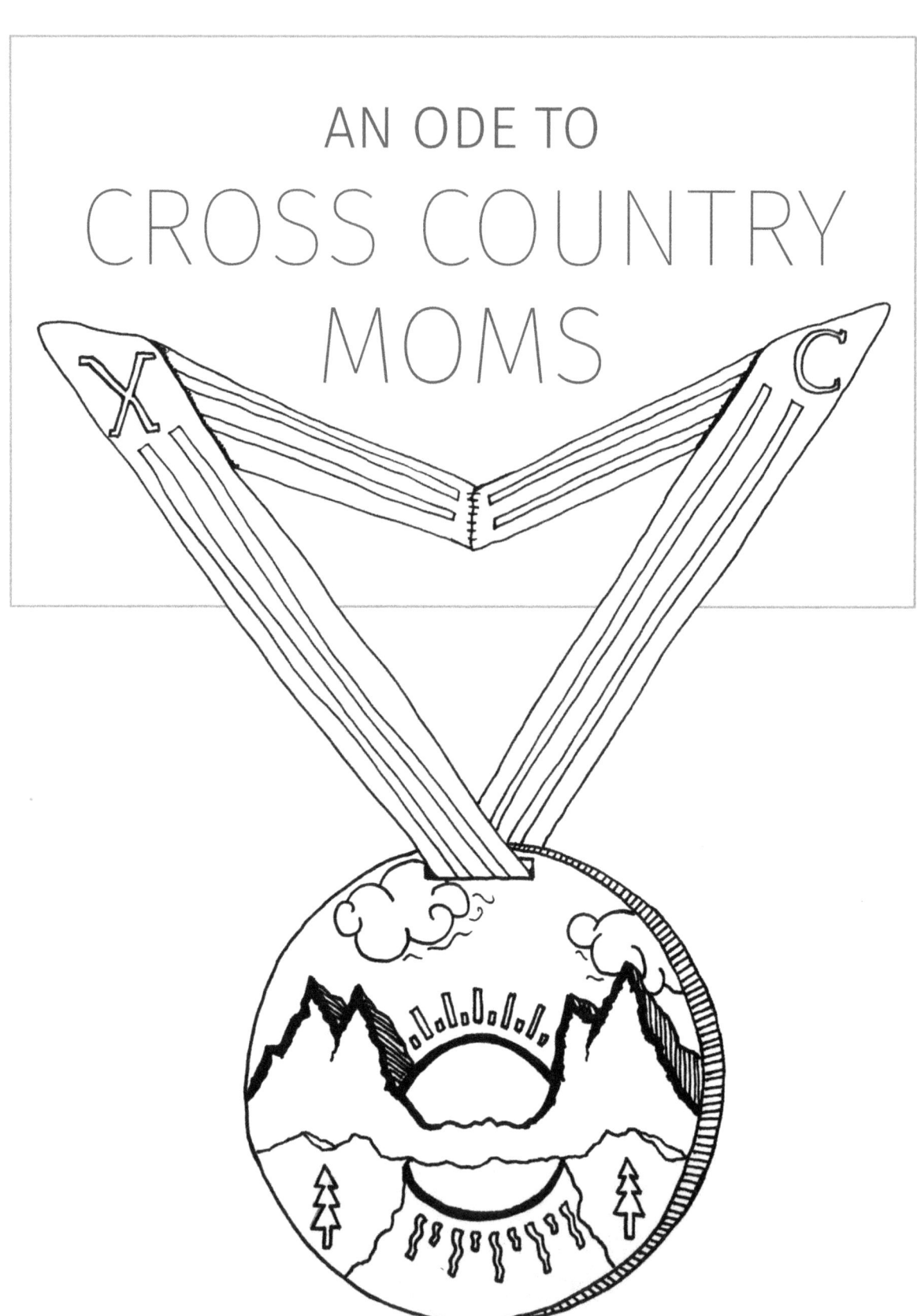

A framed photo, hanging on the wall,
Brings back memories of those far off Falls.
Snapshots taken of mom and me,
Post-race, and smiling, and content just to be.

From high school to college, and well beyond,
Singlets, tank tops, "civilian" clothes donned,
It didn't matter the race, didn't matter the time:
Mom, always ready with a hug, no matter the grime.

When hair ties broke, or the uniform was dirty,
Mom was ready, set to work in a flurry,
Helping us all to get back on our feet,
To make that next goal, to race that next meet.

The miles I've covered in the years since
Might have made my younger self wince.
But Mom knew that I had it in me,
Helping me dream of what could be.

So thank you to all the Cross-Country Moms,
Developing young runners, with both excitement and calm,
Teaching this hidden lesson all the time:
That we're running our way to the starting line.

Words by Mikhaila Redovian
Illustration by Jeremy Hendricks

Boulder Trail Running Festival

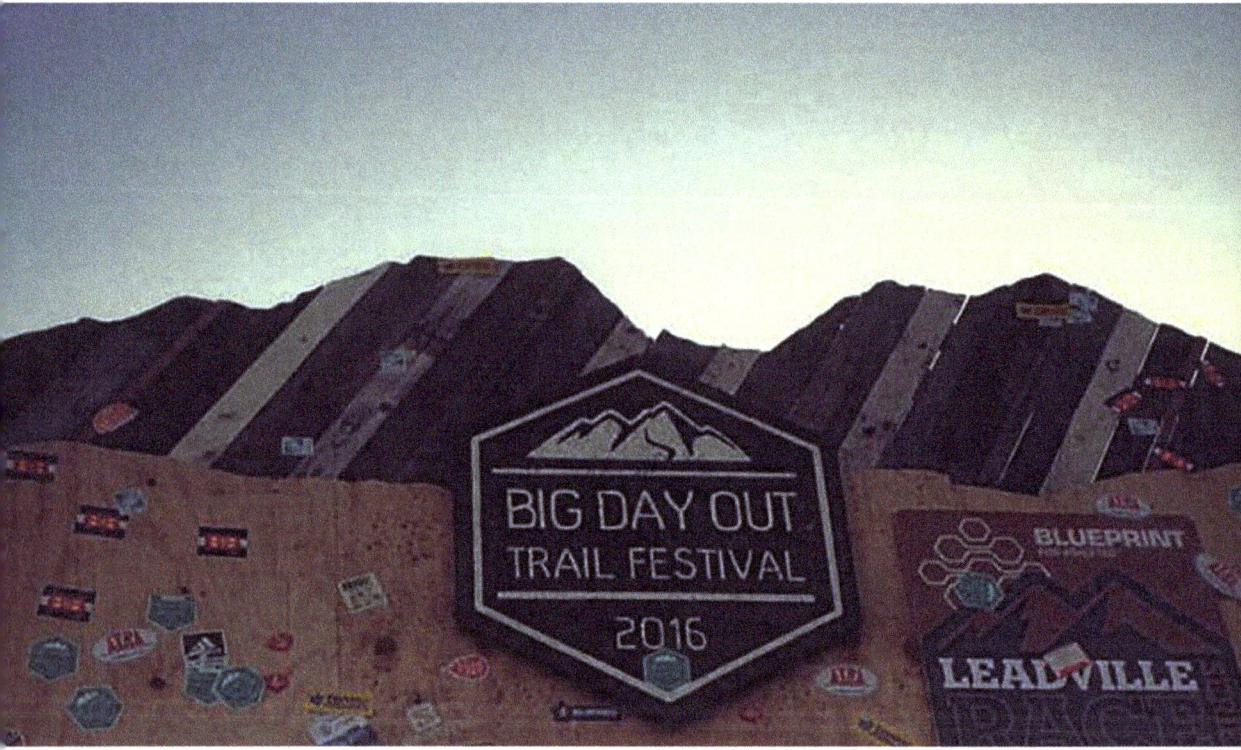

On Sept. 10, the first Trails In Motion Big Day Out Trail Running Festival took place, becoming Boulder's first trail-inspired community event. Like-minded runners gathered at Foothills Community Park to hang out with each other and some of the sport's stars, check out and demo some of the latest trail running gear, enjoy local food from Zeal Food and local pours from Shoes & Brews and watch the world's finest trail-running films. There were also breakout sessions on trail topics and a kids' fun run. The festival will return in 2017.

TRAILRUNFEST.COM

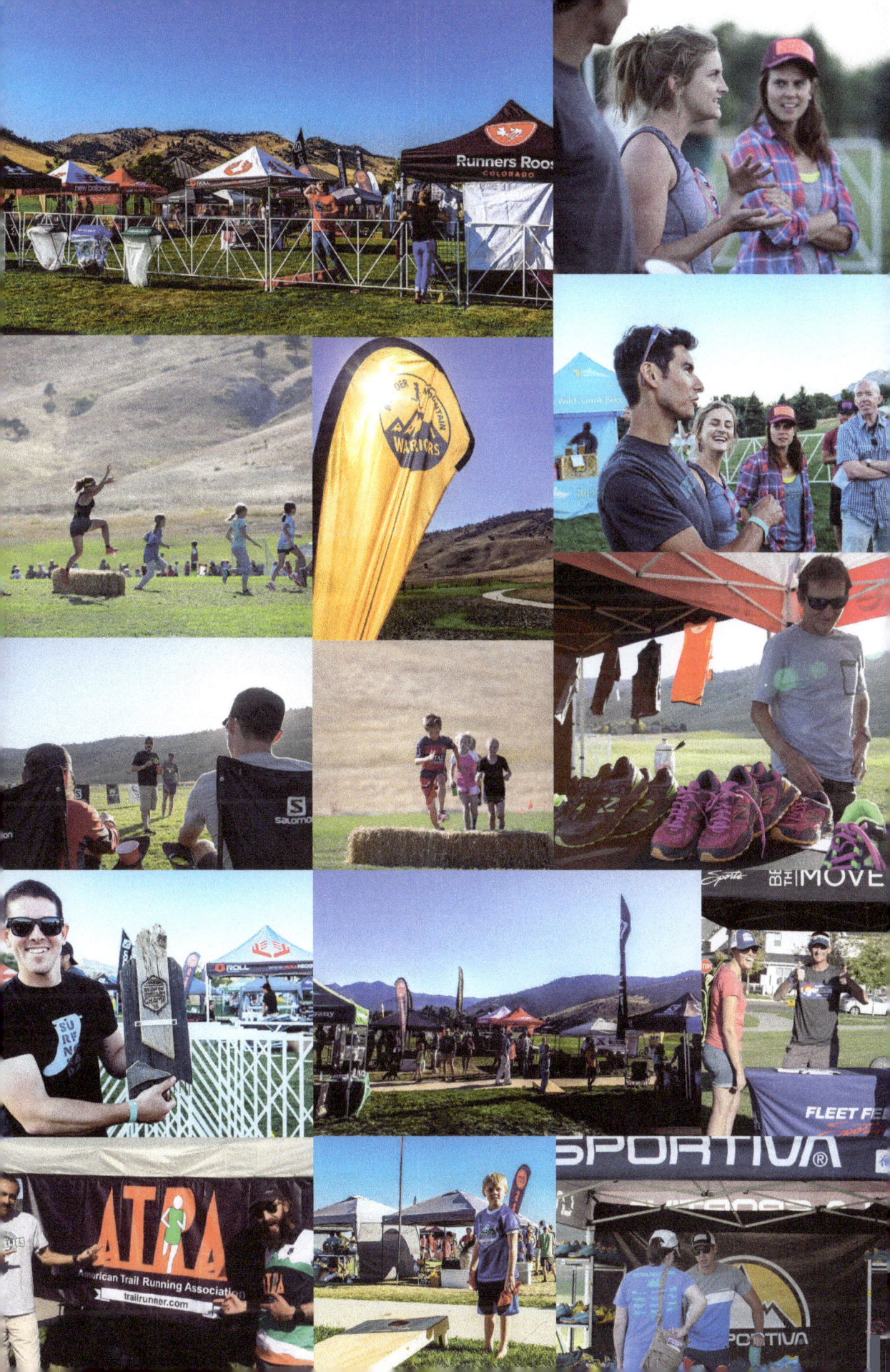

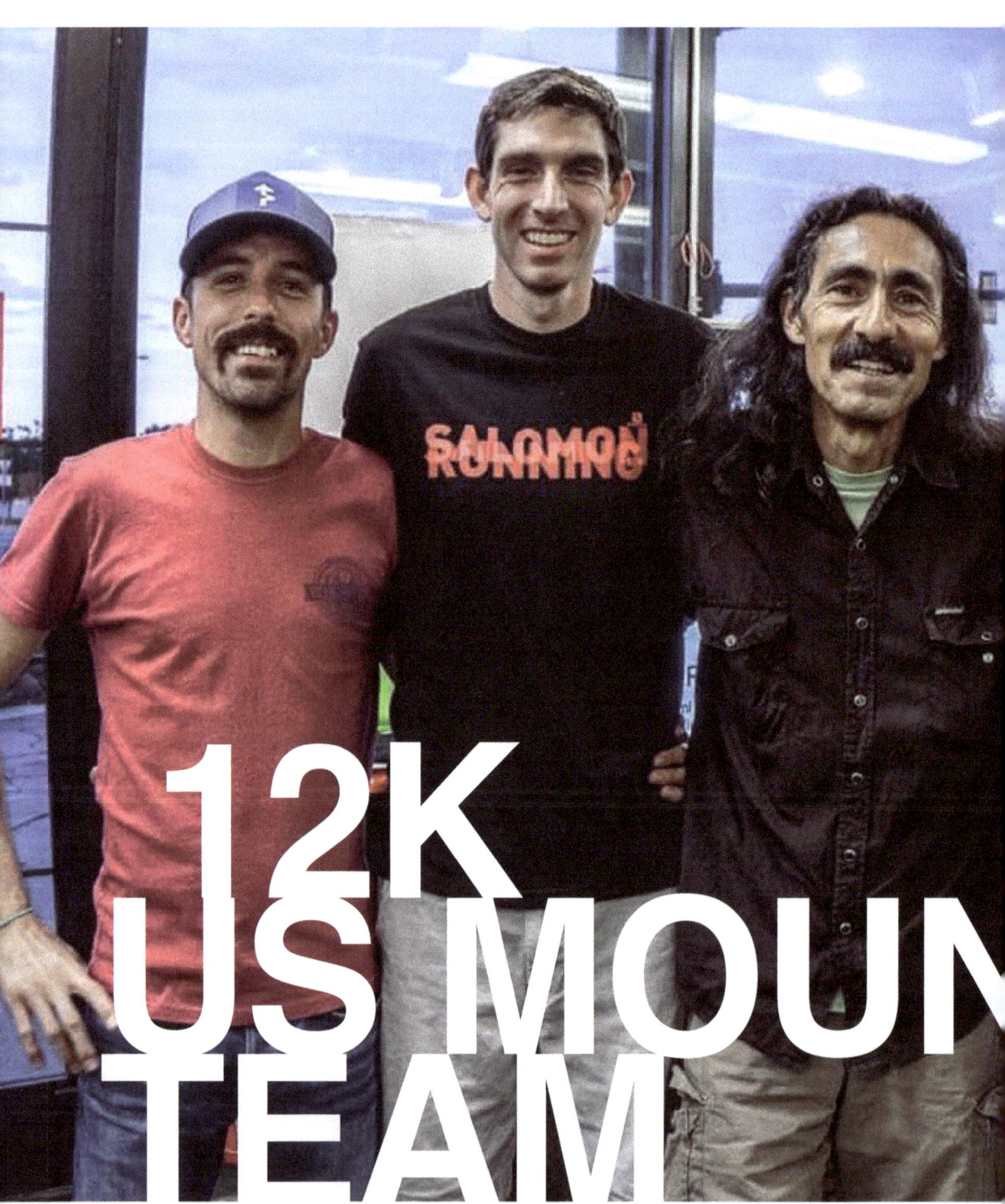

Pictured from left to right: David Fuentes, Matt Daniels, Pablo Vigil, Addie Bracy, Andy Wacker from the team send off party held at the Boulder Running Company.

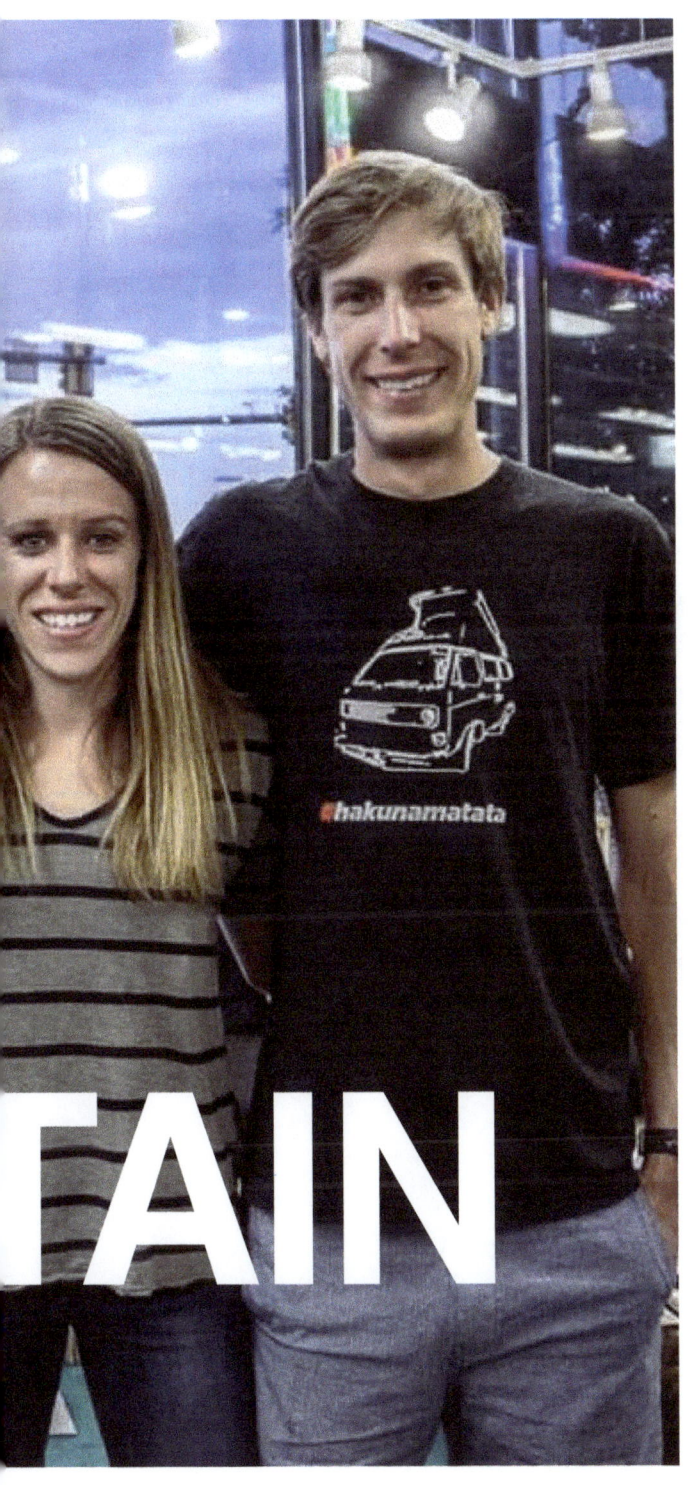

Four Boulder area runners helped to make for strong teams at the 32nd World Mountain Running Championships held in Sapareva Banya, Bulgaria in September: veteran mountain runner Andy Wacker, Matt Daniels, David Fuentes, who was in Boulder to train in the mountains, and Addie Bracy.

Qualifications for Team USA were held at Loon Mountain Race in Lincoln, NH. All of these runners are track and road superstars who turned their focus to the trails. For Fuentes and Bracy it was their first trail race ever. For Daniels, it was his second; he won the Golden Dirty 30 12 mile in June.

Despite being a novice on the trail, Bracy brought her strong steeplechase and road racing skills to the mountain and ran the second-fastest time overall up the hardest section of the course. On her success:

"I didn't really have any technique at all. I was just trying to get up the mountain. It's very different from the track. For the short steep stuff, there is never a point that it feels good. When I am fit for a 10k or a half-marathon I feel good at the start. But with this you basically hit your redline at like 2 minutes, then you run that for like 45 minutes.

"Yeah, you are only running 10 minute pace but it's some of the most I've ever hurt before."

The men's team took Gold from the support of Wacker as the 3rd American to score. Joe Gray from Colorado Springs took the Gold overall. Bracy was the 2nd American in the women's race, helping her team take home the Bronze.

"Our goal going into the race was to put four guys in the top 16. I did my best today and gave it everything I had. We all knew that this year was about the team so it's awesome to follow through on that dream and win team gold," said Wacker.

#FoundOnMyRun

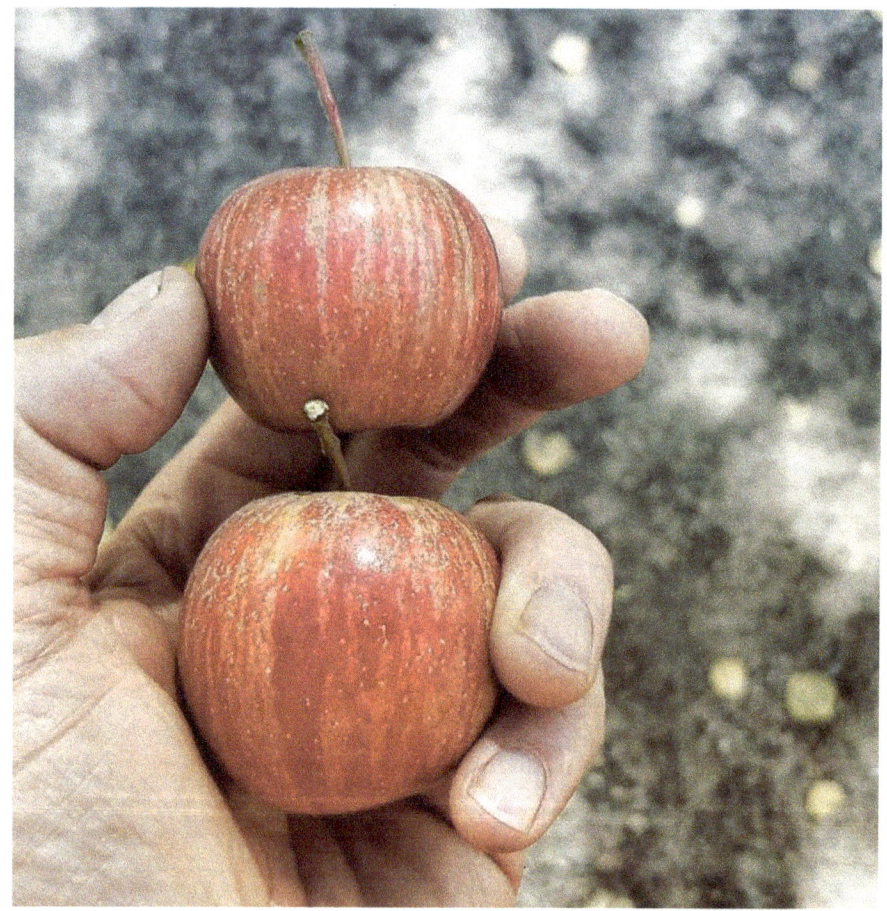

Fall Harvest
Todd Straka

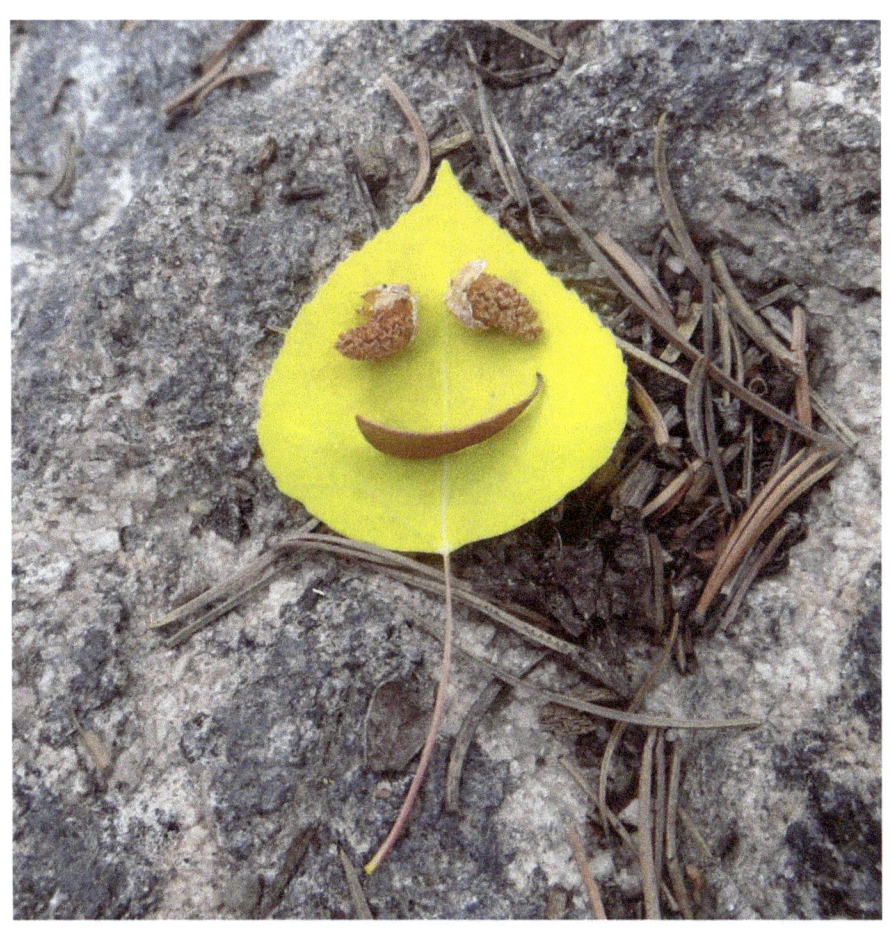

Happy Fall
Andy Ames

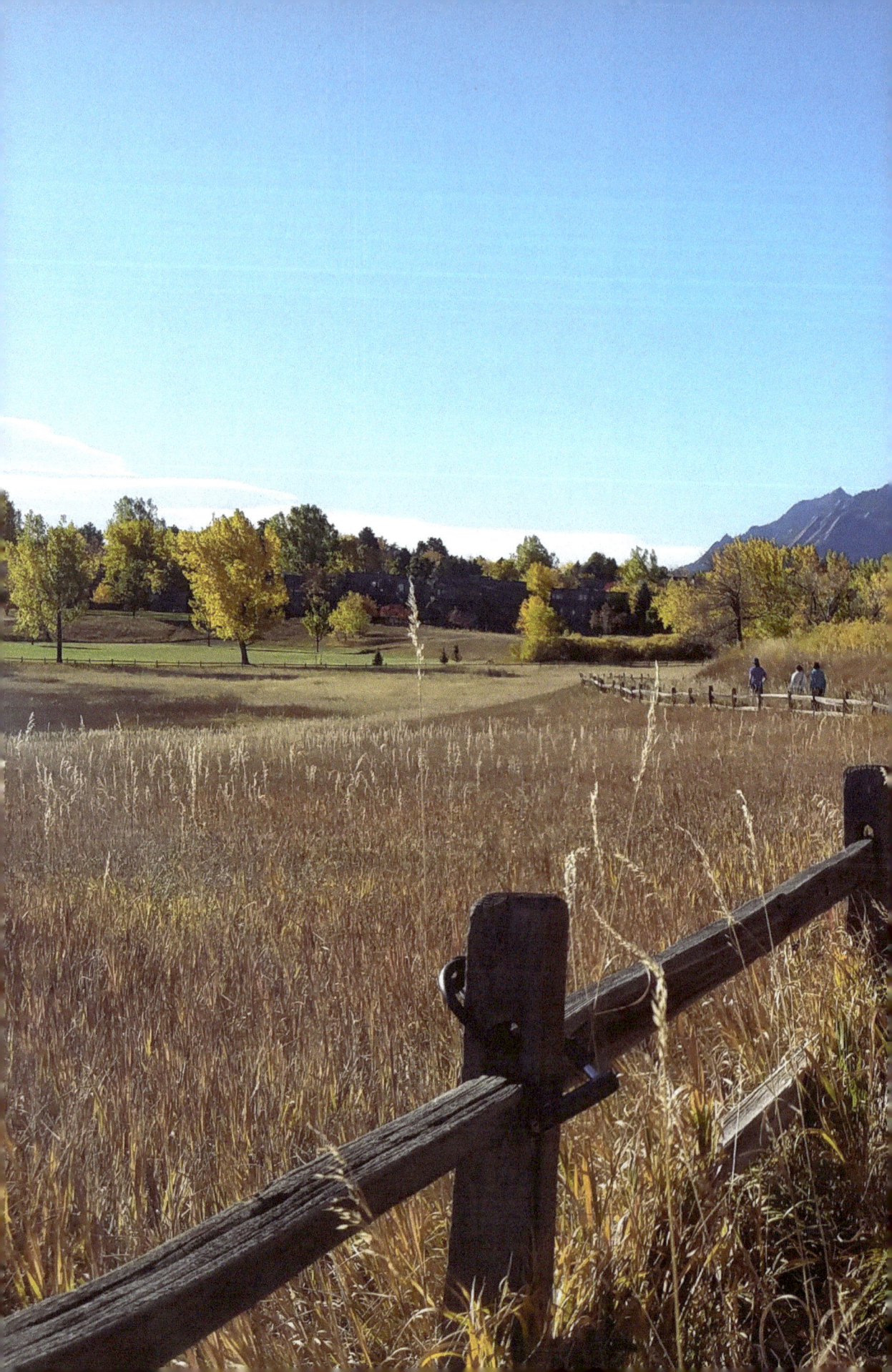

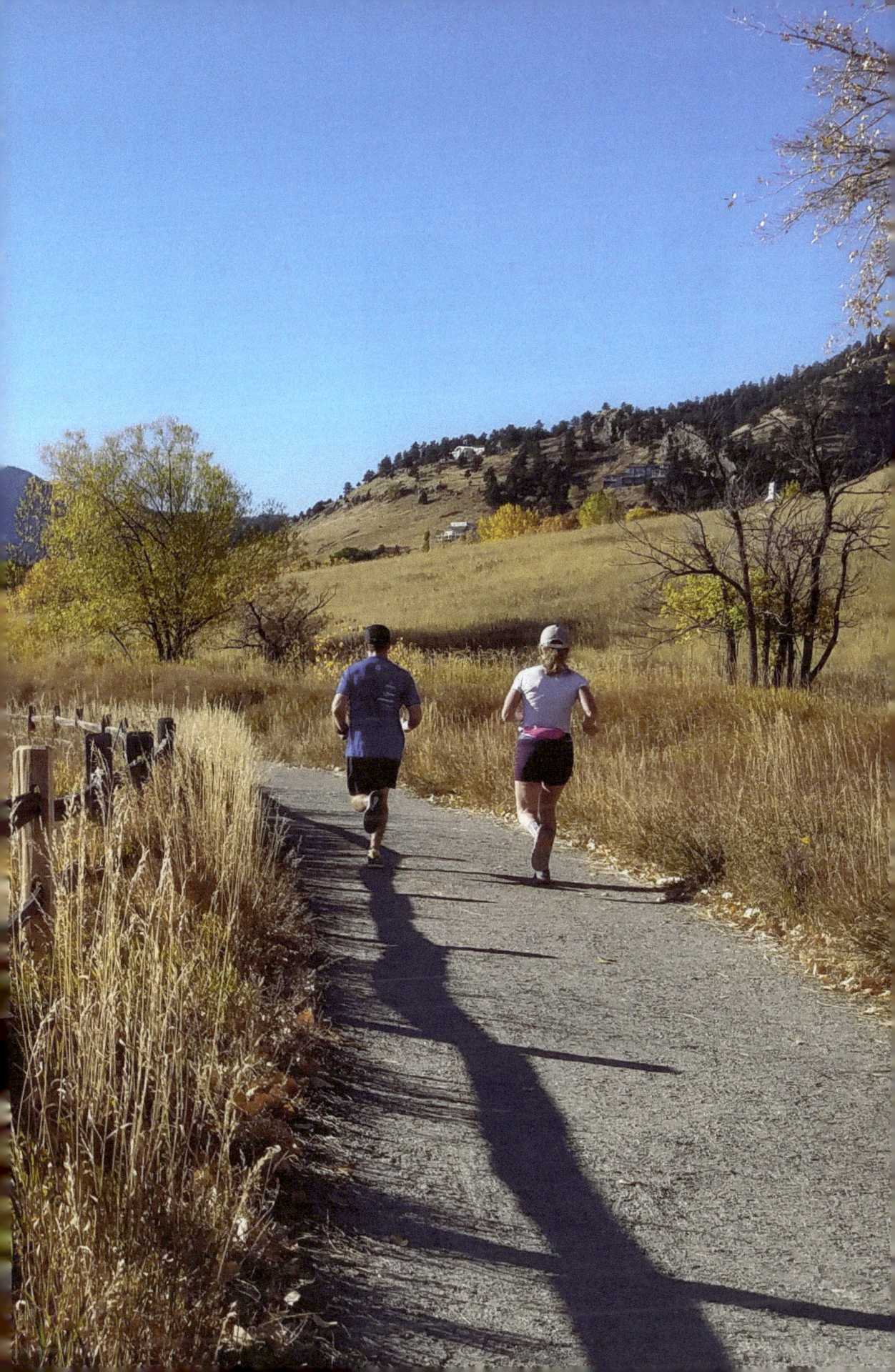

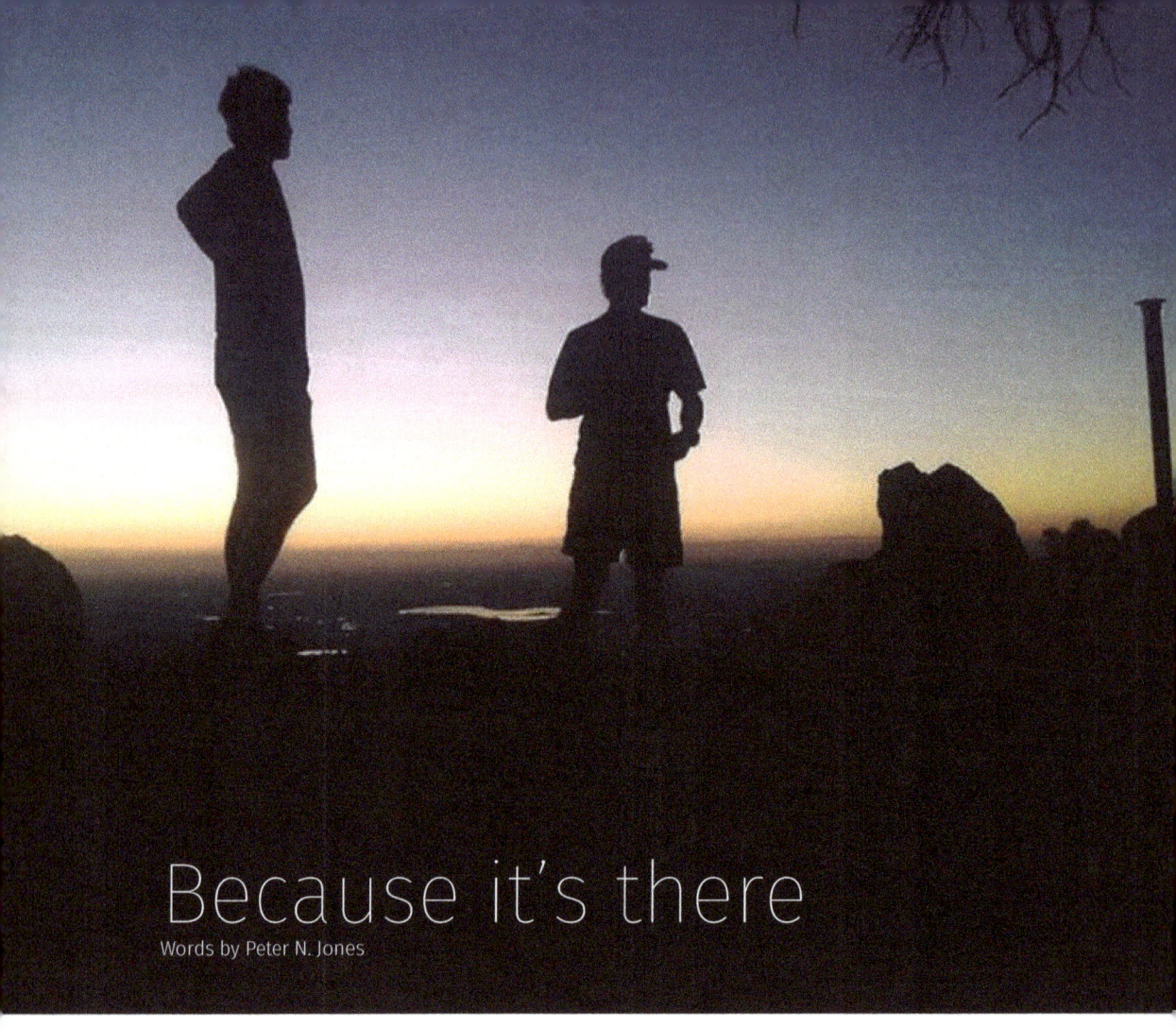

Because it's there
Words by Peter N. Jones

Runners are a goal-oriented lot.

We like to pick a goal – often a race – and train for it, putting our focus on that end result and working towards it. But runners are also an adventurous lot, and races don't always fulfill that need for achievement. So we pick other goals: contrived, repeatable, long-term, distance-oriented, speed-focused, you name it, it's a goal that becomes a Project.

Projects are unique to the individual runner who comes up with the idea – to summit Mt. Sanitas 100 times in a year, to run the mile under 4:30 as a Masters runner, to complete the insane Leadman or Leadwoman series, to qualify for the Olympic Trials three times in a row, to scale all of Colorado's 14,000' mountains by human power. You name it, a Project can be as ridiculous as the runner, and it is only the imagination that stops one from coming up with a Project and going for it. This year saw no shortage of runners picking Projects and going after them.

Some projects were completed while others are still on the horizon – that is the beauty of a project, it is always there until it is achieved.

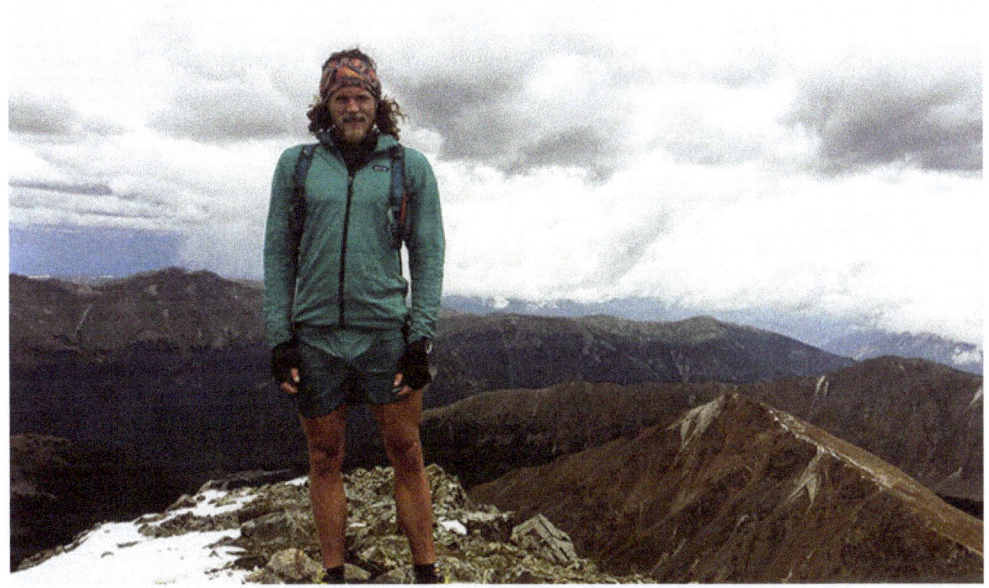

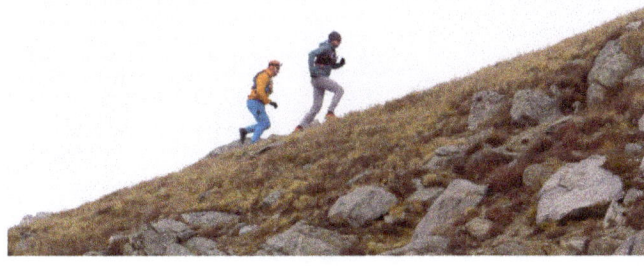

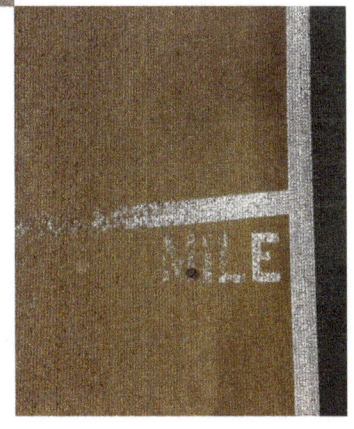

Opposite: Leo Lesperance aimed to summit Mt. Sanitas 100 times. Photo by Leo Lesperance

Joe Grant on top of Torreys Peak during his run to summit all of Colorado's 14ers by human power.
Photo by Ron Braselton

#BeatModay pushes the idea of "weekend warrior" to the limits. You have 64 hours between 5pm on Friday until 9am Monday morning to go really big, really big.

Todd Straka aimed to run a personal best in the mile.

BOULDER BACKROADS
Marathon - Half - 10k

Photos by Glen Delman and Todd Straka

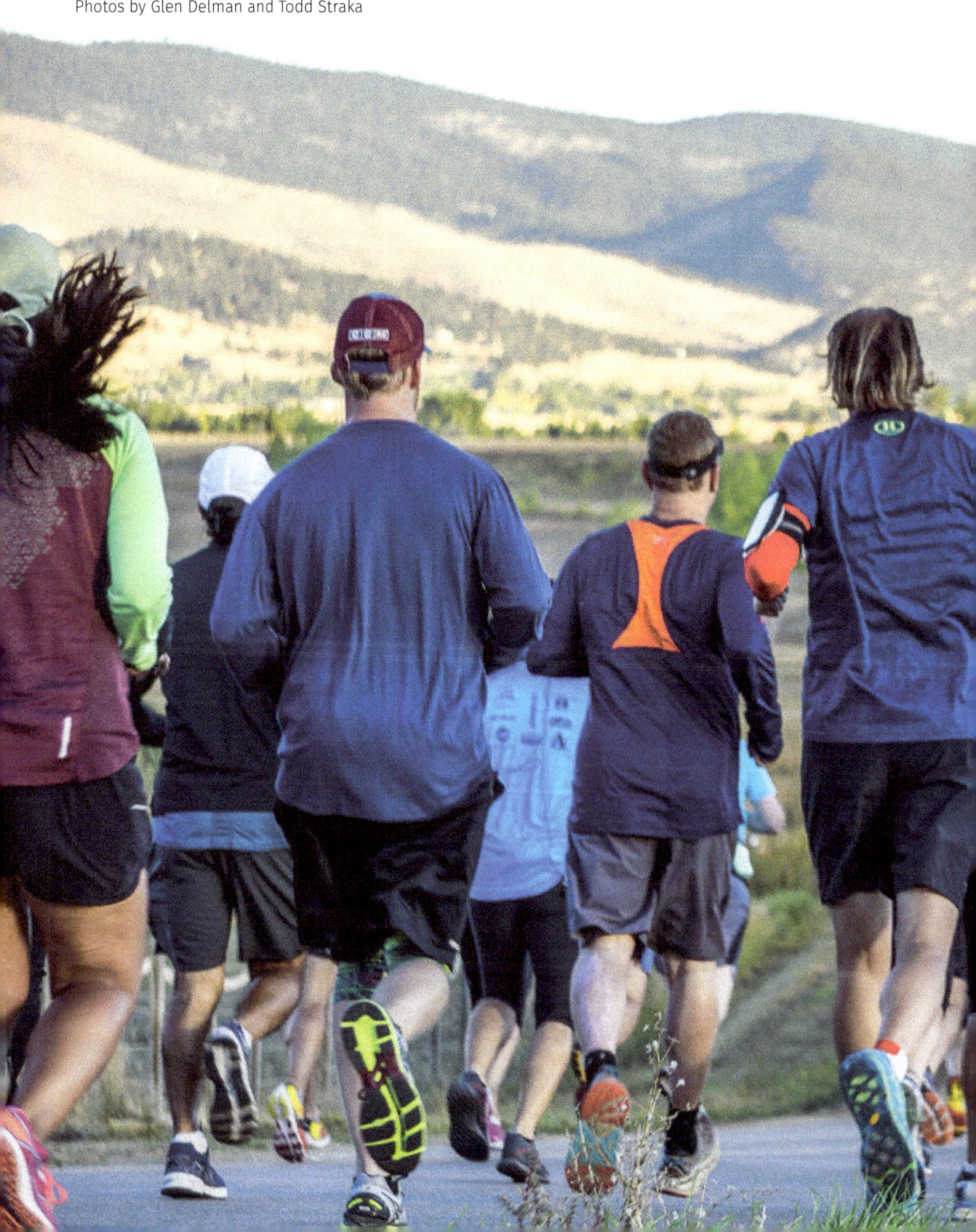

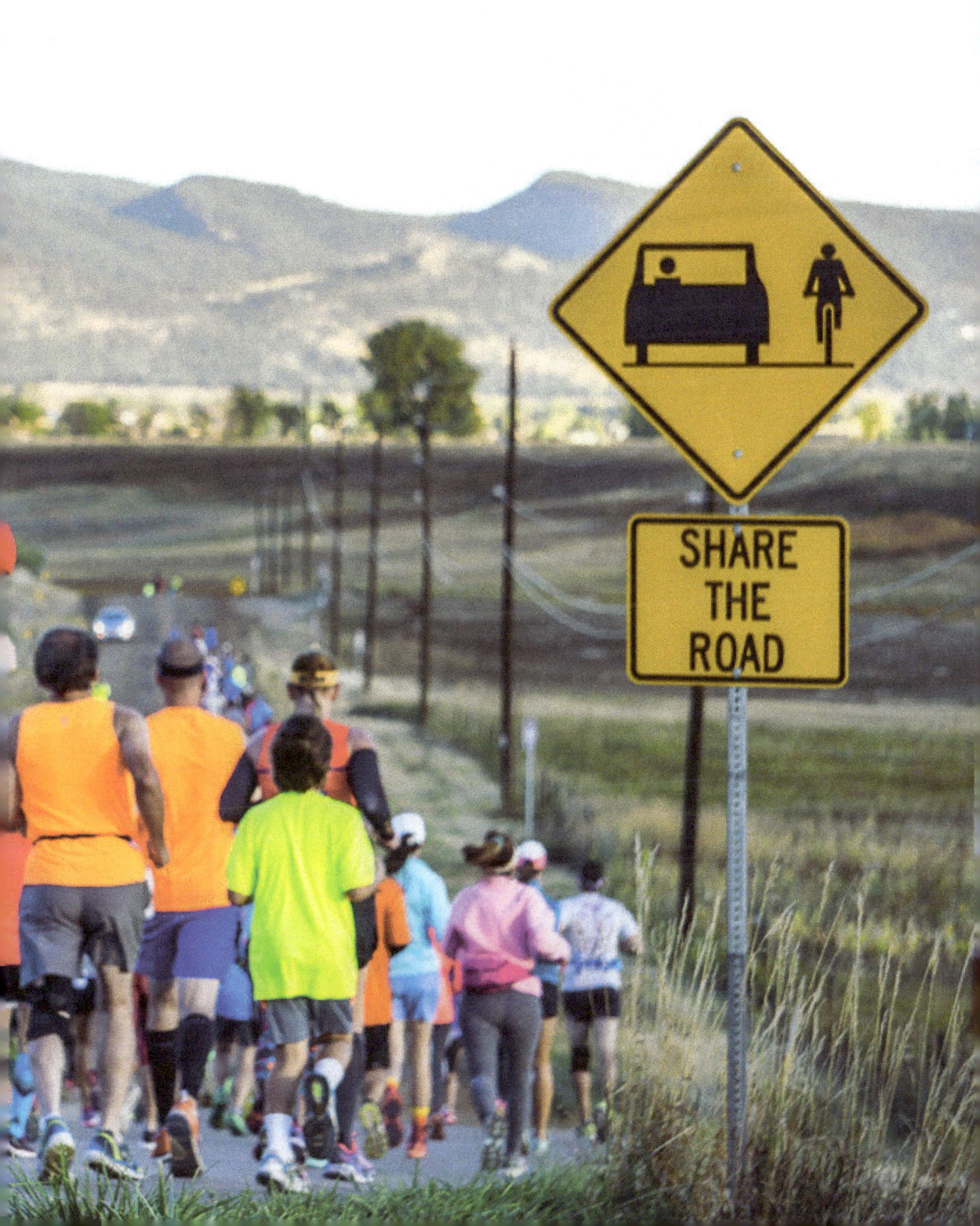

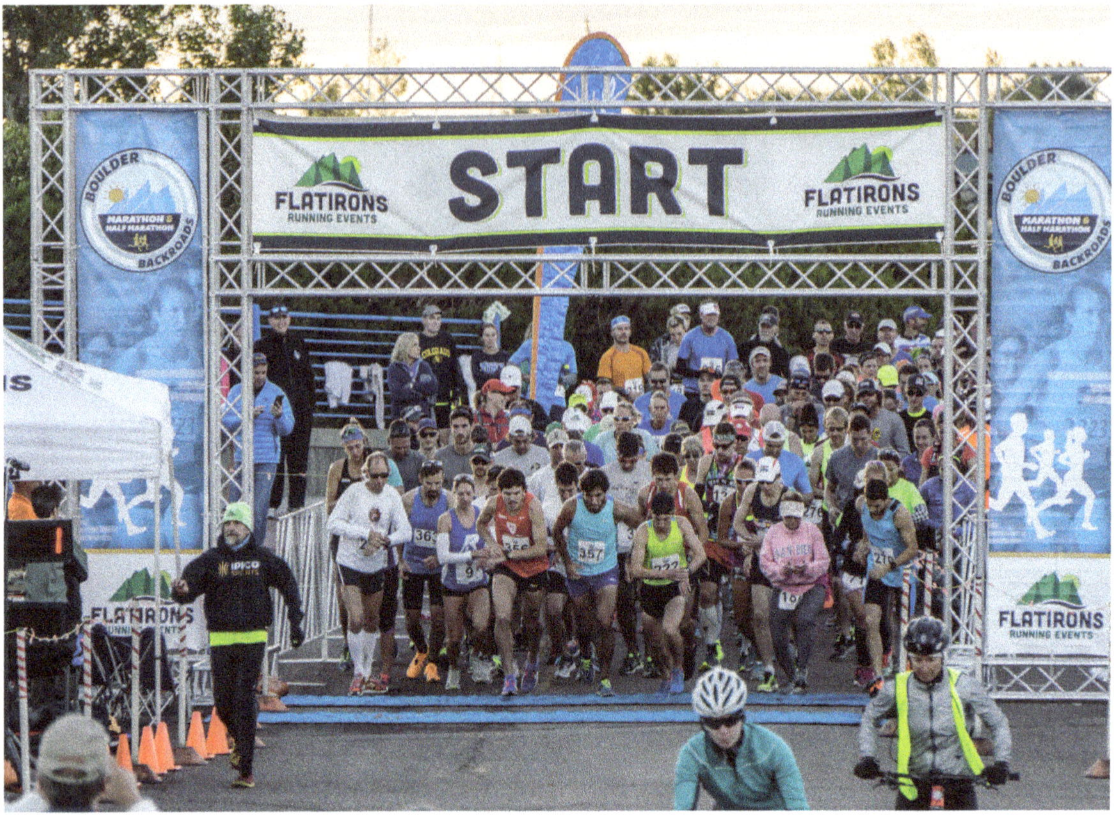

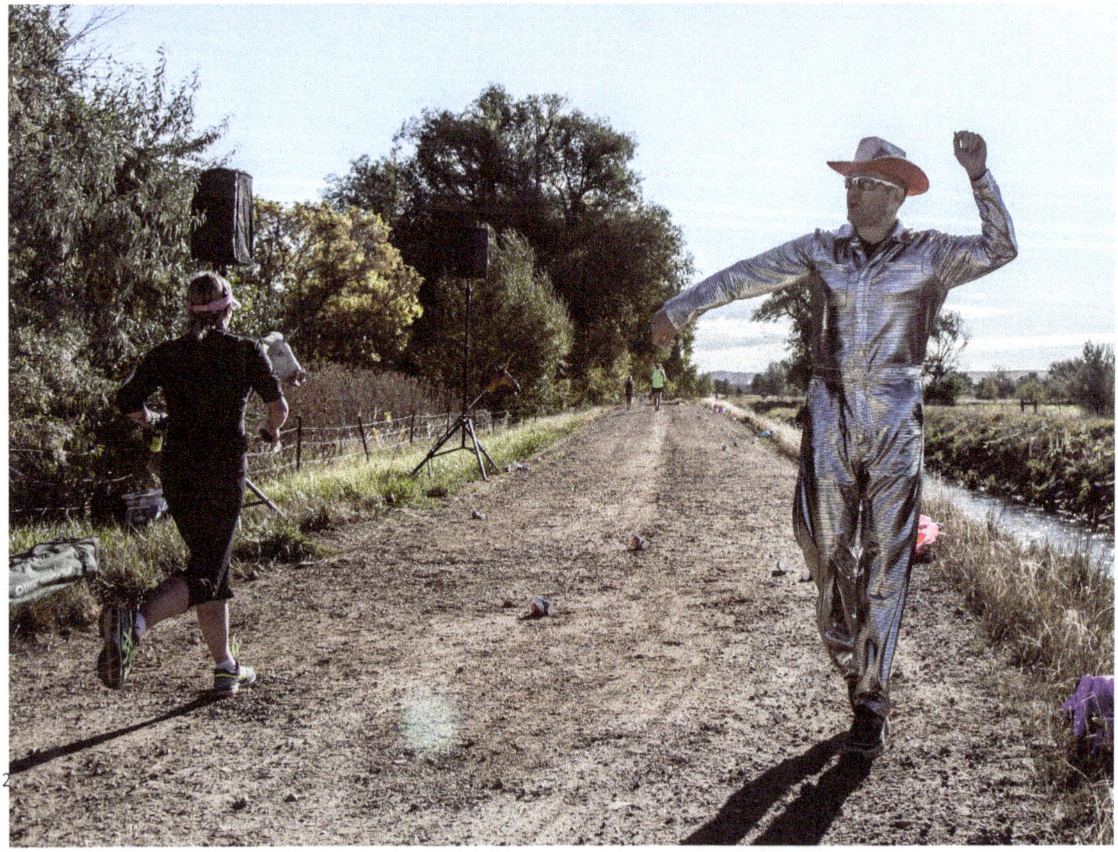

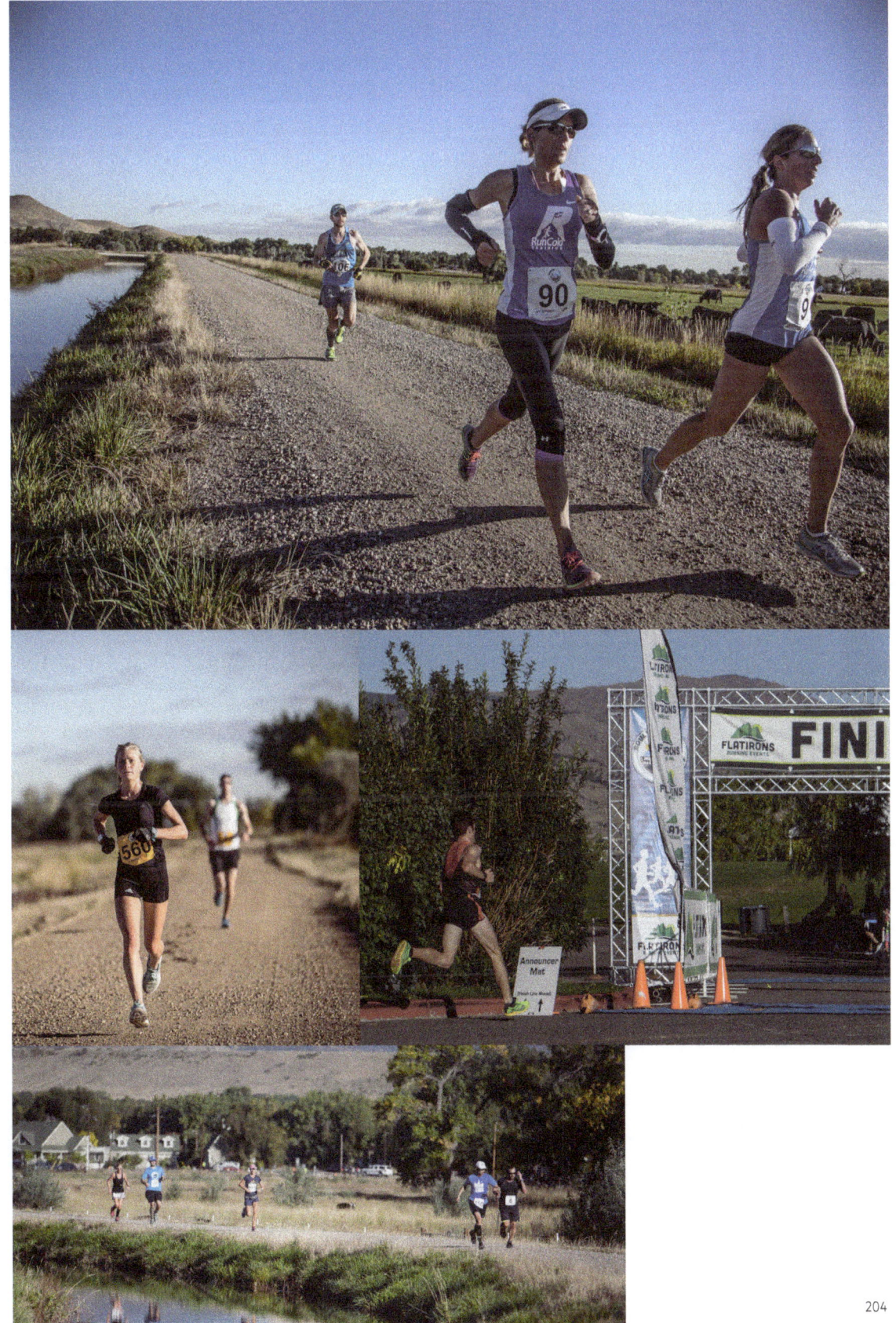

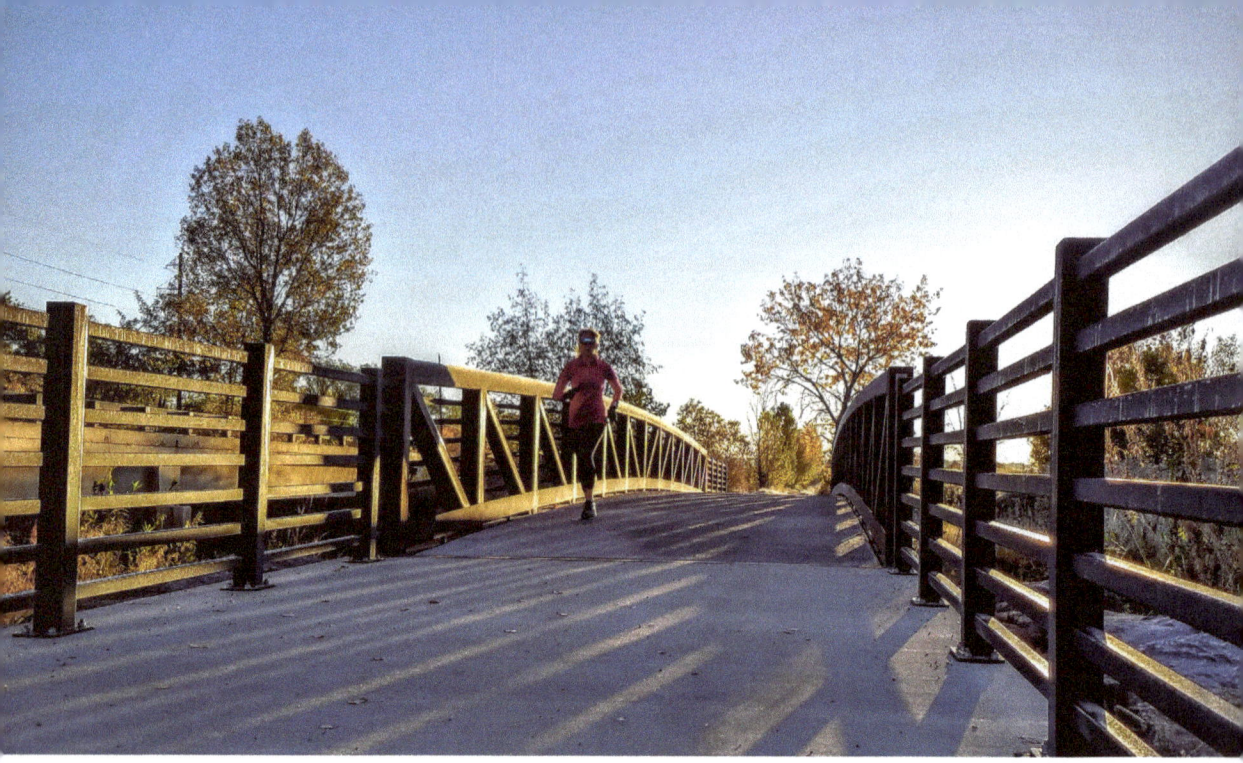

Evolution of a Runner

Words by Sunnie T. Glaister

Running has had a different meaning in each decade of my life, but from my teens to my 50s the sport has helped me evolve into a whole person and a complete athlete. Here's how that evolution unfolded:

In the mid-1970s, I was in my teens and running was part of PE. I dreaded it.

I even tried to skip out of running a lap around the track. Instead of turning left to go out the double doors to the track, I turned right into the girls' locker room. I thought I was safe but the door opened slightly, and I heard Mr. Jackson say, "Sunnneee, go out and run a lap." I replied, "That will make me tired for basketball practice." He said, "No, it won't." And he was right.

The one lap helped me warm up. So that was the start of my running career: Running to warm up for other sports.

I entered adulthood as running became mainstream in the 1980s. A short but fast run with my boyfriend (now husband) and his sister resulted in a runner's high. After that, running became a regular habit.

After college, now working, I found running relieved the stress of long, hectic days. Almost every day, I went for a run on the street in the wooded area of Mercer Island, Washington. My company announced a Corporate Cup competition in the Seattle area. The idea of competing intrigued me. I signed up for the 5K race. When race day arrived, the women lined up at the start. The excitement in the crowd of runners fueled my pace. I pushed through the discomfort and finished in 22 minutes, placing 10th! It is my 5K PR to this day.

"You paaayyy to run?" my sister asked in disbelief that I paid the registration fee for an upcoming race. I joined the millions who enter foot races each year. The craze of running was so much a part of who I was that I entered the inaugural Emerald City Marathon in Seattle in 1987. Unfortunately, a long-term illness interrupted my training, and I did not run the marathon.

With marriage came a move to Los Angeles, and then Albuquerque, two very warm places, too warm for me to run. I switched to team sports. That changed when I moved to Boulder in the late '90s. At first, running was mainly done to lose weight from my pregnancies. My supportive husband would return home for lunch to watch our little kiddos so I could run. Within a year, I was running long distances again. I set out to train for a marathon in the hopes of running Seattle at last. Training on my own, I tried and failed.

In 2001, I joined a marathon training program, Boulder Fit. The program included a complete training schedule, speakers on nutrition, hydration, equipment, and speed training with Olympic Coach Bobby McGee. The runners I met in this program became my friends even to this day. Chris, Susan, Julie and I trained for the Boulder Backroads Marathon. We were on our last long run (of 20 miles) together when I suspected something. My friends suspected the same thing since I was stopping to pee every 30 minutes. A trip to WalMart to purchase a test proved that I was pregnant again: a temporary set back to my marathon goal.

As time went on, I raised my three children and found time to run around my favorite 2-mile loop. The joy of running never left me. I met up with a neighbor mom, Amy, who was training for a marathon. Our time together running inspired me to train again for one. I ran the Seattle Marathon in 2005, so happy to have finally accomplished this goal.

I set a new goal in 2006: qualifying for the Boston Marathon. Race conditions were perfect at the California International Marathon in Sacramento, and I finished with the exact time (3:50:49) necessary for this 43-year-old female to qualify. Running Boston in 2008 was the highlight of my running career.

I have run for more than 30 years now. Half of the time, I run solo; the other half, I schedule runs with friends, the same group of ladies from 15 years ago. I appreciate both the solitude and the camaraderie. Running is my lifestyle. It makes me feel like a kid again — even though I am now 53 years old.

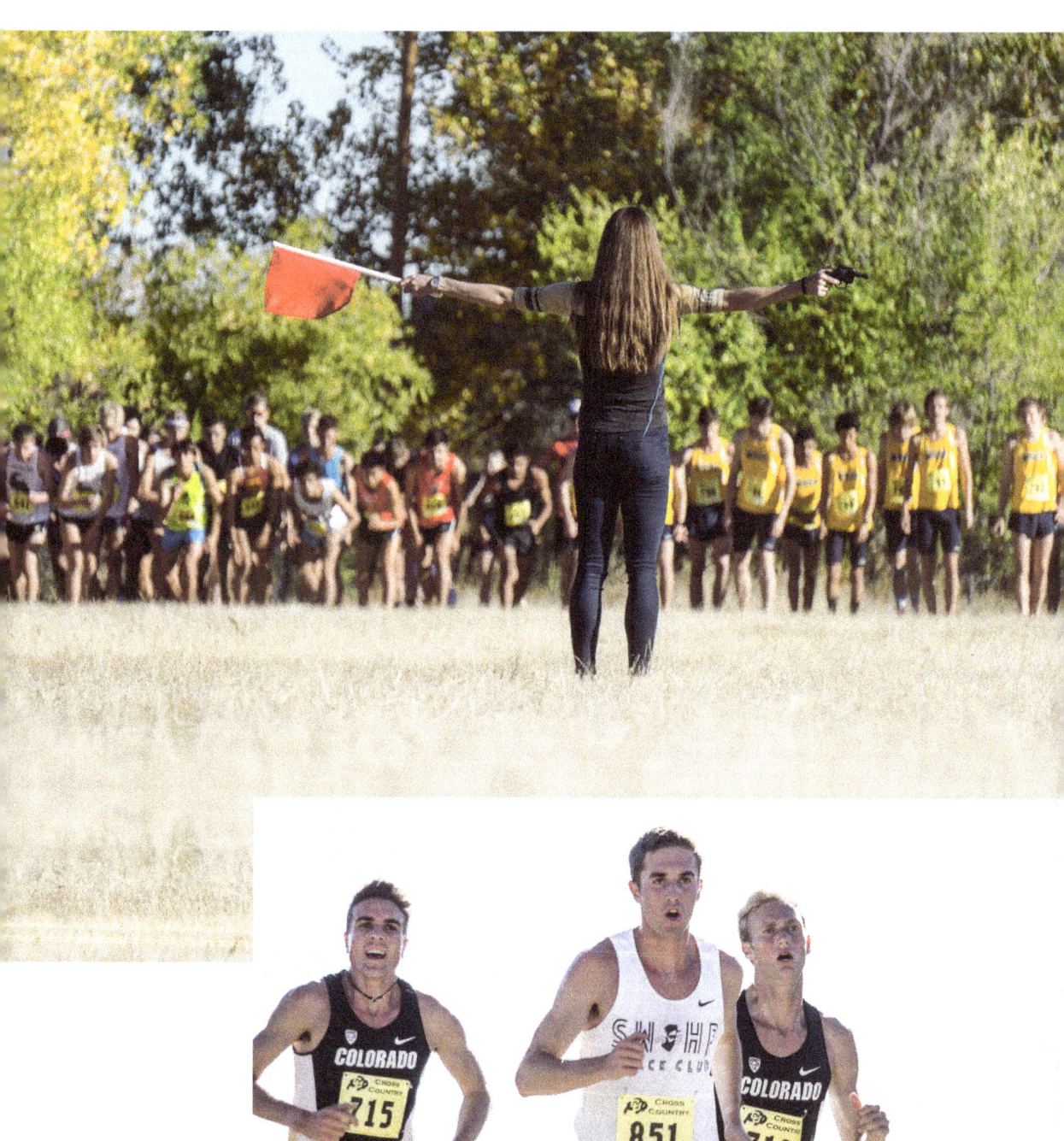

ROCKY MOUNTAIN

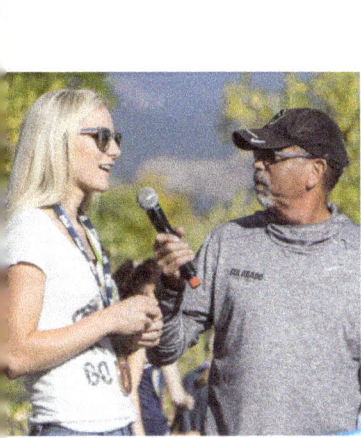
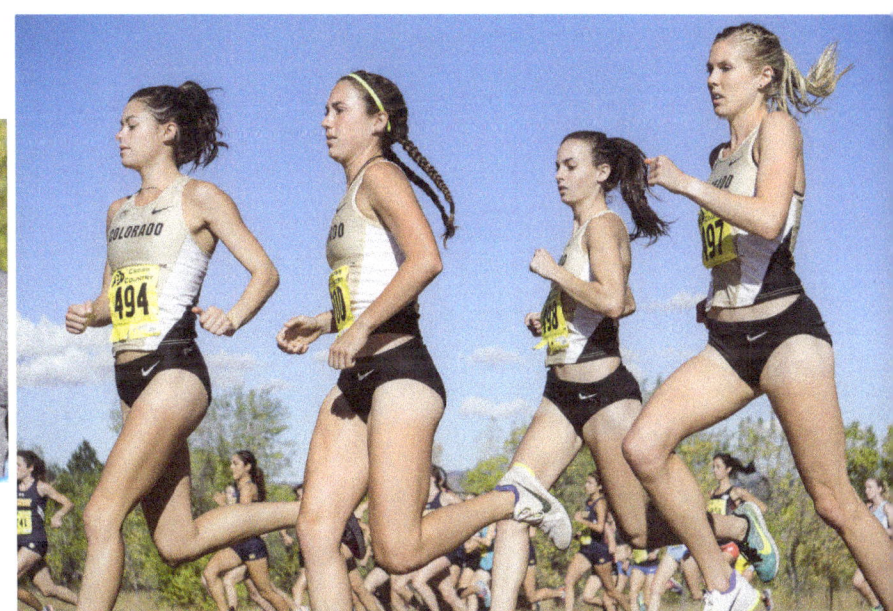

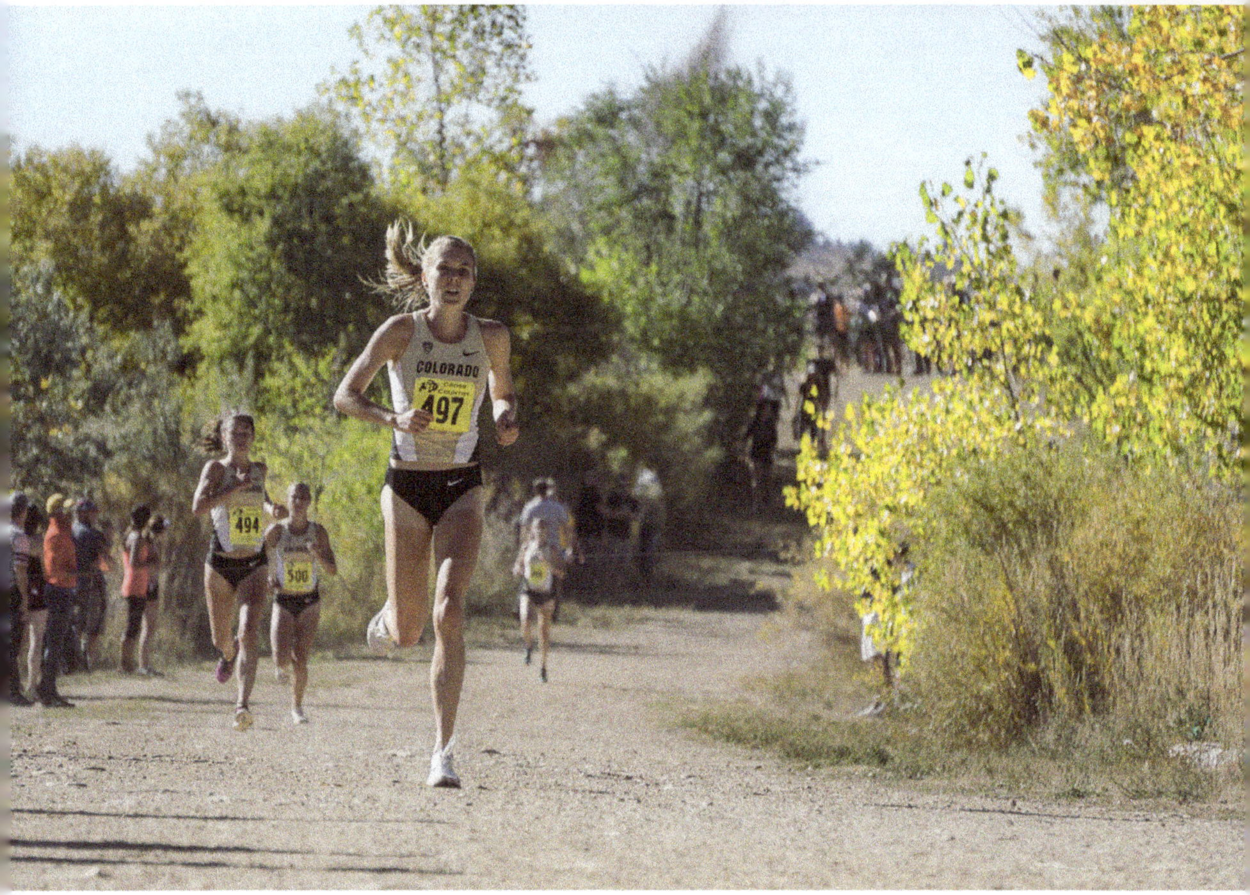

SHOOTOUT

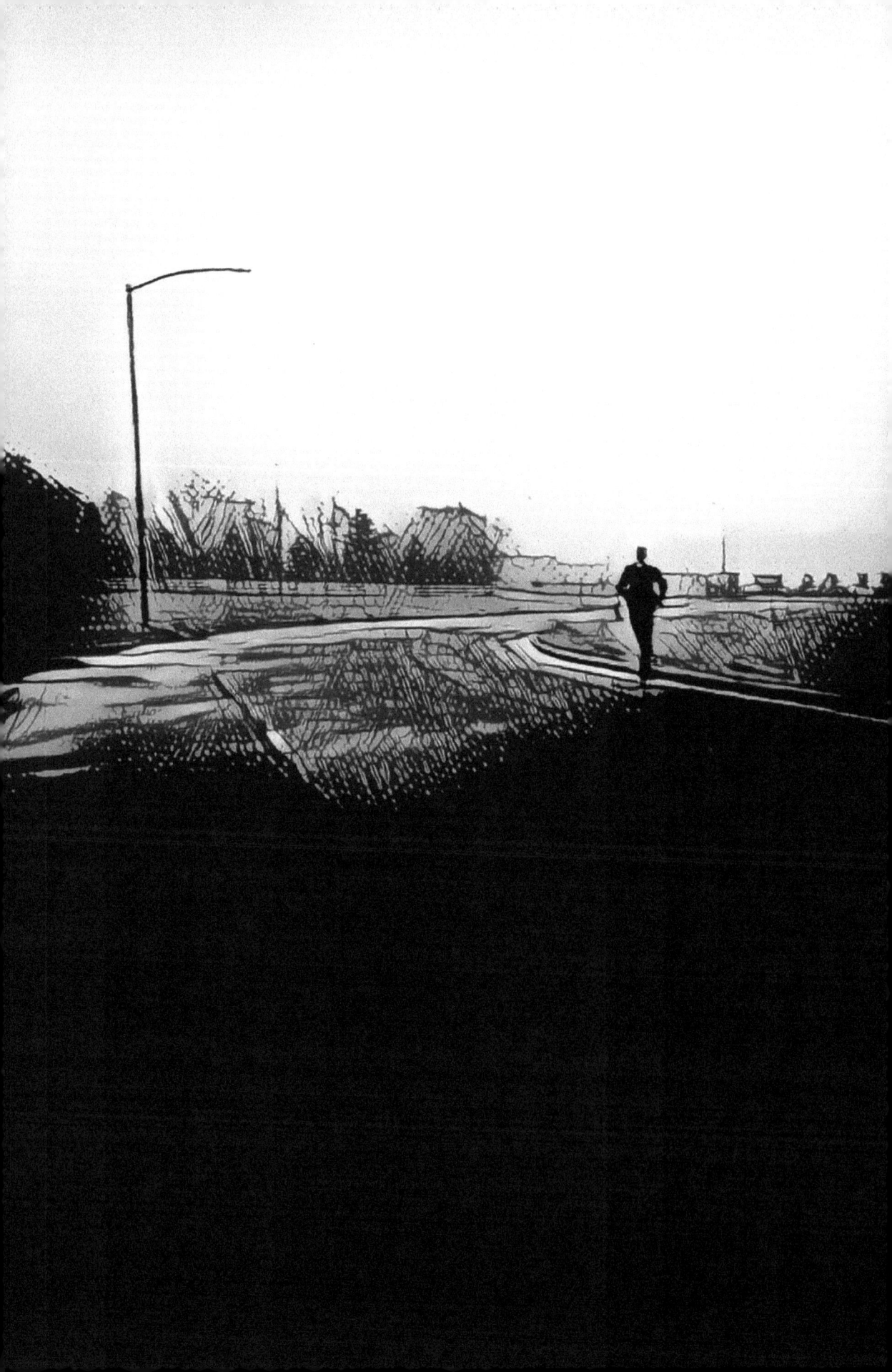

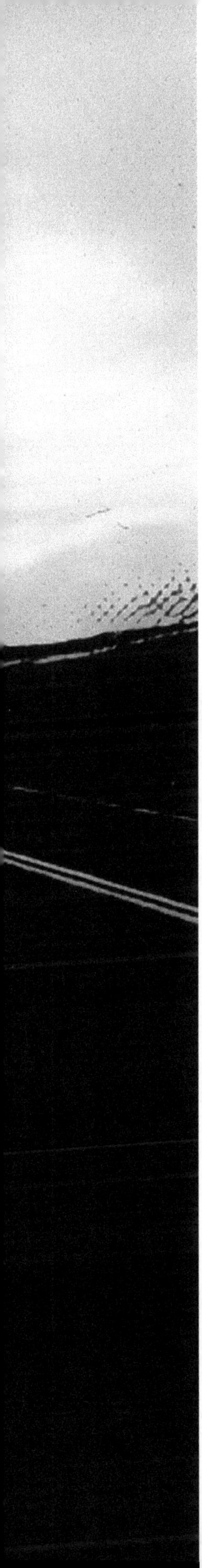

Saturdays in the fall
are electric with football games. For me, all my distance runs are dedicated to the dark fall nights.

I bike up 28th street at about 9:30pm, park my bike at Jay Rd. Against 36 I go. 15 miles is my goal, 6:50's.

I'm seshing miles really well, stride wide, about 4.5 mi up 36, when the hardest hail storm I have ever seen hits. I turn back down.

Cars are pulling to the side. I'm the only one in motion. Completely soaked, crazy. Running against the traffic, I see drivers' faces as they see me, with their eyes boggled. I'm shirtless, in my zone.

The hail looks like streaks of white, like painting a landscape.

My only concern: "These splits aren't very even."

Words by @raddrunning

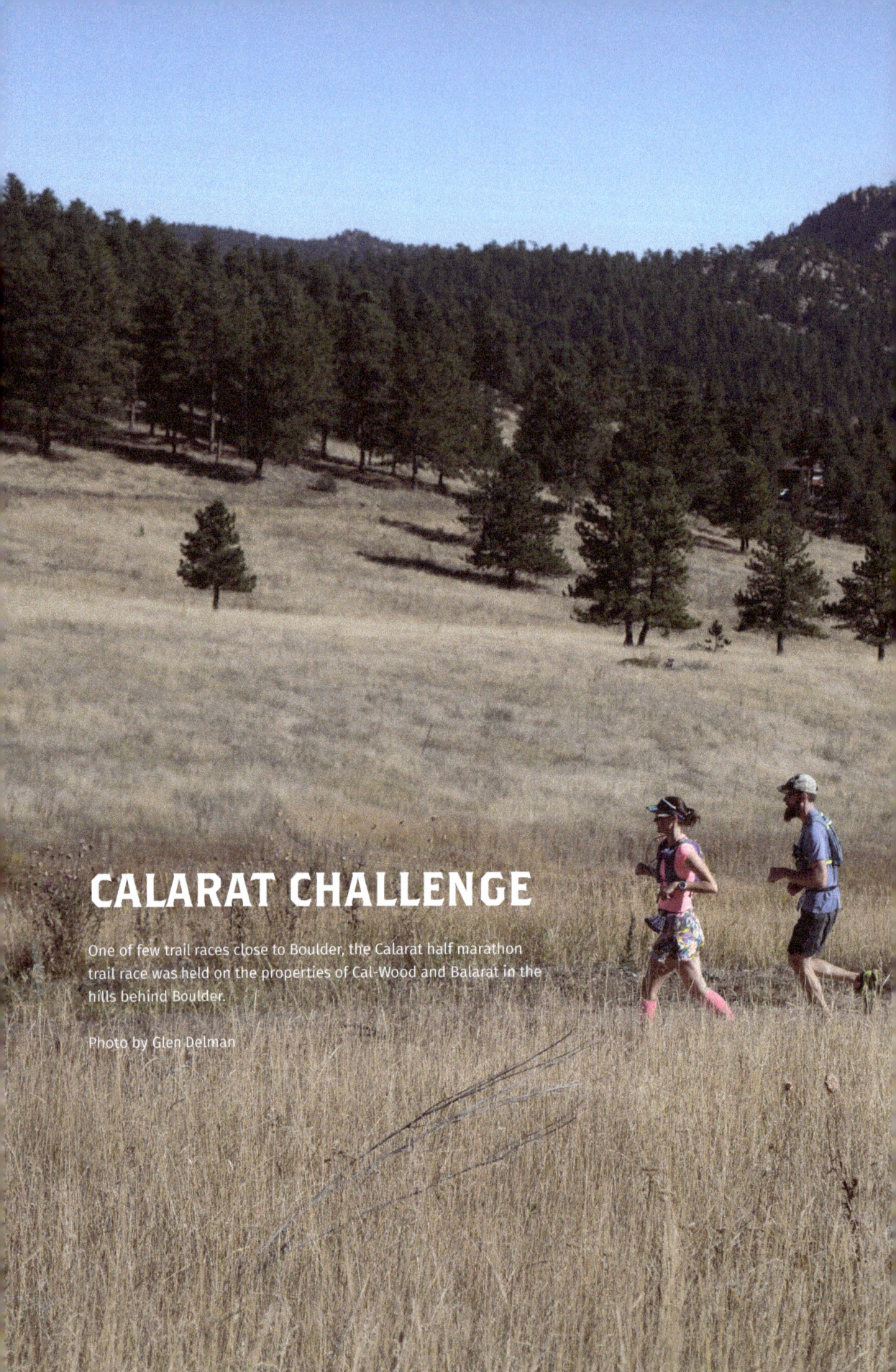

CALARAT CHALLENGE

One of few trail races close to Boulder, the Calarat half marathon trail race was held on the properties of Cal-Wood and Balarat in the hills behind Boulder.

Photo by Glen Delman

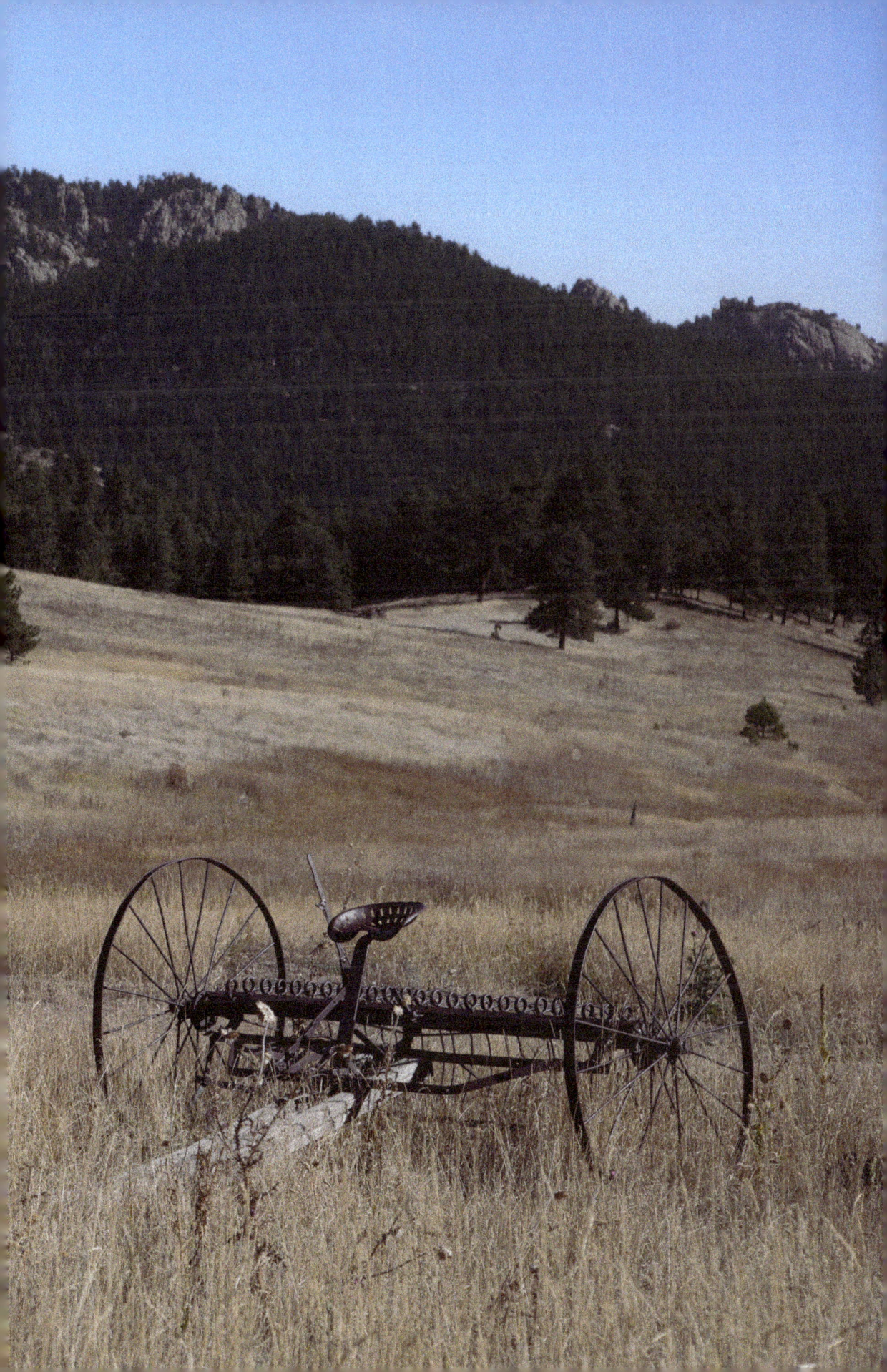

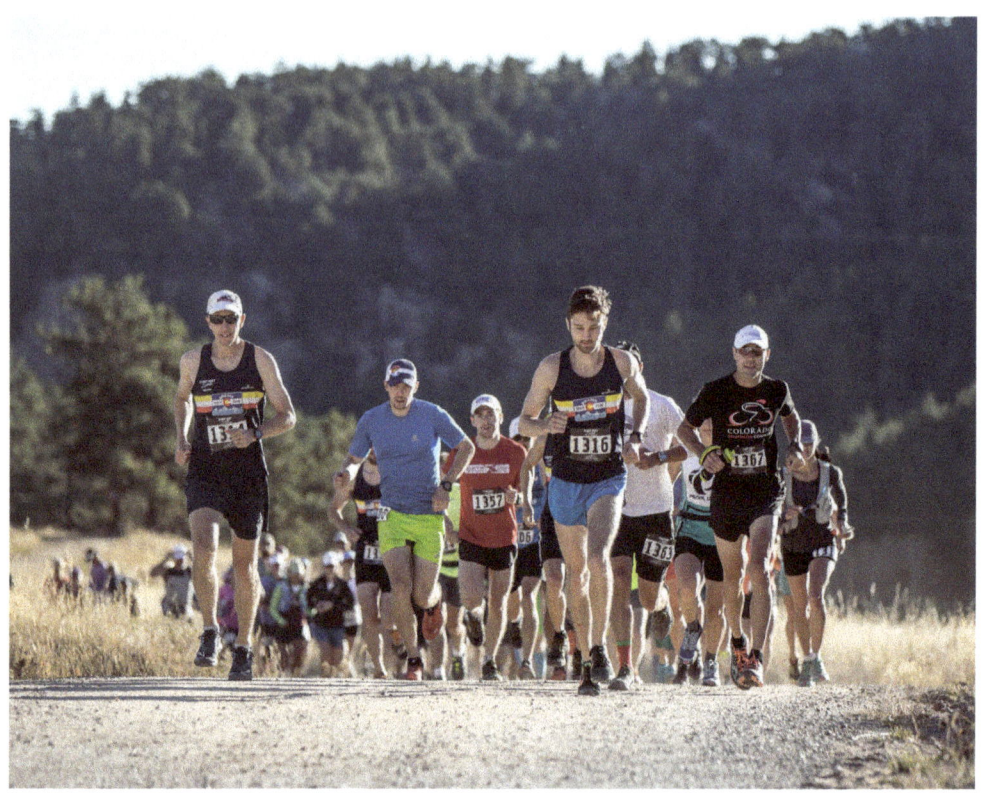

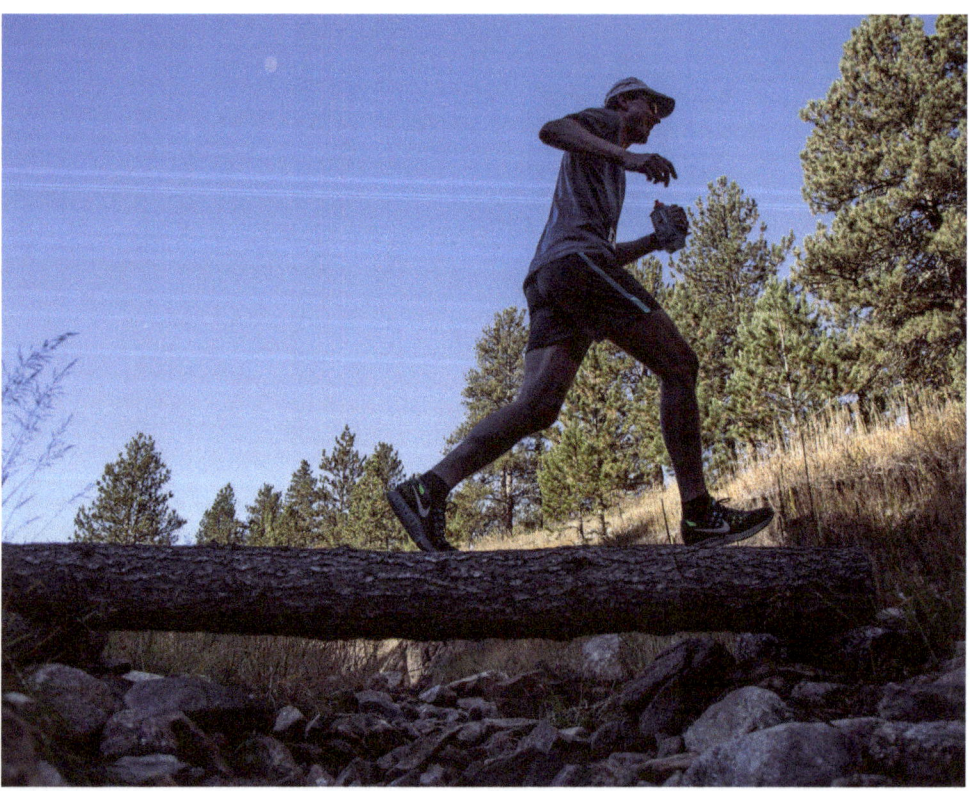

Photos by Glen Delman

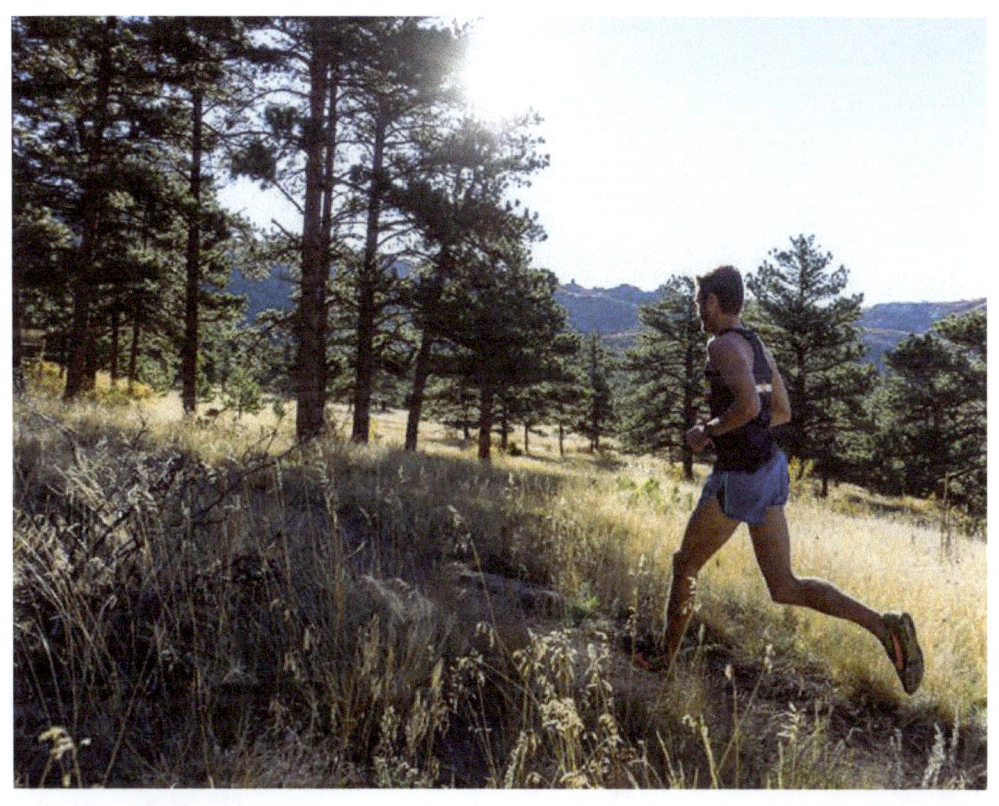

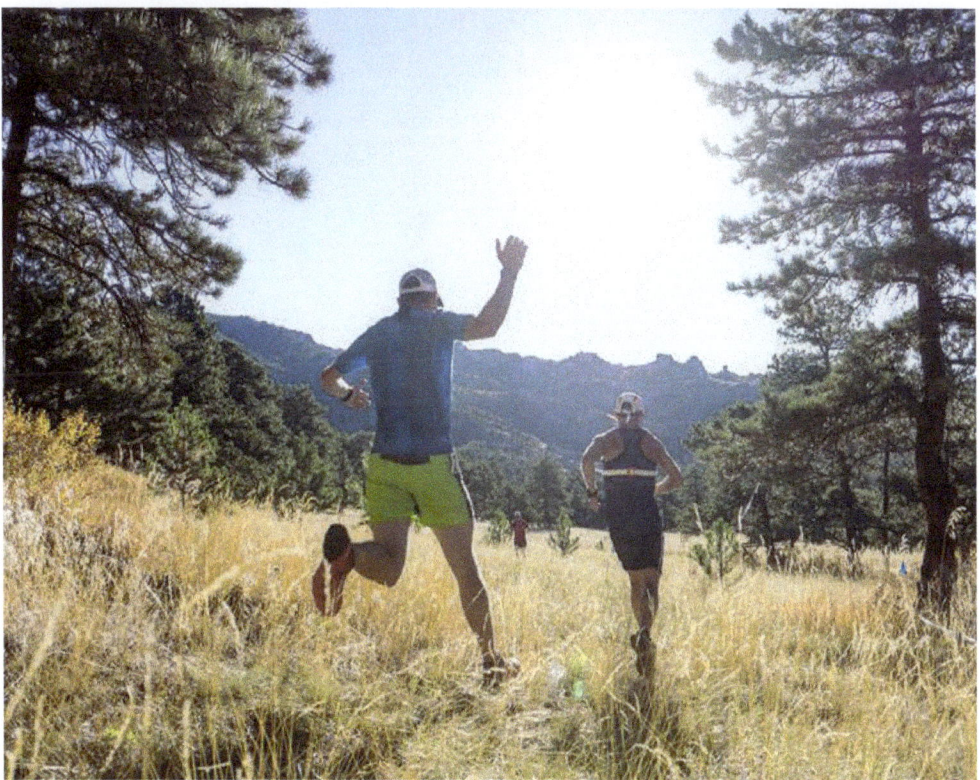

Photos by Todd Straka

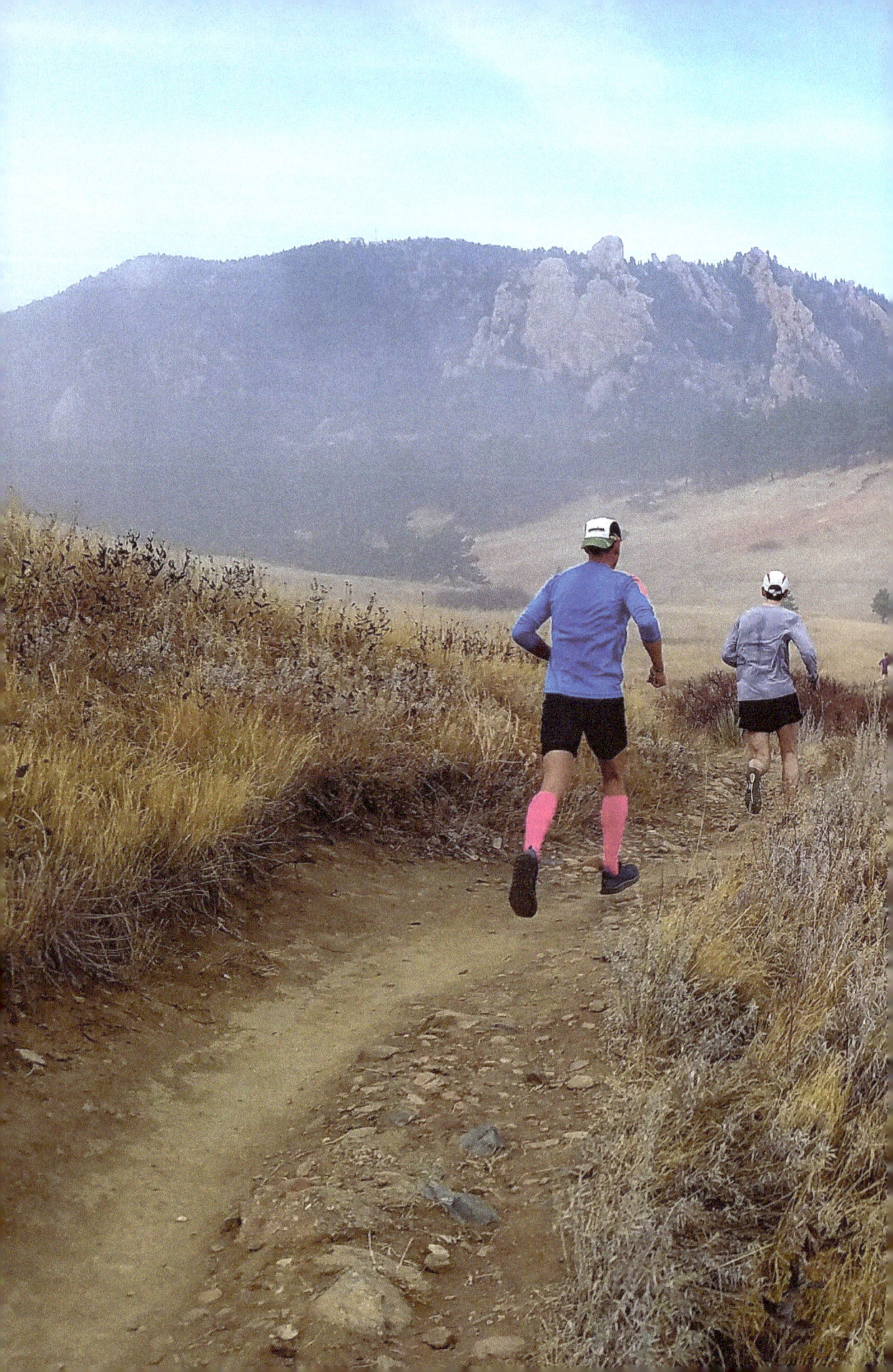

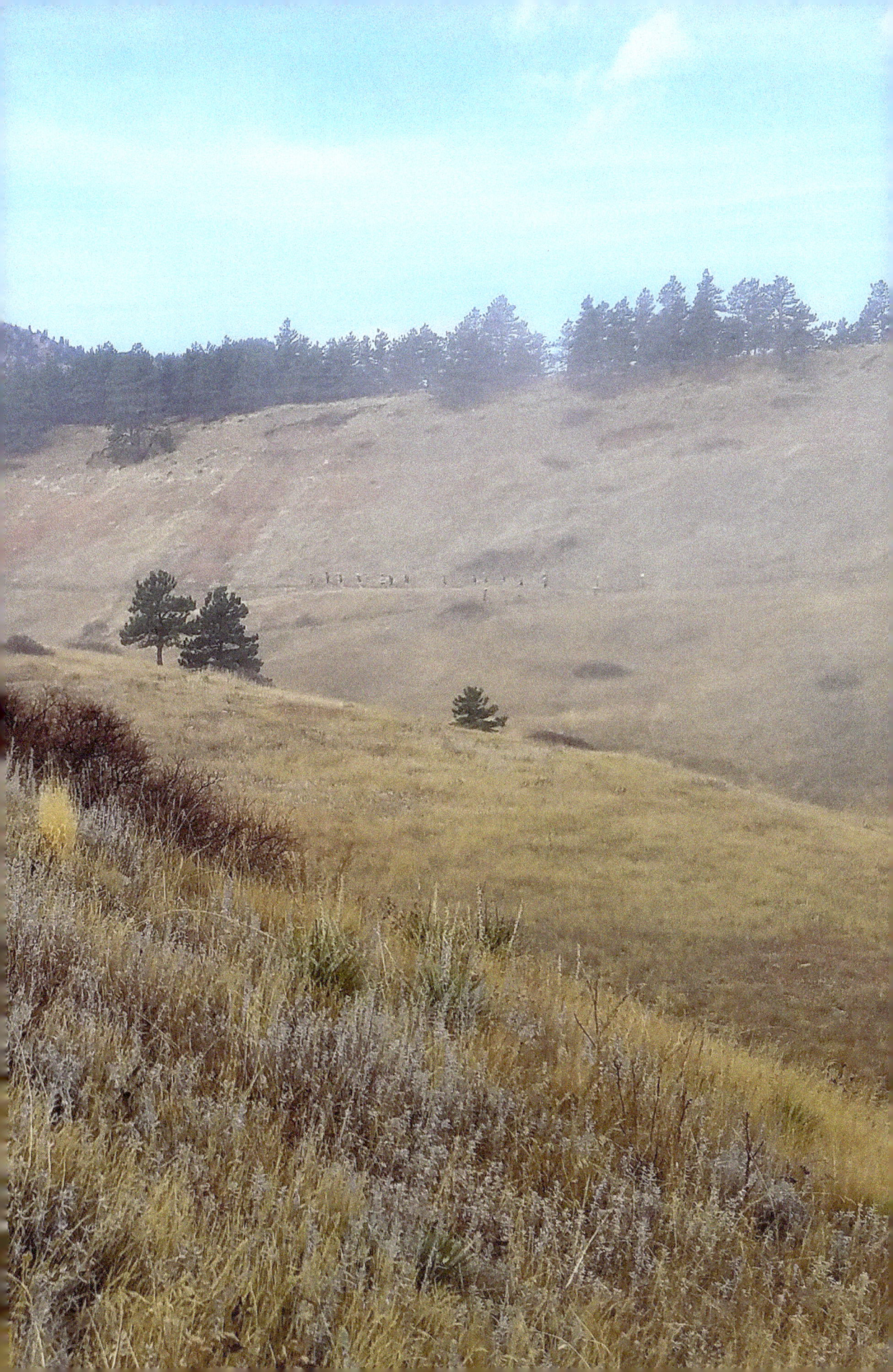

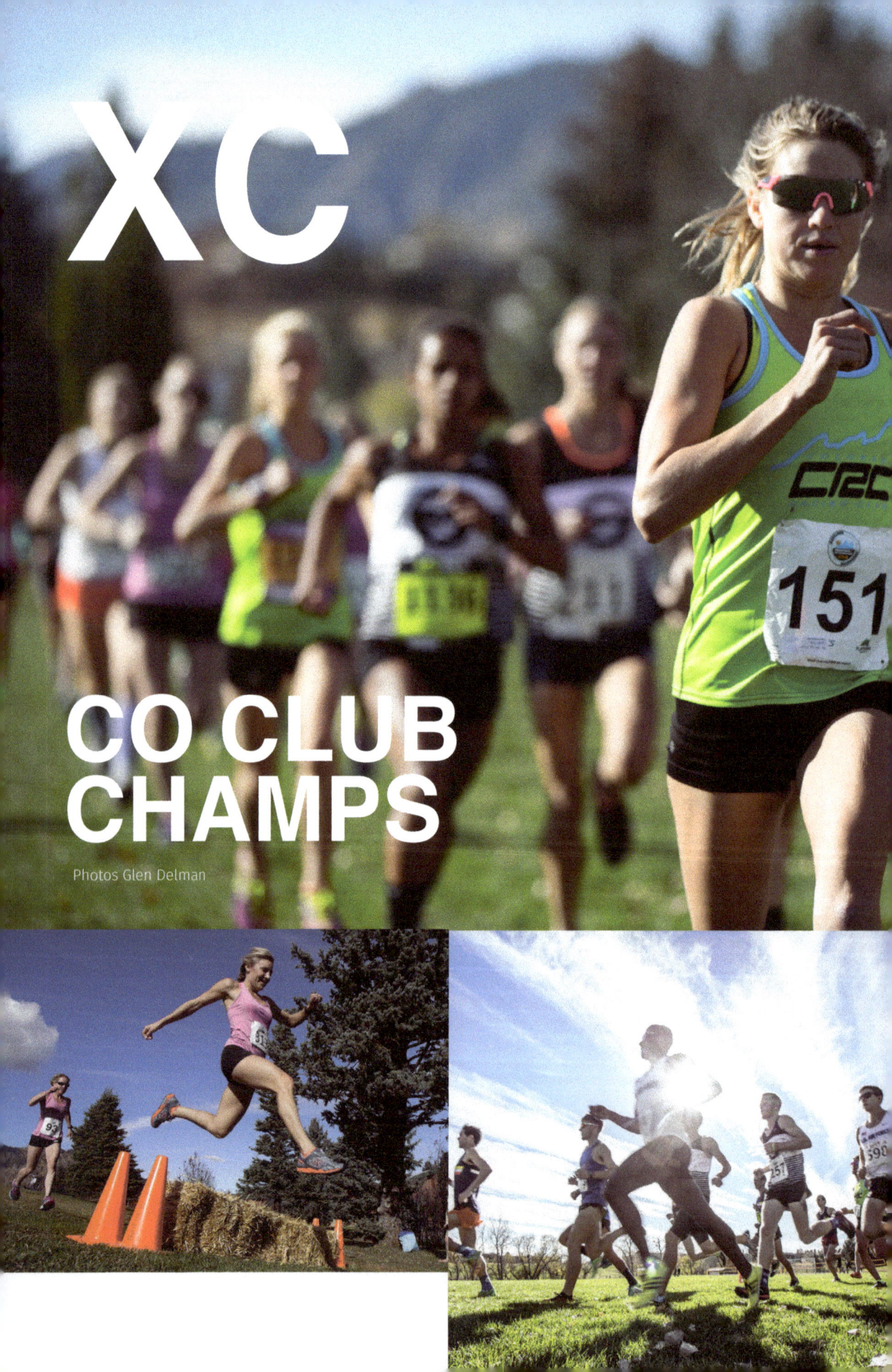

XC
CO CLUB CHAMPS

Photos Glen Delman

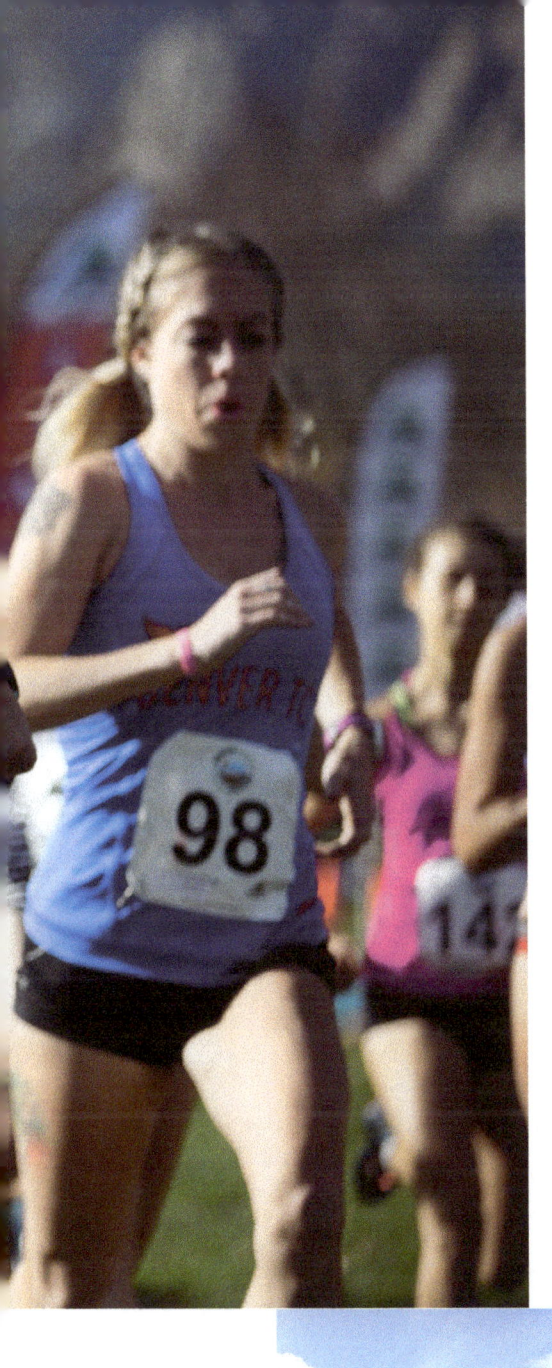
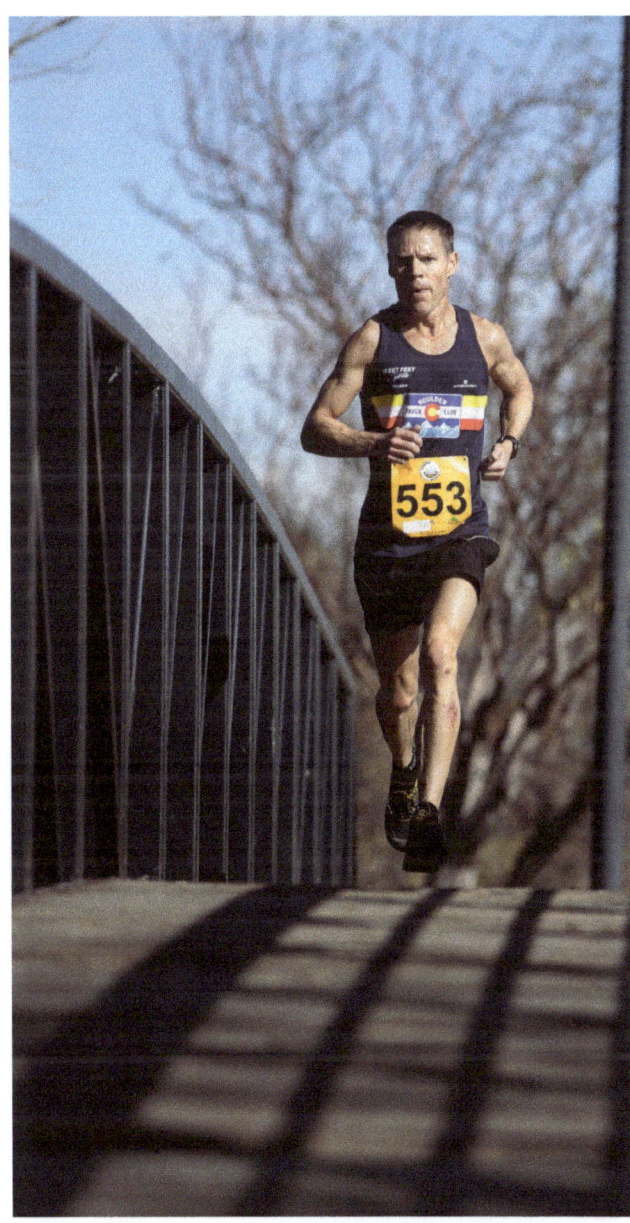
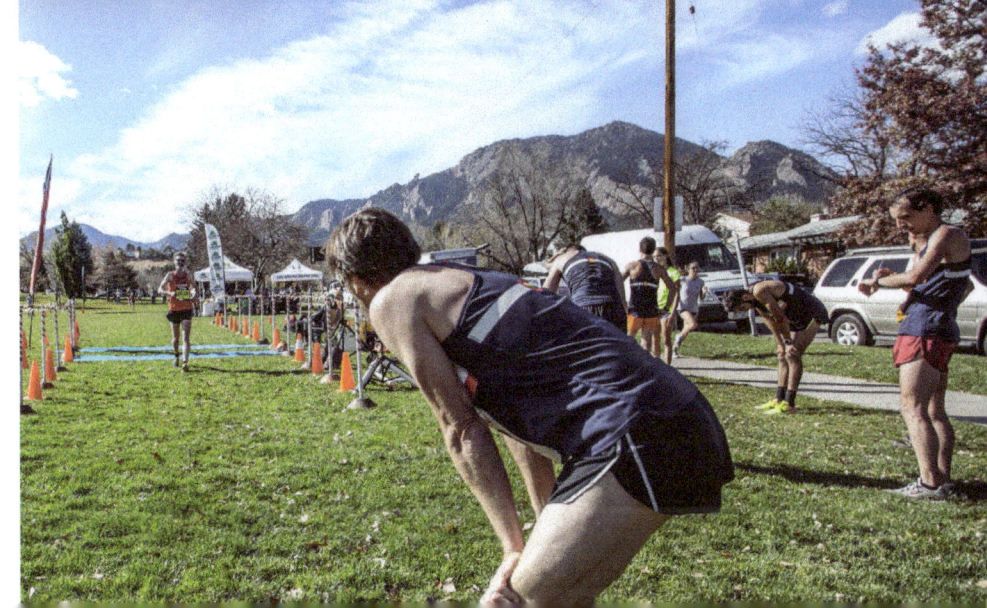

Top Results
September - November

At the 36th running of the New Balance Fifth Avenue Mile in New York City, Olympian **Jenny Simpson** came away with her fifth win there in a time of 4:18.3. Olympian **Emma Coburn** was 9th in a time of 4:23.8, and **Sara Vaughn** was 15th in a time of 4:27.1. **Jason Simpson** came away with a 6th place finish in a time of 4:12.5 at the NYRR Road Mile Championships, held at the same time.

On Sept. 5 in Kauai, HI, at the Kauai Half-Marathon, Boulder's **Tyler McCandless** broke his own course record and came away with another dominating win with a time of 1:06:47.

That same day, at the 39th Faxon Law New Haven Road Race, which served as the USA 20K Championships, **Brianne Nelson** of Golden ran to a 3rd place finish in a time of 1:07:53, while **Alia Gray** of Boulder finished 9th in a time of 1:09:57.

At the Rock 'n' Roll Virginia Beach Half-Marathon, held Sept. 6, **Jonathan Grey** of Louisville ran a stellar race, covering the distance in a time of 1:04:26.

Up in Fort Collins at the Black Squirrel Half-Marathon, held on Sept. 10, Boulder's **Erik Nau** ran to a 3rd place finish in a time of 1:37:21. **Amanda Lee**, also of Boulder, came away with the win for the women in a time of 1:48:56.

Between September 9-11, Boulder's **Nick Pedatella** became of only a handful of people to successfully complete the Nolan's 14 challenge. Starting at Blank Cabin and heading north over fourteen 14,000' mountains, Nick arrived at the Leadville Fish Hatchery after 57 hours and 31 minutes.

At the ever competitive Run Rabbit Run 100 Mile, Golden's **Courtney Dauwalter** came away with the win in a time of 21:23:37.

Up in Idaho on the same day at the Idaho Mountain Trail 100 Mile race, Boulder's **Sam Ritchie** had a solid performance, placing 2nd in a time of 20:36:35.

On Sept. 17 at the GNC Live Well Liberty Mile in Pittsburgh, PA, Boulder's **Sara Vaughn** had a solid race, finishing 5th in a time of 4:38.

Up in Northport, NY on Sept. 17 at the Great Cow Harbor 10K, **Brianne Nelson** once again had a stellar race, finishing 2nd in a time of 33:32.96. **Stephen Pifer** of Superior was 2nd for the men with a time of 29:37.53 while **Clint Wells** finished 11th in a time of 32:50.

Down in Lakewood at the Bear Chase 100K, Boulder's **Joshua Stevens** came away with the overall win in a time of 10:18:36, while in the 50K it was **Stephen Clark** of Boulder who took home the win in a time of 3:55:12.

At the 31st Rocky Mountain Shootout held Oct. 1, CU's men and women had outstanding races. **Joe Klecker** came in 2nd for the men in a time of 24:42 while **Zach Perrin** was 3rd with a time of 24:56. **Erin Clark** finished 1st for the women in a time of 19:54, while **Kaitlyn Benner** was 2nd in a time of 20:02 and **Makena Morley** was 3rd in a time of 20:11.

On Oct. 9 at the Staten Island Half-Marathon, **Neely Gracey** of Louisville ran away with the win in a time of 1:13:03.

On the same day at the Medtronic Twin Cities 10 Mile, which served as the USA 10 Mile Championships, Boulder's **Noah Droddy** ran to 2nd place with a time of 47:28. **Mara Olson** of Boulder finished 5th for the women in a time of 54:18.

On Oct. 15 at the USA Trail Half-Marathon Championships, held in Bellingham, WA, Boulder's **Andy Wacker** came away with a strong win, completing the rolling course in 1:21:02.

Down in Denver, on Oct. 16 at the Rock 'n' Roll Denver Half-Marathon, Golden's **Marty Andrie** ran to a second place finish in a time of 1:07:43, while **Sean Quigley** of Lafayette came in 3rd with a time of 1:08:35 and **Tyler McCandless** finished 4th in 1:09:20. In the 10K event, **Krystalanne Curwood** dominated the field, winning in a time of 37:01.

On October 23rd at the Metro Health Grand Rapids Half-Marathon Boulder's **Julia Viel** ran an outstanding race, finishing 3rd in a time of 1:23:43.

In Tulsa, Oklahoma at the Tulsa Run 15K, which served as the USATF Masters 15K Championships, Boulder's **Melody Fairchild** made a strong return to racing with a 3rd place finish in a time of 1:00:00. **Edie Stevenson** of Boulder won the 65-69 age group division with a time of 1:12:30.

At the 41st running of the Marine Corps Marathon in Washington, DC, **Mark Jones** of Boulder had a solid run, finishing 5th in a time of 2:30:04.

On November 5th at the Moab Trail Marathon, which served as the USATF Trail Marathon Championships, Boulder's **Sage Canaday** came away with the title in a very competitive field, finishing the race in a time of 2:58:25. **Addie Bracy** of Longmont took home the women's title with a time of 3:40:28. Masters runner **Chris Grauch** of Nederland finished 2nd in the 40-44 age group.

At the Colorado Club Cross Country Championships on Sunday Nov. 6, **Morgan Pearson** and **Lauren Goss**, both of Boulder took the individual wins over the challenging course and deep fields. The **Boulder Track Club** Men's and the **Hudson Elite** Women's teams captured the club titles.

At the New York City Marathon the same day, **Neely Gracey** ran a strong time of 2:34:55 to finish as the second American and 8th overall.

On November 6th in the Sierra Nevada foothills outside of Sacramento, Boulder's **Cat Bradley** had a spectacular race at the Rio del Lago 100. Despite the warm conditions, she flew along the trails, finishing 6th overall and setting a new course record for the women in a time of 18:48:09.

What were your top results?

WRITING PROMPT
FALL
Who are your favorite people to run with and why?

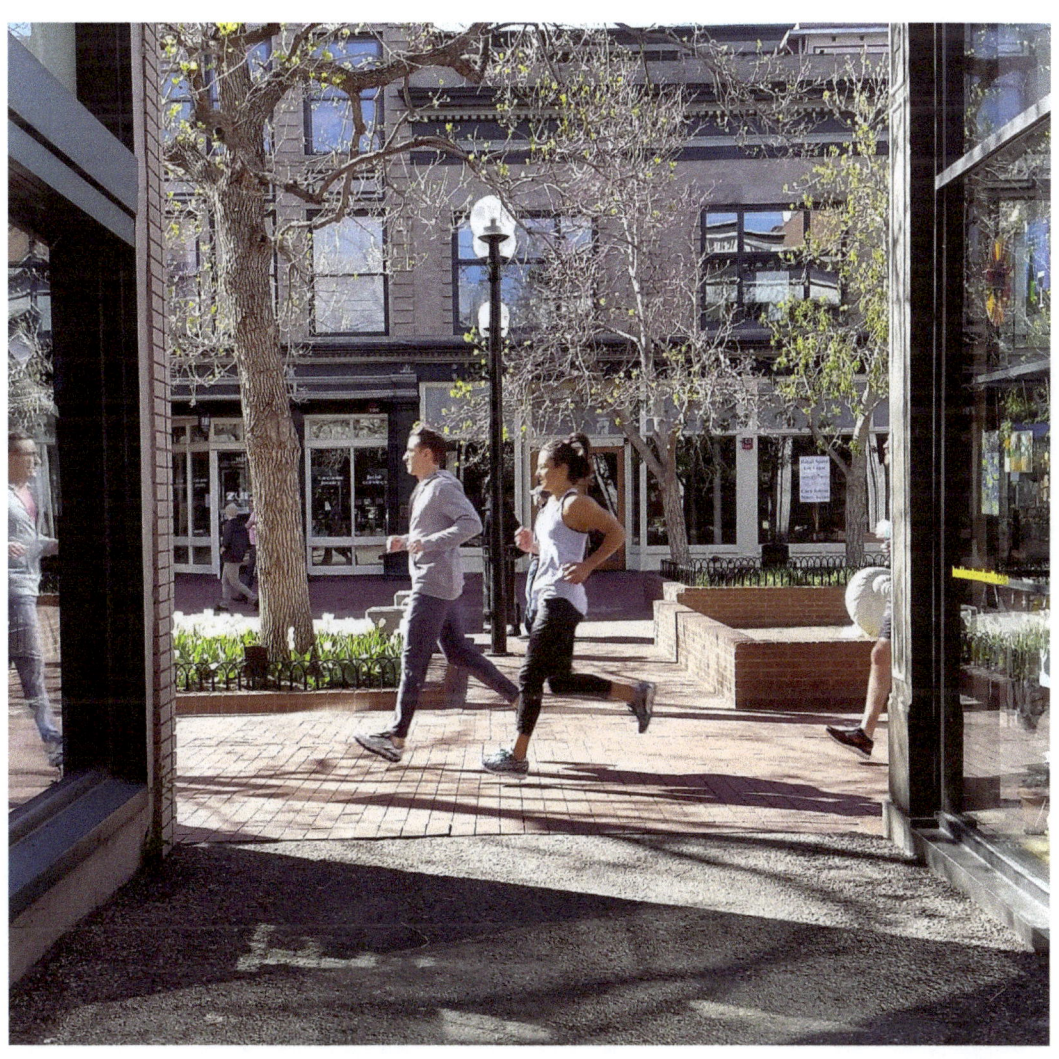

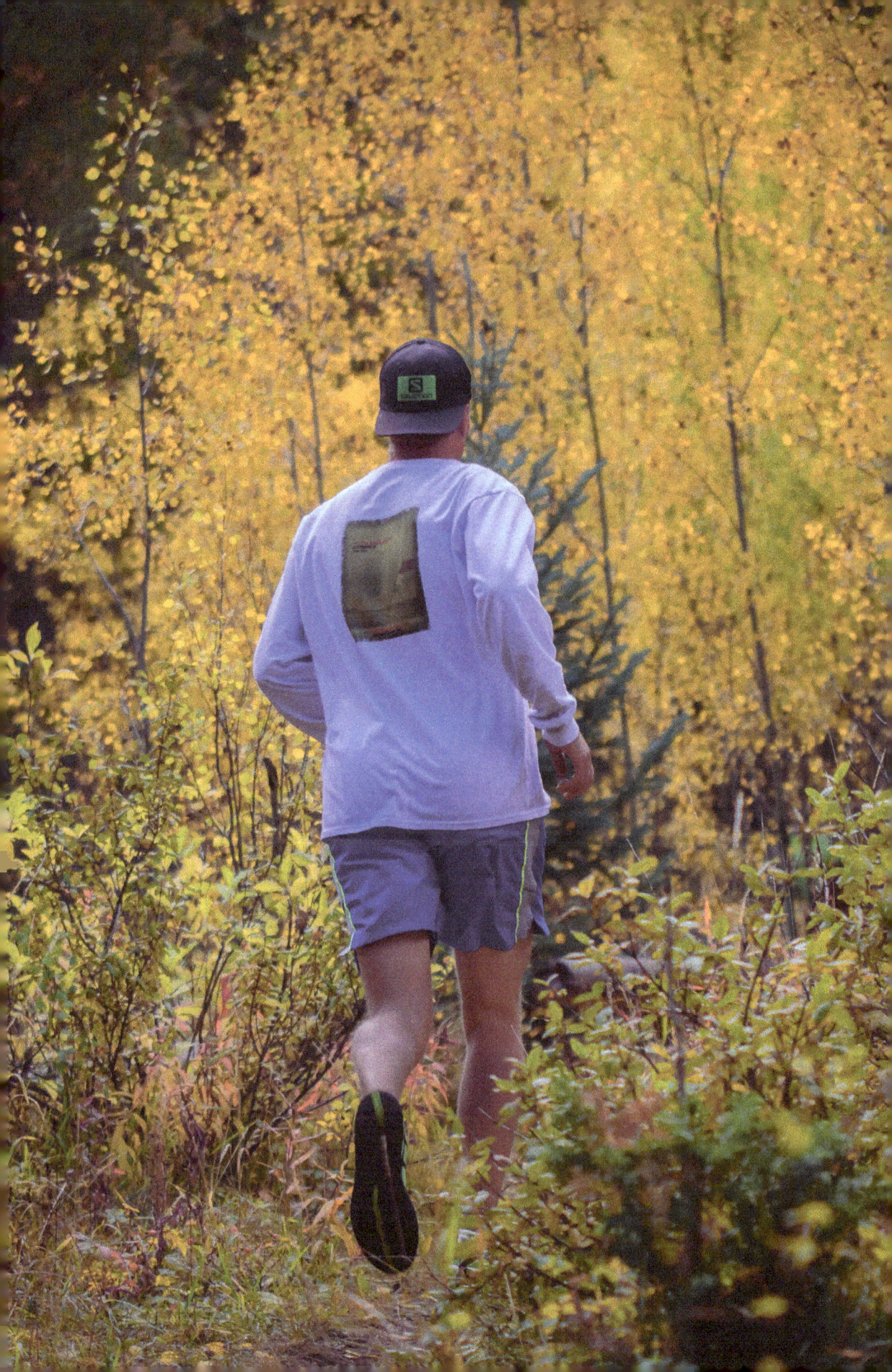

Without limiting the rights under copyright, no part of this publication may be reproduced, stored in or introduced into a retrieval system, or transmitted, in any form or by any means (electronic, mechanical, photocopying, recording, or otherwise), without the prior written permission of both the copyright owner and the publisher of this book
Copyright © 2016

Library of Congress Cataloging-in-Publication Data

Straka, Todd; Jones, Peter N.; Becker, Terzah
Boulder Running Journal 2016
Volume 2, Issue 1

p.cm

1. Sports, Running. 2. Boulder, Colorado. 3. Outdoors, Sports

ISBN 13: 978-1-936955-18-3

All Rights Reserved. All copyrights remain with original owner. Photographs and articles used with permission.

Boulder Running
250 Mohawk Drive, Boulder, CO 80303
www.boulderrunning.com

www.ingramcontent.com/pod-product-compliance
Lightning Source LLC
Chambersburg PA
CBHW040546220526

45473CB00017B/3034